HISTORICAL SOCIOLOGY

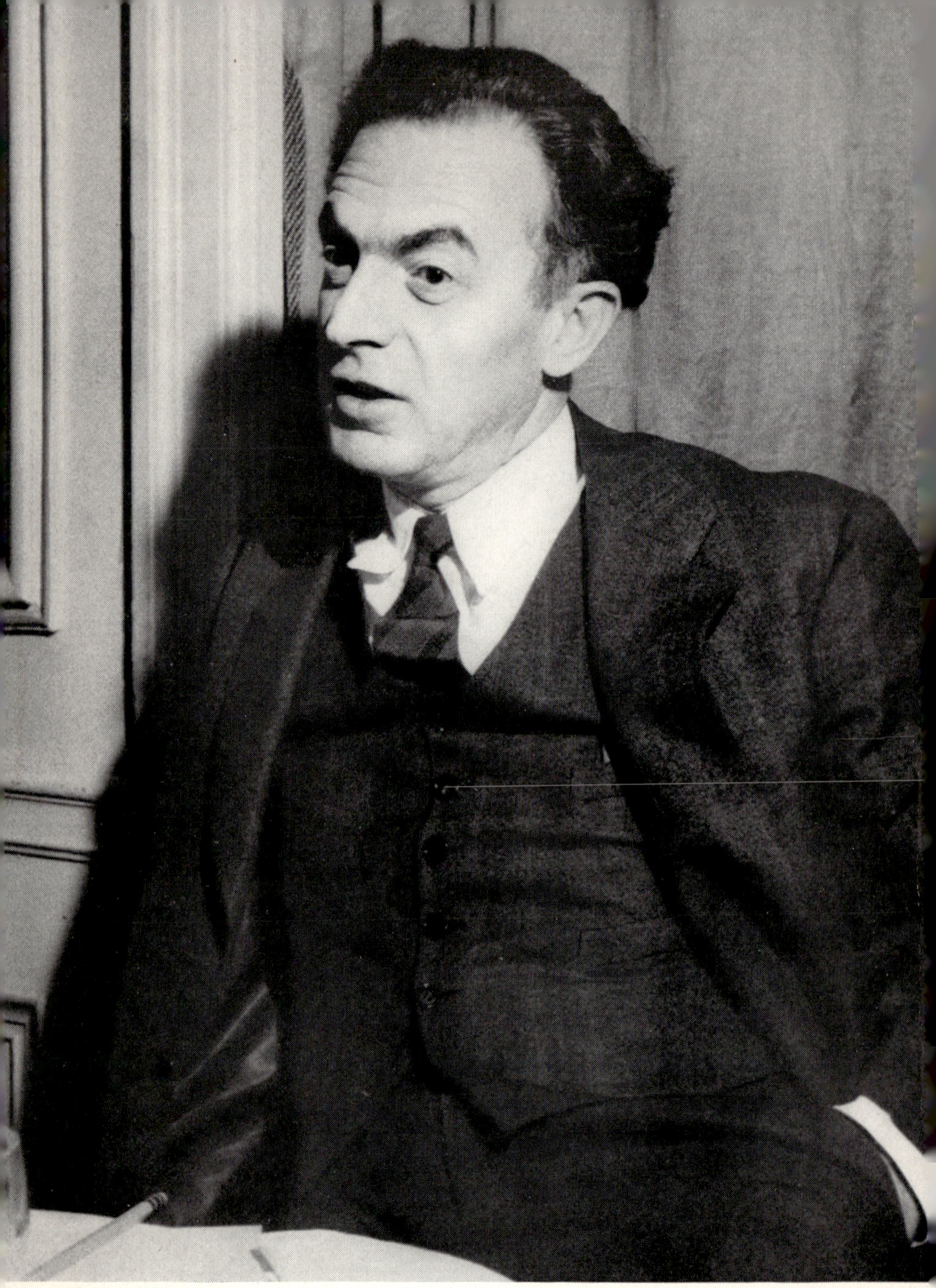

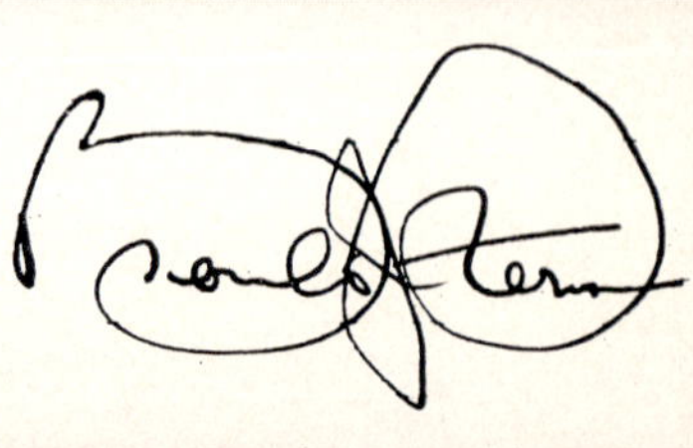

HISTORICAL SOCIOLOGY

The Selected Papers of
Bernhard J. Stern

THE CITADEL PRESS
NEW YORK

The Sponsoring Committee of the Bernhard J. Stern Memorial Fund initiated this memorial volume as a tribute to a great American sociologist, teacher and scholar. Members of the Sponsoring Committee were Dr. Edmund M. Braun, Professor Arthur K. Davis, Albert Deutsch, Dr. Leslie A. Falk, Professor Alvin Johnson, Dr. Corliss Lamont, Dr. Milton I. Roemer, Henry Schuman, Professor Vincent Whitney, and Joseph H. Crown.

First Edition

Copyright © 1959 by The Citadel Press. Library of Congress Catalog Card Number 59-14764. Manufactured in the United States of America. Published by The Citadel Press, 222 Fourth Avenue, New York 3, N. Y.

Contents

          Introduction vii

Part One **PERSPECTIVES**

          Concerning the Distinction Between the Social and the Cultural 3
          Some Aspects of Historical Materialism 15
          History and Sociology: A Comment 33
          The Scientist as Product and Agent of Change 36

Part Two **SOCIAL ASPECTS OF TECHNOLOGY**

          The Frustration of Technology 47
          Restraints Upon the Utilization of Inventions 75
          Science and War Production 102
          The Challenge of Advancing Technology 122
          Freedom of Research in American Science 133

Part Three **SOCIAL THOUGHT IN PERSPECTIVE**

          Lewis Henry Morgan: American Ethnologist 163
          Lewis Henry Morgan: An Appraisal of His Scientific Contributions 185

A Note on Comte   191
The Liberal Views of Lester F. Ward   200
Franz Boas as Scientist and Citizen   208
Alternative Proposals to Democracy: The Pattern of Fascism   242

Part Four   THE FAMILY

The Family and Cultural Change   263
Engels on the Family   277

Part Five   HEREDITY AND ENVIRONMENT

The Relationship of the Social Sciences to the Biological Sciences From the Point of View of the Sociologist   307
Human Heredity and Environment   316
Genetics Teaching and Lysenko   328

Part Six   SOCIOLOGY OF MEDICINE

Resistances to Medical Change   345
The Health of Towns and the Early Public Health Movement   386
The Physician and Society   395
Socio-Economic Aspects of Heart Diseases   401
The Need for National Health Legislation   412
Toward a Sociology of Medicine   419

Bibliography   425
Index   429

Introduction

This volume brings together posthumously a selection of articles by Bernhard J. Stern which, with one exception, have not hitherto appeared in book form. Their range is remarkably wide, including such diverse topics as sociology, anthropology, race relations, genetics, psychoanalysis, medical sociology and medical care, science and technology, higher education and the theory of historical materialism. So extensive a range in another writer might imply superficiality or merely the popularization of difficult scientific or sociological concepts. With Dr. Stern, however, the very diversity and breadth of his interests enriched his contributions to scholarship. His insights and erudition in one field stimulated his understanding of other fields; his ideas "cross-fertilized" one another.

Born in Chicago in 1894, Dr. Stern's intellectual journey started at the University of Cincinnati where he received his Bachelor's and Master's degrees. His interest in sociology was kindled at the University of Michigan (1920) where he studied under the noted sociologist, Charles Horton Cooley. Although he prepared to enter medical school, he abandoned the plan because of poor health and determined instead to study and teach sociology and anthropology. After a year in Europe at the University of Berlin (1923) and at the London School of Economics (1924), he matriculated at Columbia University where he was influenced by the ideas of Franz Boas and William Fielding Ogburn. Here he received the degree of Doctor of Philosophy in sociology and anthropology (1927). He became an assistant editor of the *Encyclopedia of the Social Sciences* (1931) and was appointed, in the same year,

Lecturer in Sociology at Columbia University and in Anthropology at the New School for Social Research. Except for a brief period as Instructor at the College of the City of New York (1926) and as Assistant Professor of Sociology at the University of Washington (1927-1930), his life of research, writing and teaching was spent at Columbia University. His connection at Columbia and the New School continued for twenty-five years until his death at the age of sixty-two.

Dr. Stern made notable independent contributions to social science research. In anthropology he investigated the culture of the Lummi Indians of the Pacific Northwest; he wrote on the concept of culture and published a standard text (with Melville Jacobs) in anthropology. He was the first American sociologist to work seriously and intensively in the field of the sociology of medicine. His doctoral dissertation, *Social Factors in Medical Progress* (Columbia University Press, 1927), and his first book, *Should We Be Vaccinated?* (Harpers, 1927), anticipated the field of specialization to which he was to devote some of his ripest years and in which he did what many consider his most significant research. Dr. Stern wrote six books and many papers in medical sociology. These works had wide influence and remain authoritative sources. In 1948, at the request of the Puerto Rican government, he studied the hospital needs of the island and made recommendations for the establishment of Puerto Rico's first industrial hospital.

A distinguishing mark of Dr. Stern's thought and teaching was his emphasis on the importance of environmental influences on mankind's advance. As early as any of his contemporaries in the social sciences, he took issue with those who held that there were inherently inferior characteristics in certain races. Often against vigorous opposition he supported the view, now generally held, that a favorable environment may outweigh an apparent genetic handicap in the development of an individual and, indeed, a race; likewise he held that an unfavorable environment may render superior genetic inheritance useless. Combatting prevalent ideas that the Negro race was inferior, he became a staunch defender and lifelong advocate of racial equality and integration of Negroes. His deep respect for the dignity of the individual and his abiding faith in man's ability to mold his environment for social betterment became the basic motifs of his life and work.

Linked closely with these views was Dr. Stern's Marxist orientation. At a memorial meeting at Columbia University on November 29, 1956, Dr. Corliss Lamont spoke of his career with the affection of a friend and the insight of a scholar:

> Basically Bernhard had a Marxist viewpoint. He believed in a materialist interpretation of history and society, and he advocated democratic socialism as the most intelligent way of solving the unprecedented problems confronting this country and the world at large in the 20th century. These views, which he maintained uncompromisingly during the latter part of his life, marked him, of course, as a non-conformist on the American scene. [But] he was an independent Marxist who did his own thinking. . . . Those who were well acquainted with him knew that he was neither dogmatic nor propagandist in his opinions.

Thus, Dr. Stern remained skeptical about the genetics of Lysenko. Obligated by the scientific method, he had to see experimental proof of Lysenko's hypotheses before he would reject the accepted Mendelian interpretations. His essay on Lysenko, published in the heat of the controversy, is reprinted here.

Dr. Stern's service in the clarification of what might be called the ideology of a science was not limited to genetics. In an early essay, "Concerning the Distinction Between the Social and the Cultural," published in 1929 and included in this volume, he defined his concept of culture. Twenty-three years later, his colleague at Columbia University, Professor A. L. Kroeber, pointed out the significance of this article. In his volume *Culture: A Critical Review of Concepts and Definitions* (1952), Professor Kroeber wrote:

> In 1929 . . . Bernhard Stern published his important article explicitly distinguishing society from culture and pointing out conceptual deficiencies due to the ambiguity of using "social" to cover phenomena of both society and culture. It is evident that for a decade or more previously there had been half-conscious uneasinesses and stirrings against the conceptual haziness and undifferentiation of social and cultural phenomena; but the explicit partition appears

not to have come until 1929. Once it had been effected it was natural that it should be reflected in . . . formal definitions.

The importance of this essay lay not only in the distinction made between the concepts of the social and the cultural but also in its rejection of the determinism that then dominated sociology under the influence of Herbert Spencer's social Darwinism. In due time the distinction made here became one of the refutations of Spencer's theory. Two decades later, in "Some Aspects of Historical Materialism," Dr. Stern presented his concept of culture more fully and demonstrated his profound grasp of historical materialist analysis.

Dr. Stern's broad human sympathies had early led him to reject the views of such influential sociologists as Franklin H. Giddings, William Graham Sumner and Albert E. Keller, whose philosophy was essentially social Darwinism. He sought instead to uncover the roots of American sociology and anthropology in the works of its earlier democratic-minded founders: Lewis Henry Morgan, Lester Frank Ward, Albion Small, and E. A. Ross. To keep alive their democratic concepts in an age when elitist and irrationalist views were gaining currency, he unearthed, edited, and published their correspondence with colleagues at home and abroad. On Morgan, he wrote several papers—two of which appear here— as well as an extensive critique: *Lewis Henry Morgan, Social Evolutionist* (University of Chicago Press, 1931); he edited *Young Ward's Diary* (Putnam, 1936) which he discovered among Lester Ward's papers. In these contributions, he sought to clarify the vague democratic concepts of the earlier sociologists and place them in their historical setting.

Dr. Stern's interdisciplinary approach enabled him to relate every subject of study to social change and the social welfare. In probing the factors affecting social change, he directed his attention to the influences of technology, and noted that scientific developments often were impeded and, perhaps, even lost to our society because of its economic and social structure. In his essays on science and technology, printed here, he emphasizes the cultural and technological obstacles to advances in scientific knowledge, research and techniques.

As in his other fields of special interest, Dr. Stern's approach to the sociology of medicine was historical. By tracing the development of medical ideas or problems in the organization of medical care he shed light on the basic social goals of medicine in society and contributed a fresh perspective on contemporary medical problems. He probed the social dynamics of disease and health services and the effect of social attitudes on medical practice. Unlike the current fashion in medical sociology of using research in the social institution of medicine for the study of interpersonal relations, his research illuminated the real and pressing problems to be faced. He lent his great scholarship, in fact, to the general movement for improved financing and distribution of medical care in the United States. His papers not only reveal important facets of the place of medicine in American society, but they demonstrate that accurate description and objective analysis can be combined with a clear effort toward social progress. "The many now at work in the sociology of medicine," his colleague Professor Robert K. Merton wrote shortly after Dr. Stern's death, "are all the beneficiaries of his pioneering studies begun only twenty years ago. . . . We sociologists have taken particular pride in having Bernhard Stern represent us to disciplines which otherwise knew little or nothing of our work or of our capacities."

In 1936, Dr. Stern joined with others in the founding and editorship of the quarterly journal, *Science and Society*. He gave his immense energy, zeal and enthusiasm to developing it into a magazine of high academic standards for the expression of Marxist and left-wing scholarship in every discipline. Many of the essays that appear here were first published in this journal to which he gave steadfast devotion until his death. However, he also found time to write for other publications and to participate in professional societies. Elected secretary of the Eastern Sociological Society in 1943, he served it for nine years, and he was an ardent member of the Teachers Union from its earliest days.

Dr. Stern's Marxist views intensified his already keen interest in world affairs. Alarmed at the rise of fascism in Germany and Italy, he feared, if Hitler triumphed, that a similar pattern might emerge in America and watched events overseas to determine their implications for the domestic scene. The article, "Alternative

Proposals to Democracy," included in this collection, was written prior to the United States' entry into World War II.

A prime source of stimulus to Dr. Stern's scholarship came through his associations with his students. Teaching was one of the deepest of his interests and he looked upon it not only as a profession but as an art to be constantly improved with new and finer techniques. He applied the Socratic method in his classes, and teaching became an exciting enterprise of joint participation. In this sense, he was both sharer and shaper. Mrs. Ruth Kitchen, an anthropology student, summed it up:

> His influence upon his students was profound, for he taught them, not his way of thinking but how to think for themselves, not apathetic acceptance of old ideas, but how to make critical evaluations. The combination of magnificent scholarship, intellectual integrity, and boundless, infectious enthusiasm made anthropology alive, not a study of the past but a tool with which to understand the present.

This admiration for him was shared by students and colleagues alike. After his death, his associates at *Science and Society* wrote:

> ... Ever conscious of the community of scholars, believing that scholarship obligated the common acceptance of scientific method rather than a common body of dogma, he was as desirous of training scholars as of being one himself. ... Always forthright in the expression of his views, he gained respect because he also genuinely recognized the right of others to dissent. Himself a dissenter from stereotyped opinions and prejudiced attitudes, he could respect views different from his own, provided they were honestly based upon facts. Free from evasiveness himself, he disliked hypocrisy wherever he found it. He associated freedom of speech with freedom of research, and both as scholar and as citizen opposed the hypocrisy of denying or perverting our democratic heritage of law and tradition.

In the essays that follow, readers will find a scholarly and masterful confirmation of these principles.

Acknowledgments

Charlotte Stern acknowledges the invaluable assistance of Dr. Milton I. Roemer, Charles Madison, Dr. and Mrs. Robert V. Sager, Dr. Edwin Berry Burgum, Mrs. Ethel S. Brook, and of her daughter, Dr. Mira Wilkins, in assembling these essays for publication and in preparation of the introduction; and extends thanks to Florence Heath Stevens for her constant, devoted secretarial help. The unfailing dedication, advice and guidance of Joseph H. Crown, secretary-treasurer of the Bernhard J. Stern Memorial Fund Committee, in all stages of the work is gratefully appreciated.

part one

PERSPECTIVES

Concerning the Distinction Between the Social and the Cultural

The distinction between the social and the cultural is predicated on the distinction between the organic and superorganic, the biological and the cultural. It implies acknowledgment of the premise that there is a sharp and distinct cleavage between the mechanisms of biological inheritance that perpetuate the physiological characteristics of the human species and the factors that underlie cultural change. Culture, it holds to be traditionally accumulative, independent of change in biologically inherited traits, acquired anew in its changing manifestations by each succeeding generation. Individuals, born into a cultural as well as a physiographic environment, are thought to possess at birth, the same physiological characteristics, unique to *Homo sapiens,* as has the human species for centuries. Differences in the behavior of persons in various historical periods and contemporary varied culture areas are ascribed to the conditioning of culture at that time and place. Culture is believed to have its own processes and mechanism of change and interrelation of traits, which can be studied and which will eventually be formulated.[1]

---

[1] The recognition of culture as an objective entity is anticipated with varying degrees of emphasis, clarity and consistency in the concept of "achievement" of Lester Ward, in the "mores" of Sumner, in W. I. Thomas' essay on "The Mind of Woman and the Lower Races" and among European writers in the "collective representations" of Durkheim and in the writings of Vierkandt. It is implicit in the works of the "historical materialists" following Marx. The recent formulation of the subject is due to the work of Kroeber in America and Rivers in England, elaborated upon and brought to the attention of American sociologists principally through the agency of W. F. Ogburn's *Social Change,* Clark Wissler's *Man and Culture,* R. H. Lowie's

The failure to distinguish between the biological and the cultural, still widespread, led Lewis Henry Morgan to maintain that "the custom of saluting by kin, the usage of wearing the breech-cloth and the usage of sleeping at night in a state of nudity, each person in a separate cover" were "transmitted with the blood"[2] and Max Mueller to declare that language arose from a certain number of phonetic types "which had been implanted in the human mind by the hand of God."[3] Social scientists no longer argue about the question which once aroused much controversy, as to whether deaf-mutes have any inborn notions of theology,[4] but much of the eugenic literature is not far removed from this discussion. Witness the following typical confusion of the biological and cultural extracted from a widely circulated volume on eugenics.

> Our main conclusion is that if we would save the world from calamity, we must not merely *teach* people religion and common sense, we must begin at once to *produce* people possessing those qualities by inheritance . . . the only road lies along the path of biological wisdom. The intellectual, the imaginative, creative, and artistic faculties of the mind must be biologically combined with the faculties which insure survival. They must blend harmoniously with the practical ability which makes people able wisely to manage their own affairs and above all with an innate religious and moral tendency which causes people to reverence one another and respect the rules of conduct which have been laid down by the accumulated wisdom of the ages.[5]

The same fallacy is found in the writings of many biologists too critical to accept the eugenists' creed. The late Professor Bateson once declared that "superstition is due to a specific ingredient in

---

Culture and Ethnology, and M. M. Willey and M. J. Herskovits, "The Cultural Approach to Sociology," *American Journal of Sociology*, xxix, 189–199.

[2] *Systems of Consanguinity*, pp. 274–5.

[3] *Lectures in the Science of Language*, pp. 427 *sq*.

[4] J. Kerr Love, *Deaf-mutism*, pp. 259 *sq*. Cited by R. Briffault, *Mothers*, I, 68.

[5] Ellsworth Huntington and Leon F. Whitney, *The Builders of America*, pp. 271–2.

the germ cell."[6] Goldenweiser lapses into the prevalent confusion when he interrupts a discussion of the nature of civilization to write:

> The talent of an Edison is a congenital gift. Even though born in early pre-history he would have been an Edison, but he could not have invented the incandescent lamp. Instead, he might have originated one of the early methods of making fire. Raphael, if brought to life in a Bushman family, would have drawn curiously realistic cattle on the walls of caves as well as steatopygous Bushman women. Had Beethoven been a Chinaman, he would have composed some of those delightfully cacophonous melodies which the seeker for the quaint and unusual pretends to enjoy in Chinatown.[7]

This quotation reflects a common belief in talent which implies an organic propensity for a cultural institution. But can a culture trait be anticipated in the germ plasm of a species that attained its physiological attributes prior to the existence of that culture? Does not the infant organism respond to cultural institutions only as a combination of wave lengths of physical energy and is not meaning derived only through the cultural setting? To consider only one of Goldenweiser's examples, there is certainly a great disparity between the stimuli playing upon the individual from fire and from an incandescent lamp, arousing different physiological responses. Fire and an incandescent lamp are culturally, and only remotely physiologically, related; neither is organically anticipated. For while culture is limited by the ability of the

---

[6] William Bateson, *Methods and Scope of Genetics*, p. 34.

[7] Alexander Goldenweiser, *Early Civilization*, pp. 18–19. On the other hand see his statement: "Those who insist on the social being a phenomenon *sui generis* and on culture being in its nature historical, base their opinion on a real fact. While the content of culture, in so far as it counts, lies in the psychological level and can only be understood and interpreted through the attitudes and tendencies in that level, it cannot be derived from it nor from the attitudes and tendencies embedded in it. A psychological interpretation of a culture can explain its content (explanation here standing for interpretive description) but it cannot account for it. This is a corollary of the fact that the cultural content is an heritage of the past and that it is cumulative. This cumulation is an historical and objective phenomenon." "History, Psychology and Culture" *Journal of Philosophy, Psychology and the Scientific Method*, XV, 566 n.b.

organism to respond to it, no cultural institution can be considered organically anticipated.[8]

Discussion of the objective reality of culture has hitherto centered around the fact that it is distinct from individual behavior. The treatment is often ambiguous, however, because cultural behavior is improperly designated by the term social. For the sake of clarity, the two concepts, social and cultural, must be rigidly distinguished and their meanings sharply defined.[9]

II

Social life precedes culture and is distinct from it. Anecdotal anthropomorphisms still persist in ascribing to the lower animals, especially to the social insects, cultural behavior. However, although great plasticity and adaptability of animal behavior to physical environmental stimuli are now recognized, dispelling the erroneous belief that animal behavior is rigidly predetermined by "instinct," careful investigators are generally agreed that the social activities of insects and other living sub-human social

[8] Cf. C. M. Child, *Physiological Foundations of Behavior;* L. L. Bernard, *Instinct.*

[9] It is frequently maintained that "scientific progress will not be made by mere voting about words." Science is, of course, not a mere matter of lexicography; the scholastics excelled in definition. But certainly sociology has suffered as a science because of the lack of precision of its fundamental concepts due to the ambiguity of its word meanings. Most of the terminology of sociology has been taken over directly from the vernacular. No science has had greater difficulty in coining new symbols to indicate with increasing exactitude its accumulative control over its subject matter. In view of the difficulty of creating new words, it becomes necessary for sociologists to become exegetes of meanings of old words, to defy customary associations which have become attached to terms and to insist on rigid exclusive connotations. Unfortunately, this often casts the sociologist into the rôle of an extreme literalist, a scholiast who seems merely to manipulate word masks to hide insufficient evidence. Upton Sinclair was but manifesting the impatience of the non-academic world at this procedure when he declared sociology to be "an elaborate structure of classifications, wholly artificial, devised by learned gentlemen in search of something to be learned about." Yet in science symbols must have exact significance to have value; it remains for sociologists to devise a method whereby standard symbols can be agreed upon that the energies devoted to wrangling over meanings may be devoted to more fruitful channels. Until then, one must risk the accusation that he is engaging in casuistry and "word-polishing" when he insists on distinctions which he considers pertinent.

animals are derived through heredity. Professor Wheeler, who examined ants preserved in Baltic amber of the Lower Oligocene period of from fifty to seventy-five million years ago, declares that the evidence shows conclusively that: "ants . . . had at that time developed all their various castes just as we see them today, that the larvae and pupae were the same, that they attended plant lice, kept guest beetles in their nests and had parasitic mites attached to their legs in the same peculiar position as our living species. . . ."[10]

Kroeber, cognizant of this evidence and its significance, asserts:

> Social the ant is, in the sense that she associates; but she is so far from being social in the sense of possessing civilization, of being influenced by non-organic forces, that she would better be known as the anti-social animal.[11]

The use here of the word *social* with dual meaning obscures the important distinction which Kroeber is making. All the mechanisms of social behavior are present in the social insects and other sub-human species without culture being present. Conflict and accommodation, leadership, rivalry, subordination, control, cooperation, parasitism and other aspects of social life are manifested among them as among men. The processes underlying the social behavior of men remain hereditary but associative patterns are modified by cultural stimuli. The use of the term *social* should be confined to these processes. For, when it is used to embrace not only the processes but the cultural pattern which acts as a stimulus as well, there is a slurring of the important rôle that culture plays independently of social processes, and an obscuring of the changes that occur within culture.

The cultural life of man as distinguished from the social life of sub-human groups is dependent on articulate language.[12] Animals

---

[10] Wm. Morton Wheeler, "Social Life of Insects," *Scientific Monthly*, XIV, 497–524. See also *Ants; their Structure, Development and Behavior; the Social Insects;* and the notes to his translation of Reaumur's *Natural History of Ants;* Auguste Forel, *The Social World of the Ants.*

[11] A. L. Kroeber, "The Superorganic," *American Anthropologist*, XIX, 176–7.

[12] Articulate language has its antecedents in the emotional cries and calls of the sub-human species. Learned recognized thirty-two sounds or elements of speech among the anthropoid apes relating to food, drink and other ani-

not possessing articulate language manifest all the social processes observable in human society, indicating that it is not indispensable to social life. Once present, however, it accelerates and heightens communication which facilitates individual and group interrelations. Substituting sign words for highly complex images or association of images, speech enormously facilitates the formation of those associations which are the basis of cultural life. The most important influence of language on social life is derived through its making possible the accumulation and transmission of culture. Recent studies of sub-human animals, especially of anthropoid apes, reveal the presence of many factors upon which culture depends, learning, inventiveness, memory, even the beginnings of symbolic abstraction.[13] But the absence of an articulate language prevents cultural life in the sense possessed by men. Articulate language alone offers sufficient symbolic abstraction to permit conceptual projection beyond individual experience and substitution of symbol for behavior making possible the accumulative retention, transmission, and diffusion of culture. With the inception of culture, human behavior responds to artificial, external patterns; social behavior becomes culturally modified and variable.

Cultural phenomena do, therefore, not create man's social behavior but presuppose man's organic potentialities for social life.

---

mals and persons. R. M. Yerkes, *Almost Human*, p. 137 *sq*. But there is a vast development in language from these rudimentary beginnings to flexible human speech. As Professor Boas writes: "Although means of communication by sound exist in animals, and even though lower animals seem to have means of bringing about co-operation between different individuals, we do not know of any case of true articulate language from which the student can abstract principles of classification of ideas." Franz Boas, *Mind of Primitive Man*, p. 96.

[13] W. Koehler, *Mentality of the Apes;* R. M. Yerkes and M. S. Child, "Anthropoid Behavior," *Quarterly Review of Biology*, II, 33–57; R. M. Yerkes, "The Mind of a Gorilla," Genetic Psychology Monographs, Clark University; P. M. Descamps, "Les differences sociologiques entre les sauvages et les anthropoides," *L'Antropologie*, XXX, 137–147; A. L. Kroeber, "Sub-Human Culture Beginnings," *Quarterly Review of Biology*, III, 325–342. That the significance of this material is yet not fully grasped is seen by the fact that a writer of the standing of Griffith Taylor can still write: "The chief difference between man and the lower animals is in the development of the reasoning faculties." *Environment and Race*, p. 40.

Social life is a *sine qua non* for cultural development and transmission. But culture traits once established have their own history and causal relations apart from the individuals or groups that initiate and perpetuate them. These culture traits afford factors additional to the physical environment, which modify the original functioning of the mechanisms of individual and group interrelations by establishing diverse patterns. Forms of social organization are imposed upon a *human* community by culture and not by nature.[14] The mating, rutting, and spawning of sub-human animal species, with the ape perhaps excepted [15] is purely physiological pattern behavior; there are fixed seasons for sexual activity and inactivity, fixed forms of sex association. For man, a culture pattern enters and restrains, inhibits and conditions the forms of mating by a variable artificial set of conditions. Among some of the lower animals there are well defined divisions of labor which are organically determined although they are adaptable to varying physiographic conditions. In human communities, division of labor is variable according to the culture pattern. When sub-human animal and human associations appear analogous, upon investigation it is seen that they are so only in their superficial external manifestations. Man's social behavior is always conditioned by the additional factors imposed by culture in its material and non-material manifestations, with its artificial taboos, historically derived restraints and sanctions. These factors are cultural products as distinct from social processes. They impinge on and determine the social behavior of their possessors but they are independent of any group or any individual. External to psychological "aptitudes" and physiological equipment, they have objective reality; they have their own geographic distribution and diffusion history which may be studied without regard to the organic characteristics of those whose behavior they affect.

[14] See especially the discussion of this point by B. Malinowski, *Sex and Repression in Savage Society*, pp. 190–191. Cf. John Dewey, *Human Nature and Conduct*, pp. 58–9.

[15] G. S. Miller, "Some Elements in the Sexual Behavior in Primates and Their Possible Influence on the Beginnings of Human Social Development," *Journal of Mammalogy*, IX, 273–293.

III

A further need for a precise distinction between the social and the cultural arises from the fact that a specific culture trait is not always correlated with the same social behavior. The elements of culture cannot be conceived of as static standardized products but must be thought of as fluctuating variable forms. When a culture trait diffuses, its meaning may be modified although it retains a similar external form, and in its new meaning acts as a stimulus for different social behavior. Ruth Benedict found that the vision-guardian spirit concept had associated itself with puberty ceremonies in one region, with totemism in another, in a third with secret societies, in a fourth with inherited rank, in a fifth with black magic.[16] There is great external similarity of detail in the Navajo and Hopi ceremonies that indicates extensive borrowing, but among the former, the ceremonies are focused on the healing of the sick and among the latter are directed on the production of fertility for the fields.[17] Spier found that the sun dance had a variety of meanings among the different tribes of the Plains; it was undertaken to purchase the right of the sacred bundle, it was a tribal seasonal ceremony, it was performed in fulfilment of a vow in time of distress.[18] Examples could be multiplied indicating the changes in meaning and hence in provoked social response of culture traits and complexes in different historical situations and in different areas during the process of diffusion.[19] These changes have often been vaguely ascribed to the psychology of the different peoples possessing the culture trait, but this must be finally resolved into the effect of cultural conditioning. The culture pattern standardizes social behavior which then acts as a selective factor for the rejection or adaptation of new cultural elements. There is no specific form of social behavior which is "inherent in the nature of" any human group. Its social behavior at any time is determined by the culture pattern then

[16] *The Concept of the Guardian Spirit in North America*, p. 84.
[17] H. K. Haeberlin, *The Idea of Fertilization in the Culture of the Pueblo Indians*, p. 9.
[18] Leslie Spier, *The Plains Indian Sun Dance*, passim. For his conclusions see pp. 520–522.
[19] Franz Boas, *Anthropology and Modern Life*, pp. 131–163.

prevailing, not by any postulated racial or group psychological variations. The proof lies in the evidence of extreme modifiability of all races and groups under diverse cultural stimuli. Each race or group is the potential basis of many diverse cultures.

IV

It is often assumed that if one goes back far enough in culture history, he must eventually find the source of culture in the physiological equipment of man.[20] Those who speak in terms of "basic needs," "basic instincts," "drives" and "tendencies" postulate them, not merely as functioning within the pattern of culture but as being the prime causes of culture. It is simple to indicate that the existence of a "need" or "drive" does not imply its gratification and hence the concept of physiological propulsion is not a satisfactory explanation of cultural origins. For this reason also, the postulated "psychic unity" of the human species, leading to like social behavior, if unmodified by cultural stimuli, may be granted without considering it the "cause" of the universal culture pattern.[21] It must be recognized that the fossil precursors of man, from whom

[20] Wissler states that he is "frankly puzzled" at this problem and then falls back on Woodworth's "drives" and "a functional pattern for inborn human behavior" to explain the universal culture pattern, begging the question by asserting "it seems reasonable to suppose that what all men have in common is inherited. Hence in so far as their behavior is uniform, we may expect it to be grounded in original nature." He recognizes the weakness of this position when he asserts: ". . . we cannot adequately define, least of all visualize the universal (native) pattern. The categories and other terms of classification, we used in Part II (where the form and content of culture are discussed, B. J. S.) are expressed in terms of culture data, whereas the universal pattern is something of another order, to be defined, if at all, in terms adequate to the expression of biological relations. Hence it should not be assumed that the facts of culture are inherited, or that the categories we used when considering culture objectively, are themselves integral parts of the germ plasm." *Man and Culture*, pp. 260–280.

[21] Bastian conceived of universal "elemental ideas" which were tendencies and potentialities in the human species, which anticipated but only found expression in the form of "folk ideas," but he does not explain how. Goldenweiser writes of Bastian: "To him original nature comprised much more in absorptive power and creativeness than do the denuded psyches of Watson's infants or those of the half-witted morons postulated by the diffusionists" but grants that clarity was not one of Bastian's virtues. "Anthropology and Psychology" in W. F. Ogburn and A. Goldenweiser, *The Social Sciences and Their Interrelations*, p. 71.

Homo sapiens was a biological variant, already had a culture, and that probably human behavior was culturally conditioned from the very start. If the monogenic origin of the human species is held, the universality of the pattern of culture may be explained by the assumption that as man migrated in early quaternary times, he carried his then existing culture with him. Upon this basic culture pattern, accretions were made and differentiations took place, leading to the diversity of the Old World and American culture patterns, and further variations within these two large areas due to both independent invention and diffusion.[22] If these hypotheses are correct, man's social behavior was culturally modified from his appearance on earth, and culture had pre-human origins.[23]

V

To state that culture had existential reality independent of, although always found in conjunction with, the social aggregation of individuals who respond to and modify its ever changing patterns, posits psychological mechanisms underlying social behavior and does not ignore them as has already been indicated.[24] The tendency has been, however, for sociologists to think less frequently of culture than of the associations of individuals that carry culture, the social processes underlying those associations and the

---

[22] Franz Boas, "America and the Old World," XXIe *Congres International des Americanistes*, pp. 22–28; also "Migrations of Asiatic Races and Cultures to North America," *Scientific Monthly*, XXVIII, 110–117.

[23] It is recognized that this merely shifts the problem of cultural origins to pre-human groups. That this is what must be done is indicated in the previous references to anthropoid behavior. See especially A. L. Kroeber, "Sub-Human Culture Beginnings," *Quarterly Journal of Biology*, III, 325–342.

[24] Critics often charge those who lay emphasis on cultural objectivism with neglecting the psychological factors involved in cultural transmission and in individual and group interrelations. The charge is hardly justified. With the exception of the work of Graebner and of the extreme diffusionists such as G. Elliott Smith, whose work is not given credence by any critical anthropologists (See the *Diffusion Controversy*, Smith and others), the importance of the psychological is repeatedly stressed. Cf. Franz Boas, *Primitive Art*; and *Anthropology and Modern Life*, pp. 131–163; Robert H. Lowie, "Psychology and Culture," *American Journal of Sociology*, XXI, 217–229; W. H. R. Rivers, "Sociology and Psychology," *Sociological Review*, IX, 1–13; A. L. Kroeber, "The Possibility of a Social Psychology," *American Journal of Sociology*, XXIII, 633–650.

psychic experiences of individuals conveying culture. Because the term social is used for both the processes underlying and the content comprising culture, cultural elements are often regarded as mere aggregations of psychic phenomena rather than superorganic determinants of associative patterns. This criticism may be especially leveled at the sociologists following Simmel who conceive sociology to be exclusively a science of the "forms of socialization" or the "forms of human relationship." Originally acknowledging the importance of "content" but ruling it out of the province of sociology, many of these sociologists later attempted to reduce all cultural phenomena to social processes. But to avoid Procrustean disposal of ill-digested cultural data into preconceived social-psychological categories, one must first study the cultural factors that determine the functioning of the social-psychological processes. In the words of Rivers: "Confusion reigns in the sociology of today through the attempt to formulate the psychological explanations of social (the context indicates that the word "social" is here used in the sense of the cultural, B. J. S.) phenomena before we have determined the course of the historical development of the phenomena with which we have to do."[25] He later illustrated his contention by his critical analysis of Westermarck's misinterpretation of the blood-feud.[26] The most vivid corroboration of the value of distinguishing between the cultural and the social and of the need of studying the cultural before making social-psychological generalizations is the recent work of Malinowski.[27] By revealing how the "family complex" or "nuclear complex" varies with the distribution of authority in the family and the different modes of counting kinship, he has been able to prove the untenability of the Freudian view of the universality of the Oedipus complex.

The recognition of the objective reality of culture and the understanding of the distinction between the cultural and the social are fundamental to a precise formulation of the problems of sociological research. Revisions of social-psychological cate-

[25] "Survival in Sociology," *Sociological Review*, VI, 293–305.
[26] *Op. cit.* Vol. IX, 2.
[27] B. Malinowski, *Sex and Repression in Savage Society*.

gories will probably ensue when these discriminations are more generally accepted as basic.

Some Aspects of Historical Materialism

The doctrine of integrative levels is either tacitly or explicitly accepted by many sociologists and anthropologists. Its underlying hypothesis that every level of organization of phenomena has its own regularities and principles not reducible to those appropriate to lower levels of organization is implicit in their use of the concept of culture. Most social scientists acknowledge that there is a sharp and distinct cleavage between the mechanisms of biological inheritance, which transmit physical and physiological characteristics of the human species, and man's cultural traditions that are historically transmitted. Cultural change is now generally recognized as occurring independently of change in biologically inherited traits, and as having its own underlying processes and laws. Racial and physiographic determinist explanations of human behavior have been discredited as the significance of the culture concept has come to be appreciated. There has likewise been a recognition of the fact that human group life and forms of association are patterned by a historically derived cultural tradition rather than by the genetic transmission of behavior patterns as among the social insects.

That cultural phenomena require analysis on a level distinct from the psychological was noted by Marx as early as 1859 in his preface to *A Contribution to the Critique of Political Economy*. It has been advocated repeatedly in different contexts and with varying degrees of explicitness since Tylor's *Primitive Culture* (1871), Durkheim's *Les Règles de la méthode sociologique* (1894), and by Kroeber and other anthropologists in their formation of the "superorganic" in the first decades of the twentieth century. Nevertheless, controversy on the nature of the relation between cultural and psychological processes in human behavior has persisted, and has recently mounted in intensity as interest in personality studies has grown. In 1916 Wissler stated more sharply than most of his contemporaries the limitations of psychological interpretations of culture:

> When we are dealing with phenomena that belong to original nature we are quite right in using psychological and biological methods; but the moment we step over into cultural phenomena we must recognize its historical nature. . . . We often read that if cultural phenomena can be reduced to terms of association of ideas, motor elements, etc., there remains but to apply psychological principles to it to reveal its causes. This is a vain hope. All the knowledge of the mechanism of association in the world will not tell us why any particular association is made by a particular individual, will not explain the invention of the bow, the origin of exogamy, or of any other trait of culture except in terms that are equally applicable to all.[1]

This quotation hits upon what is significant in the doctrine of integrative levels. It does not negate the importance of the psychological processes underlying all cultural phenomena just as biological processes underlie all psychological phenomena. However, it stresses the fact that reduction to a psychological level cannot explain any specific aspect or pattern of culture, for each is a historical product; and that, to interpret properly the forms and functions of culture as they condition the behavior of humans, one must understand their historical backgrounds. Few contemporary sociologists now deny the correlative generalization that, once humans invented culture, a process with its own distinctive characteristics came into being which is not organic, however intimate may be the reciprocal relations between the organic, the psychic, and the cultural.

Some social scientists who are preoccupied with psychological, and especially psychoanalytic, studies have, however, focused on the fact that, since man is the active functioning agent in culture,

[1] Clark Wissler, "Psychological and Historical Interpretations for Culture," *Science*, 43:200–201 (1916).

cultural change consists, in the last analysis, of changes in the attitudes and habits of the individuals who compose society. They have thus tended to conceive of culture merely as a methodological abstraction, and to regard study of the psychological processes of the individuals and group carriers of culture as the crucially important area of study. While a few social scientists have discussed culture schematically, ignoring the fact that it is always the possession of individual human beings interacting in groups in society, the critics of such formalistic analysis, who would confine their studies to the behavior of individuals, have sometimes negated the concept of culture by seeking to reduce all cultural behavior merely to psychological processes.

There has been considerable unrewarding controversy, therefore, around the contrast of culture as a thing in itself, and culture as an activity of persons participating in it. Actually both approaches are valid, and are required to supplement each other for a rounded understanding of cultural behavior. It is necessary to renounce both a reduction of culture to the level of psychology and an overdrawn demarcation between the psychological and cultural-historical sciences. There is special danger that the social psychologist in his studies of the processes in the growth of personality and in interpersonal interactions will lose sight of the fact that the cultural media in which these take place—that is, the cultural patterns which condition individual and group behavior—are historical products. On the other hand, when culture is conceived to be something entirely unrelated to the participation of people who manipulate it with varying degrees of creativeness, and who respond diversely to the inventions and innovations of others, it can be composed of nothing but empty, formal categories. Some of the studies of the distribution of culture traits merit such criticism.

Marett long ago warned that the study of culture might result in a "bloodless typology." In urging that the methods used in the social sciences conform to the subject matter, rather than the subject matter to method, he argued cogently that the respective methods of geology and human history must needs be poles asunder because the earth is dead while man is alive. He went on to say:

It is quite legitimate to regard culture, or social tradition, in an abstract way as a tissue of externalities, as a robe of many colors woven on the loom of time. . . . Moreover, for certain purposes, which in their entirety may be called sociological, it is actually convenient thus to concentrate on the outer garb. In this case, indeed, the garb may well at first sight seem to count for everything, for certainly a man naked of all culture would be no better than a forked radish. . . . Human history (nevertheless) is no Madame Tussaud's show of decorated dummies. It is instinct with purposive movement through and through. . . .

According to the needs of the work lying nearest to our hand, let us play the sociologist or the psychologist, without prejudice as regards ultimate explanations. On one point only I would insist, namely that the living must be studied on its own right and not by means of methods borrowed from the study of the lifeless. If a purely sociological treatment contemplates man as if there were no life in him, there will likewise be no life in it. The nemesis of a deterministic attitude towards history is a deadly dullness.[2]

This is similar to the argument of historical materialism in its attack upon mechanists who deal with formal abstractions rather than with concrete life situations in all their complex manifestations. Historical materialists urge careful consideration of the reciprocal interaction between man and his cultural-historical and group environment, and note that man serves as an active agent in the historical process within the broad limits of the specific culture in which he lives. Man possesses psychological capacities unique to *Homo sapiens* which enable him to respond to environmental stimuli both overtly and symbolically. Capable of being motivated by goals and stimulated by natural needs and acquired interests, he introduces changes in historical situations in his effort to control and to manipulate the environment to his own advantage. This reciprocal process of interaction between culture and individual personalities and group relations results in the creative recasting of culture and the consequent transformation of personality and of group patterns. Marxists thus not only recognize the historical nature of culture but also insistently take account of man as a dynamic agent in culture. They decry all

[2] R. R. Marett, *Psychology and Folklore* (London, 1920), pp. 12–13.

efforts of mechanists to depict the cultural process as automatic and humans as passive automatons. Engels declared, for example: "In the history of society . . . the actors are all endowed with consciousness, are men working with deliberation or passion, working toward definite goals. . . . Men make their own history." He then speaks of "investigating the driving forces which—consciously or unconsciously, and indeed very often unconsciously—lie behind the motives of men in their historical actions."[3]

Lenin particularly stressed this purposefulness of human activity as the basis of the revolutionary dynamic. For persons to wait passively for cultural change to occur within the class structure of society, he regarded as a shallow depreciation of the power of men to influence the direction of cultural development. It is for this reason that he underscored the importance of leadership and organization in the struggle for power.[4]

Faith in the ability of human beings to influence the course of history, to plan the direction of cultural change, distinguishes historical materialists sharply from such American sociologists as Sumner and Keller, who have been very influential particularly through their concept of the mores. To them the mores make up a superorganic system of relations, conventions, and institutional arrangements, which are by origin chance products of a long series of minute trial-and-error adjustments to physical, social, and supernatural environments, dictated by needs and motivated by hunger, sex, passion, vanity, and fear. The mores are conceived as functioning through individuals without possible coordination by any formal authority. The effect of this concept upon sociologists of the Sumner and Keller school is best exemplified in the editorial preface to a volume of studies dedicated to Keller, which states:

> That societal adjustment is achieved in the main automatically through the operation of massive impersonal forces of which the individuals concerned are rarely more than dimly aware, is perhaps the major single contribution of Professor Keller. Social movements

[3] F. Engels, "Ludwig Feuerbach and the Outcome of German Classical Philosophy," in Karl Marx, *Selected Works* (New York, 1936–1937), 1:457–459.
[4] See especially V. I. Lenin, *What Is to Be Done?* (New York, 1929).

spring from the blind reactions of men in the mass to largely unanalyzed economic and emotional incentives. The individual can do little to thwart, direct, or accelerate such movements.

Consequent to this is the generalization:

> To the practical sociologist, awareness of the automatic character of the adjustment process proves an invaluable aid. It stimulates him to study, rather than to advocate schemes for human betterment.[5]

A comparable position is taken by the neo-positivists in sociology, such as Lundberg who proposes a social physics and declares sententiously, "The social sciences are concerned with the behavior of those electro-proton configurations called societal groups, principally human groups."[6] He advocates that sociologists analyze their data in terms of the symbolic techniques of mathematics and scorns what he derisively designates a "mentalistic" type of analysis. The result is that Lundberg's emphasis has been on quantification rather than on thinking and acting. He would even make a cipher of the social scientists, for he suggests that they should be "non-moral" and should be ready to serve any political regime that happens to be in power: "The services of *real* social scientists would be as indispensable to Fascists as to Communists and Democrats, just as are the services of physicists and physicians."[7] He would thus make scientists the passive tools of interest groups rather than active policy makers. The same result was achieved by the conventional, oft reiterated device in sociological circles of contending that the sociologist must abjure value judgments. Such a procedure if conscientiously adhered to would make the sociologist a passive sieve through which data would drain, rather than the interpretive integrator and creative reformulator of knowledge on which action can be based.

Historical materialism, by combining the concept of integrative levels with the recognition of the dynamic power of the individual agent, has avoided the pitfalls of mechanistic sociology. Contentions to the contrary show both ignorance of Marxist literature

---

[5] George P. Murdock, ed., *Studies in the Science of Society* (New Haven, 1937), pp. xviii, xix.
[6] George A. Lundberg, *Foundations of Sociology* (New York, 1939), p. 204.
[7] George A. Lundberg, *Can Science Save Us?* (New York, 1947), p. 48.

and failure to grasp the theoretical significance of the activistic role of Marxist parties in the making of recent history. Such distortion is exemplified in Goldenweiser's statement: "To them [the Marxists] culture is objective, social, historical, cumulative, dynamic, deterministic. To culture the chariot of history is harnessed. The individual is fleeting, passive, epiphenomenal, casually irrelevant."[8] This charge cannot be reconciled with Engels's famous forecast that when history passes under the control of men themselves so that they "will fashion their own history," it will mark "humanity's leap from the realm of necessity to the realm of freedom."[9] It is likewise alien to Marx's much-quoted maxim, "The philosophers have *interpreted* the world in various ways, the point, however, is to *change* it."[10]

The recognition of the reality of culture as a distinctive level of phenomena for scientific inquiry is but the first step for the historical materialist. Culture is too nebulous and omnibus a concept to be an entirely adequate tool of research. What is required is a weighting of the relative importance of its constituent elements, and an understanding of the interrelationships between these elements. Sociologists and anthropologists were long indifferent to inquiries along these lines. Little progress could be made as long as anthropologists argued that inventions were the products of fortuitous combinations of individual incentive and creativeness, favorable geographical opportunities, and the element of pure chance. Since inventions and their diffusion were regarded as unpredictable, cultures were viewed as mere assemblages of "culture traits," with causal relationships between them of little significance.

The functionalists, on the contrary, have assumed that cultures are fully integrated and self-consistent configurations, the functions of the various parts of which can be determined by direct analysis without reference to the history of a culture or its parts. Their studies have been, therefore, merely cross-sectional and

---

[8] Alexander A. Goldenweiser, *History, Psychology, and Culture* (New York, 1933), pp. 61–62.
[9] Friedrich Engels, *Herr Eugen Dühring's Revolution in Science* (Anti-Dühring) (New York, 1939), pp. 309–310.
[10] Karl Marx, "Theses on Feuerbach" (1885), *Selected Works*, 1:473.

have lacked historical perspectives which illuminate causation. In line with their assumption of actual cultural integration, they have argued that everything in a culture that functions has value to that culture and is thus justifiable. No attempt is made to conceive of the possibility of alternative, more effective modes of meeting prevailing psychological and cultural needs. This is illustrated by Malinowski's argument:

> The substance of all religion is thus deeply rooted in human life; it grows out of the necessities of life. In other words, religion fulfills a definite cultural function in every human society. This is not a platitude. It contains a scientific refutation of the repeated attacks upon religion by the less enlightened rationalists.[11]

The functionalists have generally, in a like manner, failed to evaluate what is strategic or essential in the functioning of any culture and what is incidental or peripheral. Radcliffe-Brown, for example, has conveyed the impression that the interrelationship of the clans and the kinship systems with other features of social organization is more significant for an understanding of the functioning of a culture than food collecting, agricultural or pastoral work. Similarly obscure are the sociological proponents of multiple causation who make a fetish of complexity and evade the responsibility of untangling causal interrelationships. For example, Gunnar Myrdal blandly declares, "In an interdependent system of dynamic causation there can be no 'primary cause' but everything is cause to everything else."[12]

Historical materialists on the other hand have taken a decisive stand on the weighing of the importance of different aspects of cultures. One of the most relevant passages in Marxist literature on this point is the comment of Engels in 1890: "We make our own history, but in the first place under definite presuppositions and conditions. Among these the economic ones are finally decisive." This was in a letter in which he vigorously rebuked economic determinists, stating:

[11] B. Malinowski, *The Foundations of Faith and Morals* (London, 1936), p. 59.
[12] Gunnar Myrdal and others, *An American Dilemma* (New York, 1944), p. 78.

If therefore somebody twists this into the statement that the economic element is the only determining one, he transforms it into a meaningless, abstract and absurd phrase. The economic situation is the basis, but the various elements of the superstructure—political forms of the class struggle and its consequences, constitutions established by the victorious class after a successful battle, etc.—forms of law—and then even the reflexes of all these actual struggles in the brains of the combatants: political, legal, philosophical theories, religious ideas and their further development into systems of dogma —also exercise their influence upon the course of historical struggles and in many cases preponderate in determining their *form*. There is endless interaction of all these elements, in which, amid all their endless *host* of accidents (i.e., of things and events whose inner connection is so remote or so impossible to prove that we regard it as absent and can neglect it) the economic movement finally asserts itself as necessary.[13]

Much controversy has arisen over whether Engels was justified in making the economic factor the decisive variable in culture, while not denying the causative role of other aspects of culture in the process of change. Some of this arises from a misinterpretation of the meaning of the word "economic." It is clear from the context of the quoted letter and from other consistent formulations of Marx and Engels that the term is not used in the sense of economic motivations, or the "acquisitive instincts" of an individual, a postulated economic man. Their analysis is in terms of the interrelations of aspects of culture and only secondarily in terms of the derived forms of individual behavior. The economic factor has reference to the modes of production by which people acquire their means of subsistence, and the contention of historical materialism is that other forms of social relations and cultural patterns are basically dependent upon such economic activities. This is effectively stated in a passage written by Engels in 1878:

> The materialist conception of history starts from the principle that production, and with production the exchange of its products, is the basis of every social order; that in every society which has

[13] Letter to J. Bloch, London, Sept. 21, 1890, in Karl Marx and Friedrich Engels, *Correspondence, 1846–1895* (New York, 1934), p. 475.

appeared in history the distribution of its products, and with it the division of society into classes and estates, is determined by what is produced and how it is produced and how the product is exchanged. According to this conception, the ultimate causes of all social changes and political revolutions are to be sought, not in the minds of men, in their increasing insight into eternal truths and justice, but in the changes in the mode of production and exchange; they are to be sought not in the *philosophy* but in the economics of the epoch concerned.[14]

Available evidence validates this principle for primitive societies. Comparative studies of culture substantiate the fact that the forms of social relationships, the religious and political institutions and practices, the arts and the techniques clearly tend to be correlated with the types of economic life of primitive peoples. The crucial factor found to determine the nature and rate of development of cultures is the presence or absence of surpluses, and these depend upon the mode of production.

The characteristics of the mode of production affect the density of the population, the size of the community, the social organization, the division of labor, the degree of specialization, and status and class relationships. The correlations shown in the accompanying table[15] of changes in populations and other cultural relations with changes in the amount of surplus derived from food production, are too consistent to be accidental, and give striking proof of the validity of the Marxian thesis that the economic factor is the decisive variable. It will be seen from the table that when primitive economies are more advanced the population is denser, the village communities larger, the social organization changes its structure, specialization increases, products become more unequally distributed, ownership of strategic resources passes from the community to private hands, and inequalities in the ownership of wealth develop.

The principle that the mode of production is ultimately the determining factor is substantiated by a consideration of the basic

[14] Friedrich Engels, *Herr Eugen Dühring's Revolution in Science*, p. 300.
[15] Based on data given in Melville Jacobs and Bernhard J. Stern, *Outlines of Anthropology* (New York, 1947), pp. 125–134. I am indebted to Melville Jacobs for assistance in formulating these correlations.

social conditions required for the development of arts and crafts and elaborations of social organizational forms. In simple food-gathering economies the activity of every member of the small community is required for the common task of acquiring sufficient food for survival. There is no opportunity for the cultivation of skills, because the energies of all are directed toward maintaining life. Only when food surpluses are available can persons be released to develop the more complicated techniques of the arts and crafts. Similarly, social gatherings and religious ceremonials can flourish only with leisure; hence, complexity of social organization and cultural activities is positively correlated with increases in surpluses derived from economic activities. Ritualistic behavior associated with the public transfer of property involving future obligations of the recipient—e.g., African marriages, the potlatch in Northwest America and the Kula Ring of the Trobriands—depend upon the presence of property surpluses.

The mode of production also determines in a large measure the type of discoveries and inventions made by a society. The concentration of attention upon a specific economic occupation leads to new achievements in the field, although it does not determine the specific form of those achievements. For example, the sea-hunting Eskimo has developed his boats and his weapons because his life has been centered upon procuring sea mammals for food and for heat. Similarly, cattle breeders and agriculturists have made their technical inventions in the fields upon which their energies have been focused through their economic activities. Man's knowledge of the habits of animals and of the uses of plants has been preponderantly derived from his interest in them as sources of food. The regular movements of the sun and moon have been observed and recorded and calendar systems have been developed because of their relevance to seasonal occupations. Measures of space and time become more elaborate, the more extensive is their use in technical occupations and in the regulation of daily occupations. Religious ceremonies also reflect the context of the economy in which they function; e.g., salmon-fishing peoples have first-salmon ceremonies, and agricultural peoples have fertility rites and harvest festivals.

The nature of the economy further determines whether a

CORRELATION OF MODES OF PRODUCTION TO OTHER ASPECTS OF CULTURE

	Simple Food-Gathering Economies (Hunting, fishing societies without exchangeable surpluses)	Advanced Food-Gathering Economies (Hunting, fishing societies with small exchangeable surpluses)	Simple Agricultural Economies (Primitive societies lacking pastoralism, with small surpluses)	Advanced Agricultural Economies (Societies with or without pastoralism, that had large surpluses)
Density of population	Sparse (except in California).	Many times denser than Simple Food-Gathering Economies.	About same as Simple Food-Gathering Economies.	Mostly denser.
Communities	Bands of 40-80. Temporary greater assemblages brief.	Village community 40-50. Market villages as high as 1,500-2,000.	Villages of scores or hundreds of persons. Rarely as large as 2,000.	Villages, towns, and cities numbering many thousands of persons.
Method of obtaining strategic food supply	Democratically conducted work bands of either sex. Entire community moved seasonally to obtain major food supply.	Work parties recruited, organized and led by headmen or women who could control incidental or individualistic production too. Village maintained year round, only part of population migrating.	Garden work carried on by individuals. Sometimes community joined in harvesting and other farm work. Democratic work parties for hunting and fishing.	Work carried on by individuals or by slave labor owned by chiefs or monarchs. Production for market by specialists or specialized villages.
Specializations	Simple sexual division of labor, and no other.	Some specialization in addition to sexual division of labor. Carvers, weavers, canoe makers. Beginnings of village and district specialization.	Leisure released many individuals for specialized work or craftsmanship in pottery, basketry, weaving, carving, and ceremonial interests.	Specialization increased.

Distribution of products	Economically strategic products potentially shared.	Distribution of work party products unequal. Hereditarily wealthy received better and larger products.	Garden produce kept by individual producer—shared only in time of community need.	Unequal. Owners of lands and herds and slaves received most. Tribute exacted.
Disposal of surplus products	No economically significant surplus; no money, commerce, trade, or markets. Exchange confined to gifts.	A few products sold. Trading by sea-shell money.	Economically significant surplus bartered or presented from community to community. True money absent or coming into use. No true markets.	Commodities sold in market towns. Trade facilitated by money.
Strategic resources	Ownership by entire band or community, not by individuals or lineage. Generally could be used by any member of community.	Some fishing sites and hunting districts owned by lineage headmen who were wealthy through heredity. Used only by permission of owner.	Owned by community. Cultivated land assigned democratically for long terms to lineages or individuals from which private property tended to emerge.	Agricultural lands, herds, subject persons, slaves privately owned by nobility and well-to-do upper classes.
Ownership of wealth	No significant inequalities; wide differences in ownership of personal effects, of minor social significance.	Hereditary class strata based on inequalities in ownership of productive resources. Nobles receive tribute from relatives, fellow clansmen, and villagers. Predatory raids for wealth.	Because there are no economically important inequalities in ownership, there are no notable inequalities of wealth status. Ownership of personal effects. No hereditary leader. No taxation or tribute.	Inequalities of ownership led to development of classes and castes. Wealthy rulers increased their wealth by taxes, tributes, and fines, and by waging war.

people is migratory or has a stable habitat, and this in turn has significant influence upon all aspects of culture. In the case of simple food-gathering peoples, the roving life required in order to follow the game or visit the favorite root-gathering spots according to season makes permanent dwellings impossible and precludes any but very limited possessions. On the other hand, the stable habitat of agricultural peoples provides favorable opportunity for accumulating property resources, and lays the basis for a less grim struggle for survival. While the seasonal movement of food-gathering peoples militates against the formation of large, well organized social units, the conditions are favorable for the development of social and political complexity in an agricultural community occupying a relatively small territory. The small size of the simple food-gathering communities limits the maturing of culture, for there are, as a result, fewer social contacts and thus less interstimulation of persons than in the larger agricultural communities. The sparsity of the technological base, and relatively scant margin of safety which permits few risks, the conformity demanded within closely related groups, the absence of division of labor other than along lines of sex, which diminishes the possibility of experimentation and specialization, and the isolation which limits horizons and experiences and permits few collisions with novel concepts from without, all slow the rate of change in food-gathering as compared to the more advanced agricultural societies.

Changes in the mode of production which lead to property surpluses influence the division of labor between the sexes and bring about marked change in the power and status relations between the sexes in society and in the family. In food-gathering societies, because the bearing and nursing of children impede the movement of women in the hunting of animals, they usually perform the more sedentary tasks. While men generally are busy with the hunting of large and swift animals, women gather berries and roots and other foods within reach of the camps. Although a roughly approximate equality between the sexes prevails, these societies tend to be superficially patriarchal in character because of the relative backwardness of women's knowledge and skills as compared to those of men, and hence women's lesser economic importance. The elaboration of the authority of the mother is especially characteristic of agricultural peoples, for the domestication of plants was a product of women's work, an outgrowth of their food-gathering activities. As a consequence of the development of agriculture by women, economic power and hence social importance shifted relatively in favor of women, so that many, although not all, agricultural peoples are matrilineal. The domestication of animals, on the other hand, was achieved by men as an extension of their hunting activities. When this was combined with agriculture through the use of the animal-drawn plow, and in some areas also through the specialized development of pastoralism, even larger surpluses became possible. Women then receded in economic importance, relative to men, and patrilineal descent became preponderant.[16]

The findings of V. Gordon Childe on what he calls the Second or Urban Revolution in Europe[17] bear out the correlations between economic changes and those of other aspects of culture demonstrated in the pages above for primitive societies. He shows that the bronze ax presupposes a complex economic and social structure, for "the casting of bronze is too difficult a process to be carried out by anyone in the intervals of growing or catching his food or minding her babies." Moreover, because copper and tin, the constituents of bronze, are rare and seldom occur together, they need to be imported; and this is possible only if communications and trade have been established and there is a surplus of some local product to barter for the metals. In the Near East the so-called Bronze Age is marked by populous cities in which a large number of specialized craftsmen, merchants, transport workers, and also officials, clerks, soldiers, and priests are supported by the surplus foodstuffs produced by cultivators, herdsmen, and hunters. A substantial proportion of the community is withdrawn from the primary task of getting food to engage in the

---

[16] This is discussed in considerable detail in Bernhard J. Stern, "Engels on the Family," *Science and Society*, Vol. 12 (1948), pp. 42–64. See also p. 277 in this book.

[17] The earlier domestication of plants and animals in Europe is designated by him as "the Neolithic Revolution." V. Gordon Childe, *Man Makes Himself* (London, 1936), pp. 9, 40–41.

manufacture of tools, in transportation, commerce, and administration. The change from self-sufficient food production to an economy based in addition upon specialized manufacture and external trade promoted a further marked increase in the density of the population. Social organization became increasingly complex, and the number of slaves was augmented. Sedentary life facilitated improved housing accommodations and paved the way for brick and stone architecture and the development of the arch. Artificial irrigation using canals and ditches, the sailing boat, wheeled vehicles, orchard husbandry, and the production and use of copper—important innovations of this period—all involved the application of science to production, and in turn encouraged the development of the abstract sciences. With the development of writing, social organization became further complicated by the fact that society divided into a laboring and an administrative class. The practitioners of the arts and crafts responsible for the surplus which had made urban civilization possible gradually came to form the lower strata of society. In the class division of urban society, scribes belonged to the upper classes, in contrast to the working artisans and farmers. The scribe as the adjunct to the administrator looked with contempt upon manual labor; and as the smith, the potter, and the peasant sank lower in the social scale, their unwritten lore was likewise despised. Only that which was written was esteemed, with the result that there was a separation of the theoretical and practical sciences that long had deleterious effects upon the development of the sciences and society.[18]

Sociological studies in the history of science for later periods have demonstrated that the development of science is controlled and directed by its economic milieu. A few illustrations will suffice to indicate the nature of these findings. Farrington has shown the relation of Greek philosophy to socio-economic changes:

> Milesian philosophy . . . arose in the course of a great wave of economic and political progress, and its essential character, as I shall argue, was that it applied ideas derived from the techniques of pro-

[18] *Ibid.*, pp. 211–213; Benjamin Farrington, *Head and Hand in Ancient Greece* (London, 1947), pp. 28–54.

duction to the interpretation of the phenomena of the universe. . . . If early Greek philosophy was interested in the process of change, it was not simply because nature is so changeable (that has always been true), but because man himself has never before been so active and independent an agent of change. The men who built the cities of Ionia were a new type of men, who had effected an outstanding enlargement of man's control over nature![19]

Similarly the influential anatomical work of Vesalius was a characteristic product of an age which combined humanistic intellectual activity with the new naturalist Renaissance art, fostered by a benevolent autocracy of the merchant princes.[20] The spurt in experimental science of seventeenth century England was inspired largely by the new needs of commercial enterprise of the middle class for more adequate means of transportation and communication, especially in navigation. The prevailing interest in the mechanics of the pump for waterworks and for the drainage of mines, led Harvey to think of the heart as a pump, and to explain the circulation of the blood in terms of its functioning.[21]

With this underscoring of the evidence that the economic factor is the developmental variable in history, there is no attempt to underestimate the unevenness of development in different aspects of culture, because of which there is no complete correspondence of political, religious, and other superstructural institutions at different economic levels. Each social institution has its own internal historical development which plays an important role in determining its functions. Patterns of behavior are tenacious, and forms of social relationships and ideas that grow out of the needs of one economy tend to carry over and persist although they may have little functional significance in the setting of the new economy. When economic changes occur, the readjustments of other aspects of culture are by no means automatic and require con-

---

[19] Farrington, *op. cit.*, pp. 20–21.
[20] Charles J. Singer, *Evolution of Anatomy* (London, 1925), pp. 111, 117–119.
[21] H. T. Pledge, *Science Since 1500* (New York, 1947), p. 29; Robert K. Merton, "Science and the Economy of Seventeenth Century England," *Science and Society*, 3:3–27 (1939); B. Hessen, "The Social and Economic Roots of Newton's Principia," *Science at the Crossroads* (London, 1931). See also Bernhard J. Stern, *Society and Medical Progress* (Princeton, 1941).

siderable time to be effectuated, with the result that there are "cultural lags," incongruities, and contradictions. Since society is always in flux, real equilibrium within the social structure is never attained. What can be observed, however, is a tendency toward integration, a strain toward consistency. A culture is never a mere assemblage of shreds and patches nor an aggregate of culture elements or complexes. The psychological tendency of individuals to seek to integrate into a consistent whole their various attitudes, beliefs, ideas, and actions lays the basis for cultural integration. So too does the social pressure of groups to exact conformity upon their members. But, just as few individuals attain complete integration, and few groups complete conformity, cultures too are incompletely integrated because of the disparate origin and development of their different parts. It is this fact which vitiates not merely the work of the functionalists but also the recent efforts of those who discuss "national character." Such discussion postulates cultural and psychological integration unwarranted by available evidence, and obscures incongruities and variants occasioned by differential adjustments of other aspects of culture to socio-economic changes.

From *Philosophy for the Future*, edited by Roy Wood Sellars, V. J. McGill, Marvin Farber. Copyright, 1949, by The Macmillan Company. Pp. 340–356.

History and Sociology: A Comment

In his suggestive paper, Dr. Jenks declares that historians and sociologists "don't talk the same language." Yet in a basic sense they do. It is the forlorn language of doubtful men, usually apologetic for the achievements of their disciplines, yet at times stridently proclaiming their relative virtues. They both oscillate between breastbeating for their conceptual, methodological, and literary inadequacies, and exaggerated posturing for their assumed achievements. They both publish hundreds of thousands of words (which to paraphrase Sean O'Casey rarely have on them "the glisten of a tinsel dew drop") in their effort to exorcise their disciplines of value judgments; yet most of them should be sufficiently mature philosophically to know that if the social sciences are denuded of value judgments they are really naked of value. They both waver between the discourse of shallow empiricism, which seeks refuge in the assemblage of particulars, and abstract philosophizing, often on the basis of borrowed concepts. They both continue to be overtly self-conscious about the fact that the methodologies of their disciplines differ from those of the physical sciences, whose procedures are generally mistakenly conceived. They both are querulous about the fact that others also are cognizant of their limitations and do not honor them sufficiently.

They have come to speak the same language in other ways as well. Both acclaim their frigid objectivity, yet the historian or sociologist is rare who does not strive to attain immortality by leaving the imprint of his personality upon the organization or interpretation or verbalization of his data. Both historians and sociologists have the power to influence state policy by courageous evaluation of past and present human behavior, by seeking to predict trends on the basis of special knowledge, and by their creation of symbols that define the roles which citizens may adopt. As a rule, however, they abnegate such responsibility as unbecoming to scientists. Some are cognizant of the fact that their ideas are ideologies, but are indifferent as to which interests their ideas serve and the social consequences thereof.

The vocabulary and reasoning of the founding fathers of American sociology—Ward, Ross, Giddings and Small—may sound quaint, but their method differs little from the procedures of many contemporary sociologists. Sociologists have often been occupied with semantics, not merely as a pastime, but one suspects often as an evasion. This has made sociology less humdrum than history but also more erratic and inconsequential. It has given the sociologist as false a sense of power as the medieval scholastics had in understanding and coping with reality.

Sociologists once talked of imbuing historians with correct perspectives. But now the situation is frequently reversed and it is the historian who can serve as an example to sociologists. It is assumed to be a cardinal principle of sociology that events must be interpreted in the context of the total situation. Yet the frailty of sociologists lies in their tendency to abstract from historical reality "ideal types" that are applicable everywhere and nowhere, beyond time and space, and hence in a netherworld of unreality. For instance, there were years of sociological discussion of immigration in terms of assimilation, amalgamation, adjustment, disorganization, ethnic communities, dominance, and counter-assertion, much of it aimless and commonplace, some of it insightful. Yet perhaps largely because sociologists were concerned with processes and common denominators, the countless volumes produced by the students of Park, Giddings, Ross or Fairchild in this field cannot compare, for example, with the sociological contribution of the historian Marcus L. Hansen in *The Immigrant in American History*.

Dr. Jenks declares that "it can hardly be said that sociologists as a matter of principle ignore the dimension of time or deny reality to continuity and change." But it may be said with equal truth that sociologists do not stress the great importance of the dimension of time nor underscore the reality of continuity and change. It is this lack that militated against the success of Warner's Yankee City series. It was the Achilles heel of the Myrdal study. It renders much of attitude testing fatuous. As Dr. Jenks has noted discerningly, strictly historical assumptions are made, but resort to the historical method comes "casually and inadvertently." Sociology will remain one-dimensional and hence shallow, and its concepts empty shells, however musical their verbalism may become, unless the examination of historical contexts becomes a meaningful and disciplined task of the sociologists.

I find myself especially in sympathy with Dr. Jenks' complaint of the neglect of economic history, although I would suggest that his studies on the impact of the business leader on economic and social change be supplemented by comparable studies of the impact of the labor organization. His stricture of industrial sociologists as "playing down the existence of a struggle for power and profits," and his skeptical query on whether the great formal structures of government, business, law and religion are "just epiphenomena on the sea of child training habits and other prototypical mechanisms," are to me manifestations of a live intelligence that refuses to be lured by fashions in research.

Comment on a paper by Professor Leland H. Jenks, entitled "History and Sociology," delivered to the Eastern Sociological Society, April 23, 1949.

The Scientist as Product and Agent of Change

This is a good occasion to assess the ever-changing status and prestige of the scientist. For the scientist is, of course, a social product and is cast into a role by the society of which he is a part. There is little question but that the public attitude toward science and scientists has undergone considerable change in the United States in recent years. Historically the vast resources and plentiful raw materials of the new continent, exploited profligately, created a situation in the United States in which attention to the training of scientists was not deemed urgent. Science and scientists had little status and were accorded meager prestige; lack of appreciation and suspicion of experts and even of intellectuals by practical business men were widespread. The planlessness of the development of the country was ascribed to the inevitable consequence of the pioneering spirit. Whatever engineering skills there were arose primarily out of the participation of men in the building of canals and railroads.

Early efforts to introduce scientific subjects and methods into the curricula of established American universities were fugitive and fragmentary. The sciences were associated in the popular mind with liberalism, and their introduction into the university curricula was tardy and mixed with distrust and indifference. There was little understanding of the meaning of scientific methods and no appreciation of the value of personally conducted laboratory experiments by which the student could be trained to observe and to theorize from facts he had himself demonstrated.

Persons who wished scientific training were obliged to go to Europe for an education. There, through the influence of the

French Revolution, science had been given a new spurt of activity in the high schools by the founding of the École Polytechnique. The innovation of the École Polytechnique was that, for the first time, research scholars and mathematicians were gathered under one roof to train their successors, so that science and the scientific method could have developmental continuity. Science was regarded by the founders of the École as the core and source of social progress, and talented youth of all classes, not only the sons of the wealthy, were encouraged to specialize in it. The École Polytechnique by putting these young recruits of science in direct contact with original research workers achieved fruitful results. Theory and research methods were emphasized in place of the perpetuation of formal factual learning, and students were encouraged to do their own original experiments. Scientific laboratories played a significant role in the development of fundamental theory. The teachers of the École Polytechnique refused to be submerged by the tasks of solving immediate technical problems but promoted science through novel conceptual patternings of basic theory. The influence of such laboratory and theoretical training was universal, and persisted even after the École Polytechnique deteriorated, because scholars from all countries had come to France to study under the scientists of the École Polytechnique.

Its effects were especially pronounced in Germany through the influence of Justus von Liebig who, after studying under Joseph Louis Gay-Lussac at the École Polytechnique in Paris, introduced experimental science teaching in German universities and denounced with no little heat the *Naturphilosophie* of Schelling and Hegel which had eschewed observation and experiment. Liebig's rejection of the speculative philosophy prevailing at German universities and his successful advocacy of new research methods and laboratory instruction were instrumental in transforming the German universities, which were later to influence American educational methods profoundly. His battle against the speculative excesses of *Naturphilosophie* also had the baneful influence of stimulating a scepticism on the part of scientists of all philosophy, thus narrowing the depth of science and accentuating a limited mechanistic approach to phenomena. Later this scepticism by scientists of philosophy was extended to scepticism of social thinking and activity, and the ideal type of scientist became one void of values other than devotion to the empirical solution of the specific problems under investigation. The anti-theoretic tendency of British empiricism, already apparent in the work of Boyle and Newton, which had had little influence upon German philosophers, was thus underscored. Empirical research became not merely a method but also the end of science and the formulation of theory and participation in social action were slighted. This limited conception of the scientists' role persisted until it was blasted as one of the side effects of the atomic bomb.

The first effort to counteract the exodus of the nation's talent abroad for research training was made by Yale, beginning in 1846, when Benjamin Silliman offered his proposal which led eventually to the establishment of the Sheffield Scientific School. A year later the initial grant was given to the Lawrence Scientific School at Harvard. Both schools were manned by persons who had been trained abroad. Neither innovation in science teaching was warmly welcomed by the university administrators or by the faculties of the other departments, and both ventures were given meager financial support by university authorities. This is indicated by the fact that John P. Norton was permitted by the Yale corporation to hold the chair of agricultural chemistry only on condition that "the support of this professor is in no case to be chargeable to the existing funds and revenues of the 'College'." Both Silliman and Norton provided their own apparatus and were authorized to "make such arrangements as respects remuneration from their instruction as they may think proper." A clash ensued between the advocates of liberal arts programs and those who favored laboratory instruction in the sciences. Scientific courses were opposed as too utilitarian, as of limited educational value, as out of keeping with academic traditions, and therefore as inappropriate in an educational curriculum of a liberal arts college.

To cope with the distrust and apathy which their efforts encountered, the leaders of the Sheffield Scientific School issued repeated defensive statements arguing against those who were solely for classical education. They contended that the distinctive goal of the school was not practical or technical but that its purpose was to develop "scholars in science, well trained in the higher departments of investigation, able to stand unabashed by the side of scholars in letters." They stressed the idea that the function of the school was "to teach the principles of science, the laws of application, the right method of research, the exact habits of computation, analysis and observation, and a fundamental reverence for truth—while at the same time we impart something of that literary culture which is essential to a liberal education." The battle between the humanities and the sciences in the allocation of university budgets remains part of the contemporary educational scene, but it is clear that science is no longer as much on the defensive as in that earlier period.

The turning point in scientific education in the United States was in 1876 when the John Hopkins University opened under the leadership of Daniel C. Gilman. Gilman not merely set high standards for university science teaching and research initiative, but had social purpose, for his stated objective was that Johns Hopkins would make for "less misery among the poor, less ignorance in the schools, less bigotry in the Temple, less suffering in the hospital, less fraud in business, less folly in politics." Gilman's advocacy of the German university program of research served as a ferment for research training in universities throughout the country.

Ever since the incorporation of experimental science into the curricula of American universities under the impetus of persons trained in Germany, the struggle of science to win recognition in America has been an uphill battle. Religious sectarianism at American universities has been strong, and science, identified as it is with materialism, has been regarded with suspicion. In some respects there may have been a deterioration. Where now, for example, is the president of a public university who will write a book such as the *History of the Warfare of Science with Theology in Christendom,* as did Andrew D. White as president of Cornell University.

Even more important as a deterrent to the acceptance of science was the indifference of businessmen to science. It was not until the last decade of the nineteenth century and the first decade of the twentieth that American industry financed, very tentatively, fundamental research in industrial science. Even today industrial scientific research is predominantly in narrow applied fields. Lincoln T. Work, speaking on the philosophy of industrial research, has stated that "the research division of a company is called upon to protect, maintain, and improve the company's position in business."[1] This is shown strikingly by the study of the research expenditures of 191 industrial firms studied recently by the Division of Research of the Harvard Business School. Ninety-two percent of company research funds (i.e., excluding government funds) was spent for specific products and processes leaving only 8 percent for research of a general or basic nature.[2]

Except for the important Morrill Act of 1862 which provided for Federal grants to vocational education, the Federal government did little for scientific research in universities until President Franklin D. Roosevelt established the Office of Scientific Research and Development to make financial grants for such research in connection with the military program of World War II. Again, however, almost 94 percent of the federal research and development funds, which were $2.2 billion in 1952, went for applied research and development and only 6 percent for fundamental or basic research.[3] These grants helped profoundly to utilize and apply existing scientific knowledge but the meagerness of funds for fundamental research limited the degree of extension of the horizons of science.

During the last half century, science, by its achievements, has acquired extraordinary prestige. Science has become not merely the product but the agent of change. It has extended man's life and has extended man's control over his environment and over himself. Not only has science made all forms of energy exchangeable, but energy, by becoming abundant enough, can now be converted into any kind of material we need, either directly by

[1] Lincoln T. Work, "The Philosophy and Economics of an Industrial Research Program," *Research Operations in Industry*, Edited by David B. Hertz and Albert H. Rubenstein, New York, 1953, p. 4.
[2] DeWitt C. Dearborn, Rose W. Kneznek and Robert N. Anthony, *Spending for Industrial Research*, Boston, 1953, p. 6.
[3] Bernhard J. Stern, "Freedom of Research in American Science," *Science & Society*, Vol. XVIII (Spring 1954), p. 97f.

extracting metals from their ores, or indirectly by the provision of water, fertilizer, transport, unlimited food, and biological products. Most of the world's desert regions, comprising at least twice the present cultivated area, could, if present scientific knowledge were utilized, become fertile, food-producing land. Beyond this lies the possibility of artificial food production. With energy and food enough for all of the people in the world, one can visualize an end of exhausting toil and of want and poverty. Moreover under proper social changes there can be the lifting of heavy burdens from the backs of workers by the use of automation which under the present social structure threatens industrial dislocation and massive unemployment. In recent years scientific research in the area of health has provided antibiotics and advances in medicine and in surgery that have extended life and multiplied the potentialities of living beings. Man's life on earth is now conditioned on all sides, and his potentialities are multiplied by the continuous application of science. He has come to appreciate its gifts while still not fully acknowledging the merit of its givers, the scientists who have served as the agents of these changes.

Science has been cumulative in its development, and each new generation of scientists has benefited from the work of its predecessors in all lands. There has been traditionally an international community of science from which all scientists have derived their knowledge and inspiration. Progress in science is contingent upon the availability of specialized personnel of all countries. Science has been able to advance only by the fullest freedom of research, by the unhindered dissemination of the ideas and results emanating from such research, and by the interrelation and correlation of diverse data, interpretations, and methods by independent scientists. Thus science flourishes in an environment of free research, free discussion, free movement of personnel, free exchange of ideas, free and rapid publication and wide dissemination of information. Scientists can excel in the atmosphere of such freedoms. They are the products of the doctrine of scientific precision of definition and of clarity of research methods, of questioning scepticism and unhampered criticism without which no sound advances can be made.

That is why the security program of recent years relating to scientists has been so baneful. It has worked havoc with the traditions of scientists by imposing secrecy upon scientific work and making scientists objects of suspicion. As the Board of Directors of the American Association for the Advancement of Science said in December 1954:

> Progress in science is a cumulative process in which each scientist builds upon what is already known; through research and intellectual effort he adds his bit to scientific knowledge. National boundaries and security systems simply cannot contain this process. Scientific knowledge will continue to grow as long as men are curious about the world around them. The state of learning in a nation affects the rate of scientific progress; and the state of technology affects the speed and volume with which a nation can translate scientific findings into practical applications. ... The basic fact is that there simply are no such things as permanent scientific secrets. Even the time difference is sometimes lacking; recent decades have been filled with instances in which the same fundamental discovery or the same military application appeared practically simultaneously in two or more countries.
> Once it is recognized that there is no such thing as a permanent scientific secret, the whole picture changes. If security demands scientific superiority, and if superiority cannot be achieved by attempts to keep scientific progress secret, then how can superiority be achieved and maintained? Clearly the security of the nation requires the most favorable circumstances for the advancement of science, an environment that will foster a healthier, more imaginative, more energetic development than that which serves the enemies of freedom.[4]

The relevance and truth of this declaration was verified at the International Conference on the Peaceful Uses of Atomic Energy at Geneva where American and Russian scientists discovered that both had made vast progress on the same problems even though the barriers of stringent secrecy had separated them and they had worked in ignorance of each other's work.

The recent report of the seven-man committee appointed by the Office of the President of the United States and headed by Dr. Detlev W. Bronk, President of the National Academy of

[4] The Board of Directors of the American Association for the Advancement of Science, "Strengthening the Basis of National Security," *Science*, Vol. 120, (December 10, 1954), p. 957–958.

Sciences, opposed the harassment of scientists in government service, by security checks when they are dealing with unclassified material. They declare in this important report which has received little publicity:

> We do believe that the proper objectives of Government in sponsoring basic research will be best served by concentration on scientific competence alone.... We are confident that formal confirmation of such a policy by the Federal Government would have a vastly reassuring effect upon the scientific community at large, and would contribute much to the effective utilization of our national resources for the public interest through the advancement of science.[5]

The security program also serves as a deterrent in the recruitment of new scientists who are necessary to continue the growth of science and technology in America. Potential scientists do not wish to be regarded, and to be constantly under surveillance, as potential spies. They would rather be in other fields where they can think as they please and associate with whom they please as is the constitutional right of men in a democratic society. They resent the withdrawal of federal grants from investigators who have unorthodox opinions and demands for secrecy that hinder scientific advance in the laboratory. Though they may be drawn to science, they prefer not to enter this field lest they become controversial figures when they can have relative peace and quiet elsewhere. Motivations for a life dedicated to science must be strong, for financial compensations in the academic world are not high. The security program can prove to be the blanket which chokes off the zealous fire that ignites the flame of hope to improve the lot of humanity through a scientific career.

With the end of the cold war and the recognition by people in political power that war must be prevented by all possible means lest the civilizations of all contending parties be annihilated, we are on the threshold of a new society in which science will be a greater agent of change than ever before. The present undeveloped areas of the world are demanding that they have a place in the sun, and it is science that can raise their levels of living.

[5] National Academy of Sciences, Report of the Committee on Loyalty in Relation to Government Support of Unclassified Research, March 13, 1956, p. 5 (Mimeographed).

It is up to the two societies which possess the scientific and technical resources, the United States and the Soviet Union, to share their "know-how" with these nations without requiring political commitments. Increasing the food supply and energy resources of the underdeveloped parts of the world and extending the lives of their inhabitants will in turn create new horizons for science. The idealism which led religions to speak of service to mankind has been transferred to the secular scientific arena. The scientist who has been an agent of great change will be a product of his own changes. New theoretical problems will challenge his ingenuity and these in turn will lead to concrete achievements. We are but in the beginning of a new age, on the threshold of an age of rationality, when all the people of the world will benefit from the achievements of a constantly growing body of scientific knowledge.

Address delivered at the Tenth International Students'
Weekend, Bard College, April 21, 1956.

part two

SOCIAL ASPECTS OF TECHNOLOGY

The Frustration of Technology

The annals of technological invention are replete with evidence of protracted delays in the acceptance of innovations that have been of inestimable value to mankind. Fundamental inventions have been stillborn and entire lines of potential development unrealized, not because of deficiency in engineering plans but because of factors beyond their scope. Whether technological innovations are incorporated, delayed, or rejected is determined primarily by whether an economy is static, contracting, or expanding; whether social stratification exists or is absent; and whether there is an anarchic or planned industrial order. In each situation, the socio-economic factors give the setting which provoke specific psychological responses from individuals and groups participating and tend to determine the nature of the social attitudes prevailing.

Psychological Roots of Resistance

Similar psychological processes underlie all human behavior irrespective of the social institutions under which men live, although their functioning is decisively affected by environmental conditioning. Both resistance to change and its antithesis, alertness of response to new situations, are in this sense rooted in the individual psyche. Habit, fear, and desire for personality equilibrium and for status dispose one toward conservatism. Habit is a vague label for the tendency of an individual to persist in set forms of behavior cast by initial conditioning. In spite of the illuminating experimental studies of Pavlov and others on the development of these conditioned responses, the psychological basis of various neural and muscular retention remains obscure. There is no correlation between retention abilities in and resistant attitudes to change. Conservatism is made possible by neural and muscular retention but likewise is all learning which is the basis of change. Excellent retention may be associated with agile flexibility in behavior and attitude, while the arch-conservative may have weak retentive powers.

Attitudes resistant to change cannot therefore be fully explained in neuro-physiological terms. They often arise in the interest of personality integration. No one can be adjusted to his environment if he need be continuously expending his energies and passing through crises in making decisions. Judgments once made must of necessity serve as guiding precedents. A large part of one's behavior thus becomes quasi-automatic, involving little deliberation or contemplation. Such oft-repeated behavior becomes pleasurable, particularly when it involves rhythmic or skillful movements. One's personality becomes relatively at ease when it has attained what approximates equilibration with the objects and persons with whom he comes in contact, and thus sentiments of intimacy with the environment arise. The strength of these attachments varies depending upon the degree of stability of the culture in which one lives and the presence or absence of incentives to change. Where social forms are dynamic and transient, the extent of permanency in adjustment is less than in a relatively static society. There is emotional and esthetic satisfaction derived from identification with customary forms when these provide a modicum of gratification of human wants. A specious sense of personality adjustment is very often attained through fantasy and other escape devices which obscure actual discomfort and dull receptivity to change. This is the common situation of personality adjustment, prevailing when the economics of a capitalist society provides no certainty of employment and subsistence to its masses and men live within the threatening shadow of insecurity.

Important innovations, particularly those in the field of technology, shatter the tenuous sense of equilibrium which a person has attained. They demand not only neural and muscular reconditioning but reorganization of personality to meet the needs of the new situation, involving the discomforts of readjustment. They

therefore tend to provoke repellent defense attitudes ⟨
priety, ridicule, and disparagement, or are ignored in an a⟨
to avoid the tasks of grappling with them. Adjustment attain⟨
however meager it may be, is preferred to the frank facing of th⟨
uncertainties that appear to be involved in the reorientation
process. A passage in the Declaration of Independence expresses
this thought well: ". . . all experience hath shewn that mankind
are more disposed to suffer while evils are sufferable, than to right
themselves by abolishing the forms to which they are accustomed." Unless there are potent incentives which stimulate conscious effort toward change, rationalizations are invented to
justify established behavior, excuses are contrived to sanction it.
Particularly when an innovation is considered drastic in its
novelty, when complications in its processes require fatiguing
efforts in readjustment, or when it stimulates anxiety however
temporary or slight, resistance tends to be intense and rationalizations flourish.

The tendency of persons to develop quasi-automatic pattern
responses to situations, and to use rationalizations to justify them
may, however, be counteracted by equally important aspects of
the human personality: the discomfiture at dreary monotony with
consequent yearning for and receptivity to novel experiences, and
the pleasure derived from constructive manipulation of one's environment. These cravings for change, usually subdued and
thwarted by the social environment and the educational process,
can be stimulated to support innovations. The class structure of a
society primarily determines whether it is able to offer valid incentives to this end.

Caution in the acceptance of an innovation, or opposition to it,
is not always on the quasi-automatic level. It may be based on
considered commendable deliberation. Innovations are obviously
not always efficacious, and inventors' hopes are often gossamer.
It is one of the indictments of contemporary education in our
society that it qualifies so few to evaluate the merits of an innovation. Few persons are equipped with knowledge of experimental and other scientific methods of verifying data, nor are they
trained to analyze proof as criteria of validity. Our educational
institutions divorce theory and practice. They are focused on the

perpetuation of past experience and tradition, and the adaptation of the person to the status quo, rather than on training for intelligent receptivity toward innovation and for the building up of the intellectual resources to test the merits of change. Authoritarian education leaves one at the mercy of authorities. Such recourse to authority tends to be inevitable in an age of multiplicity of skills and fields of competence. But particularly in the field of technology, the value of the authorities' judgments is diminished by the fact that those who have been known as experts have usually leaned heavily toward conservatism, have often been too biased in terms of their own narrow schooling and specific research to give reasoned judgments, and have usually been indifferent to and have lacked understanding of the social aspects of their work. The reasonable demand for scientific and practical caution toward innovation has often resulted in unreasonable rejection on spurious grounds. The task of evaluation, difficult enough under the most favorable circumstances, is thus made doubly difficult by the inadequacies of our educational system. Moreover, our educational system leaves the scientist and statesman myopic as to the social implications of technological change. What Sir Josiah Stamp has recently declared of British education applies likewise to the United States:

> . . . The training of the scientist includes no awareness of the social consequences of his work, and the training of the statesman and administrator no preparation for the potentiality of rapid scientific advance and drastic adjustment due to it, no prevision of the technical forces which are shaping the society in which he lives.[1]

The educational system of the Soviet Union is exceptional in this regard, for there, from the primary grades through the technical schools and universities, stress is laid upon the relations between science, technology, and society as they affect human welfare.[2]

Conscious vested interest in the maintenance of one's economic and social status often generates and fosters resistances even when it is known that the change is in the interests of the larger

---

[1] "The Impact of Science upon Society," Presidential Address, British Association for the Advancement of Science, Blackpool, 1936, p. 6.
[2] Beatrice King, *Changing Man* (New York, 1937).

good. Progress in the abstract, or as it affects others, usually rates insignificantly as compared to the actual, immediate effects the innovation has directly on the class or person involved. This type of opposition, which bulks large, arises not from lethargy or indolence, nor from intellectual timidity or lack of knowledge of the implications of the innovation, but from deliberate, purposeful, obstructive activity, as will be illustrated later.

The demands of social life often strengthen a person's tendency to follow established patterns of behavior. Collective behavior of persons in groups is expedited by at least a semblance of orderliness based on their ability to anticipate the behavior of others in the group. Innovations are disruptive in that they affect not isolated persons but members of groups, who influence the behavior of all with whom they come in contact. In consequence there is often group resentment against innovators who disturb established relations, upset routines, and cause temporary confusion. To exact conformity the group brings social pressure to bear upon the deviant, by using caviling criticism, ridicule and disparagement, economic discrimination, social ostracism and violence. To avoid such reprisals most persons endorse customary procedures and refrain from projecting or supporting innovations. Social approval gives tone to personal adjustment, and when restraints are imposed by group attitudes they are powerful deterrents of change.[3] The size of the community is a factor in determining the strength of its power of coercion. If it has many members, group cohesion is not as close; and the innovator, finding some support, may be able to ignore detractors. But in a small community, contacts are more immediate and the influence tends to be more direct. The deterrent effects of group criticism function not only in the general group life of the community but also within specific industrial organizations. A person is prone to continue established routines rather than to venture with innovations that will meet the resistance of his co-workers and superiors. "Not to venture, is not to lose" becomes a guiding principle unless incentives are sufficiently strong. A society may be evaluated by the manner in which it is able to meet the challenge of these inertias

[3] Cf. my discussion of resistance to change in *Social Factors in Medical Progress* (New York, 1927).

and overt resistance to change, on the part of individuals and groups, by providing incentives that are not illusory.

Socio-Economic Factors

Cultures differ from one another in their receptivity to technological change because of the nature of their social structure and the ideological currents prevailing. A brief comparative review of the situation in pre-industrial societies will here be given to bring into focus, and give the setting for, the peculiar problems attending the incorporation of technological changes in the modern industrial order.

Primitive societies have been by no means static. Their rate of change has, however, been slow because of forces which prevail not only in primitive societies but to a large extent in small isolated communities throughout history and in rural communities in the modern world. The factors which inhibit innovation are the meagerness of the technological base; the scant margin of wealth, which permits few risks; the negligible division of labor, which diminishes the possibility of experimentation and leaves dominantly non-empirical attitudes undisturbed; the concentration of power in the hands of the aged and usually the relatively wealthy men; the isolation which limits horizons and experience and permits few collisions with novel disrupting concepts and practices from without; and the close integration of different aspects of the cultural configuration. Moreover, absence of a knowledge of writing in pre-literate societies and illiteracy prevalent in isolated areas in civilization establish a need for conserving tradition through speech and behavior, making social forms more tenacious.

Technological advances such as Hero's steam engine and mechanical appliances for construction work were neglected in the ancient world. The causes for this phenomenon are at present a subject of extended controversy and remain as yet unexplained. The belief that it was degrading to put science to practical use checked technological changes, but this attitude could not have been universal, as is shown by the development of medical science and the work of Archimedes. Although there was an overabundance of labor in some periods, which served as a deterrent, this was not true of all periods of antiquity. The disparaging social attitude toward artisans and manual labor, first set forth by Plato and Aristotle, was probably a retarding factor, but the evidence is too fragmentary to substantiate the inference that this attitude pervaded all strata of the population.

The cultural retrogression of the Middle Ages in Europe which made the situation prevailing in the medieval communities approximate in many respects that of primitive societies, was not conducive to innovation, least of all in the field of technology. The static hierarchic social stratification that was sanctioned as divinely ordained by the Church, which at the same time attached spiritual value to poverty and denounced materialism and experimentation, created both an economic setting and an authoritarian attitude fatal to scientific progress and technological change. Medieval society was, to be sure, not entirely immobile. But local self-subsistence was a limiting economic frame, and the anti-scientific attitude of the Church, enforced by heresy trials, produced an environment hostile to scientific and technological innovations.

The revival of interest in classical science, slowly followed by the use of experimental methods; the discovery of new continents, the plunder of which brought vast new wealth to Europe; the rise of cities with consequent increasing power of the burghers, formed the social setting which accelerated change and led to the decline of feudal economy. Because of these changes, the sixteenth, seventeenth and eighteenth centuries were animated by the spirit of progress, and thus provided a fertile soil for technological change. But the incentives offered the inventor remained few, as the contemporary judgment of Sprat indicates:

> And here there is suggested to me a just occasion of lamenting the ill *Treatment* which has bin most commonly given to *Inventors*. . . . Nor do they only meet with rough usage from those that envy their honour; but even from the *Artificers* themselves, for whose sakes they labor: while those that add some small matter to things begun are usually inrich'd thereby; the *Discoverers* themselves have seldom found any other entertainment than contempt and impoverishment. The effects of their *Industry* are wont to be decry'd while they live: The fruits of their *Studies* are frequently alienated from their Chil-

dren: The little *Tradesmen* conspire against them, and indeavor to stop the Springs from whence they themselves receive nourishment: The common titles with which they are wont to be defam'd, are those of *Cheats* and *Projectors*.[4]

Gerald Winstanley, the leader of the True Levellers, corroborates this appraisal of the inventor's plight by his comment that "fear of want and care to pay the Rent of Taskmasters hath hindered many rare Inventions."[5]

Technological progress continued to be retarded by the policies of the medieval guilds, which not only did not attempt to introduce changes, but resisted adaptations to new conditions. Sprat aptly characterizes their attitudes:

> I have some confidence that I have sufficiently prov'd, that the *Invention* of *Trades* may still proceed farther, and that by the help of men of free lives, and by this course of *Experiments*. But yet the main *difficulty* continues unremov'd. This arises from the suspicions of the *Tradesmen* themselves: They are generally infected with the narrowness that is natural to *Corporations*, which are wont to resist all *new comers*, as profess'd Enemies to their *Privileges*.[6]

The local and political authorities not only aided the guilds in their restraints but initiated restrictions without guild pressure. The impediments placed in the way of technological change during this period can best be illustrated by the experience of the textile industry. In the sixteenth century, during the reign of Edward VI, the guilds sought to prevent the expansion of the industry and had an act promulgated fixing the length, width and weight of every kind of cloth then made in England, which act according to its preamble "was to remain firm and perfect, notwithstanding any suggestions hereafter to be made by any clothier or clothmaker to the contrary." Comparable statutes were enacted until the second half of the eighteenth century, regulating all phases of the manufacture of textiles, the raw materials, dyeing,

[4] Tho. Sprat, *The History of the Royal-Society of London*, 2nd ed. (London, 1702), p. 401–2.
[5] *The Law of Freedom* (1652). Cited by G. Clark, "Early Capitalism and Invention," *Economic History Review*, VI (April, 1936), p. 144.
[6] Sprat, *op. cit.*, p. 398.

stretching, finishing, the tools of trade and the appearances of the product. In 1553 Parliament responded to guild pressure by prohibiting the gig-mill, which used power in picking out knots in the weft of the cloth, but the prohibition was ineffectual, as is seen by the fact that attempts to interfere with its use were made again in 1630. The Reverend William Lee, who in 1589 invented the first knitting machine, the stocking-frame, was refused a patent which would have made its use possible, by Elizabeth and James I. In 1623–4 Charles I ordered the destruction of a needle machine and the needles that had been manufactured by it, and nine years later he prohibited the casting of brass buckles, at the complaint of the Company of Buckle-Forgers, Filers and Trimmers. When the London Silkweavers were permitted by their charter of 1638 to extend their control over the entire kingdom, it was agreed that the recently invented broadloom should be suppressed. By 1695–6, however, the stocking frame was declared "a very useful and profitable invention" and its export prohibited to insure secrecy, to the profit of English manufacturers. National vested interests had replaced guild vested interests. In the same year, when the Exeter Company of Weavers, Fullers and Shearmen petitioned the Commons to prohibit the use of the skey in stretching serges, its petition was refused. Guild action had thus practically ceased as an influential obstructive force in England and the stage was set for the new capitalism.[7]

On the Continent, likewise, the guilds, abetted by political authority, prohibited the use of new machines and at times had the innovators punished. In 1397 the tailors of Cologne were forbidden to use a machine to press the heads of pins. About 1579 the Council of Danzig is said to have strangled the inventor of a machine which would weave four to six pieces at once, on the grounds that his invention would reduce many workers to beggary. Giambattista Carli of Gemona was ordered to cease the

[7] The regulations affecting the expansion of the textile industry of England in this period are best given in Herbert Heaton, *The Yorkshire Woollen and Worsted Industries* (Oxford, 1920), p. 124–144. See also Eli Heckscher, *Mercantilism* (New York, 1935), I, p. 262–5; George Unwin, *Studies in Economic History* (London, 1927) p. 186–7; A. P. Wadsworth and J. D. Mann, *The Cotton Industry and Industrial Lancashire, 1600–1780* (Manchester, 1931); and Clark, *op. cit.*

manufacture of looms because of the poverty of Venetian stocking-knitters.[8] Marx lists many examples of overt resistance to the ribbon loom by displaced workers throughout the Continent during the seventeenth and early eighteenth centuries.[9] The cord and button makers' guild obtained the support of the French government between 1694 and 1700 in preventing the manufacture and sale of woven instead of hand-made buttons, to the extent of authorizing the arrest of persons who wore the unlawful buttons. Mercantilist policy led to deliberate restrictive regulations throughout the eighteenth century in France to prevent technical and economic innovations. The most drastic effort at suppression was the government's attempt to prevent the production, import and use of printed calicoes in France from 1686 to 1759. This not only involved the exclusion of Indian cottons, but also attacked the technique of the printing of colors as a substitute for dyeing. Enforcement led to armed conflict, mass imprisonment and executions. Heckscher writes: "It is estimated that the economic measures taken in this connection cost the lives of some sixteen thousand people, partly through executions and partly through armed affrays, without reckoning the unknown but certainly much larger number of people who were sent to the galleys, or punished in other ways. On one occasion in Valence, seventy-seven were sentenced to be hanged, fifty-eight were to be broken upon the wheel, 631 were sent to the galleys, one was set free and none were pardoned."[10]

The receptivity of the new capitalism in England to technological change was held in check even after the guilds began to lose their influence, by the policy of granting patents of monopoly initiated by Queen Elizabeth and carried on by her successors until checked by Parliamentary protest. George Unwin offers the abuse of patent monopoly as a reason why the industrial revolution did not occur a century earlier: "The triumph of honest

[8] Johann Beckmann, *Beyträge zur Geschichte der Erfindungen* (Leipzic, 1783–1805), tr. by William Johnston as *A History of Inventions, Discoveries and Origins*, 2 vols. (4th ed. by William Francis and J. W. Griffith, London, 1846), II, p. 371–75, 528–31.
[9] Karl Marx, *Capital*, I, tr. by E. and C. Paul (New York, 1928), p. 457–58.
[10] Heckscher, *op. cit.*, I, p. 173.

enterprise was overshadowed by the feverish delusions of speculation and the selfish greed of monopoly. A lively mood of adventure pervaded all classes, but the sound elements were counteracted by the unsound."[11] Not only did capitalists who promoted infant industries such as glass blowing, salt boiling, soap making and alum, obtain monopoly privileges, the profits of which they shared with the Crown, but similar monopolies were granted to court favorites and capitalists who paid the Crown for monopolist control of older industries. These exclusive privileges were not used to create new demands or to introduce improvement but to extinguish domestic competition and to raise prices in an extortionate manner. Industrial expansion and technological development were thus checked. Clark declares that "there does not appear to be a single instance of a monopolist who, after securing a patent for one improvement, subsequently introduced another in the same manufacture." The large capitalist chartered trading companies of the seventeenth century limited output to keep up prices. The Dutch East India Company, for example, as early as 1625 anticipated practices adopted more recently in the United States and other capitalist countries, by rooting up "redundant" clove bushes. Moreover Sir William Temple complained that the company had forbidden exploration lest its commercial hegemony be disturbed.[12]

The landed aristocracy, whose power was challenged by the rise to power of the industrial bourgeoisie, also pitted itself against technological innovation. The opposition manifested itself not merely in the attitudes of deterrent condescension and derogation toward those associated with manufacture, which led James Watt in 1787 to declare resentfully "Our landed gentlemen . . . [reckon] us poor mechanics no better than the slaves who cultivate their vineyards."[13] It took overt form, as is illustrated by the resistance to the railroads. A characteristic expression of this hostility is given in a letter of Creevey written in 1825, while he was serving

[11] George Unwin, *op. cit.*, p. 324.
[12] William Price, *The English Patents of Monopoly* (New York, 1906), especially chapters 1–3; Sir W. S. Hodsworth: *History of English Law* (6 vol., London, 1924), IV, p. 343–355; VI, p. 330–360; Clark, *op. cit.*, p. 151.
[13] Witt Bowden, *Industrial Society in England Towards the End of the Eighteenth Century* (New York, 1925), p. 155.

as a member of the parliamentary committee dealing with a bill concerning the building of the Liverpool and Manchester Railway:

> ... Sefton and I have come to the conclusion that our Ferguson is *insane*. He quite foamed at the mouth with rage in our Railway Committee in support of this infernal nuisance—the loco-motive Monster, carrying *eighty tons* of goods, and navigated by a tail of smoke and sulphur, coming thro' every man's grounds between Manchester and Liverpool. He was supported by Scotsmen only, except a son of Sir Robert Peel's, and against every landed gentleman of the country—his own particular friends, who were all present, such as Ld. Stanley, Ld. Sefton, Ld. Geo. Cavendish, &c.[14]

When the surveyors began to lay out this road they were threatened with violence by the manager of the canal properties on the estate of the Duke of Bridgewater and by Lords Derby and Sefton, and farmers were incited against them.[15] The landed classes also opposed the technological changes of the industrial revolution because they feared that the poor rates would be increased by the burden of persons whom the machines threw out of work.

After capitalism had won its battle with the guilds and with the landed aristocracy, after the practice of granting monopoly privileges had ceased and the theory of laissez-faire was triumphant, the stupendous technological advances of the industrial revolution occurred. Capitalism was thus in this period a progressive force in that it helped to throw off the restraints which feudalism imposed upon technology. But the class structure of capitalism has always checked maximum receptivity to technological innovation. With the drive for private profits as the incentive for the incorporation of technological change, innovations have been as a rule overwhelmingly, and sometimes exclusively, in the interests of the relatively few owners of industry, and to the disadvantage, sometimes temporary but often permanent, of the masses of the population. The technical innovations of the industrial revolution were introduced with callous disregard of the havoc they wrought in the lives of the workers, as have been such changes with few exceptions under capitalism ever

---

[14] Sir Herbert Maxwell, *The Creevey Papers* (New York, 1904) II, p. 87.
[15] Samuel Smiles, *The Life of George Stephenson* (Boston, 1858), p. 197–202.

THE FRUSTRATION OF TECHNOLOGY 59

since. Workers can hardly be expected to be receptive to technological changes in the specific fields in which they are employed, when they are cognizant that their skills will be rendered worthless and their status and very livelihood imperiled by the resultant unemployment. That this peril to the workers under capitalism is real and not illusory was already recognized by Ricardo in the discussion by the classical economists of the effect of the machine on the workers:

> I am convinced that the substitution of machinery for human labour is often very injurious to the interests of the class of labourers ... the same cause which may increase the net revenue of the country may at the same time render the population redundant and deteriorate the condition of the labourer ... the opinion entertained by the labouring class, that the employment of machinery is frequently detrimental to their interests, is not founded on prejudice and error, but is conformable to the correct principles of political economy.[16]

Marx documented this fact graphically, for his period, in his notable chapter in *Capital* on "Machinery and Large Scale Production." For our own time, the evidence given in the studies of the effects of technological displacement of 754 men in three industrial cities in 1928 by Lubin,[17] on 370 Chicago men's clothing cutters from 1919 to 1926 by Meyers,[18] and on 1,190 rubber workers in New Haven and Hartford in 1930 by Clague and Couper [19] supplies further testimony that when technological changes are made under capitalism, consequences to the workers involved are generally grievous.

It is little wonder that workers have repeatedly, from the early days of the industrial revolution until today, resisted displacement by technological changes. Desperation led the workers in the textile industry to express their opposition by machine wrecking.

---

[16] *Works,* ed. by J. R. McCulloch (London, 1846), p. 236, 239.
[17] Isador Lubin, *The Absorption of the Unemployed by American Industry* (Washington, 1929).
[18] R. J. Meyers, "Occupational Readjustments of Displaced Skilled Workers," *Journal of Political Economy,* xxxvii (August, 1919), p. 473–89.
[19] Ewan Clague and Walter J. Couper, *The Readjustment of Industrial Workers Displaced by Two Plant Shutdowns: After the Shutdown* (New Haven, 1934), pt. i.

In 1768 the spinners of Blackburn invaded Hargreaves' home and destroyed his spinning jennies which first operated eight and, before long, one hundred spindles. Workers demonstrated against the jenny again in 1776 and petitioned to the House of Commons to abolish its use lest it "tend greatly to the Damage and Ruin of many thousands of the industrious Poor." Beginning in Lancashire in 1776, there were repeated attacks throughout England against the use of new machines invented by Arkwright, which used water power and horse power for carding, roving and spinning, and which forced spinning out of the cottage into the factory. In their petition to Parliament in 1780, the cotton spinners of Lancashire described the threat of total loss of employment which made the patent machines a "Domestic Evil of very great Magnitude." They declared that the worker's plight was so "intolerable as to reduce them to Despair, and many thousands assembled in different Parts to destroy the *Causes of their Distress.*" They gave evidence that the work produced by the machines was inferior to hand work, and called attention to the fact that the machines were a monopoly "for the immense Profits and Advantages of the Patentees and Proprietors." The introduction of weaving machinery was responsible for what have become known as the Nottingham Luddite riots of 1811–12.[20]

Marx makes pertinent comments on the machine wrecking of the Luddites: "Time and experience were needed before the workers could learn to distinguish between machinery itself and the use of machinery by capital; and until they could come to direct their attacks, not against the material instruments of production, but against the particular social form in which these instruments are used."[21] Machine wrecking whenever it has occurred has been the spontaneous expression of resentment of unorganized workers. Trade unions, and communist and socialist parties, have been opposed to such tactics and have sought, by collective bargaining and political pressure, to diminish the impact of the tragedy of displacement through the more gradual introduction of the new machine or process, through compensa-

[20] J. L. and Barbara Hammond, *The Skilled Labourer, 1760–1832* (London, 1919), p. 49, 160, 53–56, 145–6, 149, 257–60, 301–02, 171–74.
[21] Marx, *op. cit.*, p. 458.

tion of those displaced, and through social insurance programs to take care of the unemployed. At the same time communists and socialists have sought to crystallize sentiment against increased exploitation and displacement of labor by new machinery, in preparation for a struggle for power by labor, to establish an economy in which technology will not be subject to the exigencies of a profit system but will be used to the fullest in the interests of the entire population.

Capitalism tends to discourage rather than stimulate workers' participation in technological progress because of the employers' conception of the limited role which workers should play in production and management. Workers are as a rule regarded as appendages of machines—"hands" rather than potentially creative personalities, whose skill and experience on the job make them especially qualified to improve machinery and technical processes. Rossman in a recent investigation of this subject found that of 233 large companies, eighty-nine took no active measures to stimulate invention by employees and fifty-five companies depended entirely on their engineering and research departments. Most of the others gave meager cash rewards and bonuses which bear little relation to the profits which the innovations yield. The investigation reports that particularly in the "older and well-established industries where machines and methods have been standardized" the typical attitude is "that dreamers of new inventions make poor workers." One company official's answer reveals the attitudes that are at the root of the frustration of workers' creative energies by capitalist industry:

> When inventing is encouraged generally among the employees of a manufacturing establishment and is stimulated by rewards of money and notoriety in the plant, the employees become critical of everything connected with the establishment, and most of them, being in total ignorance of the why and wherefore of the existing order of things, suggest changing everything in and about the place. This takes their minds off their duties.[22]

Workers are moreover deterred from offering innovations by the impossibility of identifying themselves in any real sense with an

[22] Joseph Rossman, "Stimulating Employees to Invent," *Industrial and Engineering Chemistry*, xxvii (1935), p. 1381.

enterprise in which they are but wage workers. When there is recognition of the fact that their improvements in processes of manufacture may lead to the discharge of their fellow workers and even of themselves, workers have little incentive to give suggestions for technological innovations.

That capitalism, thus, by its very class structure, cancels out great potentialities for accelerating technological change, is seen by the achievements of Stakhanovism in the Soviet Union. The importance of this movement, which is increasing production and improving products by the introduction of more efficient methods and the elimination of waste, lies primarily in the fact that it was initiated and is being maintained and extended by the workers themselves, sometimes against technicians and engineers who have clung to old methods and standards. The results of this release of the energies of worker-inventors, stimulated by the recognition that they are not being exploited for profit but are rather contributing, under a socialist economy, to their own advancement, underscores the weakness of capitalism as an agency for stimulating and utilizing technological innovations.[23]

The rejection and suppression of valuable technological innovations by financial and industrial interests because consequent changes may disturb profits is a far more potent cause for retardation in technology under capitalism than is the resistance offered by workers. The enterprise attributed to "capitalist enterprise" is largely fictitious in this period of relatively static or contracting markets. William M. Grosvenor testifies as to the attitude of corporate management toward the utilization of new inventions:

> I have even seen the lines of progress that were most promising for the public benefit, wholly neglected or positively forbidden just because they might revolutionize the industry. We have no right to expect a corporation to cut its own throat from purely eleemosynary motives. . . . Why should a corporation spend its earnings and deprive its stockholders of dividends to develop something that will upset its own market or junk all its present equipment. . . . When

[23] "Movements for Labor Efficiency in the Soviet Union," Bureau of Labor Statistics, *Monthly Labor Review* (March, 1936), p. 624–26; Harriet Moore, "The Stakhanov Movement," American Russian Institute, *Research Bulletin*, 1 (February, 1936), p. 1–7; *Labor in the Land of Socialism: Stakhanovites in Conference* (Moscow, 1936); *The Soviet Union: 1936* (Moscow, 1937).

development is directed by trained and experienced men responsible to stockholders for expenditures, they have little inducement to try to supersede that which they are paid to develop and improve.[24]

Harry Jerome, after a study of mechanization in industry under the auspices of the National Bureau of Economic Research, shows the situation which prevails when the primary determinant of the utilization of techniques is the creation of private profit:

> Technical progress far outruns actual practice. This margin of non-use is in part due to non-pecuniary factors, but the major explanation is simply that, on the whole, industry must be conducted with profits as the immediate goal; hence the first and major consideration in any choice of method is not merely, will it do the work, but also will it pay? [25]

Particularly when a few giant companies control production in any capitalist industry, or monopoly prevails, technological rigidity tends to set in. Louis D. Brandeis noted this fact in 1912 in his testimony before the Oldfield Hearings on Patents:

> These great organizations are constitutionally unprogressive. They will not take on the big thing. Take the gas companies of this country; they would not touch the electric light. Take the telegraph company, the Western Union Telegraph Co., they would not touch the telephone. Neither the telephone company nor the telegraph company would touch wireless telegraphy. Now, you would have supposed that in each of these instances those concerns if they had the ordinary progressiveness of Americans would have said at once, "We ought to go forward and develop this." But they turned it down, and it was necessary in each one of those instances, in order to promote those great and revolutionizing inventions to take entirely new capital.[26]

The extent to which capitalist monopoly suppresses inventions is documented beyond question by a recent patent study of the Bell

---

[24] W. M. Grosvenor, "The Seeds of Progress," in *Chemical Markets*, xxiv (1929), p. 23–26.
[25] Harry Jerome, *Mechanization in Industry*, National Bureau of Economic Research, Inc., Publication No. 27 (New York, 1934), p. 331.
[26] U. S. Congress, House Committee on Patents, *Oldfield Revision and Codification of the Patent Statutes:* Hearings, 62nd Cong., 2nd Sess. (1912) no. 18, p. 12.

Telephone Company by the Federal Communications Commission. The Commission reported that the telephone company suppressed 3,400 unused patents in order to forestall competition. Of these, 1,307 were said to be "patents voluntarily shelved by the American company and its patent-holding subsidiaries for competitive purposes." In reply to the company's allegation that the other 2,126 patents were not used because of "superior alternatives available," the Commission declared:

> This is a type of patent shelving or patent suppression which results from excessive patent protection acquired for the purpose of suppressing competition. The Bell System has at all times suppressed competition in wire telephony and telegraphy under its telephone and telephonic appliance patents, and this exclusion is extended to patents covering any type of construction. Moreover the Bell System has added to its . . . patents any patent that might be of value to its competitors. This policy resulted in the acquisition of a large number of patents covering alternative devices and methods for which the Bell System has no need. . . .
>
> Provisions tending to suppress development are found to be present in patent license contracts between the Western Electric Co. and independent manufacturing companies.[27]

In 1914 Brandeis repeated his criticism of the technological apathy of giant capitalist corporations by citing with approval the judgment of the editor of the *Electrical News*:

> . . . such innovations as are being introduced by our iron and steel manufacturers are merely following the lead set by foreigners years ago. We believe the main cause is the wholesale consolidation that has taken place in American industry. A huge organization is too clumsy to take up the development of an original idea. With the market closely controlled and certain of profits by developing standard methods, those who control our trusts do not want the bother of developing anything new.[28]

The history of the steel industry in the United States substantiates this judgment, for the United States Steel Corporation has initi-

---

[27] Federal Communications Commission, Engineering Department, Telephone Investigation, Docket No. 1. *Report on Patent Structure of Bell Telephone System* (Washington, D. C., February, 1937), Exhibit 1989.

[28] Louis D. Brandeis, *Other People's Money* (New York, 1914), p. 150–1.

ated few technological changes and has been slow to respond to innovations. Because of its vast investments in other processes, it originally rejected or ignored Gray's invention of a structural section that could be rolled together in one piece; Tytus' method of manufacturing steel sheets by a continuous process; Gayley's method of supplying a dry blast to blast furnaces; and the centrifugal process of casting ingots which eliminates ingot molds, soaking pits and blooming mills. It delayed the development of the stainless steel market. Probably because prices are calculated in tonnage, it discouraged for a long time and refused to experiment or pioneer in alloy steels which permit reduction in the weight of steel without a sacrifice of strength.[29]

The suppression of patents such as is typified by the practice of the Bell Telephone Company has been sanctioned by court rulings in the United States. In 1896 it was decided that the patentee "may reserve to himself the exclusive use of his invention or discovery . . . His title is exclusive and so clearly within the constitutional provisions in respect to private property that he is neither bound to use his discovery himself, nor permit others to use it." This decision was reaffirmed in 1909 with the judgment that "the public has no right to compel the use of patented devices or of unpatented devices when that is inconsistent with fundamental rules of property."[30] Technological change in the United States is thus retarded by decisions which place property rights, interpreted in terms of individual rights and the rights of a corporation, against the larger interests of society. In practice, it is the large corporation rather than the inventor that benefits from the legal right to suppress patents. Individual inventors are powerless to defy suppression by attempting to utilize their patents independently in fields dominated by large corporations. They usually lack the requisite capital to put their plans into effect and are moreover deterred by the fear of costly infringement suits and of harassing interference procedures.[31] Patent pools

[29] Harvey O'Connor, *Steel Dictator* (New York, 1935), p. 126–9.
[30] F. L. Vaughan, *Economics of Our Patent System* (New York, 1925), p. 161, 164.
[31] Joseph Rossman, *The Psychology of the Inventor* (Washington, 1931), p. 161–62; W. I. Wyman, "Patents for Scientific Discoveries," in Patent Office Society *Journal*, XI (1929), p. 552.

often keep patents within a small circle of large corporations and restrain independents from utilizing them.[32] Through their control of basic patents and improvements, and also of kindred patents, only a few of which they use or develop, these giant corporations prevent others from making technological changes in the fields which they preempt. The Inventors' Guild has testified to this effect:

> It is a well-known fact that modern trade combinations tend strongly toward constancy of processes and products, and by their very nature are opposed to new processes and new products originated by independent inventors, and hence tend to restrain competition in the development and sale of patents and patent rights; and consequently tend to discourage independent inventive thought.[33]

The research laboratories and other scientific departments of large corporations are widely proclaimed as powerful agencies for the promotion of technological change. The potentialities they offer are indeed prodigious. Experimentation for technological invention usually involves expensive apparatus, and moreover requires coordinated simultaneous investigations along many lines which subsidized laboratories can undertake and solo inventors cannot.[34] In spite of this fact, according to Grosvenor only twelve out of the seventy-five most important inventions made between 1889 and 1929 were products of corporation research.[35] What is most significant, however, is that these research departments augment the control which large corporations have over technological changes in industry and facilitate the suppression of patents which, if used, might disturb their immediate profits. The evidence given above on the suppression of inventions by the Bell Telephone Company, for example, illustrates the primary purpose of the research laboratories of the telephone company,

[32] U. S. Congress, House, Hearings on H. R. 4523, *Pooling of Patents*, 74th Cong., 1936.
[33] Cited by Vaughan, *op. cit.*, p. 212.
[34] The extent of industrial research in this country can be appraised from the compilation by Clarence J. West and Callie Hull, *Industrial Research Laboratories of the United States*, National Research Council Bulletin No. 91 (Washington, 1933).
[35] Grosvenor, *op. cit.*, p. 24.

which are featured in the company's publicity as its contribution to humanity's progress. The judgment of Sir Arthur Balfour of the relation between British research associations and British industry is applicable likewise to the situation in the United States:

> It is when we come to consider the relations between the research associations and the industries themselves, and the extent to which these industries avail themselves in practice of the results of research by their own associations, that we find most cause for disquietude. . . . We have laid special stress on the importance of this aspect of the question of scientific research in relation to industry, because in our opinion it is the imperfect receptivity toward scientific ideas on the part of British industry which is at the moment the main obstacle to advance.[36]

The motivations for industrial research are often to be understood in terms of Andrew Ure's comment that "when capital enlists science in her services the refractory hand of labour will always be taught docility."[37] In a like manner James Nasmyth suggested that the desire to curb the militance of labor was a prime factor in the employers' interest in new machinery:

> In the case of many of our most potent self-acting tools and machines, manufacturers could not be induced to adopt them until compelled to do so by strikes. This was the case with the self-acting mule, the wool-combing machine, the slotting machine, Nasmyth's steam arm, and many others.[38]

That planned and coordinated long range research is infinitely superior to the research of the individualistic inventor, as a spur to technological progress, when the demands of capitalism do not distort their use, is shown by the success of such research methods in the Soviet Union.[39]

In any capitalist society, be the competitive units large or small, the rivalry between alternative methods and products leads to opposition to innovation by vested interests seeking to retain

---

[36] Great Britain, Committee on Industry and Trade, *Final Report*, Comd. 3282 (London, 1929), pp. 215, 218.
[37] Andrew Ure, *The Philosophy of Manufacturers* (London, 1835), p. 367–68.
[38] Samuel Smiles, *Industrial Biography* (Boston, 1864), p. 355.
[39] See *The Second Five Year Plan* (New York, 1936).

control over a limited market. Canal and stagecoach owners opposed the railroads, and the railroad and street car corporations oppose the automobile and auto bus. Gas companies obstructed franchises for electric lighting. Lumber companies campaigned against the use of brick building construction and wooden shingle companies lobbied against laws for fireproof roofing. Brick manufacturers in turn joined with the lumber companies in discouraging the use of cement. Prefabricated houses are being denounced by all who profit from building construction materials which will be superseded. The coal industry propagandized against the use of oil for power. The silk corporations inveighed against rayon. Horse breeders attacked the use of tractors for farming, and the Rust cotton picker appears as a dire threat, not as a blessing, to the cotton industry under capitalism.[40] In the absence of a socialist planned economic order, these conflicts between capitalist interests and technological innovations are inevitable and far-reaching in curtailing technological change.[41]

Capitalist industry has moreover been unable to keep abreast of technique because of the periodic crises inherent in capitalist economy. In the midst of a crisis, with available machinery operating at but a fraction of its capacity, little new equipment incorporating inventions is introduced. This is illustrated by the fact that purchases of industrial machinery in the United States in 1932 declined 74 per cent under the annual average for 1919–29.[42] The shrinking of markets led to an abandonment of large-scale production methods in some industries in all capitalist countries. There were drastic retrenchments in research staffs, resulting in a serious problem of unemployment among tech-

[40] I have documented these and other examples of obstruction to new processes and products in my contribution on "Resistances to the Adoption of Technological Innovations," in National Resources Committee, Subcommittee on Technology, *Technological Trends and National Policy*, edited by William F. Ogburn (Washington, 1937), p. 39–66.

[41] Sir Daniel Hale, J. G. Crowther, J. D. Bernal, and others, *The Frustration of Science* (London, 1935); M. Rubinstein, *Science, Technology and Economics under Capitalism and in the Soviet Union* (Moscow, 1932).

[42] "Industry is Thirty Billion Dollars Behind on New Equipment Purchases" and "Industry Needs Modernization but Awaits Low-Cost Capital" in *Business Week*, no. 154 (1932), p. 20–21; no. 155 (1932), p. 14–16.

nologists, with the result that skilled technicians thwarted in their functioning by the very absence of jobs to develop and apply their knowledge, could hardly be vital agents in technological progress. Deliberate planning was undertaken to restrict production and thus prevent technological expansion; in fact this has been the only type of planning that has been attempted under capitalism. Such efforts were made under the N.R.A. The Research and Planning Commission of the N.R.A. reported in February 1935 that all construction was restricted by code provisions in the following industries: cordage and twine, petroleum, glass container, excelsior, American glassware, crushed stone, floor tile, alloys, iron and steel, carbon black, pyrotechnics, candle, tool implement, and ice. Ten of these codes stipulated that no construction be made without authorization of the code authorities, and six permitted "modernization." Code amendments also restricted construction in the cotton textile and lace manufacturing industries.[43] These efforts were not altogether successful because the raising of wage levels by the N.R.A. led many employers to substitute machinery for labor and to rationalize their plants.[44]

There was an attempt to solve the problem of unemployment during the crisis by the advocacy of the return to earlier mechanical processes, especially in public works. Schmitt reported in the *Engineering News Record* in 1930 that replacement of machines by hand labor was

> a burning question with many city engineers and administrative officials. Some have already answered it in favor of hand labor. . . . Minneapolis is planning to use pick-and-shovel men instead of machinery in its winter program of municipal improvements. Boston proposes to abolish the use of snow-loading machines in clearing the streets after a snowfall. Newark has just begun hand excavation

[43] U. S. National Recovery Administration, Research and Planning Division, *Report on the Operation of the National Industrial Recovery Act* (Washington, 1935), p. 53.
[44] L. S. Lyon and others, *The National Recovery Administration*, Brookings Institution, the Institute of Economics, Publication no. LX (Washington, 1935); Standard Statistics Co., *Standard Trade and Securities*, LXXI, no. 2, sec. 1 (Jan. 3, 1934), p. M5–M8; LXXXVI, no. 35, sec. 3 (June 19, 1935), PMA-9–MA-11; John Strachey, "The Two Wings of the Blue Eagle," in *Nation*, CXXXVII (1934), p. 42–43.

in converting the abandoned Morris Canal to a subway roadbed. Akron and Sacramento have put the pick-and-shovel plan into practice. . . . And so the list goes.[45]

Representative William I. Sirovich, chairman of the House Committee on Patents, commented on this trend in a reply to Representative Hatton W. Summers of Texas, who had urged before the hearings of the Committee that the Patent Office should cease granting patents to those "who will devise methods for taking away jobs of persons now engaged, who will have to be supported either by charity or from the Public Treasury." Sirovich declared:

> One of the western states last year entered into a number of contracts for paving roads containing the specific stipulation that labor-saving machinery should not be used, with the intention of increasing the number of jobs provided. I am not informed whether the men were required to dig up and remove the dirt with their hands, or whether they were allowed to do two or three times as much work with a shovel.[46]

Albert Kelsey, technical adviser to the Pan-American Union, declared in 1931, that several South American countries were contemplating steps to abolish machine work and to substitute hand labor; that Bolivia had practically penalized the use of machines in mining; and that Chile was considering the abolition of motor trucks.[47] In most capitalist countries there have been repeated requests for "scientific holidays" and a "moratorium on invention," such as that advocated by Bishop Burroughs of Ripon before the British Association for the Advancement of Science in 1927. These have found echo in certain business and scientific circles. Joseph Caillaux, for example, in 1932 warned that the "machine is devouring humanity," and urged, "It is necessary to take control of technique. It is necessary to prevent

---

[45] F. E. Schmitt, "Hand Against Machine Work," in *Engineering News Record*, cv (1930), p. 915.
[46] U. S. Congress, House Committee on Patents, *Patents: Hearings on General Revision of Patent Laws*, 72 Cong., 1st Sess. (1932) p. 39–46.
[47] *New York Times*, Dec. 29, 1931, p. 7.

inventions suddenly upsetting production."[48] In the United States, as elsewhere, a literature has developed in which flight from the present takes the form of a fantasy reconstruction of the past, and the Middle Ages is idealized as an escape from the depressing conditions of the crisis of capitalism.[49] Technological advance can receive little nourishment from such barren soil as this.

There have been conflicting currents toward technological change in Nazi Germany. A popular campaign was undertaken in the early years of Nazi rule in defense of *autarchy* or local subsistence economy, occasioned by the collapse of national and international markets. The techniques required by mass production methods were denounced, small workshop and craft production was praised as superior to factory production and peasant farms were favored over large scale agriculture. Such a return to small scale production methods in industry and agriculture could not help but curtail technological progress; technology has in fact retrogressed whenever it has occurred. It was rationalized in the anti-machine polemics of Spengler who wrote, "The flight of the born leaders from the machine is beginning."[50] On the other hand, as part of the Nazi war program to prepare Germany for national self-subsistence during the conflict, new laboratories and factories are being set up to make extremely costly experiments on *Ersatz* substitutes for foreign raw materials. Moreover, there has been expansion and rationalization in the munition and other war industries. Such technological advance as occurs under fascism is thus primarily a handmaiden of militarism.

The substitution of socialized ownership of the means of production in the Soviet Union for private ownership under capitalism has completely altered the class setting of technology and has decisively affected the rate of technological change. The financial hazards entailed by technological advance under an

---

[48] Cited by R. Palme Dutt, *Fascism and Social Revolution* (3d. rev. ed., New York, 1935), p. 70.

[49] See for example the sentiments of the Southern Agrarians in Herbert Agar and Allen Tate, eds., *Who Owns America* (Boston, 1936), and the works of the Catholic "distributionists" in many countries.

[50] Oswald Spengler, *Der Mensch und die Technik* (Munich, 1931) tr. by C. F. Atkinson as *Man and Technics* (New York, 1932).

anarchic system of production built upon the demand for immediate profits on private investments, are eliminated by socialized planning. The vast concentrated resources of a socialized economic system are utilized according to a progressive plan for the technological expansion of socially necessary industries, not haphazardly upon those which yield huge speculative profits as under capitalism. Cyclic crises inherent in capitalism which, as shown above, make the introduction of new technique perilous because of the instability of the market, are effaced in the socialist economy of the U.S.S.R. by the fact that the improvement of wages and living standards of the masses is regarded as an important part of the plan of expansion.[51] The wealth derived from the vast increases in productive capacity concomitant with large scale rationalized production is regarded as social property, part of which is distributed in increased wages permitting the absorption of the new products, and part invested in technological expansion. Costs of depreciation and obsolescence occasioned by the introduction of new techniques which render the older machinery relatively obsolete, are borne without difficulty because, with a constantly expanding market, the volume of the output permits a wide spread of the expense. Sir Josiah Stamp has noted how the problem of obsolescence is tied up with the nature of the social structure:

> An overrapid series of innovations may mean the scrapping or unprofitability of much excellent capital for very small marginal gains. A responsible socialist community would see each time that the gain was worth while, but competitive individuals have no collective responsibility.[52]

Moreover when the market is not narrowed, as under capitalism, by unemployment and static or lowered wages, while production is accelerated—but expands because workers share increasingly in industrial advance—the old techniques may in many instances

---

[51] See for example *The Second Five Year Plan*, p. 431–459; Beatrice and Sidney Webb, *Soviet Communism: A New Civilization* (New York, 1936), p. 767-71.
[52] Sir Josiah Stamp: "Must Science Ruin Economic Progress" in *Hibbert Journal*, xxxii (1933–34), p. 395.

be utilized simultaneously with the new, rather than junked before their costs are met. The effects upon technological advance of potent socialist incentives, of planned industrial research adequately financed by government funds, and on an educational system orientated toward preparing the masses for effective and enlightened participation in a modern world of socially owned machinery, are incalculable.

The permanence of the acceleration of technological change under a socialist economy in the Soviet Union is being challenged by the argument that Russia is temporarily receptive to new techniques because it is passing through its delayed industrial revolution and that, upon the passing of this limited period, its markets will become saturated and crises will recur as under capitalism. This surmise is based upon at least two important fallacies, one historical, the other psychological. Even the most casual reading of the history of the industrial revolution of the eighteenth and nineteenth centuries would indicate the contrasts between the introduction of new machinery under a capitalist and under a socialist economy. Because of the ruthless disregard of the interests of the workers during the capitalist industrial revolution already discussed, whatever benefit accrued to the proletariat from the increase in wealth occasioned by the technological advances, was incidental and usually percolated to them through indirect channels. The capitalist market was "saturated" then, as now, by the inability of low-paid workers to absorb the products which their labor with improved techniques made available. Cyclic crises are not a new phenomenon of capitalism but, because of the individualistic anarchic nature of capitalist production, likewise occurred in the early stages of the industrial revolution, when potentially profitable markets remained untouched. The chaos that characterizes contemporary capitalism, though intensified in an age of imperialism, was present in the early period of the industrial revolution as Heaton testifies:

> Enterprise there was, but not always triumph, and the industrial field was strewn with the wreckage of men who failed. The trouble with machinery that broke down, with workmen who refused to

use it, with customers who demanded long credit yet refused to pay their debts, with booms that burst, with banks that refused any more loans, with wars that closed markets, all made the road stony. Inadequate supplies of working capital wrecked many a venture, and when a successful period came, the profits had to be plowed back into the business. The industrial revolution has not yet been studied through the records of bankruptcy, but enough is known to show on what a treacherous sea the entrepreneur of the early machine age launched his boat.[53]

The planned utilization of advanced technologies in the Soviet Union clearly bears little relation to this type of industrial revolution. The circumstances arising from capitalism's failure to utilize techniques adequately and to avoid crises which smother technological advance are avoided by the very organization of socialist economy.

Moreover the inference of these critics that technological advance under socialism must inevitably slow down because of the limitations of human needs, is unsupportable on psychological grounds. A comparison of the needs of contemporary man and men of the Stone Age shows that men's needs are not static but infinitely plastic, that they are not rigidly preformed but are determined by cultural conditioning. Capitalism has barely acknowledged, let alone satisfied, the potential needs of the expanding personalities of the masses of the people. As these potentialities are released by a socialist economy in which the masses are participants, the possibilities of technological advance to satisfy their requirements are well-nigh limitless.

[53] Herbert Heaton, "Industrial Revolution," *Encyclopedia of the Social Sciences*, VIII, p. 12.

From *Science and Society*, Vol. II, No. 1 (Winter 1937), pp. 3–28.

Restraints upon the Utilization of Inventions

The importance of free research, publication, and utilization in the applied sciences can hardly be overestimated. The rate of technological change and hence the economic development of any country rests to a large extent on the degree to which this freedom prevails. The presence or absence of direct or indirect restraints determines whether the creative potentialities of inventors will be nurtured or inhibited, and whether the application and utilization of their inventions will be encouraged or deterred. The basis of such freedom or restraint lies primarily in the economic and industrial structure of a society, in governmental policy, and in public attitudes toward science and toward social change. Within recent centuries there have been vast transformations in all these spheres which have decisively affected the problem of freedom in the applied sciences, and it is therefore imperative to present historical perspectives, however scant, before appraising the contemporary situation in the United States.

Progress in the applied sciences is inextricably intertwined with advances in the pure sciences. Until freedom of inquiry and publication had been won in the pure sciences, development in the applied sciences was hindered. It is important to note, if only in passing, that we are the beneficiaries of the victories of the experimental scientists over the authoritarian traditions of scholasticism, and over the coercive restraints of the churches. The successes of these scientists as well as the secularization of life associated with modern industrialism and urbanization, have made direct interference of religious authorities in the physical sciences negligible and have thus removed one important restraint upon freedom in the applied sciences.

CHANGES THROUGH TECHNOLOGY

From the sixteenth century onward, economic and cultural developments have stimulated scientific progress and offered a fertile soil and a vast arena for technological changes. The prodigious number of technological innovations that have since occurred, cumulative in their rate and effects, have transformed the earth's surface and man's role upon it. The inventions of steam, electric, and internal combustion power-engines have mechanized production on farm and in factory and accelerated transportation with startling economic and social consequences. Recent advances in applied chemistry have made possible the utilization of coal-tar distillates for the synthetic manufacture of a multitude of products. They have led to the fixation of nitrogen; the conversion of cheap oils into valuable fats; the production of wood alcohol; the artificial nitrate industry; the production of cellulose and its diversified textile and paper products; synthetic rubber; synthetic resins; important progress in the phosphate and potash industries, and in petroleum production and refining; and a vast host of other improvements that have not only revolutionized agriculture, industry, and medicine, as well as the modes and customs of men, but also furnished the agencies of their destruction. Applied physics has transformed metallurgy, facilitated communication by telephone and radio, developed air-conditioning and artificial refrigeration processes, and provided other changes that have had equally significant consequences. Engineering design and construction methods have changed so phenomenally that those of even a short time ago appear naive.[1]

Changes have been so rapid and significant that it is commonly assumed that there has been uninhibited freedom of in-

[1] See Robert K. Merton, "Science, Technology and Society in Seventeenth Century England," in *Osiris*, Vol. IV, pt. 2 (Bruges, 1938), 360–632; G. N. Clark, *Science and Social Welfare in the Age of Newton* (Oxford, 1937); Abraham Wolf, *History of Science, Technology and Philosophy in the 16th and 17th Centuries* (London, 1935); H. E. Howe (Ed.), *Chemistry in Industry*, 2 vols. (New York, 1924–25); Lancelot Hogben, *Science for the Citizen* (New York, 1938).

quiry, publication, and practice in the field of applied sciences. Justifiable elation over achievements has partially obscured the fact that the history of technology has been marked by the rejection of many important and valuable inventions and by protracted delays in the utilization of others. These resistances have not been exceptional, but have generally characterized the response to innovation. The railroad, automobile, street car, steamboat, iron ship, screw propeller, submarine, airplane, typewriter, telegraph, telephone, cable, steam engine, Diesel engine, gas for lighting, incandescent lamp, alternating current; important processes in the manufacture of iron and steel and of textiles; the sewing machine; the iron plow, mechanical planting and threshing machines, tractors, the cotton gin and mechanical cotton picker—these are but a few of the important innovations upon which modern living rests that have met opposition of varying degrees of intensity.[2] . . .

SUPPRESSION OF PATENTS

Especially in recent years the suppression of valuable technological innovations by financial and industrial interests has been far more potent in limiting freedom of research, publication, and use of inventions than has been the resistance offered by workers. The reality of such suppression of invention has repeatedly been questioned. It has been dismissed as rumor, having its source in the stories of impractical and embittered inventors. It has been denied as contrary to industrial policy. The Committee on Patent Revision of the American Bar Association declared in 1929: "It is not believed that in all the discussion that has taken place about the 'suppression of patents' it has been adequately proved that there has been a single instance of such suppression," and cites in corroboration the testimony of Thomas A. Edison at the hearings of the House Committee on Patents on the Oldfield Bill in 1912. Edison then stated:

[2] I have documented these and other oppositions in "Resistances to the Adoption of Technological Innovations," in National Resources Committee, *Technological Trends and National Policy* (Washington, D. C., 1937), pp. 39–66.

I have heard and read numerous statements that many corporations buy valuable inventions to suppress them, but no one cites specific cases. I myself do not know of a single case. There may be cases where a firm or corporation has bought up an invention, introduced it, and afterwards bought up an improvement and ceased using the first patent—suppressed it in fact. Why should that not be done? . . . Let the objectors cite instances where injustice has been worked on the public by the alleged suppression of patents for other reasons than those which were due to improvements.[3]

More recently, in 1935, Gerard Swope, president of the General Electric Company, testified in a similar vein before the House Committee on Patents in answer to questions by Representative Amlie. The record reads:

>Mr. Amlie: . . . Do you know of any instance where with your company, or has there come to your attention in your cross-licensing, any instance where the Radio Corporation, the General Electric, and the A. T. & T. have made important discoveries but have purposely kept them out of use because they would render obsolete existing equipment?
>
>Mr. Swope: That, of course, has been said in the public prints and discussions again and again. In all my experience I do not know of any such instance; . . . because, if you do not bring it out, somebody else will, and then you will have more difficult competition. As soon as we can develop the art by new inventions, we try to bring them on the market so as to get the first benefit of them. I mean just from a selfish policy we do that.
>
>Mr. Amlie: If you had the patents, you would be in a position to prevent any one else doing so, would you not?
>
>Mr. Swope: Yes; if our patent controlled; certainly. But we would do it ourselves, if we had the patent.[4]

EVIDENCE OF SUPPRESSION

Although specific reference is difficult by the very nature of the problem, adequate proof is available to controvert these cate-

[3] American Bar Association, *Advance Program of 52nd Annual Meeting, 1929*, p. 81.
[4] U. S. Congress, House Committee on Patents, *Pooling of Patents*, Hearings on H. R. 423 (Washington, D. C., 1936), Part I, pp. 325–26.

gorical denials of suppression. One source of evidence is decisions of the Federal Courts. In 1897 the National Harrow Company was found to control 85 patents, some of which were shelved, on spring-tooth harrows. A circuit court in 1906 ascertained that the Indiana Manufacturing Company had acquired 105 patents relating to straw stackers which could not be used conjointly, and hence many of them had been suppressed. In 1909 a court decision declared:

> It is a fact familiar in commercial history that patent rights have a commercial value for purposes of extinction; that many patents are purchased in order to prevent the competition of new inventions and of new machines already installed.

In the case of *Heaton-Peninsular Button Fastener Company* v. *Eureka Specialty Company* suppression of patents was acknowledged, as it was likewise in the case of *Continental Paper Bag Company* v. *Eastern Paper Bag Company*.[5]

Suppression of patents is likewise corroborated by other governmental inquiries. The Commissioner of Corporations found in 1909 that the American Tobacco Company had acquired a patent for a tobacco-stemming machine by purchase of a majority of the stock of the Standard Tobacco Stemmer Company, and had not only not manufactured the machine but had prevented its development and use by competitors.[6] At the hearings before the Committee on Interstate Commerce in 1914 suppression of patents to curtail competition was condemned:

> Paper patents, patents covering inoperative devices, and dormant patents (that is, patents not used, but applied for and held for the purpose of preventing the manufacture of the devices of improvements therein described) are at the foundation of much of the most injurious monopoly and trade restraint . . . Again, there are thousands of patents lying dormant, having been acquired by established concerns whose business was threatened by competition.[7]

[5] Appellate Division 21 N.Y. 290; 148 Fed. 21; 166 Fed. 560; 77 Fed. 301; 210 U. S. 430.
[6] U. S. Commissioner of Corporations, *Report on the Tobacco Industry* (Washington, D. C., 1909), Part I, p. 84.
[7] U. S. Senate, 63rd Congress, 2nd Session, Committee on Interstate Commerce, *Hearings on Bills Relating to Trust Legislation* (Washington, D. C., 1914), Vol. II, p. 1078.

Cases of Suppression

The most detailed and conclusive evidence of the suppression of patents is given in the report on the patent structure of the Bell Telephone System made after an extensive inquiry by the Federal Communications Commission.[8] The report cites the testimony of Thomas D. Lockwood, then general patent attorney for the Bell System, in the case of *Western Union* against *American Bell Telephone Company*, on December 7, 1907, when he acknowledged voluntary suppression of patents:

> Question: Has the Bell purchased to any extent patents it has not used itself, or which have not actually been used in the business?
>
> Answer: Certainly. Quite a number.
>
> Question: Will you state personally to what extent it has purchased such patents, and why it has purchased them?
>
> Answer: The Bell Company, through persons delegated to look after such matters, has always thought it well to give itself the benefit of any doubt that might arise in such connection. It has not always been possible to tell, when an invention has been offered to it for consideration, whether, though perhaps not immediately and obviously useful, it might not be useful and valuable as the business advanced, and consequently it has seemed prudent to purchase all inventions offered, of either present or potential or prospective value, or possibly of value or usefulness. A great many, or I would say a very fair proportion of these, have turned out to be of use in later stages of the business, after they have been held without being used for a number of years; and so it has seemed best to take this

---

[8] Federal Communications Commission, Engineering Department. Telephone Investigation. Special Investigation, Docket 1. *Report on Patent Structure of Bell System. Its History and Policies Relative Thereto,* Feb. 1, 1937 (Exhibition 1989). From the point of view of a study of freedom of inquiry and publication, it is of interest to record that this important study, as well as other reports compiled in connection with the investigation of the telephone industry, has not been made available for distribution. T. J. Slowie, secretary of the Commission, who attributed this fact to the Commission's limited appropriation, likewise refused the author of this article permission to photostat pages of the report. The contents have been summarized in Federal Communications Commission, *Proposed Report, Telephone Investigation,* Pursuant to Public Resolution No. 8, 74th Congress (Washington, 1938), Chap. 8.

precaution and buy patents, if they could be obtained at a fair price, whether they were to be immediately put to use or not.

Question: Has the Bell purchased patents at all on the theory that they might be dangerous in the hands of competitors?

Answer: It has, both as regards telephone patents and apparatus patents.

Question: To what extent roughly?

Answer: To the very largest possible extent; in fact, I can only recall one instance in which we have failed to purchase patents or inventions of that character and order, and in this connection I refer to the automatic exchange patents; but as regards them we were reasonably sure that they never would be dangerous or valuable to competitors. In this, however, it has turned out that we were mistaken.[9]

Proof is likewise given from letters in the files of the Bell Telephone System that specific patents were purchased with the object of preventing use by others. Among these are the patent covering a brake key attachment for a magneto generator and the Collier patent for a telephone receiver. In his recommendation on the purchase of the former, accepted by the Company, Lockwood argued:

> The only advantage then (of the purchase of the patent) would be, that by the possession of the patent opposing interests *would be prevented from using it,* and the Western Electric could, if it pleased, sue them as committed infringements subsequent to the assignment. (Emphasis supplied by the Commission.)[10]

The motives which led to the purchase of the Collier patent are revealed in a letter written by W. W. Swan, general counsel for the American Bell Telephone Company:

> *It would be well to buy it to prevent its falling into the hands of persons wishing to establish rival companies.* A party going into the telephone business a year or so hence will probably undertake to use magneto transmitters, or, probably, ignoring the Berliner and Edison patents, will use some carbon transmitter that is about as

---

[9] Western Union Telegraph Company v. American Bell Telephone Company, Vol. 2, "Evidence for Defendant," pp. 488 et seq.

[10] Letter to Hudson, Oct. 5, 1896. Federal Communications Commission, *op. cit.,* p. 113.

good as the standard Blake. Now if such a party can control the Collier receiver it will be a great help to such a party to show that their receiver is a much better instrument than the one in common use by the Bell Company. Indeed such a showing would make it necessary for the Bell Company to take out the receiver now in use and substitute the "100" receiver. (Emphasis supplied by the Commission.)[11]

Other of the early patents of the Bell System that were suppressed are nine Irwin patents, for which the System paid the sum of $118,952.03 for exclusive license privileges over a period of fifteen years. The Bell System delayed thirty years before adopting as standard an anti-sidetone subscriber station circuit, during which period the company made a determined effort to prevent the use of such circuits by independents through the ownership and suppression of patents. The Commission also found that intention to suppress was involved in the purchase, in 1915, of a group of six patent applications from J. L. Wright.[12]

The American Bell Telephone Company reported to the Commission that on December 31, 1934, the Bell System owned and controlled 9,234 patents, of which but 4,225 or 45.7 per cent were in use. Failure to use the 5,009 patents was explained as follows: development incomplete, 608; practical application depends upon other developments, 237; awaiting the determination of commercial application, 660; superior alternative available, 2,126; no public necessity, 1,307. (75 of the unused patents are not classified.) Of the last-named group the Commission concluded:

> The question immediately arises: who determines "public necessity"? In the present case the American Company and its patent-holding subsidiaries have determined that there is no public necessity for the use of devices or methods covered by the 1,307 patents. The determination by the holder or owner of a patent, that there is no public necessity for the device or method covered by the patent, represents in itself patent suppression or patent shelving. It is better to say that the 1,307 unused patents held by the Bell System

[11] Letter to Hudson, Sept. 8, 1893. Federal Communications Commission, *op. cit.*, p. 114.
[12] Federal Communications Commission, *op. cit.*, pp. 115–19, 122.

as of December 31, 1934, are patents voluntarily shelved by the American Company and its patent-holding subsidiaries for competitive purposes.

Of the group of 2,126 patents classified as unused because of superior alternatives available, the Commission declared:

> This is a type of patent-shelving or patent-suppression which results from excessive patent protection acquired for the purpose of suppressing competition. The Bell System has at all times suppressed competition in wire telephony or telegraphy through patents. It has always withheld licenses to competitors in wire telephony and telegraphy under its telephone or telephonic appliance patents and this exclusion is extended to patents covering any type of construction. Moreover, the Bell System has added to its telephone and telephonic appliance patents any patent that might be of value to its competitors. This policy resulted in the acquisition of a large number of patents covering alternative devices and methods for which the Bell System had no need.[13]

Evidences of comparable excessive patent protection leading to suppression are available for other companies. The International Harvester Company reported to the House Committee on Patents in 1935 that approximately two-thirds of its patents were not in current use, and the Ingersoll Rand Company acknowledged that they were not operating under the great majority of their patents.[14] Vaughan's study of the patents of the A. B. Dick Company showed that in 1916 this mimeograph company controlled 128 patents relating to only a few subjects and suppressed alternatives.[15]

Conflicting Court Decisions

The freedom to suppress patents is sanctioned by United States Supreme Court decisions. Until the Supreme Court had acted, the lower courts had given conflicting decisions. In 1898 the

[13] Federal Communications Commission, *op. cit.*, pp. 121–22.
[14] U. S. Congress, House Committee on Patents, *Pooling of Patents*, Hearings on H. R. 4523 (Washington, D. C., 1936), Part IV, pp. 3412, 3453.
[15] Floyd W. Vaughan, "Suppression and Non-working of Patents," *American Economic Review*, Vol. 9 (1919), pp. 694–95.

circuit court declared the suppressed patents were entitled to scant recognition in law:

> It has long appeared to the court, as constituted for hearing of this cause, that a patent for an invention which the patentee refuses to make available himself, and refuses to allow others to make useful, is not within the spirit of the provision of the Constitution which assigns as a reason for securing exclusive rights to authors and inventors a desire "to promote the progress of science and the useful arts," and that patents so held are entitled to scant recognition at law, though necessarily to some, but to none whatever in equity. They are not, as claimed by the plaintiff, the equivalent of a highly cultivated field, surveyed, plotted, and fenced in by the owner; but they constitute, for all useful purposes, a waste from which the public is sought to be excluded for reasons of which equity takes no cognizance.[16]

In 1909 another circuit court decided that an attempt to make profit by suppressing an invention was contrary to the spirit and intent of the patent law:

> The grant of letters patent confers upon the patentee no right not to use his own invention, or to make an agreement in restraint of trade in that article, save in connection with an assignment of the rights conferred by the letters patent ... An attempt to make profit out of letters patent by suppressing the invention covered thereby is outside the patent grant, and is so far removed from the spirit and intent of the patent law that the mere fact that an inventor may make a profit by suppressing his invention is not a sufficient reason for holding the Sherman Act inapplicable to agreements affecting patented articles. If there is secured to the patentee all profits legitimately arising from the manufacture, use, and sale of his invention, this is all that is within the terms of the grant. ... The profit which arises from suppressing an invention, from non-use, flows from commercial tactics and not from the use of the invention. The public interest which forbids contracts in restraint of trade, arises from no right in the public to create trade by compulsion, but only from the expectation of the ordinary course of conduct and the harmful results of interference with it by monopolistic schemes.[17]

[16] *Evart Mfg. Co.* v. *Baldwin Cycle-Chain Co.*, 91 Fed. 262.
[17] *Blount Mfg. Co.* v. *Yale and Towne Mfg. Co.*, 166 Fed. 560.

On the other hand, The Circuit Court of Appeals in 1896 declared that the patentee has exclusive property rights in his invention and is neither bound to use it nor to permit others to use it:

> A patentee may reserve to himself the exclusive use of his invention or discovery. If he will neither use his device, nor permit others to use it, he has but suppressed his own. That the grant is made upon the reasonable expectation that he will either put his invention to practical use, or permit others to avail themselves of it upon reasonable terms, is doubtless true. This expectation is based alone upon the supposition that the patentee's interest will induce him to use or let others use, his invention. The public has retained no other security to enforce such expectations. A suppression can endure but for the life of the patent, and the disclosure he has made will enable all to enjoy the fruits of his genius. His title is exclusive, and so clearly within the constitutional provisions with respect to private property that he is neither bound to use his discovery himself, nor permit others to use it.[18]

Suppression Sanctioned

The right to suppress was upheld by the Supreme Court in the case of *Continental Paper Bag Company* v. *Eastern Paper Bag Company*. The Court declared that the patentee had the privilege of any owner to use or not to use his property:

> ... Can it be said, as a matter of law, that a non-use was unreasonable which had for its motive the saving of the expense that would have been involved by changing the equipment of a factory from one set of machines to another? And even if the old machines could have been altered, the expense would have been considerable. As to the suggestion that competitors were excluded from the use of the new patent, we answer that such exclusion may be said to have been of the very essence of the right conferred by the patent, as it is the privilege of any owner of property to use or not use it, without question of motive.[19]

The doctrine of the right of the non-user was again enunciated by Justice Brandeis for the Supreme Court, when he said in 1931

---

[18] *Heaton-Peninsular Button Fastener Co.* v. *The Eureka Specialty Co.*, 77 Fed. 294–95.

[19] 210 U. S. 429 (1908). See also Walker on Patents (6th Ed. by J. L. Lotsch, 1929), Section 742.

that "if the patent is valid the owner can, of course, prohibit entirely the manufacture, sale or use" of a patented article during the term of the patent.[20]

These decisions place private property rights clearly above the other interests of the community and above the needs of technological progress. That the patentee has absolute property rights which place him under no moral obligation whatsoever to the public is explicitly stated in the case of *United States* v. *Bell Telephone Company:*

> Counsel seem to argue that one who has made an invention and thereupon applies for a patent therefor, occupies, as it were, the position of a quasi trustee for the public; that he is under a sort of moral obligation to see that the public acquires the right to the free use of that invention as soon as is conveniently possible. We dissent entirely from the thought thus urged. The inventor is one who has discovered something of value. It is his absolute property. He may withhold the knowledge of it from the public, and he may insist upon all the advantages and benefits which the statute promises him who discloses to the public his invention.[21]

Corporate Control of Patents

In practice, the freedom here involved is not the freedom of the individual inventor, but a freedom of corporations who control the utilization of patents; for, in an age of large-scale enterprise requiring concentrated capital resources, few individuals are free to promote their own inventions independently, because of lack of requisite capital.[22] Whatever the value of his invention may be, the patentee is prevented in his efforts to reduce it to commercial practice for his own profit except under conditions laid down by the corporations which dominate the market. Because of their control over other patents, these intrenched

[20] Carbide Corporation of America v. American Patents Development Corporation, 283 U. S. 27, 31 (1931). See also Frank L. Schechter, "Would Compulsory Licensing of Patents Be Unconstitutional?" *Virginia Law Review*, Vol. XXII (1936), pp. 287–314.
[21] 167 U. S. 224.
[22] Joseph Rossman, *The Psychology of the Inventor* (Washington, D. C., 1931), pp. 161–62; W. I. Wyman, "Patents for Scientific Discoveries," *Journal of the Patent Office Society*, Vol. XI (1929), p. 552.

interests are able to deter independents from capitalizing inventions for fear of infringement suits. It is therefore very difficult for an inventor to obtain outside capital with which to exploit and develop his invention. This situation was recognized by President Taft, who declared in his message to Congress in 1912:

> Large corporations, by absorbing patents relating to particular arts, have succeeded in dominating entire industries, and the only market to which an inventor of improvements upon such machines may offer his patents for sale is to such corporations.[23]

Comparable sentiments were expressed by President Roosevelt in his message to the Seventy-fifth Congress in 1938:

> There are practices which most people believe should be ended. They include . . . the use of patent laws to enable larger corporations to maintain high prices and to withhold from the public the advantage of the progress of science.[24]

The dependence of the inventor upon corporate interests was stressed by Thomas A. Edison, who said:

> The long delays and enormous costs incident to the procedure of the courts have been seized upon by capitalists to enable them to acquire inventions for nominal sums that are entirely inadequate to encourage really valuable inventions. The inventor is now a dependent, a hired person to the corporation.[25]

Threat of Infringement Suits

This is especially true in fields dominated by patent pools and cross-licensing agreements, where the inventor's real market is decisively restricted, and the implied threat of patent litigation stands, ever more than in other situations, as an insurmountable obstacle to securing independent capitalization. In many fields, the extensive scope of patent pools makes it very difficult to predict free and untrammeled operation of any patent, regardless

---

[23] Cited in U. S. Congress, House Committee on Patents, *Pooling of Patents,* Hearings on H.R. 4523 (Washington, D. C., 1936), Part I, p. 1076.

[24] *New York Times,* Jan. 4, 1938.

[25] U. S. Congress, House Committee on Patents, *Oldfield Revision and Codification of the Patent Statutes,* Hearings, 62nd Cong., 2nd Sess. (Washington, D. C., 1912), No. 23, p. 32.

of its merit. Prior patents ever remain a potential threat of expensive and long-drawn-out litigation. As the engineer and inventor Edward Chandler testified before the House Committee on Patents in 1935:

> There is a growing belief by private capital that even a meritorious patent, in a competitive field, is vulnerable, or at least extremely costly to prove otherwise should its rights tend to run counter to those of some well-entrenched interest.[26]

The effect of fear of infringement suits and their high costs is shown in the experience of the Wrights and of Edward Weston. The secretiveness and suspicion of the Wright brothers, which did much to retard the advance of aviation in its early years, was generated in part by this fear. One of the Wright brothers is quoted as saying that they concealed the developments of their airplane for five years after they had made a successful flight, because "we decided that we would be absolutely lost if our patent became known before we had $200,000 to fight with. Our experiences in the courts have indicated that we did not overestimate the money needed."[27] Baekeland asserted that Edward Weston, who took out three hundred patents between 1873 and 1886, rarely patented after 1886 because he was troubled by patent infringers. The defense of one set of patents alone is said to have cost him $400,000.[28] Few inventors are able financially to defend their rights in such expensive patent litigation with large corporations.[29]

LIMITATION OF INDUSTRIAL RESEARCHERS

The control of monopolistic corporations and patent pools over patent outlets is held not only by blanket patent ownership and by the coercive threat of infringement suits which the inventor has not the funds to combat, but also by legally sanctioned duress-

---

[26] U. S. Congress, House Committee on Patents, *Pooling of Patents*, Hearings on H. R. 4523 (Washington, D. C., 1936), Part I, pp. 665–66.
[27] *Outlook*, Vol. 106 (March 21, 1914), p. 607.
[28] L. J. Baekeland, "Edward Weston's Inventions," *Science*, Vol. XLI (April 2, 1915), p. 492.
[29] See also Joseph Rossman, *Psychology of the Inventor* (Washington, D. C., 1931), p. 170.

terms and tying clauses in contracts. Such contracts require, as a condition of purchase or lease, the use of other equipment or commodities not manufactured under the same patent, but sometimes indispensable to make that patented equipment operative, as for example in the case of the United Shoe Manufacturing Company.[30] Intrenched corporations are in this way able to prevent any invention in the industry from being marketed by potential competitors.

With his market thus drastically curtailed, the inventor is dependent upon these corporate interests. And when there is little danger of a competitor's purchasing the inventions and utilizing them to the disadvantage of the members of the patent pool or of the participants in the cross-licensing agreement, the inventions can be rejected with impunity or bought up at a figure far below their worth.[31]

The engineers, the technicians, and the specialists in the industrial laboratories in the United States engaged in organized research and invention are less free than independent inventors, both in the choice and pursuit of their inquiries and in the power to exploit their discoveries and inventions. Research work financed by the profits of large corporations is usually for the specific purpose of perpetuating and extending their control of the market and of increasing their profits. The researcher's work is therefore largely confined to the development of practical improvements on devices in current use, and is not directly concerned with novel developments that will change decisively established manufacturing processes. This limitation is not necessarily inherent in industrial research. Very significant and profitable results can be achieved by well-equipped, subsidized laboratories that make possible coordinated research beyond the

---

[30] William H. S. Stevens, *Unfair Competition* (Chicago, 1917), pp. 54–67; F. L. Vaughan, *Economics of Our Patent System* (New York, 1925), pp. 210–11; Testimony of Milton Handler, U. S. House Committee on Patents, *Pooling of Patents* (Washington, D. C., 1936), Part I, p. 1037; Arthur R. Burns, *The Decline of Competition* (New York, 1936), pp. 11–18.

[31] U. S. Congress, House Committee on Patents; *Pooling of Patents*, Hearings on H. R. 4523 (Washington, D. C., 1936), Part I, pp. 665–70. See also corroborative testimony of Willis B. Rice, *ibid.*, p. 1139, and of Charles N. Warner, *ibid.*, pp. 681–82.

powers of a sole inventor, as is demonstrated on the largest scale by the accomplishments of planned research in the Soviet Union during the First and Second Five Year Plans.[32] But the underlying spirit of these scientific departments of large capitalist industries is revealed by William M. Grosvenor, chemical engineer and inventor. . . .

According to his calculations, only twelve of the seventy-five basic and radically new inventions made between 1889—when corporate investigation may be said to have started—and 1929 were produced by corporation research.[33]

Assignment Contracts

This channeling of efforts toward the solution of immediate problems does not permit the freest play of the creative abilities of the scientist employed by the laboratories. Many of the problems are none the less extremely interesting, and offer an outlet for creative energies. They would be able to do so far more successfully, were the inventor able to identify himself more fully with his work through a consciousness of his participation in the rewards derived from it. It is, however, a common practice for employers who operate industrial research laboratories to require the employee to sign a contract assigning all inventions and all patent rights which he may achieve during the period of his employment. The contract in use by the Ingersoll-Rand Company in 1935 is typical:

> In consideration of one dollar ($1) paid to me by Ingersoll-Rand Co., the receipt whereof by me is hereby acknowledged, and of my employment by that company during such time as may be mutually agreeable to that company and myself, I agree to assign and hereby do assign to said company, its successors and assigns, all my rights to inventions which I have made or conceived or which I may hereafter make or conceive, either solely or jointly with others, in the course of such employment, or with the use of the time, material, of facilities of said company, or relating to any method,

[32] U.S.S.R., State Planning Commission, *The Second Five Year Plan,* New York, 1937.
[33] William M. Grosvenor, "Seeds of Progress," *Chemical Markets,* Jan. 1929, pp. 23–25.

substance, machine, article of manufacture, or improvements therein within the scope of the business of that company; and I further agree that, without charge to said company, but at its expense, I will disclose such inventions to the said company as soon as practicable after they are made, and execute, acknowledge, and deliver at the request of the company all papers including patent applications which may be requisite for obtaining patents on said inventions in any and all countries and to vest title thereto in said Ingersoll-Rand Co., its successors or assigns, and do all other acts and things which may be necessary and proper to be done in furtherance of these ends, the inventions to remain the property of Ingersoll-Rand Co. whether patented or not.

In order that further disputes may not occur, all patents issued prior to the date of my employment with Ingersoll-Rand Co., are excluded from this agreement, and all other inventions which I wish to exclude therefrom are listed within.

Witness my hand and seal this..........day of.......................19........

....Seal

Witnesses:

Printed on the contract is the following comment:

The men who are asked to sign this agreement are those who in the natural course of events may be brought in touch with the problems which are from time to time presented to Ingersoll-Rand Co. for solution and with the efforts which are being made by various engineers attached to the company to solve these problems. Without an agreement to assign inventions along the line of the company's activities it would be impossible to put these men in any such relations with the company's work and to bring them into free and open relations with those engineers who are regularly assigning inventions to the company.

While the company holds out no promise of additional compensation for assignment of inventions, its policy is to recognize all good service of whatever nature, by proper adjustment of the salaries of employees, by advancement in opportunity and responsibility, and otherwise, and inventive ability is in general recognized as an element of value just as designing ability, executive ability, and other similar traits are recognized.

As the employee is to assign inventions which he makes after he enters the employ of the company, then for his own protection as well as in the interests of the company it is desirable that records should be made of the inventions which he possesses at the time of employment and which he would therefore naturally wish to exclude from the operation of the contract and to take up specially with the company if they were such that the company would be likely to be interested in them.

It is obvious that during this employment a man may acquire many records and data and much confidential information which under no circumstances should be used after the termination of the employment. There is also much that is marginal, or as to which doubt may arise. It is difficult exactly to draw the line in writing; a man's own sense of propriety is usually the safest guide in each particular case. The more experience he has the more careful he becomes in such matters. The company will in many cases be glad to have the employee use such information but expects the employee to obtain permission in each case when doubt arises.[34]

The extent to which large companies utilize these contracts was investigated by Rossman, who found that of 201 companies, 99 required the contract and 102 did not. The companies that did not demand assignment in their contracts declared that shop rights were ample for their purposes and that they found little trouble in having their employees voluntarily execute their assignments to them.[35] The courts have sustained employment contracts requiring the assignment of inventions and patents as not contrary to public policy, on the ground that the employee is free to contract and sell his services, and that the employer's business must be protected within the scope of normal or expected activities.[36]

Compensation for Inventions

"Freedom of contract" is hardly applicable as a description of the bargaining relationship between a large-scale employer

[34] U. S. House Committee on Patents, *Pooling of Patents, op. cit.*, Part IV, pp. 3454–55. For comparable contracts see also Clark A. Nichol, *Annotated Form Book* (Chicago, 1925), pp. 861–62.
[35] Joseph Rossman, "Stimulating Employees to Invent," *Industrial and Engineering Chemistry*, Vol. 27 (1935), pp. 1512–14.
[36] Lindley D. Clark, "Rights of Employees to Their Inventions," *U. S. Monthly Labor Review*, Vol. 22 (June, 1926), pp. 1188–99; E. Adler, "Inventions of Employees and the Austrian Patents Act of 1925," *International Labor Review*, Vol. 13 (Jan. 1926) pp. 1–20.

and a scientific worker pressed by economic need. Professional and technical workers resent contracts requiring the assignment of inventions, and one of their major grievances is the fact that in most instances, whatever the value of their inventions, they receive only their salaries. The attitude of most employers financing research activities is epitomized by the comment of George Folk, general patent attorney of the American Telephone and Telegraph Company, in his testimony before the House Committee on Patents. When questioned by Congressman Dunn on whether employees who invented some new kind of apparatus, which in the opinion of the telephone officials would be very advantageous to them, received any extra compensation, he replied:

> I know of no extra compensation except the normal credit a man would get for doing his job well; in other words, irrespective of any contracts at all, it is an established principle of law that when you hire a man to do something for you and pay him for doing it, when he finishes a job it belongs to you.[37]

This widespread legalistic, impersonal attitude toward the members of research staffs does not produce an environment conducive to the stimulation of free creative participation on the part of scientists and technicians.[38]

In some cases inventors may receive additional compensation for notable inventions, but they are barred from exploiting their inventions independently for their own benefit. Even more than the independent inventors, they are helpless to prevent the shelv-

---

[37] U. S. Congress, House Committee on Patents, *Pooling of Patents*, Hearings on H. R. 4523 (Washington, D. C., 1936), Part I, p. 721. See also testimony of Frank Jewett, director of Bell Laboratories, *ibid.*, pp. 275–76; and statement of the Socony-Vacuum Oil Company, Part IV, p. 3814.

[38] See also H. Stafford Hatfield, "The Encouragement of Invention," *Psyche*, Vol. 10, No. 3 (1930), pp. 103, 111; Rossman, *op. cit.*, p. 515. Thorndike has recently investigated the incomes of the 72 scientists who were starred by Cattell in 1935 for their notable contributions and who are employed by business concerns. Of the 45 on whom information could be obtained, 29 appear to earn less than $15,000 yearly. E. L. Thorndike, "The Salaries of Men of Science Employed in Industry," *Science*, Vol. 88 (Oct. 7, 1938), p. 327.

ing and suppression of their inventions. One of the important functions of industrial research laboratories is, in fact, to extend the control of corporations over the patents in their industries. Moreover, inventors derive no additional returns when the patented inventions which they develop on a salary basis for one concern are placed at the disposal of members of a patent pool or participants in a cross-licensing agreement.

Contract of the Mellon Institute

When companies do not operate their own research departments but finance research through institutes such as the Mellon Institute of Industrial Research, they likewise require the assignment of inventions and patents made by the scientist during the period of his researches. The following clauses in the contract of research fellowships at the Mellon Institute oblige the recipient of such a fellowship to forfeit his rights of independent publication and the use of his findings, in favor of the company financing the investigation:

> Any and all discoveries, germane to the subjects of this investigation, made during the term of this Fellowship, as well as all relevant information obtained, by the Fellow of this Fellowship, or the Executive Staff of the Institute, separately or conjointly, shall become the property of the Donor, subject to the terms and provisions of this Agreement, and such member of the Institute making such discovery or obtaining such information shall promptly and without demand make revelation of all such information and discoveries. Such revelations shall be made to the duly designated representatives of the Donor directly, or through the Director, as the Director may determine.
>
> The members of the Institute . . . making a discovery or invention germane to the subjects of the Donor's investigation, shall at any time, upon the request and at the expense of the Donor, apply for letters patent, and shall assign such letters patent and any and all rights to such invention to the Donor under the conditions of this Agreement. In case the Donor desires to keep secret any discovery or invention, or for any reason desires that letters patent shall not be applied for, such member of the Institute making such discovery or invention shall not at any time apply for patent or

patents in his own name and shall not disclose such discovery or invention to others except as herein provided.[39]

Weaknesses of the Patent System

It is occasionally urged that industrial research has rendered the patent system obsolete, and that for this reason patents be abolished. The judgment of the British Science Guild on this matter, after its investigation of reforms of the British patent system, is cogent. The Guild declared:

> In the absence of a patent system the practice of secret working grows apace, often with the result that the maintenance of secrecy costs the manufacturer, and ultimately the public, more than open working under a sound patent system, while postponing or even preventing publication and free working.[40]

Reforms in the patent laws of the United States to meet the needs of the new situation, and especially such revisions as would require compulsory licensing to prevent suppression, have met vigorous opposition from vested interests. Within recent years the bills requiring compulsory licensing which have been introduced into Congress—the Oldfield bill in 1912, the Stanley bill in 1922, the King bills in 1928, 1929, and 1935, and the McFarlane bill of 1938 have received little support and vigorous attack. In 1935 the American Bar Association, which has consistently disapproved of these bills, appointed a Public Relations Committee whose designated functions were:

> To act in conjunction with the various local patent law associations, and otherwise, in presenting to the public facts as to the value to the public of the United States patent system in encouraging the making of inventions and their commercial exploitation, in order that the public may not be misled by certain incorrect and unfounded criticisms and attacks upon our patent laws and operations under them, now being made by some who are either hostile

---

[39] U. S. House Committee on Patents, *Pooling of Patents, op. cit.*, Part III, p. 2913.
[40] British Science Guild, *Report on the Reform of the British Patent System* (London, 1928), p. 8.

to patents in general or to the privileges granted pursuant to our present patent laws.[41]

The procedure of the Patent Office, which permitted secrecy of inventions for excessive periods during which the patents were pending, has also been subject to criticism. The classic example is the Fritts patent on the talking motion picture, which was first filed in 1880, and not granted until 1916. The large steel companies were able to keep several important patents pending from five to sixteen years, and the Carson patents on a copper-smelting furnace were kept pending eight and a half to twelve years, thereby prolonging the monopoly on the patent long beyond the seventeen years set by Congress. The average time of pendency of patent applications was, in 1929, two years and ten months, but it is reported that this period has recently been reduced.[42]

UNPROGRESSIVE CORPORATIONS

There are many factors restraining receptivity to innovations which do not involve patent rights. Giant corporations are prone to be apathetic to technological changes by the nature of their complicated setup. . . .

For example, evidence of technological rigidity in the metallurgical industries is given by Furnas:

> Once in a long time a revolutionary process enters industry. Often it comes in by the back door—that is, from someone outside the

[41] American Bar Association, *Report of Los Angeles Meeting, July 16–19, 1935* (Baltimore, 1935), p. 134. See also Frank Schechter, "Is Compulsory Licensing Unconstitutional?" *Virginia Law Review*, Vol. XXII (1936), pp. 287–314. The most recent blast against compulsory licensing is the Report of the *American Patent Law Association Opposing the McFarlane Bill, H. R. 9259* (Washington, 1938).

[42] For a record of the length of time pending of the patents of 143 important inventions, see U. S. House Committee on Patents, Hearings, 72nd Congress, First Session (Washington, 1932), pp. 287–89. See also testimony on this subject by the Commissioner of the Patent Office, Conway Coe, U. S. House Committee on Patents, *Pooling of Patents* (Washington, 1936), Part I, pp. 1055–57. For criticism of the existing interference system frequently utilized against the interests of the inventor by large corporations, see American Bar Association, Advance Program of 52nd Annual Meeting at Memphis, Tennessee, Oct. 23–25, 1929; Minority Report, pp. 99–100.

particular industry involved. It seems strange that this should be true, particularly for those industries which maintain competent, alert research staffs. Nevertheless, outside individuals frequently come along with absurd ideas which any expert knows cannot work for a dozen perfectly good reasons but which eventually do work and become important despite all opposition. . . .

Most steel men knew that Henry Bessemer's ideas of making steel by blowing air through molten iron was absurd. Despite universal ridicule Bessemer built his own plant, and revolutionized steel making. The ridiculers are lost to history. William Siemens knew that his open-hearth process for making steel was fundamentally sound. No one else believed it until he had demonstrated its success in the steel plant he built himself. After the steel makers had all climbed on the wagon with him many of them contended that they had thought of its first. Hadfield discovered that steels containing 13 per cent of manganese were strong, tough, and very desirable. He couldn't convince even his own father, a foundry owner, that this was true. Eventually, Hadfield's work led to the opening of the entire field of alloy steels. Not many years ago all electro-experts knew that chromium plating could never be practical—all but one or two. Millions of automobile bumpers show evidence of the experts' errors. Before 1908 it was known that it was impossible to make ductile tungsten wire, but in that year Dr. W. D. Coolidge, of the General Electric Laboratory, forced that tradition out of the window.[43] . . .

REASONS FOR APATHY TO INNOVATIONS

The factors leading to the delayed response of large organizations to innovations lie not only in the "clumsiness" of their structure or in the psychological inertias born of complacency, timidity, and industrial bureaucracy. These are of course potent, for an innovation demands troublesome readjustments, risks, and responsibilities, disturbs established routines, causes realignments in authority, and often deflations of the prestige of those who are in a position to maintain their status by interfering with the

[43] C. C. Furnas, "Metallurgy," in National Resources Committee, *Technological Trends and National Policy* (Washington, D. C., 1937), p. 355. See also Louis C. Hunter, "Factors in the Early Pittsburgh Industry," in Edwin F. Gay, *Facts and Factors in Economic History* (Cambridge, Mass., 1932), p. 44; W. T. Jeans, *Creators of the Age of Steel* (New York, 1884), p. 104.

new practice. Another significant cause is that large-scale production and productive enterprise are as a rule highly specialized and standardized, with the proportion of fixed costs large as compared to variable costs. Innovations often incur large obsolescence costs, and therefore although an innovation may be more efficient than the process already in use, it may be, temporarily at least, less economic. The writing-off of depreciation costs depends to a large extent on the available and potential market. On an expanding market the depreciation charges of drastic technological changes can be spread widely, but the handling of obsolescence becomes more difficult on a saturated and contracting market. The fear of the consequences of periodic capitalist crises is a deterrent of technological change even at the peak of production, for few want to scrap existing capital equipment when the prospects for more profit on the innovation are not certain. During a crisis, with markets glutted, there is less motivation for the installation of new machinery. This is the opinion of Haberler in his study for the League of Nations:

> It is very likely that during the contraction, when investment was at a standstill, new inventions may have been made which, in spite of the fact that (at the ruling prices) they would reduce the cost of production, have not been put into application because they necessitate more or less heavy investments which the entrepreneur is not willing to make when he expects a fall in demand and prices.[44]

That the recent crisis occasioned technological lag is shown by the fact that purchases of industrial machinery in the United States in 1932 declined 74 per cent under the annual average for 1919-29,[45] a figure which takes no account, however, of new rationalization processes, as distinct from machinery, installed

---

[44] Gottfried von Haberler, *Prosperity and Depression,* League of Nations Intelligence Service (Geneva, 1937), p. 290. For a study of socio-economic problems of rates of invention and shifts of immediate interest see Robert K. Merton, "Fluctuations in the Rate of Industrial Invention," *Quarterly Journal of Economics,* XLIX (1935), 454-74.

[45] "Industry Is Thirty Billion Dollars Behind on New Equipment Purchases," and "Industry Needs Modernization but Awaits Low-Cost Capital," *Business Week,* No. 154 (1932), pp. 20-21; No. 155 (1932), pp. 14-16.

to increase production and lower labor costs. Deliberate attempts on the part of N.R.A. boards to prevent technological expansion were in some instances circumvented by companies to nullify the effect of the increase in wage levels.[46] In public works and in certain private industries there was a trend toward reversion to earlier mechanical processes, to production methods geared to small-scale industry and to hand labor.[47] The problem of technological innovation is otherwise intimately tied up with the nature of the social structure, as Sir Josiah Stamp has noted:

> An overrapid series of innovations may mean the scrapping or unprofitability of such excellent capital for very small marginal gains. A responsible socialist community would see each time that the gain was worth while, but competitive individuals have no collective responsibility.[48]

RIVALRY BETWEEN ALTERNATIVES

Be the competitive units large or small, the rivalry between alternative methods and products under capitalism leads to opposition to technological innovation by vested interests seeking to retain or gain control over a limited market. Westinghouse throws light on the nature of this rivalry in his answer to Edison's vigorous opposition to the use of alternating currents for electric lighting:

> Four large corporations were started almost simultaneously upon a career of competitive business (of supplying electric lighting). The energy and money since expended by each of these corporations *in efforts to thwart the progress of the others* has mutually embittered the interested parties to a degree that can with difficulty

---

[46] U. S. National Recovery Administration, Research and Planning Division, *Report on the Operation of the National Industrial Recovery Act* (Washington, 1935), p. 53; L. S. Lyon and others, *The National Recovery Administration,* Washington, D. C., 1935; John Strachey, "The Two Wings of the Blue Eagle," *Nation,* Vol. CXXXVII (1934), pp. 42–43.

[47] F. E. Schmitt, "Hand Against Machine Work," *Engineering News-Record* (1930), p. 915.

[48] Sir Josiah Stamp, "Must Science Ruin Economic Progress?" *Hibbert Journal,* Vol. XXXII (1933–34), p. 395.

be comprehended by those not immediately concerned in the strife. [Italics supplied.][49]

Canal and stagecoach owners similarly opposed the railroads, and the railroad and street car corporations have opposed auto and air transportation. The coal industry propagandized against oil for power. The silk industry campaigned against rayon. Manufacturers of alternative housing materials have sought to capture and restrict each other's market.[50] Such competition interferes with free research, publication, and utilization, as well as does its counterpart monopolistic control for private profits discussed above.

EFFORT TO RETARD INVENTION

There has been a recurrent demand on the part of individuals in the United States that there be a "scientific holiday" or a "moratorium on invention" such as that advocated by Bishop Burroughs of Ripon before the British Association for the Advancement of Science in 1927. Recently, Representative Hatton Sumners introduced a bill in the House of Representatives to stop the issuance of patents on labor-saving devices.[51] The antimachine polemics of Spengler[52] have moreover found echo in the United States in the writings of the Southern Agrarians, in which flight from the present takes the form of a fantasy reconstruction of the past.[53] Technological change can find no roots in such barren soil as this, and should the views of these or

[49] George Westinghouse, Jr., "A Reply to Mr. Edison," *North American Review*, Vol. 149 (1889), p. 655. For Edison's attack see Thomas A. Edison, "The Dangers of Electric Lighting," *ibid.*, pp. 625-34.

[50] For documentation of these and other obstructions to new processes and products see my article "Resistances to the Adoption of Technological Innovations," in National Resources Committee, *Technological Trends and National Policy* (Washington, D. C., 1937), pp. 39-66. See also Sir Daniel Hale, J. G. Crowther, J. D. Bernal, and others, *The Frustration of Science*, London, 1935.

[51] *Congressional Record*, Nov. 23, 1937, pp. 483-85.

[52] Oswald Spengler, *Der Mensch und die Technik* (Munich, 1931), tr. by C. F. Atkinson as *Men and Technics*, New York, 1932.

[53] Herbert Agar and Allen Tate (Eds.), *Who Owns America?* Boston, 1936.

comparable publicists prevail, freedom of research and publication in the applied sciences would be increasingly curtailed.

Some deletions have been made in this article in places where it overlaps with the previous essay.

Science and War Production*

There has been much publicized discussion recently of the prodigious advances in science as applied to industry as a result of the war program.[1] These accounts are doubtless correct as far as they go, for the achievement is spectacular when measured by prewar standards. But they do not tell the full story. They are, in fact, misleading, for they give the impression to the uniformed that the full scientific resources of the country are now in play, that science is being channelized creatively to the limit in the war effort. This is far from true. Factors outside the field of science, but in the structure of American economy in which the sciences must function, have held back scientific and technological developments to a mere fraction of their actual potentialities. It will be the purpose of this paper to delineate some of the major impediments to the full realization of science's contribution to the winning of the war. These reside in the abuses of the patent system by certain monopolistic groups; the persistence of the monopolists' prewar policy of curtailment of production to maintain high prices and market control; the failure to utilize small plants, and the lack of centralized planning of the production program.

* This article is an extension of a paper, originally prepared as part of a symposium on "Science and the War Effort," arranged by the American Association of Scientific Workers in connection with the annual meetings of the American Association for the Advancement of Science that were held in New York in December, 1942.

[1] See for example the widely distributed address before the American Chemical Society on September 6, 1942 by Charles M. A. Stine, Vice-President, E. I. du Pont de Nemours and Co., entitled "Molders of a Better Destiny." Reprinted from the *Chemical and Engineering News*, xx (September 10, 1942), p. 1085 f.

In discussing patents before a group of scientists, it is particularly fitting to recall the intentions of the founding fathers who initiated the system. The constitutional provision under which patents are granted stipulates that "Congress shall have power . . . to promote the progress of science and useful arts by securing for limited times to authors and inventors the exclusive right to their respective writings and inventions." George Washington sponsored patents to give "effectual encouragement . . . to the exertion of skill and genius at home." Jefferson promoted them that "ingenuity should receive liberal encouragement." Abraham Lincoln paid tribute to them in his often quoted words: "The patent system added the fuel of interest to the fire of genius."[2]

It is a far cry from this conception of promoting the progress of science and rewarding inventive genius through patents to the patent policy of modern corporations. Patents have instead become a major instrument of business policy, an agency for the attainment and maintenance of monopoly power. This purpose is boldly stated in a communication from the files of the Hartford-Empire Company, an engineering and development concern engaged in developing machinery for making glass containers. A memorandum which was brought to light during the hearings of the Temporary National Economic Committee, dated February 18, 1930, reads as follows:

> In taking out patents we have three main purposes—(a) to cover the actual machines which we are putting out, to prevent the duplication of them . . . (b) to block the development of machines which might be constructed by others for the same purpose as our machines, using alternative means . . . (c) to secure patents on possible improvements of competing machines, so as to "fence in" those and prevent their reaching an improved stage.[3]

Far from stimulating science, patents are here being used to block its progress. As Walton Hamilton writes:

[2] U. S. Department of Commerce, Patent Office, *The Story of the American Patent System, 1790–1940* (Washington, U. S. Government Printing Office, 1940), pp. vii, i, ii.

[3] U. S. Senate, 75th Congress, Third Session, Temporary National Economic Committee, *Hearings*, Part 2 (December 6–16, 1938), p. 386–91.

The grant of a patent is intended to protect an invention; in practice it repeatedly operates to block off a whole technology.... The incentive it releases is not the propensity to tinker and contrive, but the urge to make fast the barriers about the corporate estate; any genuine technical advance it prompts is a by-product of the acquisitive arts. In such employment a wayward patent system has strayed far from the office to which it was appointed by the Constitution.[4]

The public relations departments of the large corporations still utilize the symbol of the benefits accorded to the struggling scientists and inventors when they seek popular support for their patent practices. But it is the corporations, not their scientists, that are the beneficiaries of the patent privileges.

The following colloquy before the Senate Patents Committee is relevant to this discussion:

Senator Clark of Idaho. What has become of the inventor, the fellow who used to visualize these things, the little fellow working in his laboratory, which he probably made with his own hands? He was the inspiration for those very words that are used in the Constitution and later in statutory law. Does he exist any more?

Mr. [Thurman] Arnold. He does. He is the third assistant to the patent expert.

Senator Clark of Idaho. Or is he on the pay roll in some gigantic research laboratory?

Mr. Arnold. Yes; as third assistant to the patent expert. Of course, there are independent inventors running around, but they are caught sooner or later in this same machine.

The Chairman (Senator Bone of Washington). Well, it can hardly be characterized, with the most generous attitude toward it, as a free enterprise system.

Mr. Arnold. No. The inventor has become a kind of front for this whole system. He is the painting on the outside of the building. That is what he really is.

Senator LaFollette. He takes the place of the widows and orphans.[5]

[4] Walton Hamilton, *Patents and Free Enterprise*, Temporary National Economic Committee, Monograph No. 31 (Washington, U. S. Government Printing Office, 1941), p. 161 f.

[5] U. S. Senate, Seventy-seventh Congress, Second Session, Committee on Patents, *Hearings* on S. 2303, Part 2 (April 20–25, 1942), p. 968 f.

It is generally recognized that the age of the successful solo inventor is well-nigh past and that a much greater proportion of commercially applicable discoveries are made in industrial research laboratories than previously. Less well known is the control which the larger corporations have over industrial research. Organized research is highly concentrated, because of the large capital outlay required for equipping laboratories and financing their operating expenses. In 1938, 13 companies employed one-third of the industrial research personnel, 140 companies, representing 10 percent of the number reporting, employed two-thirds of the workers. The remaining third was employed by 1,582 concerns. This concentration of research means that a relatively small number of enterprises have been in a position to make scientific advances serve their special purposes, by determining the directions of the fields of inquiry and by restricting the use of the findings. Large scale enterprises through their industrial research are thus able to have vast technical advantage over smaller enterprises which are without research facilities. It becomes practically impossible for the small companies to keep apace with scientific developments, for the information becomes the commercial property of the large corporations.[6]

It is the common practice for employers who operate industrial research laboratories to require employees to sign contracts assigning all inventions and all patent rights which they may achieve during the period of their employment to the company. The companies that do not demand such assignment contracts contend that shop rights are adequate for their purposes, for under shop rights the employer has a non-exclusive, nonassignable license to use inventions made by persons in their employ.[7]

This situation has made possible patent abuses by corporations, which have disastrously affected our war effort, since they prevented the full utilization of our technological resources for the winning of the war. Through these abuses, significant segments

---

[6] George Perazich and Philip M. Field, *Industrial Research and Changing Technology* (Philadelphia, W. P. A. National Research Project, 1940).

[7] Bernhard J. Stern, "Restraints Upon the Utilization of Inventions," *The Annals of the American Academy of Political and Social Science*, cc (November, 1938), pp. 13–31. See p. 75 in this book.

of our economy have been involved in cartel systems both foreign and domestic, in a manner that has obstructed the flow of strategic materials vital for war and for internal security. The production and distribution of the most basic elements of a war economy such as magnesium, zinc, rubber, aviation gasoline, beryllium, titanium, electrical equipment, plastics, dyestuffs, tungsten carbide, have been seriously impaired, and in some cases, totally blocked by patent restrictions. The cartels, by the use of patents to suppress competition, and also to restrict production, have been responsible for America's crucial delay before the war in developing important light metals, chemicals and plastics which are now important in the winning of victory and in the safety of our fighting forces.

Thurman Arnold in his testimony before the Senate Patent Committee[8] has given an interesting summary of the devices used by corporations to protect their monopolies through patents. He described the use of the "patent *blitzkrieg*," a term actually used by one company to describe its procedures in a communication found in its files. By means of "patent *blitzkriegs*," cartels coerce entire industries by the oppressive use of infringement suits or threats of such suits. This is made possible because banks will not lend money for the development of an industry while infringement suits are threatened. Because their customers are intimidated, the business of independent companies collapses. Infringement suits are costly, and whatever the merits of the case, the independents cannot face the battery of counsel of the giant cartels. The Anti-trust Division of the Department of Justice declares that it has observed such patent *blitzkriegs* at work in the radio, chemical, metal, optical goods and electrical goods industries among others.

Patent *blitzkriegs* are facilitated by the use of "umbrella patents," "accordion patents" and "bottleneck patents" and by the existence of patent pools. Umbrella patents are so broad that they really cover industrial ideas. Recently in the case of the manufacture of hardboard, an umbrella patent was used to destroy whatever independent enterprise existed and to prevent

[8] U. S. Senate, Committee on Patents, 77th Congress, Second Session, *Hearings* on S. 2303 and S. 2491. Part 7 (July 31, 1942), pp. 3295–3324.

new types of hardboard from being manufactured. The patent in this case was so comprehensive that it included the idea of making hardboard from any vegetable substance with fibers. An "accordion patent" starts with a simple invention and is extended to control unpatented processes associated with the invention until a complete vertical cartel is contrived. An invention of a lens segment in bifocal spectacles, for example, led to the patenting of the finished spectacles and this was extended to the processes of grinding and polishing and even to the methods of merchandising. Control is thus exercised through patents from the manufacturer to the customer. In the case of "bottleneck patents" crucial inventions are used in restraint of trade, to hold up all other techniques in the industry.

Patent pools have a legitimate function in breaking up patent impasses arising from the fact that patents on various parts of a single complex machine or process are often owned by different individuals. Through patent pools, however, giant corporations have been able to keep smaller manufacturers from producing unless they abide by discriminatory rules and regulations concerning division of the field, production and prices. The power of these patent pools is prodigious because of the number of patents controlled. The patent pool of Standard Oil-I. G. Farbenindustrie cartel, for example, embraced thousands of patents, and over 15,000 patents are in the General Electric, A. T. and T. and R.C.A. patent pool. Conflicting and competing patents are absorbed by these pools; anyone who stands in the way is crushed. Even the major members of the pool limit each other by restrictive licenses.

Inventions in one field frequently have uses in others. It has been to the financial interest of some patent-owning groups to restrict the use to which a process may be put instead of permitting the utilization of the invention to the full. The use of this procedure as it affects the war effort is dramatically revealed by testimony before the Senate Patents Committee, in the document of the Standard Oil-I. G. Farbenindustrie cartel. The process which makes butadiene, an essential of synthetic rubber, is also capable of making aviation gasoline. I. G. Farbenindustrie, which is closely controlled by the Nazi government, was able, by its pact with Standard Oil, to narrow Standard's rights to the process for the use of the process only in gasoline. It was, in fact, brought out in the hearings of the Senate Patent Committee that full technical information on butyl used in synthetic rubber was given by Standard Oil to I. G. Farbenindustrie and so to Hitler's government on March 15, 1938, four days after the invasion of Austria. Similar information was consistently refused to manufacturers in the United States and even to our government until it was taken from the files by the Anti-trust Division.[9] I. G. Farbenindustrie also placed a restriction on the use of a process to manufacture hydrogen and carbon monoxide, limiting its use to the manufacture of ammonia for agricultural fertilizers, and so preventing its use for the manufacture of nitric acid which could be used in the preparation of TNT. Through cartel arrangements organized around patents, Nazi Germany was thus able to impede the scientific and industrial development of synthetic rubber in this country, and to restrict our production of munitions.

Licenses restrict production in other respects. In its cartel agreement for carving up the world market with I. G. Farbenindustrie and Rohm and Haas of Darmstadt, Germany, the American firm of Rohm and Haas of Philadelphia was forbidden to manufacture dyestuffs, artifical rubber and pharmaceuticals. In its domestic patent agreement with DuPont, Rohm and Haas restricted the production of certain plastics utilized, among many other important uses, as glass substitutes in making bomber noses and other aircraft parts. DuPont was by this agreement permitted to manufacture cast sheeting at no more than one-half of the output of Rohm and Haas, and all others were kept out of the field. Moreover, prices were rigidly maintained at identical levels. Clearly this policy neither promoted science and the useful arts, which is the avowed purpose of the patent system, nor did it contribute to the adequate preparation of the United States for the great war of survival which the country was about

[9] U. S. Senate, 77th Congress, Second Session, Committee on Patents, *Hearings* on S. 2303 and S. 2491, Part 6 (May 20–22, 1942).

to face. As a result of this limitation, for example, DuPont failed to meet the military demand for cast sheets during 1941.[10]

II

Closely joined with the utilization of patents to limit production is their use to fix prices. By means of a patent cross-licensing agreement the Krupp Co. of Essen, Germany, and the General Electric Company were able to restrict the number of producers of tungsten carbide (trade name Carboloy) in this country, to eliminate those who attempted to compete independently, and to raise the price from $48 a pound to $453 a pound so that its use was thoroughly discouraged. Tungsten carbide is strategic in the war program because it is a metal alloy second only to diamonds in hardness, and therefore invaluable for the tips of cutting tools, and for wear resistant dies. While this restrictive agreement was in effect, tungsten carbide was serving as one of the keys to the Nazi armament program, and over twenty times as much of the material was being used in Germany as in the United States. An interesting sidelight in this instance was the fact that when a test of the patents was made in court, after the cartel had delayed such an examination of their merits for twelve years, they were declared invalid. But in the meantime, America's armament program, as well as its industry, had been weakened by the restrictive uses of the patents.[11] Efforts of the Anti-trust Division of the Department of Justice to set the Carboloy case for trial on charge of restraint of trade in the early months of 1942 were blocked by the company on the grounds that the trying of the case would embarrass the war

[10] For evidence of the nature and effect of this international cartel on plastics, see U. S. Senate, 77th Congress, Second Session, Committee on Patents, *Hearings* on S. 2303. Part 2 (April 20–25, 1942), p. 663–932.

[11] For the documentary evidence of the character and effects of this contract as presented by the Anti-Trust Division of the Department of Justice, see U. S. Senate, 77th Congress, Second Session, Committee on Patents, *Hearings* on S. 2303, Part 1 (April 13–17), p. 36–52. General Electric sought to counteract by inserting full-page paid advertisements in the leading newspapers of the country which told an inspirational story of its development of the metal without mentioning the Committee's evidence. The misrepresentations of this advertisement were exposed in further hearings before the Committee, *ibid.*, Part 4 (May 7, 1942), p. 1871–1906.

production program by taking officers of the company away from their war work.[12] At the same time that this stay was granted the General Electric Company was active in court seeking to restrain the development of fluorescent lighting by Hygrade Sylvania.[13]

The case of the magnesium patents illustrates in its varied phases the functioning of an international patent cartel and its consequences for science and technology. Magnesium, one of the most abundant natural resources in this country, was until recently controlled completely by a patent pool organized in 1932 in the form of the Magnesium Development Corporation jointly controlled by I. G. Farbenindustrie and Aluminum Corporation of America.[14] By a joint licensing agreement with the Dow Chemical Company the price of magnesium was consistently kept at a level of about one-third higher than aluminum. In addition the Aluminum Corporation of America agreed not to produce more than 4000 tons a year without the consent of I. G. Farbenindustrie, and Dow's production was limited by an agreement not to export metal to any European country other than to Germany, with the exception of a maximum of 150 tons a year to a licensee of I. G. Farbenindustrie in England, and that at a fixed price higher than I. G. Farben's price. In this way I. G. Farbenindustrie was able to use a patent pooling arrangement not only to limit production in this country but to retard the development of the magnesium industry in Europe outside of Germany. In the United States, moreover, the patent pool made it necessary for all fabricators to purchase their magnesium from Dow, so that any other potential contributors of raw magnesium were blocked.

The manner in which this cartel agreement built on patents retarded the war production program is highly significant. Magnesium is a crucial war material. It is the lightest metal which has physical properties adequate for structural purposes when alloyed with other metals, for it is one-third lighter than an equal

[12] For the correspondence showing the efforts of the company, the insistence of the Department of Justice that the trial be held, and the intervention of the War Department, see *ibid.*, Part 5 (May 13, 1942), p. 1987–1998.
[13] *Ibid.*, Part 5, p. 1999–2000.
[14] For the testimony and documentary evidence on the magnesium cartel, see *ibid.*, Part 2 (April 20–25, 1942), p. 934–1140.

volume of aluminum. Because of its light weight and because it is easy to work hot or cold, to machine and to weld electrically, it is invaluable for parts of aircraft engines and bodies. Magnesium is also ideal material for incendiary bombs because in certain forms it burns well and it is also useful in flares and star shells because of its intense white light. It is also valuable in portable tools, and in machine parts. The aircraft industry used about 80 percent of the magnesium alloys produced in the United States in 1939-40.

Yet in spite of the abundant supply of magnesium in the United States the patent pool which the Aluminum Corporation of America formed along with the Nazi-controlled I. G. Farbenindustrie, in order to protect its market for aluminum, was able to dwarf America's production of magnesium in relation to that of Germany. While German production increased from 12,080 metric tons in 1937 to 19,000 tons in 1940, the production in the United States amounted to only 2,059 tons in 1937 and 5,680 tons in 1940. In 1940, when France fell, Germany was producing over half of the world's production while the United States was producing only 14 percent, and was prohibited by the patent agreement from producing more. As a consequence there was a severe shortage of this strategic material for war purposes.

This patent cartel was the partner in a consent decree entered into with the Department of Justice on April 15, 1942. The decree provided for compulsory licensing of the strategic patents, and for exemption of licenses from royalties during the period of the emergency for the production patents and for all time for the fabrication patents.[15] This was admittedly a victory for the patent pool, which was under indictment for violation of the Anti-trust Act. By pressure upon the War and Navy Departments the sentiment had been created that anti-trust prosecutions should cease for the war period, because it has been alleged they diverted corporation officials, important in the war production program, from their major work. As a result the Department of Justice took what it could get. The decree does not provide as did an earlier consent decree with another company, that the "know how" and the industrial processes be exposed for general

[15] *Op. cit.*, Part 2, p. 582-89.

use; a valuable clause, for when patent rights are granted it does not mean that the "know how" is revealed also. The significance of this fact is shown before the Senate Patent Committee in the testimony by the Department of Justice agent who drew up the decree: [16]

> We had drawn up a decree which gave us the know-how, and the representatives of the Dow Company said that that was nothing other than servitude; that they would be made to give their know-how for the development of magnesium principally for the Government by being forced to do so and that was, in effect, industrial servitude. They became very excited.

It will be remembered that this incident occurred three months after Pearl Harbor. One of the companies responsible for the scarcity of a strategic material was still holding back, and was moreover strong enough to make a government agency back water in its demands for full revelation of the patent processes. The remarks of Senator Homer Bone, chairman of the Senate Patent Committee, subsequent to this testimony are highly pertinent:

> This is no pink tea that we are engaged in now; this is a life and death struggle. We have no business calling the boys to defend the country when we permit anybody in the country who is supplying vital necessities in this conflict to hold back. At least in part, the draft should touch them.[17]

And again:

> We are not dealing with 130,000,000 people in this problem; we are dealing with a little group of men and they present a dismal picture. I do not want to see a boy placed in the penitentiary for refusing to serve his country with 100 percent of his body, and see some other fellow, who has something of vital importance in the way of knowledge that will make that boy an efficient soldier holding back. There ought to be 100 percent cooperation.[18]

This there certainly has not been.

[16] *Ibid.*, p. 1121.
[17] *Op. cit.*, p. 1125.
[18] *Ibid.*, p. 1135.

It should be emphasized that the illustrations given here of patent practices that have impeded the progress of science by restrictive licenses, hindering development of industry in the interest of monopoly profits and control, and which have directly affected our preparation for the war by preventing the production of basic war materials, are not unique and unusual. They are in fact characteristic.

The layman, unversed in the strategy and tactics of big business, will have asked himself as he has read these accounts of discriminatory contracts arising from cartels: Why did American corporations let I. G. Farbenindustrie and Krupp do this to them? The sad fact is that they were willing partners in permitting the Germans to use the patent laws of this country to gain economic preeminence for their country. The anti-democratic philosophy and behavior of the Nazis did not deter the American corporations from negotiation of these contracts, nor did the interests of this country as a power in case of war enter as a factor in affecting decisions. It is not that the corporation executives were malevolent men. Big business policy dictated that their primary concern be with carving up the world markets, and with maintaining higher prices and low turnover, rather than with developing the products and extending their use in the United States. As long as American corporations could be assured that the Germans were not going to upset the cartel arrangements on markets and high prices, they were willing to agree to many restrictions. They were, as the evidence shows, willing to make any sort of an alliance, to avoid competition and maintain their domination of the market.[19]

[19] Since the attack on Pearl Harbor and the entry of the United States into the war, the patents taken out by nationals of the Axis or of countries occupied by the Axis, which had not already been assigned to American companies in anticipation of that development, have been taken over by the Alien Property Custodian. The policy of the Alien Property Custodian, Leo T. Crowley, as enunciated on December 18, 1942, is to license without delay to American industry every patent important to the war industry. Patents are not being sold or titles released, and licenses are non-exclusive and royalty free for the duration of the war and for six months thereafter. For a statement of the role of the Alien Property Custodian see the testimony of Leo T. Crowley before the Senate Patent Committee, *op. cit.*, Part 2, pp. 1181–1190.

In view of these disclosures, it is difficult to be sympathetic to Dr. Robert E. Wilson's unequivocal defense of the existing patent system in his address on January 8, 1943 before a joint meeting of several scientific societies in New York, upon his receipt of the Perkins Medal for outstanding industrial research processes. He raises the bogey of alarm that the patent system is to be emasculated and that there will be "a reversion to the Dark Ages of secret processes."[20] On the contrary, the current patent agitation is directed toward achieving more publicity for the now secret licensing arrangements that have served the purpose of circumventing the anti-trust laws. In none of the proposed patent legislation has there been the slightest suggestion that patents should be abandoned, and that the interests of the inventor and of the entrepreneur who promotes the patent should not be protected. The contention of the proposed legislation is to make illegal the restraint of trade involved when the holders of patents on an industrial project combine those patents in order to dominate the industry, to control price and supply and handicap the development of an industry. Where a patent owner has used his patent in violation of the Sherman Act in order to dominate an industry, the proposed law would make it impossible for him to collect royalties until the effect of that patent abuse had been dissipated. The right is asked to cancel any patent which has been used as an instrument to create a domestic and international cartel.[21]

III

From the beginning of the war program that segment of big business whose major concern was profit failed to put its shoulders full weight against the wheel. Donald C. Blaisdell wrote in his monograph on *Economic Power and Political Pressures* written for the Temporary National Economic Committee:

> In the 1940 national defense crisis, business displayed much the same attitude that it had shown 23 years earlier. Business would

---

[20] *New York Times* (January 9, 1943), p. 28.
[21] For the text of Senate bill 2303 see *op. cit.*, Part 1, p. 1. For the proposed draft of the bill drawn by Thurman Arnold see *ibid.*, Part 7, p. 3315.

help the government and the people, but the basis of payment therefor would have to be fixed before the wheels would begin to turn. Profits, taxes, loans and so forth, appeared to be more important to business than getting guns, tanks and airplane motors into production. . . . Steel, aircraft, motor and chemical companies created the impression in the summer of 1940 that the Nation's rearmament program could wait until the fixing of satisfactory financial terms and that time, far from being of the essence of success, was of secondary importance.

Bluntly speaking, the Government and the public are "over a barrel" when it comes to dealing with business in time of war or other crisis. Business refuses to work, except on terms which it dictates. It controls the natural resources, the liquid assets, the strategic position in the country's economic structure, and its technical equipment and knowledge of processes. The experience of the World War, now apparently being repeated, indicates that business will use this control only if it is "paid properly."[22]

The question of the rates of profits was settled in the interest of the business man by the government, which was desperate to get its war program under way. The statutory provisions of the Vinson-Trammell Act which had been passed in 1934 in order to limit profits on the construction of naval vessels and aircraft were suspended at the insistence of manufacturers who refused to go along unless this was done. The result was shown by the Truman Committee report which declared after an analysis of contracts that "a considerable number of firms doing business with the Government have begun to reap a harvest of excessive and unconscionable profits in the tremendously increased program of expenditure for national defense."[23]

Even high profits were not a sufficient lure for some monopolists to utilize the processes which science had made available.

[22] Donald C. Blaisdell, *Economic Power and Political Pressures*, Temporary National Economic Committee, Monograph No. 26 (Washington, U. S. Government Printing Office, 1941), p. 171 f.
[23] House of Representatives, Seventy-seventh Congress, Second Session, Committee on Naval Affairs, *Preliminary Report* pursuant to H. Res. 162, Investigation of the Naval Defense Program Parts 1 and 2 (January 20, 1942), p. 34-36. Complete statistical tables on profits are given in the Appendices. See also Office of Price Administration, Division of Research, *War Profits Studies*, No. 1-4, December, 1942, mimeographed.

There was, and still is, in some quarters, a hesitance to participate fully in war production lest expansion interfere with their domination of industry after the war. Thurman Arnold wrote in the Annual Report of the Anti-trust Division of the Department of Justice for the year 1940-41:

> Looking back over ten months of defense effort we can now see how much it has been hampered by the attitude of powerful business groups dominating basic industries who have feared to expand their production because expansion would endanger their future control of industry. These groups have been afraid to develop new production themselves. They have even been afraid to let others come into the field. They have concealed shortages by optimistic predictions of supplies and talked of production facilities which do not exist.
>
> Anti-trust investigations during the past year have shown that there is not an organized basic industry in the United States which has not been restricting production by some device or other in order to avoid what they call "the ruinous over-production after the war." [24]

It is, in large part, the fear of overproduction after the war, augmented by psychological factors of inertia, that has led industrialists to fail to respond fully to many technological innovations [25] that would be of great importance to the war effort. Secretary Harold L. Ickes writes in his Department of Interior report of 1941-42:

> Our proposals for the complete utilization of certain domestic minerals . . . did not meet with whole hearted welcome. In some instances, temporary expedients seemed to be preferred by some groups to imaginative, full-scale adoption of novel, though proven methods. We endeavored to work closely with the War Production Board in order that war industry might have the full benefit of the work of our scientists and technical bureaus. The inertia of the old

[24] Mimeographed release (January 3, 1942).

[25] For an analysis of comparable opposition to technological innovations prior to the war see: Bernhard J. Stern, "Resistance to the Adoption of Technological Innovations," in National Resources Committee, *Technological Trends and National Policy* (Washington, U. S. Government Printing Office, 1937), p. 39-66. See also my article, "The Frustration of Technology," SCIENCE & SOCIETY, II (1937), No. 1.

way, the weight of industrial tradition, the following of the established pattern, frequently induced heavy industries to postpone technical innovations.[26]

Among the processes that have been resisted in spite of the great needs of the war production program is the development of aluminum from domestic clays instead of only from the limited supply of bauxite which must be imported from South America. Yet scientific plans for such production got a minimum of attention from the War Production Board and the National Academy of Sciences.[27] The use of sponge iron to help meet the stupendous steel requirements of the war program has encountered the opposition of some representatives of the steel industry.[28] The Bureau of Mines has also been unsuccessful in getting its plans for the domestic production of manganese from low grade ores accepted. These plans would make the United States independent of other countries on this strategic metal, but they have not been accepted because of the opposition of the larger manganese and steel producers. Similarly, its plans for the expansion of copper, zinc and nickel production have been blocked.

Secretary Ickes in his testimony before the Senate Small Business Committee on January 13, 1943 emphasized that this situation arose because war business was being concentrated in the hands of the big companies.[29] He pointed out that in 1939, 170,000 small plants in the United States were turning out 70 percent of the nation's production and the 100 largest companies

[26] Harold L. Ickes, *Resources for War: A Report by the Secretary of the Interior to President Franklin D. Roosevelt* (Washington, U. S. Government Printing Office, 1942), p. iv.

[27] Testimony of Ralph Miller before the Kilgore Committee, U. S. Senate, Seventy-seventh Congress, Second Session, Committee on Military Affairs, *Subcommittee Hearings* on S. 2721, Vol. II (November 25), p. 359–80, 404–46.

[28] Testimony of H. A. Brassert before the House Merchant Marine Subcommittee (October 20, 1942).

[29] In the last half of 1940, 140 concerns had received 95 percent of the prime contracts or $6,700,000,000 out of the $7,000,000,000 expended. Previously, 68 companies had received about two-thirds of the $14,200,000,000 defense orders let by March 14. Later figures are not available. See House of Representatives, 77th Congress, First Session, *Hearings* of Select Committee Investigating National Defense Migration, pursuant to H. Res. 113, Part 16 (July 15–17, 1941), p. 6490.

did only 30 percent of the business. As a result of the monopolistic influence in the awarding of war contracts, the 100 large companies are now doing 70 percent of the business, and the small plants were being liquidated. When the Bureau of Mines offered proposals to the War Production Board for expanding raw materials production through small companies by the use of new processes, its plans were consistently rejected. The opinion of Mr. Ickes was that "it may be that if we freed technology from the restrictions of interlocking corporate control and the ideology of monopoly, we would reap a harvest of new, highly efficient and self-contained medium and small sized operations."[30] One of the biggest obstacles to the fuller use of smaller plants in war production is the shortage of steel, copper, aluminum and other basic materials that constitute the life blood of war effort.

A most serious defect of the war production program has been the failure to utilize the skills and machinery available in the plants of the small manufacturers. The army has piled up contracts in the big companies, even when they could not be handled for months, instead of giving them to little companies, literally begging for work, who could have done them at once. This has often been in spite of specific recommendations of regional ordnance offices. The explanation given by the army authorities is that it is easier to deal with a limited number of large concerns than with thousands of smaller ones which would require the protracted task of breaking down the contracts into parts. But this is too simple. As Arnold declared in his previously quoted annual report: "If we are to scatter these contracts there must be a vigorous curb on all concealed coercions and combinations which have created this problem."

Monopolies are still patterning their economic behavior after the pre-war idea of low production and high prices, and are resisting the competition of the small producers whose output would expand production to fit the needs of the war, lest it endanger their post-war control of the markets. Their influence has been so strong that the Smaller War Plants Corporation, established under the Smaller War Plants Act in the summer of 1942

[30] Testimony before Senate Small Business Committee (January 13, 1943).

after pressure by the House and Senate Small Business Committee, has been a conspicuous failure. After six months of work, only $2,000,000 of the Small War Plants Corporation's capital of $150,000,000 had been loaned to small business, and only 234 out of 2200 distressed companies who had provided a list of their facilities had received contracts. This was during a period of a drive for all-out production, while our soldiers and our allies desperately needed more guns, ships and planes to hasten victory.

IV

It is difficulties of this sort that led Senator Kilgore to introduce his Technology Mobilization Bill in the last Congress. This bill aims to secure the full and immediate utilization of the most effective scientific techniques to improve production facilities for the successful prosecution of the war, by the establishment of an independent Office of Technological Mobilization. The stated purposes of the bill give an excellent summary of the tasks that face America in its utilization of its scientific and technological resources. These are:

> To mobilize for maximum war effort the full powers of our technically trained manhood; and similarly to mobilize all technical facilities, equipment, processes, inventions and knowledge; and to accomplish the above objectives:
> (1) by breaking the bottlenecks that today choke up these technical forces and result in the diversion of vast amounts of material, time, and effort from war and essential civilian use to less essential and non-essential uses; by making fully available all patents and all applied technical knowledge for full war use;
> (2) by fully utilizing the facilities of small business, technological laboratories, inventions and inventors, and maximizing the output of war goods and essential civilian supplies;
> (3) by providing adequate supplies of substitutes for goods normally containing critical materials and by discovering and developing new sources of critical raw materials;
> (4) by stimulation of new discoveries and inventions, developing more efficient materials and products, and improving standards of production, and in general,
> (5) by promoting the use and development of those processes,

products and materials most efficient for the successful prosecution of the war to a speedy and secure victory.[31]

That such a centralized agency is imperative to coordinate and integrate and extend the scope and power of existing government agencies has been strikingly evident in recent hearings before the Senate and House committees, investigating the progress of the production program. The National Inventors Council and the Office of Scientific Research and Development have not conceived of their function in this broad sense, but act merely in an advisory capacity.[32] The failure to use scientists effectively is shown, for example, in the notable Baruch report on the production of synthetic rubber issued on September 10, 1942 which declared in one of its striking passages:

> The production of synthetic rubber represents an investment exceeding $600,000,000 and is one of the most complicated, technical projects ever undertaken in this country. Yet in none of the Government agencies has there been a clearly recognized group of independent experts to make the technical decisions. Reliance has been placed on one part-time technical adviser, aided by committees drawn from industry. This technical adviser has testified that on more than one occasion he requested the appointment of an adequate technical staff in vain. The committee has found many evidences of procedures bordering on the chaotic in which non-technical men have made decisions without consulting with subordinates nominally in the positions of responsibility.

The drastic consequences of this type of insufficient attention to scientific and technical men in the planning of the war program in the United States and of the dominance of the program by industrialists concerned with profits and the maintenance and extension of their economic power are now a part of history.[33]

---

[31] U. S. Senate, 77th Congress, Second Session, Committee on Military Affairs, Subcommittee, *Hearings* on S. 2721, October 13–27 (November 17–18, 1942), Vol. I, p. 1 f.

[32] *Op. cit., passim.* See also Harry Grundfest, "The Utilization of Scientists," SCIENCE & SOCIETY, VII (1943), no. 1.

[33] Our ally the Soviet Union had, of all nations, least difficulty in turning from a peace-time to war-time economy, because its Academy of Science served as an integral part of the government in the planning of scientific and technological expansion. The development of industrial growth was not per-

It is clear that technical mobilization is not enough. This mobilization must be part of a larger pattern of centralized war production. Such has been the objective of the Tolan-Pepper bills, which would establish an Office of War Mobilization to coordinate more effectively both military and economic strategy involved in materials, machines and manpower. An evaluation of the specific proposals of these bills lies outside of the scope of this paper. But the need for an all-over plan for the more effective scheduling of military and essential civilian requirements is glaringly evident from the developments of the last year. Anarchic production methods based on individual procurement practices geared to peace-time methods of purchasing; chaotic expansion while valuable machines lie idle; haphazard manpower allocation —all of these point up the need for more effective coordination of our war program.

The winning of the war is ahead of us. It is a task which will command our utmost resources. The people who are making the sacrifices on the battle front and at the home front, the common man and woman who are financing the war by the payment of taxes, have a right to demand that the stupendous advances in human knowledge and ingenuities be used efficiently and planfully to bring the war to a speedy and successful end. The task of mobilizing our scientific and technical resources in the interests of winning the war and in the interests of the post-war security has just begun. There is a saying current in certain win-the-war circles in Washington: "The difficult we do at once; the impossible takes a little longer." Centralized and scientific technical planning is one of such "impossibles."

---

mitted to be haphazard, disjointed and incomplete because of the interests of special economic groups. See testimony of Waldemar Kaempffert before the Subcommittee of the Committee on Military Affairs, *op. cit.*, p. 67–69; also J. D. Bernal, *The Social Function of Science* (New York, 1939); Maurice Dobb, "Economic Planning in the Soviet Union," SCIENCE & SOCIETY, VI (1942), no. 4.

From *Science and Society,* vol. VII, No. 2 (Spring, 1943), pp. 97–114.

The Challenge of Advancing Technology

Even before the announcement of the unlocking of atomic energy, it could be said that advances in technology during the years of the war had been far greater than during many preceding decades. The spectacular discovery of a method of unharnessing atomic energy for the uses of man has catapulted the world into an uncharted tomorrow. It has dwarfed the technological changes prior to it, which, however important, were for the most part mere modifications of previously known forms of power and processes and types of materials and products.

The effects of these prior changes upon the lives and communities of men, if properly utilized, would alone have marked the dawn of a new era. Supplementing the constructive use of the phenomenal development of atomic energy, they are capable of creating a new epoch of plenty in which cities will be distributed rationally to permit the full development of man's potentialities and the effective use of environmental resources. Conditions prevailing in the structure of our economy and psychological conservatism that impede the most fruitful application of these changes increase the challenge to an enlightened leadership to use the vast power of the new technology for the social good.[1]

[1] For a tabulation of technological changes during the war see U.S. Senate, Subcommittee on War Mobilization of the Committee on Military Affairs, 79th Cong., 1st sess., *Wartime Technological Developments* (Washington: Government Printing Office, 1945). For opposition to technological change see Bernhard J. Stern, "Resistances to the Adoption of Technological Innovations," in National Resources Committee, *Technological Trends and National Policy* (Washington: Government Printing Office, 1937), pp. 39–66; *idem*,

Atomic Energy

It has long been known by scientists that the nuclei of atoms are reservoirs of tremendous energy; that the power which resides within them, when released, would make the energy obtained from the combustion of gasoline by chemical action negligible in comparison. Now that the release of this energy has been achieved by the planned, cooperative pooling of the scientific and engineering knowledge and skills of many men and women, financed at a cost which only the funded resources of governments are able and willing to risk, the social responsibilities of the governments which have tapped its strength are stupendous. The conquest of the atom may well be but an initial step in a chain of events which will lead to a comparable conquest of man's social irrationalities which affect urban development as they do all other aspects of man's social life.

With the advent of peace, never before in the history of man has the world situation been more opportune for such developments. Aspirations for a creative, rational social life surge in the hearts of common men and have a better chance than ever before for fulfillment. This can become one world, not merely because its span can be traversed by the airplane in the time it once took to go from village to village, but also because governments with diverse social structures and traditions have laid the basis for fruitful, peaceful, economic and political collaboration. Everywhere human energies as well as physical energies have been released and democratic forces are gaining ascendancy throughout the world which will permit the greater participation of masses of the people in the achievements made possible by man's manipulation and control of his environment. The energy of the atom has made man vastly more powerful in a physical sense. It makes imperative a social order and a humane and rational approach to human resources that will be able to cope with its power.

It is mere conjecture at this time to discourse on the postwar

---

"The Frustration of Technology," *Science and Society*, Vol. 2 (Winter 1937), pp. 3–28; *idem*, "Restraints upon the Utilization of Inventions," *The Annals*, Vol. 200 (Nov. 1938), pp. 13–31. See also pp. 75–101 in this book.

uses of atomic energy. The basic data have not yet been released from which forecasts could be derived. The relative costs of producing atomic energy as compared with the costs of the same amount of energy derived from coal or water power will be a factor determining the speed with which it will be utilized. In view of the extraordinary power of atomic energy, per unit cost seems certain to be less. More important from the point of view of the future of cities will be man's ability to control the rate of release of energy from the atomic breakdown to permit its transmission and distribution as motive power. Until this becomes public knowledge, one cannot state the degree to which the use of atomic energy will accelerate the mounting trend toward large-scale production, or whether it will promote concentration of manufacturing units or lead to their dispersal. Also not yet accessible is information on the amount of uranium needed and available and its present ownership and control, and whether or not the knowledge of how to release energy from uranium 235 can soon be extended to the release of energy from the nuclei of the atoms of other metals.

The shape of cities to come depends on the answers to these questions. Even after they are answered, it rests upon whether the new discovery and other technological changes will be held by governments to improve the earning power, the creative opportunities, and the standards of living of all the people, or whether they will be given over to monopolists to exploit. These sociological considerations cannot for one moment be ignored, for they are crucial to the entire problem of the future patterning of urban centers.

PRIOR WARTIME CHANGES

The release of atomic energy would not have been possible without an infinite number of prior technological changes. The very organization of the atomic experiment is relevant to the problem of the influence of technological changes on urbanization. Federal hydroelectric projects enabled the Government to localize cities of as many as 75,000 workers in previously isolated areas in Tennessee and Washington. At these sites were installed productive facilities utilizing the most advanced industrial processes, materials, and products.

Recent changes along all these lines have been extraordinary. The need for rapid production of war materials necessitated, and government financing of research and application made possible, numerous innovations which otherwise would have required a much longer period for development. Increased experimentation led to great progress in manufacturing techniques. Critical shortages of conventional materials and great advances in techniques for producing or fabricating materials led to the development of new or improved materials. Designs of planes, ships, trucks, and other mechanized equipment have steadily improved; jet propulsion and the gas turbine have been effectively developed; instruments have been made vastly more precise; and there has been tremendous progress in the development of radar and other electronic devices.

Each and all of these advances and many others will influence the design of the future city as they have already affected the developments of cities during the war. They will influence the distribution and growth of populations, the intercommunication of communities, and the ideas, attitudes, and standards of living of countless millions. As a result of the interwebbing of the peoples, trade, and industry of the world, the planning of cities, to be fully effective, will have to be in the context not merely of state, regional, and national planning, but of international planning as well. At the same time, world planning, to be rational and fruitful, will be obliged to take into consideration not merely the plans of nations, regions, states, and cities, but the interests of neighborhoods, of families, and of the individual personality. Recent technological changes make it possible for centralization and decentralization to be not antithetical but complementary processes.

It is impossible within the scope of this article to review even a meager fraction of the wartime technological changes that are capable of transforming human living. A few illustrative developments in manufacturing processes and in materials will be discussed without the implication that they are the most important or far-reaching.

PLASTICS

Even before the war, the chemical industry had emerged as an important producer of substitute materials which were displacing or competing with metal products and other natural products of mines, quarries, forests, and agriculture. Its rapid expansion was given impetus during the war because plastics were needed for their own unique qualities and as substitutes for scarcer materials. Plastic substances recently developed possess various combinations of desirable properties such as colorability, translucency, flexibility, lightness, dielectric strength, resistance to physical stress of various kinds, and resistance to water, petroleum, heat, aging, and corrosive chemicals. New and revised formulas and fabricating processes have multiplied the uses of plastics. They are no longer novelties supplementing other materials, but have become an important feature of contemporary economy.

Plastics are significant not merely because they have introduced new and useful products; they affect the use of our labor force profoundly. For example, by the substitution of a cellulose-acetate plastic for aluminum in the cockpit ventilator of a fighter plane, production time was cut in half and less skilled labor was required. The use of plastic hand wheels for destroyers to replace aluminum wheels which operate valves reduced required work by more than 280 man-hours in the building of each ship, released machine tools and foundry space for other purposes, and resulted in the employment of women in their production. In general, considering the extraction as well as the manufacturing processes, chemical production of plastics reduces drastically the number of man-hours required per unit as compared to mechanical production of metal products.

The development of plastics, moreover, may influence the location of cities. Urban communities have traditionally been fixed by the availability of raw materials, and so settlements have concentrated in the neighborhood of coal, iron ore, and other metal supplies. Improved transportation facilities and electric power have only partially freed communities from this dependence. Materials required for some types of plastics are practically ubiquitous, and the communities that are engaged in their manufacture are not rigidly confined but may be located according to planned requirements.

SYNTHETIC RUBBER

After considerable fumbling and delay, due largely to the competition of conflicting industrial groups, the synthetic rubber program financed by the government has been able to make up for the shortage of natural crude rubber brought about by the Japanese conquest of the Malay Peninsula and the Dutch East Indies. The production of synthetic rubber, which totaled 12,000 tons in 1941 and 30,000 tons in 1942, had reached over 900,000 tons early in 1944. Because the most advanced large-scale manufacturing processes have been utilized, only between 18,000 and 19,000 workers of all classes were to be employed in the new industry when all facilities of the war production program had reached capacity operation.

It is difficult to forecast whether in the postwar period synthetic rubber will displace natural rubber or merely supplement it. Such imponderables as the future of colonial policy in Asia and the consequent effect upon wages and standards of living of rubber workers in the jungle are involved. The plant amortization policy of the government, so generous to industrialists, will narrow the present disparity in the cost of production of synthetic as compared to natural rubber. Under any circumstances, the development of the product has freed man from complete dependence upon natural rubber, and has multiplied the availability of crucial materials essential for expanding transportation and for many types of consumers' goods.

VARIOUS MATERIALS

Between 1938 and 1944 the annual production of magnesium increased from 4 million to 368 million pounds. Magnesium is 35 percent lighter than aluminum and is very strong when alloyed. It is therefore an effective material where lightness and strength are desirable. Great progress has been made in the improvement of processes of extracting, alloying, surface treating, casting, forming and drawing, and welding magnesium. These and later improvements in production may enable magnesium to compete with aluminum, steel, plastics and plywood. Whether or not it does so depends to a considerable degree on the ability of the competing industries—particularly its closest and most powerful competitor, the aluminum monopoly—to control government postwar policy in relation to the disposal of magnesium plants during the reconversion period. Other than answers to technical engineering questions will therefore play a role in determining the degree to which magnesium will affect the development of postwar cities.

Aluminum production capacity has also expanded greatly during the war through improvements in manufacturing techniques and the development of methods to permit the recovery of the metal from lower-grade ores. Some of these methods were known before the war but were not utilized because of the patent, price, and marketing policies of the aluminum monopoly. Whether or not new aluminum-producing plants will be abandoned in the postwar period in the interest of maintaining such monopoly control remains to be determined.

Plywood has emerged during the war as a versatile material to compete with metals, plastics, and solid wood, especially in housing construction. During the war, prefabricated plywood housing units, insulated against heat and cold, were transported overseas for use of the armed forces.

The increase in war requirements for the lighter alloyed steel trebled alloy-steel ingot production between 1939 and 1942, and alloy steels rose from 6 per cent of total steel tonnage in 1939 to 13 per cent in 1942. New discoveries and techniques have introduced new alloying materials and have helped to make available supplies of alloying elements for which the United States had been previously dependent on other countries. Improved metallurgical methods have vastly bettered the quality of steel in ways that permit an increase in its usefulness for manufacture and construction in the postwar period.

ADVANCES IN MANUFACTURING PROCESSES

During the war, established manufacturing techniques were improved and new methods introduced. Advances have been made primarily, but by no means exclusively, in metalworking processes: in the joining of metal by riveting, welding, and stitching; in heat-treating procedures which result in superior metal products and help to reduce the need for scarce alloying materials; in metal spinning, which is often more economical than stamping or other fabricating methods, since costly dies and presses are not required; in powder metallurgy, a technique for converting dust-fine metal particles into finished mechanical forms through pressure and heat without the melting, casting, forging, rolling, or hammering required in conventional metal production; in centrifugal and continuous casting; and in metal spraying. The actual and potential influence of these processes on metal manufacture and products, on the use of the labor force, and thus not only upon communities whose subsistence is derived from mining and metal manufacturing but upon working and living conditions of all communities, is prodigious.

Even more important are the changes that have occurred in industrial mass production methods. These methods, which were already well established in some American industries, have been improved and introduced in new industries. Designs have been standardized, line or belt production systems developed, prefabrication and subassembly increasingly employed, and many new special-purpose machines introduced. Work simplification methods have standardized processes, materials, and tools and equipment; rearranged work space and equipment; divided the production processes into small successive operations; and coordinated the work process to eliminate unnecessary movements and motions, as a continuous flow of materials is maintained through various stages of fabrication.

Manufacturing and extractive processes have become increasingly automatic through the use of power-driven special-purpose machine tools. The inspection process, which formerly required the use of human labor even where production was highly mechanized, has also become increasingly automatic through the use of electronic devices and pneumatic gauging devices.

This rationalization process has been extended not only into all the major fields of industrial production during the war but also into office procedures. Agriculture is likewise undergoing unprecedented revolutionary changes. Many labor-saving agricultural machines that were merely discussed theoretically before the war have been put into commercial use. Vast migration of agricultural labor has ensued and an increased proportion of the agricultural labor that remains has taken on the characteristics of industrial labor.

Bane or Blessing?

These developments were undoubtedly a potent factor in winning the war. In the postwar period, however, they evoke memories of the "ghost cities" of the depression and arouse fear of vast technological unemployment. As long as the war expenditures of the Federal Government paid for 44 percent of a total gross national production of 155 billion dollars, as it did in 1943 according to an estimate of the Department of Commerce, and provided for full employment, these technological changes offered no hazard to workers. As government war spending ceases, a peril is undoubtedly present that our cities will be blighted, not by bombs but by economic distress due to mass unemployment.

It is not merely a question of the unemployment occasioned by failure to provide an effective reconversion program from wartime to civilian production. It is the question of coping with a permanent problem of how to have full employment in the face of the technological proficiency of modern industrial society. Before defense and war production got under way, actual production had exceeded 1929 levels while about ten million persons remained unemployed. The hearings and monographs of the Temporary National Economic Committee brought the implications of these developments sharply to public attention. President Roosevelt was cognizant of the further effects of the wartime technological changes upon mass unemployment, and sought to make every effort through the National Resources Planning Board to cope with them. However, Congress ordered the dissolution of the Board and specifically denied the President the right to establish a similar agency by Executive order. As a result, the nation is not adequately prepared with long-range comprehensive plans or machinery to meet the situation brought on by the end of the war.

The task is too great for improvisation. If the technological progress made during the years of the war is to be preserved and extended, and its benefits spread throughout the population, social legislation will have to be enacted enabling the government to play as decisive a part in maintaining peacetime employment as it did in winning the war. If it does not, it is fantasy to discourse on the reconstruction and redesigning of our cities in terms of our new techniques.

The potentialities for better living which recent technological changes afford are so great that they are worth striving to realize. Such aspirations need not be confined to city development programs concerned with the elimination of slums. City congestion could have been conquered before the war if the technical knowledge of that period had been applied. Present technology permits a bridging of the chasm that has been wrought between the city and the country during the last few centuries. It makes it possible to bring to the countryside the benefits of urban life, and to transform urban communities so that they may have all the positive values of the countryside. Cities can now readily obtain the benefits of favorable location at or near focal points where access to materials, persons, institutions, specialized services, and products, and communication and transportation are easy and economical.

It should be emphasized that this is no longer a mere theoretical assertion. The Soviet Union's transposition of cities from the Ukraine to the Urals, its building of new cities in previous wastelands, and our own TVA and the building of new communities for war production show how cities can be located planfully.

With the development of prefabricated houses, transport and passenger planes and helicopters, quick-frozen, dehydrated, and other processed and packaged foods, improved gasoline, and new and improved types of power for industrial production, for transportation, for illumination, and for easing household burdens, cities can be freer to develop functionally in terms of the harmonious living of their populations. Advances in public health and in medicine have made possible precipitous declines in death and morbidity rates, so that healthy city populations can enjoy the leisure which shorter working hours make available to them. Illiteracy and ignorance, long anachronisms in industrial societies, can more easily be liquidated through advances in human psychology and in educational processes.

The tools are ready. Will we be thwarted in their use? Never before was an answer to a question so important for the future of civilization. If our economic system is unable to meet the challenge of modern technology to facilitate the building of the cities of the future, another must supersede it. The war has awakened many more people to the significance of this fact.

From *The Annals of The American Academy of Political and Social Science*, Volume 242 (November 1945), pp. 46–52.

Freedom of Research in American Science*

I

Participation of the Federal government in scientific research initiated by the founding fathers, encountered vigorous opposition from the beginning. There were many causes for this resistance. America was rich in natural and human resources, and industry, reckless and wasteful in the use of them, had little patience with the advice of scientists, although it made use of the mineral and other resources government scientists located. The view was sedulously propagated that public service was associated with corruption, political control and incompetence, illustrations of which were not hard to find. Able scientists were therefore reluctant to enter government service. The prevailing mood of the country was *laissez faire* saturated with anti-intellectualism. Great wealth was being made through the empirical methods of the self-made, poorly educated entrepreneurs whose anti-intellectualist attitudes persisted even after corporate production became dominant in American economy. The practical man was extolled, the research scientist disparaged.

The importance of this climate of opinion was evidenced not merely in the disdain of industrialists for government scientists, but in their failure to initiate and finance scientific research in their own plants. Capitalist industry was woefully backward and unimaginative in this respect. It was held to be uneconomical to support scientific research because its profit yield could not be anticipated. The first professionally trained chemist in

* Part III of this paper was read at the annual meeting of the Eastern Sociological Society held in New York City, April 3, 1954.

the American petroleum industry was employed less than 65 years ago.[1] Up to 1894, when the General Electric Research Laboratory was founded, there was not a single industrial laboratory in the country dedicated to fundamental research. The earliest organized research in the American chemical industry was by the Du Pont Company in 1902. The Corning Glass Works formed its research laboratory in 1908 after some earlier experimentation. Westinghouse did not have a special building devoted to chemical, physical and magnetic research until 1910. The Kodak Research Laboratories were not set up until 1912, the General Laboratories of the United States Rubber Company until 1913, and the laboratory of the Aluminum Corporation of America until 1918.[2] World War I stimulated considerable industrial research especially in the field of chemistry, and during the 1920's the research work particularly of the Bell Telephone Company, Du Pont and Westinghouse expanded.

American universities were responsible in part for the low status and meager use of research science and scientists. Throughout most of the nineteenth century, it was necessary for a student to go abroad, usually to Germany, to get scientific training, and few had the means to do so. Yale had, in 1860, instituted the degree of Doctor of Philosophy to "enable us to retain in this country many young men, and especially students of Science who now resort to German universities for advantages of study no greater than we are able to afford." Its scientific program, however, received little support. The turning point in scientific education in the United States was in 1876 when the Johns Hopkins University opened under the leadership of Daniel C. Gilman. Gilman not merely set high standards of university

---

[1] He was Dr. William Burton: employed by the Standard Oil Company. Robert E. Wilson, "The Petroleum Industry," *Industrial Science: Present and Future*. Arranged and edited by Allen T. Bonnell and Ruth C. Christman, Washington, 1952, p. 17.

[2] For a history of industrial research see Howard R. Bartlett, "The Development of Industrial Research in United States," National Resources Planning Board, *Research. A National Resource, II. Industrial Research*, Washington, 1941, p. 19 f., C. E. K. Mees and J. A. Leermakers, *The Organization of Industrial Scientific Research*, New York, 1950, p. 121 f., C. G. Siuts, "Seventy-Five Years of Research in General Electric," *Science*, vol. 118, 1953, p. 451 f.

science teaching and research initiative, but had social purpose, for his stated objective was that Johns Hopkins would make for "less misery among the poor, less ignorance in the schools, less bigotry in the Temple, less suffering in the hospital, less fraud in business, less folly in politics." Gilman's advocacy of the German university program of research by mature scholars served as a ferment for research training in universities throughout the country.

During the decades that followed the prestige of science mounted. The pioneers of university science teaching had encountered indifference, disparagement, and overt opposition from industrialists on the boards of trustees and from faculty members who conceived of science teaching as too utilitarian to be taught in a liberal arts university. The continuing controversy over the relative educational values of the sciences and the humanities had its values in that it obligated the science faculties in universities to direct their attention to the training of "scholars in science," to stress scientific theories, principles and methods of research rather than practical applications. While this tended to have the effect of divorcing the university from industry and agriculture, it directed university research to fundamental inquiries into the vast, unexplored areas of science. The basic discoveries in chemistry, physics and biology, which modern industry is now utilizing, were made by university scientists on sparse university budgets, with little financial support from the business men and industrialists of America.

The impact of the Federal government upon private university education was first felt when the Morrill Act of 1862, which provided for Federal grants to vocational education, gave such grants to the Yale Sheffield Scientific School, Cornell, and to the state universities. There was little consensus among university authorities as to the scope, value, functions and methods of science and technical teaching within their schools. It became clear, however, that the universities would have to emerge from being hothouses for the cultivation of the children of the leisure class, if they wished to serve the larger needs of the democratic community. In the major conflict that ensued between those who regarded university instruction and research in fundamental principles and underlying theories as the only adequate basis for successful and ever improving practice, and those who urged direct practical training of farmers and mechanics on farms and shops, the first emerged victorious. The vapid formalism that had gripped the universities was challenged and more scientific subjects were brought into the academic curricula. There was also eventually an effort to bring students into the context of real concrete working situations by the utilization of specialized laboratories on farms and some comparable educational procedures for industries. The universities concentrated, however, on making basic contributions to the fundamental sciences, and left the practical developmental work to the factories. In the process of the controversy, American universities matured slowly but they still depended largely upon the theoretical contributions of foreign scientists. Scientific departments were established with a somewhat larger share of the university budgets. Significant discoveries were made that had the potential to enlarge man's power over his environment, and to enhance man's resources substantially. By the time of the outbreak of World War II, theoretical knowledge was far ahead of its use.

In this informal environment of the university the scientist developed his ethic. His time and his tasks in research were not routinized, except as he alone would impose discipline upon himself to achieve his goals. He could follow through what he might consider an interesting scientific lead without being asked to justify appropriations. His work was unstandardized and not geared to a production program. He was responsible only to his fellow scientists, and his incentives were more in the joy of his work and prestige of achievement than in the monetary reward which might accrue from his efforts. He regarded his scientific scepticism to be the embodiment of intellectual honesty and disinterestedness, and any interference which could be interpreted as an invasion of these sentiments was deeply resented. Robert K. Merton has commented that

> Although it is customary to think of the scientist as a dispassionate, impersonal individual—and this is not inaccurate as far as his technical activity is concerned—it must be remembered that the

scientist, in company with all other professional workers, has a large emotional investment in his way of life, defined by the institutional norms which govern his activity. The social stability of science can be ensured only if adequate defenses are set up against changes imposed from outside the scientific fraternity itself.[3]

Valiant efforts are being made by scientists to maintain this independence in the face of strenuous pressures from government and industry. The process through which the present perilous situation has developed takes on deeper meaning when placed in historical and socio-economic perspectives.

II

The Federal government had established machinery for contact with scientists outside of the government long before World War II. The National Academy of Sciences had been chartered by Congress in 1863 and approved by President Abraham Lincoln as a completely independent self-perpetuating body "to investigate, examine, experiment, and report upon any subject of science or art desired by any department of Government." Prior to the outbreak of World War I, in 1916, President Woodrow Wilson requested the National Academy of Sciences to set up the National Research Council to assist the government in coordinating the scientific resources of the government. Two years later, after the war had ended, he asked that the Council be established on a permanent basis in view of the "new and important possibilities" in science and research in time of peace as well as war. The National Research Council, as an agent of the Academy, operates under its charter which stipulates that "the Academy shall receive no compensation whatever for any services to the Government of the United States."[4] The insistence

[3] Robert K. Merton, *Social Theory and Social Structure*, Glencoe, Ill., 1949, p. 298 f.
[4] Senate Committee on Military Affairs, Subcommittee on War Mobilization, *The Government's Wartime Research and Development 1940–44. Part I. Survey of Government Agencies*, Washington, 1945, p. 234 f. For the research situation prior to World War II see National Resources Committee, *Research. A National Resource. I. Relation of the Federal Government to Research*, Washington, 1938, and President's Scientific Research Board, *Science and Public Policy. I. A Program for the Nation*, Washington, 1947, p. 9 f.

of the National Academy of Sciences and the National Research Council to retain their complete independence from government control reflected the deep suspicion by scientists of government interference in scientific inquiry.

Congress had also established in 1915 the National Advisory Committee for Aeronautics to supervise and direct the scientific study of the problems of flight. The Committee constructed laboratories and wind tunnels, developed a research staff of professional and semi-professional members under Civil Service, and made a limited number of contracts with educational institutions for studies and reports. In June 1939, by order of President Franklin D. Roosevelt the NACA became a consulting and research agency for the Joint Army and Navy Aeronautical Board.

It was as chairman of this committee that Vannevar Bush, once a professor of electrical engineering, the former vice-president of the Massachusetts Institute of Technology, and president of Carnegie Institution of Washington, conceived the idea of the National Defense Research Committee. This Committee was established by an Executive Order of the President in June, 1940 to "conduct research for the creation and improvement of instrumentalities, methods and materials of warfare." The Committee was authorized to utilize the laboratories, equipment and services of the National Bureau of Standards and other government institutions, and to enter into contracts with individuals, educational or scientific institutions and industrial organizations for experimental investigations and reports. In June, 1941, the President added to the National Defense Research Committee, a Committee on Medical Research and designated the combined committees the Office of Scientific Research and Development.[5]

It was the Office of Scientific Research and Development that was responsible for mobilizing the scientists for participation in World War II. Motivated by their desire to help the government in its battle against fascism, scientists relaxed their antagonism against working for the government and bore, not without complaints or ungrudgingly, the bureaucratic restraints which impeded normal scientific practices of communication and pub-

[5] For the text of the Executive Orders establishing these committees see James Phinney Baxter 3rd, *Scientists Against Time,* Boston, 1946, p. 451 f.

lication. They adjusted themselves also to team work involving sharp division of labor, often without knowing what the end-product would be, or where their segment might fit into the design of the work.

The Office of Scientific Research and Development originally adapted itself to the prevailing attitude of the scientists. It hoped to decentralize research and to leave the scientist free to work in his own university environment. In December, 1941, Bush described the agency as one that conducted research through cost-basis contracts with academic institutions and industrial companies which in most cases permitted scientists to work in their own laboratories. Soon, however, the need became apparent for laboratories in which various specialists could pool their knowledge and skills by being in constant contact with other specialists. Laboratories of sizable proportions were developed at various universities throughout the country. The typical contract arrangement was that the university should furnish space, management and a portion of the scientific personnel, some of whom might continue their university teaching. Sometimes the management of a project as well as most of the personnel were recruited from other academic institutions, as in the case of the Radio Research Laboratory at Harvard and the Radiation Laboratory at the Massachusetts Institute of Technology. By 1945 large groups of scientists worked full time on some segment of a National Defense Research Committee contract, and had no other relation with the academic institutions which paid for their services. They were not receiving grants-in-aid for pure research for the advancement of science. As Baxter notes:

> They were hired to hit an assigned target in an organized effort to create new instrumentalities of war. The government money which paid them was not expended to advance pure science or to aid the institutions from which they came or at which they worked, but to speed the day of victory.[6]

The work of these scientists was of utmost importance in the winning of the war. A pattern was set, however, for the post-war

[6] Baxter, *ibid.*, p. 21 f.

period that has jeopardized the future of science and changed the lives of scientists pronouncedly.

The contracts of the Office of Scientific Research and Development with academic institutions involved large sums of money which greatly affected university finances and made some universities later dependent upon government support for survival. The total dollar value of government contracts to the largest contractors up to June 30, 1945 were: Massachusetts Institute of Technology, $116.94 million; California Institute of Technology, $83.45 million; Harvard University, $30.96 million; Columbia University, $28.52 million; University of California, $14.38 million; Johns Hopkins University, $10.57 million; University of Chicago, $6.74 million; and George Washington University, $6.56 million. Seventeen other universities and research institutes each had contracts which involved over a million dollars.[7]

From the beginning and even after the mechanics of liaison relationships had been established between the two groups, there were difficulties arising out of what the civilian scientists considered to be the bureaucracy and excessive secrecy of the armed forces. The rigid hierarchical structure of the military, the necessity of going through channels and the slowness of decision-making at various levels impeded scientific work and its full utilization. For example, Harvey H. Bundy, the Army representative in the Office of Scientific Research and Development, submitted a memorandum to the Secretary of War on February 18, 1942, which called attention to the fact that

> various modern inventions have been kept so secret and their development has been so rapid that important officers of the General Staff and especially those in the War Plants Division have not been and are not currently advised of their existence, functions and effect on strategy.[8]

The Joint Committee on New Weapons and Equipment, which held its first meeting on May 12, 1942, helped to facilitate the more effective use of science in the winning of the war, but the committee was never brought into contact with staff planners.

[7] Baxter, *ibid.*, Appendix C, p. 456.
[8] Baxter, *ibid.*, p. 29 f.

The reaction of scientists to this war experience is reflected in the results of a poll in 1947. Only 11 percent of all scientists (including those in government, industry and universities) preferred a government career in terms of satisfactions, while 31 percent preferred industry and 48 percent the university environment. The remaining 10 percent preferred consulting work or some other activity.[9]

The most herculean task undertaken by the Office of Scientific Research and Development was the scientific work leading to atomic fission on which about $1,500,000 was spent before the project of the development of the bomb, which cost over $2 billion, was undertaken by the Manhattan Engineering District of the War Department with the aid of scientists and engineers. Scientists adapted themselves readily to the security regulations involved in the scientific and development work in the production of the bomb, and the secret was kept. After the war, atomic secrecy and the spy mania associated with it have enmeshed scientists in a web of political demagoguery that has sullied their characters and reputations and done grave damage to their scientific work. When directly after World War II was over, the War Department proposed the May-Johnson bill to continue the military control of atomic energy, the scientists, backed by democratic forces in the country, defeated it. Scientists recognized that the continuance of military controls would destroy the basic source of the strength of science, the free interchange of information, "the right to knowledge and the free use thereof," that it would end freedom in research, and impose controls over teaching. Although scientists won the initial skirmish against the military, they are being defeated in the battle for scientific freedom through administrative decrees which intensify regulations involving compartmentalization of workers, classification of information and of documents and loyalty and security checks. In the meantime Congressional committees intent on exposing "subversives" have kept the country aroused by their charges which are featured by the press, radio and television. The cloud

[9] President's Scientific Research Board, *Administration for Research*, Washington, 1947, p. 142.

of the atomic bomb has come to envelop increasingly larger areas of government, education and industry.

The President's Scientific Research Board in 1947, after noting that "scientific progress depends upon the full and free interplay of ideas and exchange of knowledge," declared:

> Fortunately, there is recognition among leading military men of the importance of scientific freedom; and among the scientists for some degree of secrecy. Nevertheless the conflicting points of view are a constant source of friction. Security regulations hamper governmental recruitment of scientists in peacetime. Industrial and university laboratories hesitate to accept Government contracts which involve secrecy. . . . However important secrecy about military weapons may be, the fundamental discoveries of researchers must circulate freely to have full beneficent effect. . . . We need have no fear of the widest circulation of basic ideas. . . . Security regulations, therefore, should be applied only when strictly necessary and then limited to specific instruments, machines and processes. They should not attempt to cover basic principles or fundamental knowledge.[10]

This advice has been ignored and rejected and the regulations have become more exacting and burdensome, not only over scientists in government service but over scientists remotely connected with government contracts in universities and in industry.

III

There has been a tremendous expansion in research and development expenditures in the United States on a scale never previously contemplated. The statistical facts on such expenditures are startling and, taking into account the decreasing value of the dollar, show an increase since the beginning of World War II, greater than the over-all expansion of American economy.[11]

---

[10] The President's Scientific Research Board, *Administration for Research*, Washington, 1947, p. 35 f.

[11] These generalizations have been derived from the following sources: U. S. Department of Defense, *The Growth of Scientific Research and Development*, Washington, 1953. U. S. Department of Labor, Bureau of Labor Statistics and U. S. Department of Defense, *Scientific Research and Development in American Industry*, Washington, 1953. National Science Foundation, *Federal Funds for Science I. Federal Funds for Scientific Research and*

The tabulation which follows shows the relative roles of the Federal government, industries and universities in research and their interrelations in recent years. A discussion of the significance of these developments, which are having a dramatic impact upon the social, industrial and educational life of America, will follow.

The nation's total research and development expenditures, of government, industry and universities combined more than quadrupled from $900 million in 1941 to $3.75 billion in 1952:

1. The federal government's share in this expenditure increased during the war years from 41 percent in 1941 to 70 percent in 1945, declined to 51 percent in 1946 and increased again to 60 percent in 1952.

2. The federal government's research and development expenditures grew from $97 million in 1940 to $2.2 billion in 1952 or more than a twenty-fold increase in 12 years. The recent declines have been slight.

3. Not only have federal expenditures for research and development increased in absolute terms, but during this period the relative proportion of the total federal budget for these purposes has increased from roughly 1 percent of the total budget in 1940–43 to about 3 percent in 1952–54.

4. Military research and development made up approximately 90 percent of federal research expenditures in 1954, the Department of Defense accounting for 76 percent, the Atomic Energy Commission about 10 percent and the National Advisory Committee for Aeronautics about 4 percent, of the total. Only four other government agencies, the Department of Agriculture, the

---

Development at Non-profit Institutions, 1950–51 and 1951–52, Washington, 1953. National Science Foundation, *Second Annual Report for the Fiscal Year 1952*, Washington, 1953. DeWitt C. Dearborn, Rose W. Kneznek and Robert N. Anthony, *Spending for Industrial Research, 1951–52*, Boston, 1953; American Council on Education, *Higher Education and National Affairs*, Bulletin No. 193, November 12, 1952. L. A. DuBridge, "Science and Government," *Chemical and Engineering News*, Vol. 3, April 6, 1953, p. 1384 f, President's Commission on the Health Needs of the Nation, *Building America's Health: Financing a Health Program for America*, Vol. 4, Washington, 1952. John E. Deitrick and Robert C. Berson, *Medical Schools in the United States in Mid-Century*, New York, 1953; Irving Ladimer, "Trends in Support and Expenditures for Medical Research, 1941–52," *Public Health Reports*, Vol. 69, 1954, p. 111 f.

Department of Health, Education and Welfare, the Department of Interior, and the Department of Commerce had expenditures of more than 1 percent of the total research budget, and the last three of these shared in the decline of research expenditures in 1954.

5. Non-military research expenditures increased from 1940 to 1952 by a little over four times, but military research and development, including the activities of the Atomic Energy Commission, had grown by 40 times over the same period.

6. Almost 94 percent of the federal research and development funds go for applied research and development and only 6 percent for fundamental or basic research.

7. The federal government paid for nearly one-half of the 1951 research and development costs in industry. The government's share of the research expenditures ranged from 85 percent in aircraft manufacturing to a low of 3 percent in petroleum refining.

8. Industry increased its own research and development expenditures from $510 million in 1941 to $1.43 billion in 1952. While industry spent out of its own funds only 38 percent of the total nation's outlay in 1952, Federal financing of research and development in industry raised its share of research performed in that year to 68 percent.

9. The total cost of research performed by industry, including the $1.14 billion paid for by the government, was $2.5 billion in 1952. The electrical machinery, aircraft and chemical industries, which were the leading employers of research personnel, also had the greatest dollar volume of research costs, altogether more than $1 billion.

10. Approximately one-half of the 96,000 research scientists and engineers employed by nearly 2,000 industrial companies in January 1952 were working on projects financed by the federal government. Almost all of these were sponsored by the Department of Defense or the Atomic Energy Commission. The number employed on government contracts was more than 50 percent higher in January 1952 than in January 1951.

11. The concentration of industrial research scientists and engineers in large organizations is marked. Approximately 40 percent of the 96,000 employed in January 1952 worked for the 44

largest companies (2 percent of the total surveyed) each of which had at least 25,000 employees. Two-thirds of the research scientists and engineers were employed by 222 companies (11 percent of the total) with more than 5,000 employees. In contrast, only 4 percent worked for 642 companies (33 percent of the total) with fewer than 100 employees. The concentration of research scientists and engineers in large companies was greatest in the aircraft, motor vehicle and petroleum refining industries, in each of which about 90 percent are working for companies with 5,000 or more employees. The 34 companies with the largest professional research staff (500 or more) employed approximately 48 percent of all research scientists and engineers.

12. Industrial firms spent for company-financed research a median percentage of sales amounting to 1.1 percent in 1951 and 1.3 percent in 1952. The highest median figure of 4.9 percent in 1951 was reported by firms in the drug industry, as contrasted with 0.3 percent reported by the food industry.

13. Only about 2 percent of funds committed by industry to research and development were used to support scientific and development programs at non-profit institutions in 1951.

14. Universities and colleges increased their expenditures for research and development from $20 million in 1941 to $80 million in 1952. While their research and development expenditures were only 2 percent of the nation's total in 1941 and in 1952, federal and industrial financing brought their share of the cost of research performed up from 5 percent in 1941 to 11 percent in 1952.

15. The federal government spent in 1951, $338 million dollars for research at non-profit institutions or about 15 percent of the total spent by government for research and development in that year.

16. Eighty-eight percent of the federal research funds spent in 1951 at non-profit institutions ($229 million) were administered by the Department of Defense and the Atomic Energy Commission.

17. Approximately one-half of the federal research funds granted to non-profit institutions in 1951 was spent on 24 research centers all but one of which were managed as separate

agencies by the universities and other non-profit institutions for the Department of Defense and the Atomic Energy Commission. They thus contributed little to the teaching and training objectives of educational institutions.

18. Only about 1 out of every 5 dollars of federal research funds granted to non-profit institutions in 1951 was spent for basic research that might lead to the long range progress of science; the other 4 dollars were utilized for applied research and development and for additions to the research and development plants of non-profit institutions.

19. Seventy-two percent of federal research funds to non-profit institutions in 1951 was spent on the physical sciences, 19 percent on the life sciences, 3 percent on the social sciences, and 6 percent for additions to the research and development plants.

20. In numerous instances 25 percent or more of an educational institution's annual income in 1952 was derived from research subsidies granted by the federal government, industry and foundations. The proportion in one institution reached as high as 69 percent.

21. Of the nation's $173 million expenditures for medical research in 1952, 42 percent was spent by the federal government, 35 percent by industry, 14 percent by philanthropy and 9 percent by hospitals and medical schools. Of the federal expenditures, almost 60 percent was expended by the Public Health Service for research conducted by its personnel and for grants to non-federal research institutions and investigators. The combined research expenditures of the federal government, industry and philanthropy in 1952, were less than one-fifth of the research expenditures of the Department of Defense alone in that year, and about 5 percent of the nation's total research expenditures.

22. The gifts and grants for research to the 59 four-year medical schools in the United States in 1950 were $14.5 million from the federal government compared to $12 million from industry and philanthropy. The funds granted for medical research by all groups had increased nine times in a decade, yet they were only 22 percent of the $116.7 million spent by the Atomic Energy Commission alone for research and development in that year.

To recapitulate the outstanding conclusions of the foregoing tabulation: there has been a prodigious increase, in recent years, in the nation's expenditures for scientific research and development; the federal government pays the largest share of these expenditures predominantly for applied research with military objectives to the neglect of basic scientific research; industrial research, about half of which is paid for by the federal government, is highly concentrated in large corporations, which expend only a very small proportion of their research and development funds outside of their plants; university and college expenditures for research and development make up a minor share of the nation's total expenditures for this purpose, with the federal government's support of military research in these institutions playing an increasing role in stressing research in applied, as contrasted with the fundamental sciences, and finally expenditures for medical research, which has made important contributions to the health and longevity of the people of the United States, are insignificant compared to those spent for the military program. The scientific and socio-economic life of America is being profoundly affected by the impact of these developments.

The dominant note that runs through these findings on federal research expenditures and performance is the fact that the program is preponderantly military. This is consistent with the characteristic feature of the federal budget as a whole. Those who stress the need for greater attention in the budget to peaceful objectives are constantly reminded that government economies are being made in all areas because of an "emergency." This often leads to self-imposed stringent economies by the heads of government agencies as is shown by the following colloquy between a member of the Appropriations Committee of the House of Representatives, Congressman George B. Schwabe of Oklahoma and Dr. Leonard A. Scheele, Surgeon General of the United States Public Health Service, at the budget hearing of this agency on January 28, 1952:

> MR. SCHWABE: Dr. Scheele, I notice that there is a considerable decline in the requested appropriations under the item of venereal

diseases, namely $1,429,360 in 1953 as compared with actual appropriations for 1952. Is that due to the fact that it is considered that less assistance may be necessary to States and communities in handling these diseases?

DR. SCHEELE: No sir; that is due to the necessity for our cutting the cloth of our whole Public Health Service operation into the cloth of total money which we are permitted to ask for, and represents a sum of money below that which we originally asked for for venereal disease work. . . .

MR. SCHWABE: As a matter of fact, in view of the general statement that you have made before the committee this morning, this reduction would seem to be bordering on a situation that might be dangerous to the further spread of venereal diseases throughout the country, is that right?

DR. SCHEELE: Yes sir; that is exactly correct. . . . We appreciate the problem that the committee has in finding enough money to maintain all good activities in this period when our total national expenditures are especially high because of the military program.[12]

With the mood reflected in these hearings prevailing in Washington, department and bureau heads are reluctant to ask for appropriations for fundamental scientific research. When they do so, their requests are likely to be cut out by the Appropriations Committee. An illustration of this process is in the treatment of the budget of the National Science Foundation.

The National Science Foundation was established after several years of persistent efforts on the part of scientists to have the federal government encourage more basic long-range research as opposed to immediate, applied research. To justify its need to receive adequate appropriations, its director, Alan T. Waterman argued:

> The general goal of the Foundation is to make certain that the scope and quality of basic research in the United States meet the requirements of national security, national welfare and continuing progress in science and technology. In particular, the Foundation lays great stress upon the fact that adequate general support of basic research and training in the sciences is indispensable to the

[12] House of Representatives, Eighty-second Congress, Second Session, Subcommittee of the Committee on Appropriations, *Hearings on Federal Security Agency, Part 2, Public Health Service*, Washington, 1952, p. 391, 393 f.

emergency effort. It constitutes a *defense in depth* which is essential to establishment and maintenance of technological supremacy.[13]

In spite of this plea, which ties up basic research to the military program, the Congressional grants for support of the work of the Foundation to develop basic research have been meager. Its budget request in 1952 for $14 million was reduced to $3.5 million; in 1953 its request for $15 million was cut to $4.75 million. In 1954 it was granted $8 million and its $15 million ceiling upon annual appropriations was removed. With this small budget the Foundation awards fellowships and grants, analyzes the present status of different fields of science, and encourages interdisciplinary symposia on selected subjects to pool existing knowledge and to discover which problems will yield most effectively to research.

The federal government, indifferent to fundamental research, has rather directed its attention to applied research in the military field and is expending a vast amount to subsidize research in industry, $1.14 billion in 1952. Such large research subsidies are a new development in the American economy.

Industrialists have been consistently candid about their concepts of the function of industrial research. They have been primarily interested in research that would yield relatively immediate profits and would contribute to the maintenance of their competitive position. Lincoln T. Work, speaking on the philosophy of industrial research, has stated that "the research division of a company is called upon *to protect, maintain, and improve the company's position in business*" (his italics).[14] This is shown strikingly by the study of the research expenditures of 191 industrial firms studied by the Division of Research of the Harvard Business School. Ninety-two percent of company research funds (i.e. excluding government funds) was spent for specific products and processes, leaving only 8 percent for research of a general or basic nature. Small firms typically spent none of their research dollars for this latter purpose. In the largest firms (50,000 or more employees), research undertaken to improve

[13] National Science Foundation, *Second Annual Report for the Fiscal Year 1952*, Washington, 1952, 10 f.
[14] Lincoln T. Work, "The Philosophy and Economics of an Industrial Research Program," *Research Operations in Industry*, Edited by David B. Hertz and Albert H. Rubenstein, New York, 1953, p. 4.

existing products or processes absorbed more than twice as many dollars as did research on new products or processes.[15] That such research is profitable is shown by a statement in 1949 of Robert E. Wilson, chairman of the board of Standard Oil Company of Indiana:

> The present day petroleum industry is largely a demonstration of what research has done to improve products, increase yields, cut costs, and increase the scale of operations. If we tried to evaluate what research has done for our industry, the figure would run into the billions of dollars. ... We have also seen what happens to companies that do not carry on research. They gradually drop out of the picture because they can not keep up with their competitors' better products and lower prices. ...[16]

The concentration of research in the large companies (see p. 145) gives them great competitive advantage, and accelerates the concentration of economic power. Generally, the mass of specialized information on products and processes assembled in the course of industrial research does not become accessible to anyone except to the owners of the research laboratory. A few of the large concerns, which carry on studies in the fundamental sciences as part of their research activity publish some of the results of their experiments, but this is not typical of industrial research. The findings published by the concerns having industrial laboratories are meager compared to those published by academic and governmental laboratories. Even in cases where permission is granted to individual scientists working in industrial laboratories to publish their experimental findings care is taken that no advantage is lost. The corporation usually reserves the right to scrutinize such technical papers, modify their contents, and approve their publication only when it finds that this would not jeopardize the firm's competitive position. It is because of the industrialists' desire to have exclusive rights to the findings of all scientific research which they finance, and their eagerness

---

[15] DeWitt C. Dearborn, Rose W. Kneznek and Robert N. Anthony, *Spending for Industrial Research*, Boston, 1953, p. 6.
[16] Robert E. Wilson, "The Attitude of Management Toward Research," *Chemical and Engineering News*, Vol. 27, 1949, 274 f; see also idem, "The Petroleum Industry," *Industrial Science, Present and Future*. Arranged and edited by Allen T. Bonnell and Ruth C. Christman, Washington, 1952, p. 13 f.

for secrecy to preserve these rights, that such a very small part of the funds allocated for industrial research are spent outside the plants of the company. Such scientific secrecy is very wasteful, for each industrial concern must make its own independent investigations, duplicating equipment, instruments and personnel. Moreover, scientific knowledge cannot flourish in an atmosphere of secrecy, and industrial secrecy is as pernicious for science as is military secrecy. It impedes the free flow of ideas and discoveries from one scientist to another, and thus slows the rate of scientific progress. The emphasis on secrecy is multiplied on government contracts to industry by the fact that industry has not only screened, for loyalty and security, persons employed on classified military work, but, in some instances, has sought to have these clearance procedures extended to civilian workers.

Industry has not welcomed government intervention in industrial research. It has accepted government contracts only when they have yielded large profits and when the government has borne the risks and has given generous amortization allowances.[17] The hostile attitude of industry toward government support even during World War II is shown by the remarks of a speaker before the American Chemical Society in 1949 who declared that industrial research departments "were thrown out of stride by the war; they spent many months in an unnatural regimented existence; they were subsidized by a paternalistic government."[18] Industry has particularly resented the complications involved in securing and protecting patents on products developed with the aid of federal funds, and has been bringing pressure on the Atomic Energy Commission and Congress to secure a relaxation of patent policy.[19]

The allocation of a disproportionate share of federal funds for applied research as compared to fundamental research in uni-

[17] Bernhard J. Stern, "Science and War Production," *Science and Society*, Vol. VII, Spring, 1943, p. 97 f.

[18] Quoted by Lincoln T. Work, "The Philosophy and Economics of an Industrial Research Program," *Research Operations in Industry*, Edited by David B. Hertz and Albert H. Rubenstein. New York, 1953, p. 5.

[19] Congress of the United States, Eighty-third Congress, First Session, Joint Committee on Atomic Energy, *Summary of the Hearing on Atomic Power Development and Private Enterprise*, Washington, 1953.

versities (see p. 144) raises, on a higher level, the same question that the universities had to face after the passage of the Morrill Act. The problem is further intensified by the use of university laboratories by industrial corporations to develop and to test their products. There is some question as to whether it is a proper function of colleges and universities to perform such utilitarian and short-range practical tasks. If the major function of an educational institution is to enlarge the horizons of knowledge, to push back the boundaries of ignorance, to develop new theoretical approaches and to make new discoveries that will give man greater power over his environment, then to occupy their science faculties with practical tasks is wasteful of scientific manpower. If university scientists concentrate on applied research, the mainsprings of scientific progress will dry up. For knowledge of scientific theory facilitates practical achievement and enables applied scientists and engineers to reach their goals with a minimum of wasteful activities. Empiricism is always blundering and reaches dead ends because it is not rooted in theory. It is the university scientists' attention to elaboration of theory which current emphasis on applied research imperils.

Two men, long connected with industrial research, C. E. Kenneth Mees and John A. Leermakers, of the research laboratories of the Eastman Kodak Company, have this to say about university research:

> The pre-eminence of the universities in scientific work will continue as long as research in university departments continues free from any external direction or organization. Compared with other agencies for the prosecution of scientific research—research institutes, technological institutes, industrial laboratories—universities are at a disadvantage. The investigators are often burdened with administration and with teaching; they are, on the whole, poorly paid; and it is difficult for them to get funds for equipment. . . . But they are *free*—they can explore unpromising paths and make experiments that any administrator would regard as useless, and sometimes those experiments succeed and those paths lead to new fields of knowledge.[20]

[20] C. E. K. Mees and J. A. Leermakers, *The Organization of Industrial Scientific Research*, New York, 1950, p. 14 f.

The dangers of the loss of this freedom by the acceptance of industrial and government contracts stressing applied research are seen by university administrators. The Association of American Universities at its annual conference in October, 1947, sought to develop standards for the acceptance of research subsidies and graduate fellowships from government and industry. Among the general principles on which they agreed are that the proposed research must be fundamental in nature; that the donor may indicate in broad, but not specific terms, the problems to be studied; that institutions must retain complete control over research activities of the fellows and the publication of the results of the research; "that no restrictions be placed on the right of publication by the institution, except for reasons of national security" (who is to determine when national security is threatened is not specified) and that the name of the institution must not be used in any advertising. Some of the graduate deans indicated that they were alert to the dangers of "the insidious control of research activities of the institutions by outside funds," to the fact that "certain industrial firms are willing to sponsor research activities under the guise of graduate fellowships when the real objective is to get a job done for the particular sponsor without paying the usual fees and overhead." Nevertheless, the proposal of the Committee on Graduate Work of the Association, which pointed out "the danger [in the acceptance of contractual research and subsidized fellowships] of accelerating the tendency, persistent and of long standing in some institutions, to orient the programs of graduate students in the direction of too specialized or narrowly vocational interests," and recorded the conviction that this "should be vigorously and openly resisted," was rejected by the deans lest it be "construed by benevolent industrial organizations . . . as antagonistic."[21]

Three years later the same group heard Albert W. Noyes, Professor of Chemical Engineering at the University of Rochester, complain that

> Cases could be cited of research sponsored by research agencies where graduate students and others must be cleared by the Federal

[21] Association of American Universities, *Proceedings*, Forty-Eighth Annual Conference, Iowa City, October 23–25, 1947, p. 112 f.

Bureau of Investigation, where they are required to work behind closed doors through which no one can enter who is not cleared and where they are unable to discuss the details of their research with fellow graduate students and with faculty members who are not admitted to the sanctum sanctorum. The plea is often made that the country needs individuals trained along these lines, and that in a period of emergency almost any sacrifice of academic tradition should be made for the good of the country. It seems to me that this policy is very short-sighted.[22]

He also warned that research grants by industries to universities to pursue specific problems which might have financial value can involve dangerous encroachment on university tradition. He pointed out that in order to receive a grant, a professor "must be willing not only to sign away his patent rights but also to guide his research along lines which may be of benefit to the company, rather than of value to science." Moreover, he indicated that, when as a result of such sponsorship, graduate students are not allowed to discuss their research with fellow students and faculty members, an important aspect of graduate training is curtailed.

The trend of military infringement on university autonomy in the selection of and authority over its faculty and the impact of industry on university policy and procedures, has mounted during the last few years. The resulting hazards led the Committee on Institutional Policy of the American Council on Education to issue a statement of policy in February 1953 which declared:

> Classified military research normally has no place in a college or university and can only be justified by the needs arising out of a national emergency. This type of research, imposing as it does restrictions of secrecy and diversion of manpower to short-term, "hardware" objectives, can be potentially damaging to the work of our colleges and universities. . . . Imposition of restrictions on publication of research results, either for secrecy or patent reasons, is incompatible with the basic concept of an educational institution

[22] Albert W. Noyes, "Is Sponsored Research a Danger to the Academic Tradition?" Association of Graduate Schools in the Association of American Universities, *Proceedings*, Second Annual Conference, Rochester, October 26–28, 1950, p. 40 f.

as a source and distributor of knowledge. Research contracts involving such restrictions, especially long-term or permanent restrictions, should be undertaken only for exceptional or emergency reasons; otherwise, no arrangement should be permitted which could inhibit free and effective work by the institution in any scholarly field. Normally no project should be accepted unless it is open to qualified students.[23]

This statement expresses the current judgment of those university administrators who are alertly conscious of the destructive effect of military and industrial secrecy upon the creative atmosphere which has characterized university research. Its weakness lies in its reservations for it leaves to university administrators, who are eager to share in the available research money, the decision on whether an "emergency" exists, and whether the situation is "normal." Too often expediency rather than principle determines such a decision.

Scientists themselves have not been inactive in the face of the threat to science and to their rights as free citizens. They have been impeded in their expression of resentments, by the fear that to speak out would imperil their opportunities for employment, even in non-sensitive positions, because of the rigors of security clearance and the use, by investigatory agencies, of the concept of guilt by association. Scientists have generally been indifferent to the historical and social implications of their work. Yet some three thousand originally joined the Federation of American Scientists whose function it is to treat with the social problems raised by recent scientific developments. The fact that this membership subsequently dropped to about 1000 may be ascribed to the fear of the scientists to be associated with anything controversial. In spite of this dread, which pervades the life, thoughts and associations of American scientists, many of them have nonetheless directly and indirectly protested against the restraints put upon scientists and science, although not as emphatically and as often as some would wish them to.

A few illustrations will show the nature of their manifestations

[23] American Council on Education, *Preliminary Report of the Committee on Educational Research Policy.* Approved by the Committee, February 14, 1953.

of sensitivity to the dangers that confront them. The American Association for the Advancement of Science, made up of 44,000 members, appointed a Special Committee on Civil Liberties of Scientists whose report in 1949 was endorsed by a 4 to 1 majority of the 130 members of the Council of the Association. This report protested against undue secrecy in science and urged that the areas of secrecy, and thus the number of scientists concerned with confidential data in science, be reduced to a minimum. The Committee also declared "until the loyalty order deals with the way employees act rather than with the way they supposedly think, we shall inhibit the freedom and encourage the insecurity of our public servants."[24]

In 1949 a bill was passed by Congress requiring full F.B.I. and Atomic Energy Commission clearance of all A.E.C. fellows, even though the executive committee of the American Institute of Physics had protested that this "would be an unnecessary extension to the field of education of measures appropriate only in secret work." The Council of the National Academy of Sciences, whose National Research Council administered the Atomic Energy Commission's fellowship program, then declared that "the requirement of F.B.I. investigation and Atomic Energy Commission clearance is ill advised for those fellows who neither work on secret material, nor are directly preparing for Atomic Energy Commission projects. . . . We have grave doubts whether the continuance of the Atomic Energy Commission Fellowship Program thus restricted is in the national interests."[25] The fellowship program was therefore subsequently withdrawn.

The Scientists' Committee on Loyalty Problems of the Federation of American Scientists gave publicity in 1949 and 1950 to the governmental clearance procedures and articulated the protests of the scientists to the injustices done under them. It declared that

> extension of secrecy into the field of nuclear physics would be unwise in the long run. Any security gained by general secrecy of our *fundamental* data would be rapidly overweighed by the diminished vigor of our own research. These remarks will be accepted as tru-

[24] "Civil Liberties of Scientists," *Science*, Vol. 110, 1949, p. 177 f.
[25] *Science*, Vol. 111, 1950, p. 223.

isms by most members of the scientific community; but the point is worth making in view of the widespread tendency among the laity to regard "science" and "secrecy" as synonymous . . . any extension of personnel security measures beyond the minimum and into the fields of general science threatens the national security rather than strengthens it.[26]

This committee was succeeded by the Scientists' Committee on Loyalty and Security, which, in its statement in 1953, expressed its belief that "the national security can be maintained only by a proper balance of the need for security by secrecy, where it is necessary, against the need for long-range security by continuing scientific achievement." The Committee concerns itself "with security programs as they affect individual scientists, leaving to other groups the study of such programs with respect to civil liberties and democratic processes."[27]

The American Association of Scientific Workers has likewise sought to bring to the attention of other scientists the dangers confronting American science because of the workings of the security program. In speaking of the decline of scientific freedom it contended in 1952:

Restrictions on scientific intercourse, both domestic and international, further infringe on the freedom of the scientist and limit the advancement of science itself. The frank, corrective interchange of ideas, which uncovers the mistakes and misconceptions of in-

[26] The Scientists' Committee on Loyalty Problems, "The First Year of the SCLP," *Science*, Vol. 111, 1950, p. 220 f; idem, "Loyalty and Security Problems of Scientists: A Summary of Current Clearance Procedures," *Science*, Vol. 109, 1949, p. 621 f.

[27] "The New Government Employee Security Program," *Science*, Vol. 117, June 5, 1953, p. 3. In November and December 1953, this committee released material on the investigations of the scientists and engineers of the Army's Signal Corps Engineering Laboratories at Fort Monmouth, New Jersey by the Army and the Senate Permanent Subcommittee on Investigations under the chairmanship of Senator Joseph R. McCarthy. It revealed the unproven nature of the sensational charges and declared on November 14, 1953 that "this vital defense work has been seriously disrupted by the suspension of a number of key scientists and by the atmosphere of suspicion and distrust which exists throughout the laboratories." The Council of the Federation of American Scientists also issued a statement on these developments. See also Walter Millis, "The Scandal at Fort Monmouth," *New York Herald Tribune*, December 8, 1953; and articles by Peter Kihss, *New York Times*, January 11–13, 1954.

dividual or group thinking, is seriously hampered. The large amount of secret research acts as a deterrent to open and independent work in some fields, because workers fear duplication of effort and even the imposition of restrictions if they stray into sensitive areas.

The conditions for the advancement of science, which permit no compromise, they assert to be

> 1. Scientific work must be in the public domain, freely published, taught and criticized. 2. Scientists must not be hedged about with restrictions on personal freedom. 3. Science must be supported as a public responsibility for the public welfare, whether immediate or ultimate, and not for primarily military ends.[28]

Another organization of scientists that has responded to the urgent challenge of current government policy is the Society for Social Responsibility in Science. This society was founded in 1949 by a group of scientists, mostly physicists, who objected to doing scientific work on military projects. Among its purposes is to find suitable employment for those unwilling to work on military projects. At a meeting at Haverford College in 1953 it issued a statement contending that the spirit of free inquiry is essential to scientific research and asking scientists everywhere to "speak out on the problems of the maintenance of scientific integrity, the maintenance of channels of communication and travel, and the proper direction or public support of research, as well as on the personal, moral problem of the end results of a scientist's professional work."[29]

This sampling of the expressed attitudes of the organizations of scientists shows that the government by its security policy is alienating large numbers of scientists of America upon whom the nation's scientific progress depends. Other professional organizations of scientists have also gone on record against such policies. They have been joined by scholars in other fields.[30]

---

[28] Melba Phillips, "Dangers Confronting American Science," *Science*, Vol. 116, 1952, p. 439 f.

[29] *Science*, Vol. 118, December 11, 1953, p. 3.

[30] For a review of the implications of the security program see Walter Gellhorn, *Security, Loyalty and Science*, Ithaca, 1950; and his essay "Security, Secrecy and the Advancement of Science" in *Civil Liberties under Attack*, Philadelphia, 1951, p. 85 f. See also the files of the *Bulletin of the Atomic Scientists*.

Although the tradition of freedom of science and the scientist is still in jeopardy, it has not been submerged.

Restraints upon the freedom to inquire and the extension of secrecy are products of the race for the production of atom bombs, of the "emergency" engendered by the military in its assumption of the imminence of another World War, of the selfish acquisitiveness of industrialists intent upon the extension of their economic power. To the extent that these conditions are changed will science be really free to extend man's knowledge and skills in the use of the resources of the world for the welfare of all of mankind.

part three

SOCIAL THOUGHT IN PERSPECTIVE

Lewis Henry Morgan: American Ethnologist

I

Few American scientific works have had the international popularity and influence of *Ancient Society or Researches in the Lines of Human Progress from Savagery through Barbarism to Civilization,* Lewis Henry Morgan's *magnum opus* which was first published just fifty years ago. For many years it pervaded the outlook of the ethnologists and sociologists of America and its influence still persists in many quarters. In England, W. H. Rivers' early field work was dominated by its conclusions, and Hartland and others of the classical ethnologists are still under its sway. Cunow in Germany, Elie Reclus and Letournau in France and Kovalesky in Russia may be mentioned among the many writers on the continent who have acknowledged its influence. J. J. Bachofen in Switzerland, dedicated a book to Morgan in appreciation. The character of the anthropological researches of Lorimer Fison and Alexander Howitt in Australia were directly determined by it.

Morgan's influence has extended far beyond academic circles. *Ancient Society,* referred to by Karl Marx, as corroborating his thesis of the influence of property on social organization, has been translated and taken up by socialists and communists all over the world. Karl Kautsky wrote an introduction to the German translation; Frederick Engels paraphrased it in *The Origin of the Family, Private Property and the State;* August Bebel popularized parts of it in *Woman and Socialism.* These books have had a phenomenal sale, making the name of Lewis Henry Morgan widely known. His reputation and influence were not based entirely upon or confined to *Ancient Society* and the books deriving from it. Morgan's other works, in a more restricted though not less important manner have affected the character of researches that followed them and have been lasting storehouses of pertinent facts.

II

Lewis Morgan gloried in his ancestry and collaborated avidly in the preparation of his genealogy which is found in the *History of the Family of Morgan from the Year 1089 to Present Times* by Appleton Morgan of the twenty-seventh generation of Cadevor-fawr, and in other genealogies of the Morgan family of New York. His paternal ancestors had come from Bristol in 1648 and were among the founders of New London, Connecticut. From there, his grandfather Thomas had migrated and become a farmer in Cayuga County near the village of Aurora, New York, then surrounded by the Iroquois Indians. His father Jedidiah served as state senator from the district for five years. Lewis, one of his thirteen children was born November 21, 1818. He lived in Aurora until he went to college and a few years after his return. He graduated in 1840 from Union College, in Auburn where he received a thorough training in the classics. After reading law for four years and being admitted to the bar, he moved to Rochester where he made his residence until he died. Whatever intellectual stimulus he received in Rochester, was through *The Club* composed of a select group of the prominent professional men of the city, who conducted a somewhat superior sort of "Thanatopsis Club" at which the members delivered papers and discussed current profundities.

Early in his life Morgan displayed his deep interest in matters religious and until he died was an ardent Presbyterian, serving as an active member of the church board, securing ministers when the pulpit was vacant, and attending regularly the church functions. He was sectarian enough to be accused of harboring a dislike of Episcopalians. His was more than lip service; religion was one of his prime interests and he never emancipated himself from his theological background. That Morgan was conscious of the conflict between the results and implications of his researches and his theological creed is seen in his query in 1880 to Lorimer Fison, as to whether he thought the work they were doing "was detrimental to the true religion." Funeral orations are notoriously poor biographical material but what Morgan's friend Rev. J. H. McIlvaine, said of him is borne out by a study of Morgan's correspondence and other manuscript material left to the University of Rochester:

> He presents a striking contrast to the sceptical scientists with whom he was in constant correspondence . . . . who have hardly ever lost an opportunity of speaking disparagingly and even contemptuously of Christianity.

He adds:

> Whilst his great work on *Ancient Society* was passing through the press, I called his attention to a passage which inadvertently might have found its place there, and which might be construed as an endorsement of these materialistic speculations in connection with evolution, and he immediately cancelled the whole page although it had already been stereotyped. . . . .

No one was more responsible for Morgan's orthodox religious views than McIlvaine who took upon himself the task of being the guardian of Morgan's faith and of dispelling whatever waverings Morgan may have entertained. Over a period of fifteen years, he cautioned Morgan to "guard his soul," to "be careful not to go to the bad" and pleaded "I do most earnestly desire to see you a humble-minded believer and confessor of Christ." That Morgan did not resent such pressure is shown by his continued friendship and by the fact that he dedicated *Ancient Society* to McIlvaine. Morgan's attempted reconciliation of his faith and the results of his researches is evident in the closing sentences of *Ancient Society* which read:

> Civilization might as naturally have been delayed for several thousand years in the future as to have occurred when it did in the good providence of God. Their [our precursors'] labors, their trials and their successes were a part of the plan of the Supreme Intelligence to develop a barbarian out of a savage and a civilized man out of a barbarian.

Morgan served in the New York State Assembly from 1861 to 1867 and in 1868–1869 was in the State Senate. It was here that Morgan received his lessons on the influence of property on the state which provoked him to say in *Ancient Society:* "Government and laws are instituted with primary reference to its (property's) creation, protection and enjoyment." For these were the days of great corruption in the New York Senate, the period when the Tweed Ring was in its glory. Morgan appears to have kept himself free from the graft that was shown to have been paid to Republican Senators, but when an attempt was made to investigate the charges of graft, singularly enough, it was Morgan who was responsible for quashing it. Perhaps this explains the fact that he was defeated for renomination at the election in 1870. After this Morgan held no official position but was active as a party politician all his life. He sought an appointment as ambassador to some foreign country and thrice in 1869, 1872, and 1876 he urged all his prominent friends to solicit the presidents in his behalf. He also applied unsuccessfully for other political appointments.

Morgan was a "practical" politician and that political theory to which he subscribed was a reflex of current prejudices and concepts. In his early days he was a Whig and upon the passing of the Whigs as a party, a Republican. The party's views were his views and it cannot be said that he transcended them. On the few occasions that he expressed his political opinions, his discussions were oratorical and ill-defined. During the Civil War he was rabidly jingoistic and vindictive in his attitude toward the South. His limitations are evident in his laudatory worship of General Grant even after the bungling inefficiency of his administration had been exposed.

Although Morgan lived in the days of the activity of the First Internationale in America, and at a time when liberals such as Horace Greeley were inveighing against privilege, he was irresponsive to and little affected by the stirrings of revolt and discontent among the masses. This is well explained by the fact that Morgan was very wealthy, through his interest in a railroad near Lake Superior and his investments in iron mines. His ignorance of the plight of the workers of his day and his complacent economic beliefs are revealed in an unpublished address delivered in 1871:

> I can hardly see why there should be any poor in the United States, except such as may be poor from misfortune, or owing to causes where the blame rests entirely with themselves. . . . For there is not one, I care not how low his circumstances may be, who has health but can somewhere purchase an acre of ground and draw his support from the soil. If he cannot pay outright he has credit, and a little industry and perseverance will soon place him above actual want. . . . Yet there are none of this class of poor except in cities and I think on examination that most of these are foreigners whose habits have become formed from modes of life in their native land, or the idle and dissolute whom we may pity, yet who deserve no compassion. . . . When therefore, I hear complaints from the more indigent of my countrymen whose situation curiosity has led me to inquire into, that they can get no employment, I regard it only as an idle pretext.

It is ironic that an individual with such a point of view should have contributed to socialist doctrine.

Morgan was also conservative in his attitude toward morality and that he viewed with alarm changes in the mores of his time is shown by a letter to McIlvaine in which he declared that the tendency in morals in America was toward degeneration as in ancient Roman times. His attitude toward deviations from rigid monogamy is illustrated by the abhorrence with which he viewed Mormonism which he regarded as "one of the excrescences of modern civilization . . . . a relic of the old savagism not yet eradicated from the human brain." One expects a man of Morgan's religious and cultural background to say as he did of monogamy, "The whole previous experience and progress of mankind culminated and crystallized in this preëminent institution."

In his youth, Morgan stumped his neighborhood in a temperance campaign, and hard cider, the beverage made famous by the Whigs during the Harrison campaign of 1840 was the strongest drink served in his home. He did not hesitate to indulge in a round of poker and when he renounced tobacco late in life, a friend wrote him: "I should as soon have expected the devil himself to partake of holy water."

Morgan appears to have had a persuasive geniality combined with a dignified urbanity that made him the companion alike of men of convivial and austere interests. Placid, contented, and self-possessed, he was never disquieted by revolutionary political or economic ideas. Capitalism was to him the best system, the United States government the best democracy, Christianity the only true religion in this better than all previous worlds. He approached friendship and work alike with a righteous seriousness tempered by an essential humanness. He was, in effect, a conventional, capable, middle-class individual—a "first citizen" of Rochester.

The question naturally arises as to how a man of Morgan's orientation became interested in ethnology. Morgan delighted to tell the genesis of his dominant interest. It happened thus. When Morgan returned to Aurora from college, he joined a floundering secret society called the "Gordian Knot." With his aptitude for organizing, he set to work to give the society a semblance of purpose and above all a ritual with the appertaining rites and ceremonies upon which the success of fraternal organizations depend. His material was close at hand. He patterned the society after the Iroquois Confederacy and, in the manner of Tammany Hall and other similar grand orders of today, he appointed chiefs, sachems, councils, and other dignitaries and functionaries. The necessary idealistic purpose of this secret "New Confederacy of the Iroquois," known to the initiated under the high sounding name of "We-yo-ba-yo-de-za-de Na-bo-de-no-sau-nee," was the study and perpetuation of Indian lore, the education of the Indian tribes, and the reconciliation of these tribes with the conditions imposed by civilization. Only Morgan appears to have taken this purpose with any seriousness; to the others it proved to be incidental to the fellowship and pleasure which the order afforded its members especially at the Grand Council meetings which were held by night near Aurora with much flourish and display. Huge campfires illumined the neighborhood of the meeting and the sachems and chiefs assembled in Indian panoply, with chaplets of eagle feathers, Indian tunics, scarlet leggings and decorated moccasins. It was impressive hokum, to which

Morgan contributed not only by determining the ceremonies but by preparing the addresses at the chapter or council meetings. It was therefore necessary for him to make a study of the ceremonies and customs of the Iroquois in his neighborhood which he had hitherto merely noticed with casual interest. His curiosity was aroused and his interest stimulated so that when the order became defunct his investigations continued. Lewis Morgan therefore, far from being the "born ethnologist" as he was characterized by his friend and disciple, Adolph Bandelier, was a "made" one, made, *mirabile dictu*, by a secret society.

It was not difficult for Morgan to find a definite and immediate task for his New Confederacy, for an act characteristic of the methods employed in exploiting other Indian tribes, was being perpetrated against the Iroquois. Through the connivance of the Ogden Land Company, the United States Senate had abrogated the unanimity principle of the Iroquois, by authorizing the majority of the Seneca chiefs to make a treaty for the sale of their lands in western New York. The Senecas were strongly opposed to any sale, but the land company by bribing ten of the chiefs, plying others with rum until they were intoxicated and then forcing them to sign, creating chiefs by sham elections, and representing men as chiefs who were not so in fact, secured the required majority. The Senecas protested vigorously but by the vote of the Vice-President, the Senate ratified the treaty. The Indians refused to recognize it and a compromise was offered which would give the land company the reservations of the Tonawanda and Buffalo Senecas, land worth at that time $16.00 an acre, for $1.69. To prevent this steal from being effected, Morgan was sent by the society to Washington, to plead the cause of the Indians. The success of his mission made him very popular among the Indians. As a result, he was adopted into the Hawk gens of the Senecas, as the son of Jimmy Johnson, the nephew of Red-Jacket, immortalized by William Stone. He was given the name of Ta-ya-da-wah-kugh meaning "One Lying Across" which signified that he would serve as a bond of union between the Indians and the whites. His adoption greatly facilitated his researches.

III

As suggested above, Morgan served as a sort of intellectual dignitary in the "New Confederacy of the Iroquois," and upon him as sachem Skenandoah fell the task of making the "serious" addresses to the assembled members at their council meetings. These speeches he published in the *American Review: A Whig Journal of Politics, Literature, Art and Science* in 1847–1848, in the form of fourteen "Letters on the Iroquois" addressed to Albert Gallatin, president of the New York Historical Society. These letters verbatim, with the exception of a few interpolations and minor emendations, form Book I and parts of Books II and III of the *League of the Iroquois* which appeared in 1851. Book III also contains, practically unchanged, the report on the articles which Morgan had gathered and described for the New York State Museum Indian collection. In his investigations he was assisted by Ely Parker, a full bred Indian, who acted as interpreter.

One need but compare the *League of the Iroquois* with Henry R. Schoolcraft's contemporary study, *Notes of the Iroquois,* to realize the advance Morgan's study marked in American ethnology. It was a pioneer work and so has naturally glaring deficiencies and inadequacies. It fails lamentably to measure up to Morgan's later standard on the very points which Morgan stressed, and for which American ethnology owes him its greatest debt, i.e., to describe Indian life in terms of itself and not in terms of the culture of the investigator. One cannot criticize him too vehemently for not having freed himself from the classification of political institutions of Aristotle when one is aware that the majority of the political scientists of our time have not yet done so. But the chapters on the religion of the Iroquois are especially reprehensible as ethnologic material, for not Morgan, the alert investigator with a penchant for essential fact but Morgan the Presbyterian is speaking. The result is such characteristic sentences as these:

> That the Indian, without the aid of revelation should have arrived at a fixed belief of the existence of one Supreme Being, has ever been a matter of surprise and admiration. . . . By the

diffusion of this great truth, if the Indian did not escape the spell of superstition, which resulted from his imperfect knowledge of the Deity, and his ignorance of natural phenomena, yet he was saved from the deepest of all barbarisms, an idolatrous worship.

He differs from the earlier investigators in that he is sympathetic but this sympathy and undoubtedly the purpose for which his addresses were written leads him to romanticize and sentimentalize. But what is more open to criticism is Morgan's utter failure to grasp the details of the economic life of the Iroquois and to recognize its influence on the other forms of social organization. He had his eyes on the Confederacy and its machinery as a model for his "New Confederacy" and as a result he abstracts this from its background. He gives a description that has become classic although it has had to be fundamentally revised and supplemented in fact and in nomenclature in the light of later studies. It is in his description of the fabrics and implements of the Iroquois that Morgan is at his best and his Museum reports printed after the *League of Iroquois* appeared, add to his laurels as a careful observer and an able recorder of such objects.

IV

When Morgan wrote the *League of the Iroquois,* he was of the opinion that the kinship system of the Iroquois was the unique possession of the Iroquois and the tribes with whom they came in contact. But in 1858, while on the south shore of Lake Superior on business connected with his railroad, he found that the system of tracing relationships among the Ojibwas, an Algonquin tribe, was essentially the same as among the Iroquois, although the linguistic terms were different. His great idea was born, later to become his *idée fixe:* "the *gens* was universal." (The term *gens,* as used by Morgan, is synonymous with the word *sib* as used today by ethnologists, i.e., unilateral descent. *Gens* is now used to signify specifically unilateral descent through the father, and *clan* unilateral descent through the mother.) On his return to Rochester, he consulted Rigg's *Dakota Grammar and Dictionary* and found the same kinship system. He then examined more carefully the English and Roman systems as they were set forth by Blackstone and the Pandects of Justinian. Finally, he prepared questionnaires concerning kinship terms and relations and circulated them among missionaries, teachers, traders and other persons familiar with Indian life. Professor Joseph Henry rendered him the assistance of the Smithsonian Institution, and questionnaires were sent to the United States Consuls throughout the world with the request that they be placed in proper hands.

The returns from the questionnaire were at first very meager, and Morgan, greatly excited by his discovery, determined to pursue his investigations in person. In 1859, he made an expedition through Kansas and Nebraska, and in the following year, he went over the same ground, revising his former work, supplementing his observations, and extending his journey far up the Missouri River. In 1861, he made a trip to the Hudson Bay territory and Lake Winnipeg, and in 1862 to Fort Benton and the Rocky Mountains. Completed schedules began slowly to accumulate from all parts of the world until a very large number of kinship systems were recorded by Morgan and his correspondents. Morgan systematized the materials thus collected and first brought out his conclusions before the Academy of Arts and Sciences in 1868 under the title *A Conjectural Solution of the Origin of the Classificatory System of Relationships*. The data with these conclusions were published in a quarto volume of 600 pages by the Smithsonian Institution, in 1871, under the title *Systems of Consanguinity and Affinity of the Human Family*.

This gargantuan effort, which met some strong opposition of the readers of the manuscript even before its publication, was variously received. Sir John Lubbock, in his presidential address before the Royal Anthropological Institute of Great Britain declared it to be "one of the most valuable contributions to ethnological science which has appeared for many years." The irascible McLennan, said to have been piqued because he felt that Morgan had used his work without proper acknowledgment, declared the book to be "a wild dream, not to say nightmare of early institutions." Among the letters which Morgan received that are significant in showing Morgan's influence as a result of this book are those from Edward Tylor and Herbert Spencer. Tylor wrote in part:

> I assure you that I appreciate the great value [of the book] as bearing on the difficult problem of early social relations. I shall hope to make use of your research in a work on the Morals and Politics of the Lower Races, but it will be years first. As yet the only book of yours I have profited by is the *Iroquois League*.

Spencer's letter read:

> I am much indebted to you for the present of your great work on *Systems*, etc., which lately reached me. Hitherto, I have had but time to glance through it and to be impressed with the value of its immense mass of materials collected and arranged with so much labour.
>
> I thank you for it in more than a mere formal way that is common in the acknowledgment of presentation copies; for it comes to me at a time when I am making elaborate preparations personally and by deputy for the scientific treatment of Sociology, and its contents promise to be of immediate service.

Others who praised the book, some cautiously, some extravagantly were Henry Maine, Charles Darwin, and in America, Francis Parkman, Horatio Hale, and Oliver Wendell Holmes, Jr. Most other American reviewers were outspokenly impressed with its bulk and to them unintelligible profundity; but one asserted that it was the easiest of the Smithsonian publications to do without.

In judging the value of *Systems of Consanguinity*, we must distinguish three aspects of the work *viz.*, the accumulation of the facts themselves, the arrangement of these facts, and the hypotheses based on the facts. In the first instance, the book is a very valuable addition to the source materials of primitive society, and no praise is excessive in acknowledgment of the prodigious labor involved. The materials have been and are used repeatedly to good advantage by ethnologists, Spier's recent work on *The Distribution of Kinship Systems in North America* deriving much of its data from the book. The arrangement of the material was, however, not especially fortunate. Lubbock, in his address, felt called upon to reclassify the materials as have most other anthropologists that have made use of them. The fundamental basis of his arrangement has been justifiedly questioned. Morgan distinguished between a "classificatory" and a "descriptive" system of kinship terms. The former, which required for its origin a form of "group marriage" was coextensive with savagery and barbarism and represented an earlier stage of social development. The latter, he thought to be inevitably bound up with monogamy and the institution of the family as we know it and therefore employed by all or most of the peoples who had attained civilization. Kroeber has maintained that the terms "descriptive" and "classificatory," as applied to relationship systems are really misleading, for the so-called "descriptive" system is as much classificatory as the one specifically so named and that it is only the basis of classification which differs. The basis for the peculiar categories of relationship he finds in psychology or in language. Lowie has also shown that the features of kinship terminology are distributed like all other ethnological phenomena; that differences and similarities in terminology are regional. Morgan did the best he could with the materials in his possession but he was ill-equipped to cope with them. The conclusions derived from his data are substantially the same, though in an embryonic form, as those found in *Ancient Society* and will be considered later in the critical analysis of that book.

V

While Morgan's prestige was acquired in European circles by the publication of *Systems of Consanguinity,* his recognition in America by his contemporaries came primarily through his work on a critical reconstruction of the culture of Mexico and Central America. As early as 1856, probably under the influence of Albert Gallatin, he had protested against the fictitious descriptions of Mexican life by the Spanish writers which often rivalled the tales of Baron Münchhausen for absurdity. In an article entitled: "Seven Cities of Cibola" in the *North American Review* of April, 1869, he tried to burst the bubble of exaggeration that marked the popular descriptions of Mexican dwellings as palatial residences of emperors by interpreting them as communal dwellings in terms of the Iroquois "long-house." This was followed by an article in *Johnson's Encyclopaedia*, in 1873, on Indian architecture to the same purpose. But it was at the instance of Henry Adams who felt of Hubert H. Bancroft's *Native Races of America* that it would be a "disgrace to let such a work go out as a measure of our national scholarship" that Morgan launched his devastating attack on Bancroft's uncritical use of Spanish documents which brought attention to his efforts. The two articles entitled "Montezuma's Dinner" and "The Houses of the Mound Builders" which appeared in April and July, 1876, in the *North American Review*, in the words of F. W. Putnam "took Bankcroft's scalp off down to his neck." Henry Barnard's comment characterizes the response that the articles provoked:

> You have done for the student of our aboriginal history what Mommsen did for Rome; you not only exposed the errors and speculations of the early chronicles but give us clear sunlight in which to walk with certain steps over so much that was obviously enough absurd, but which most of us could never quite clear up.

Although Morgan learned too heavily on the Iroquois in his interpretation of Mexican life these articles were valuable in that they stressed the necessity for painstaking archeological investigations and ethnological field work to establish the character of aboriginal life in America rather than dependence upon the mendacious gossip of travellers and the misconceptions and perverted accounts of missionaries. As a result of his labors in this field, Morgan was called upon to present the program for the archeological expedition into the Pueblo country undertaken by the Archeological Institute of America at Harvard which appeared as an appendix to its first report. At Morgan's request, Adolph Bandelier was appointed to undertake the work and his reports represent the results of the first extensive schematic exploration of the Southwest. Morgan's final treatment of the subject was in *Houses and House Life of American Aborigines* which appeared just prior to his death.

Along with the extended praise which Morgan received for his realistic approach to the problems of American aboriginal life was the antagonism of Bancroft and his followers. They produced a tract in which they bitterly condemned Morgan and his school and attacked the *Nation* which had published an unfavorable review of Bancroft's work as a "chronic sore-head journal." The controversy extended for some time but although the Spanish accounts of early Mexican and Central American life still are read because of their appealing romance, they are no longer given credence by scientists. It is primarily due to Morgan's efforts in this field that Professor O. T. Mason called him the "founder of the Commonsense School of Anthropology."

VI

Morgan's capacity for intelligent and accurate observation and his ability to document his findings meticulously led him to make another contribution in a diverse field in the period during which he was gathering material for *Systems of Consanguinity*. Time hung heavily on Morgan's hands during his annual sojourns at Marquette, Michigan, where he tended the interests of his railroad. Instead of spending his leisure fishing, as did his friends, he decided to devote his time recording the behavior of beavers that were constructing their homes in the streams nearby. He had had a passing interest in animal psychology since his youth; one of his earliest periodical contributions was entitled "Mind and Instinct: An Inquiry Concerning the Manifestation of Mind by the Lower Animals," and one of his papers to *The Club* was on this subject. The notes he collected at Marquette interpreted in the light of these early papers, he published with the addition of two chapters on the anatomy of the beaver by Dr. W. W. Ely, under the title *The American Beaver and Its Work*. This book was very favorably reviewed when it appeared in 1868, and remained the classic on the beaver until the recent book on the subject by Edward H. Warren.

The scope of this article does not permit an analysis of Morgan's interesting views on instinct as given in his contributions on this subject. But brief quotation from his review of Chadbourne's *Instinct: Its Office in the Animal Kingdom, and its Relation to the Higher Powers in Man* which appeared in the *Nation* in 1872, suggests how he approximated the modern view that the term instinct is misleading and scientifically useless because it substitutes verbal labels for extended analyses and discourages inquiry and investigation. He wrote:

> Dr. Chadbourne adopts the "instinct hypothesis" to explain the phenomena of animal intelligence and regards it as adequate to embrace and account for all the facts. Having adopted this hypothesis in the title of his book (which hypothesis it would be pleasant to ascribe to human laziness if it could properly be done), he was substantially released from the necessity of collecting and discussing the vast and complicated array of facts revealed by the lives of the inferior animals.

VII

In *Ancient Society*, which appeared in 1877, Morgan gathered together the materials which he had previously published with new data and certain new interpretations. The book represents the summation of his life's work and his supreme effort. As suggested previously, through it Morgan became widely known and exercised a potent influence on ethnological and sociological thought.

Morgan's general evolutionary concept is too well known to need extended exposition. Incorporated into early sociological textbooks, it has become entrenched as a dogma in many quarters. Postulating the common origin and thus the psychic unity of all races of man, which cause them to react similarly to environmental stimuli, he believed that mankind the world over passed through the successive stages of savagery, barbarism and civilization, the two earlier of which had a tripartite division of lower, middle and upper. He anticipated Tylor in saying:

> Like the successive geological formations, the tribes of mankind may be arranged, according to their relative conditions, into successive strata. When thus arranged, they reveal with some degree of certainty the entire range of human progress from savagery to civilization. A thorough study of each successive stratum will develop whatever is special in its culture and characteristics and yield a definite conception of the whole in their differences and their relations.

Forced to determine the lines of demarcations between the various stages, he was obliged to be arbitrary. He recognized this arbitrariness more than did most of his disciples but once having made the divisions, he was stubborn and rigid in their application. The "middle status of savagery" began, in his classification, with the acquisition of a fish subsistence, the "upper" with the invention of the bow and arrow. "Barbarism" came with the art of pottery; its "middle status," with the domestication of animals on the eastern hemisphere, and the cultivation of maize and plants by irrigation on the western. The "upper status of barbarism" was introduced by the invention of the process of smelting iron ore and "civilization" came with the phonetic alphabet and the use of writing.

One need but apply Morgan's scheme critically to primitive society as we now know it, to reveal its extreme tenuousness. The Polynesians who have a well developed agriculture and technology and the Micronesians who weave textiles and have a fine mythology are placed in the lowest subdivision while the far more primitive African and Indonesian peoples, because they breed cattle, would be placed in the second stage of "barbarism." Such discrepancies could be multiplied many times, for culture is too complex and the forms of combination of social institutions too variable to fit into any definite social evolutionary scheme.

Without entering into a detailed criticism of unilateral schemes such as Morgan's, it is enough to point out that any fixed sequence is completely disturbed by borrowing. Morgan acknowledged this factor. In an early museum report he wrote:

> Such is the diffusion of Indian arts and Indian inventions among the Red races that it is impossible to ascertain with what nation or tribe they in fact originated. . . . One system of trails belted the whole face of the territory from the Atlantic to the Pacific and the intercourse between the nations was constant and much more extensive than ever has been supposed.

In *Ancient Society*, he accounted for the existence of descent through the male line among the Siouan Indians as due to borrowing from the white man, probably in this case erroneously. But Morgan did not recognize the implications of diffusion in reference to his idea of development through successive stages.

One must not adopt a too critical attitude toward Morgan's evolutionism but must consider him in his historical setting. That he erred in attempting to carry over a principle which Darwin had demonstrated so effectively in biology, into the field of culture, merely reflects the tendency of his period. The persistence of the application of his methods today, is, however, inexcusable.

Morgan's views on the evolution of the family have aroused more acrimonious controversy than any other aspect of his work. Space does not permit more than a cursory presentation of his views and a summary analysis of the somewhat intricate and complicated arguments and proofs advanced in refutation of them. The discussion in *Ancient Society* depends upon and represents a direct development from the views expressed in *Systems of Consanguinity*. He distinguishes five different and successive forms of the family preceded by promiscuity, beginning with the "consanguine" family and through a series of "reformatory movements" finally attaining monogamy.

It is actually not a refutation of Morgan to point out with Westermarck and a host of others, that promiscuity cannot be found anywhere and that the horror of incest is universal among existing primitive peoples for Morgan himself maintained:

> The existence of the Consanguine family must be proved by other evidence than the production of the family itself. As the first and most ancient form of the institution, it has ceased to exist even among the lowest tribes of savages. It belongs to a condition of society out of which the least advanced portion of the human race have emerged.

His proof of the previous existence of promiscuity is a logical one derived from his interpretation of kinship terms. Morgan understood them to indicate earlier relations between the sexes, upon which the existing marriage form was "superimposed," and therefore he found evidence in the "Malayan" (Polynesian) system, which he considered the lowest existing form, of a previous "consanguine" family. He concludes:

> Finally, it will be perceived that the state of society, indicated by the Consanguine family points with logical directness to an anterior

condition of promiscuous intercourse. There seems to be no escape from this conclusion although questioned by so eminent a writer as Mr. Darwin. . . . The most that can safely be claimed upon this difficult question is that the Consanguine family was the first organized form of society, and that it was necessarily an improvement upon the previous unorganized state, whatever that state may have been. With the existence of the Consanguine family established, of which the adduced proofs seem to be sufficient, the remaining families are easily demonstrated.

In other words, Morgan's concept of the growth of the family logically required the existence of the "consanguine" family, which in turn logically required an unorganized state or promiscuity to complete the proof of evolution from the lowest to the highest form.

It is around the interpretation of kinship terms that most criticism has centered. Evolutionists following Morgan continue to see in them "survivals," the signposts of previous social conditions. McLennan, Morgan's arch contemporary antagonist, failed to see any sociological significance in the terms whatsoever, and considered them merely terms of address, a position later defended by Andrew Lang. American ethnologists show how the terms are often expressive of status or potential relationship rather than indicative of antecedent social organization, and hold them to be subject to a variety of influences of a purely linguistic character and to change through diffusion. They contend that it is exceedingly hazardous to attempt to reconstruct a form of social organization on the basis of the relationship system, for the terms often reflect the effect of diffusion and historical contact. The underlying prop of the evolutionists' system is thus undermined.

Morgan was particularly unfortunate in choosing the Polynesian family to represent the lowest in the scale of evolution, for, as pointed out above, Polynesian society is relatively highly developed. This reveals the great arbitrariness of the evolutionists' classifications. Writers such as Morgan invariably place monogamy as the highest form and latest development of the family, yet the monogamous family has been shown by Starche, Gross, Westermarck, Lowie and others to have been universal and omnipresent at all stages of culture. In fact, as Lowie points out, on the very lowest plane, among peoples such as the rude Adaman Islanders, matrimonial relations are frequently encountered that would be rated exemplary by a mid-victorian moralist. There has been no fixed universal evolution of the forms of the family; sequences such as Morgan's are superimposed and merely reflect the prejudices and preconceptions of the author.

This leads to the discussion of two other vigorously debated contentions of Morgan, first, that the *gens (sib, i.e.,* unilateral descent) was universal and could be traced to one source, and second, that the succession was always from the *clan* (maternal descent) to the *gens* (paternal descent). When Swanton pointed out that the *sib* was not even universal in North America among the existing tribes, because it was not found among the Salish, Athapascan and Eskimo groups, he did not differ from Morgan who had admitted that there were no traces of *sib* organization among these people. Morgan, not put out by this, had maintained that "since the Columbia valley was the initial point of migration of the other tribes it was probable that their ancestors possessed the organization into *gentes* and that it fell into decay and finally disappeared," an unsupported assumption. Lowie has proven that the great variability of *sibs* makes their single origin as assumed by Morgan impossible, and also that in North America alone there are several independent centers of *sib* diffusion. Swanton also ventured the judgment that the fact that the *sib* is lacking precisely among the most primitive tribes and as a rule appears only when horticultural or pastoral activities have partly or wholly superseded the chase as a basis of economic existence, completely repudiates the idea that the *sib* represented the earliest form of social organization.

Boas, Swanton, Lowie and others have been instrumental in refuting Morgan's contention that the *clan* (maternal descent) universally preceded the *gens* (paternal descent). Morgan had arrived at this view through the influence of Bachofen's *Das Mutterrecht* and by his interpretation of the importance of women among the Iroquois. Here again the argument rests heavily on the postulate of "survivals," and refutation partly on the fact that these assumed "survivals" can be explained in their own cultural setting. It appears that the *clan* preceded the *gens* in certain cases, but this does not prove that such a sequence is universal, or even that it was the rule. Furthermore, sibless tribes have been shown to have adopted the *gens* by borrowing without passing through the supposedly intermediate *clan* stage. The conclusion is obvious that the social history of any particular tribe can be reconstructed only in the light of its known and probable cultural relations with neighboring peoples and not from any generally valid scheme of evolution. The futility of armchair theorizing and the shuffling and arranging of tribes into fixed categories becomes apparent.

It was Morgan's belief that when the paternity of children became known, the fathers protested against their children being disinherited by the clan rule of inheritance and in this way descent in the female line was overthrown and patrilineal descent substituted. Morgan saw clearly that this principle was not always applicable when he wrote of the Siouan family:

> It is surprising that so many tribes of this stock should have changes of descent from the female line to the male, because when first known, the idea of property was substantially undeveloped or but slightly beyond the germinating stage, and could hardly as among the Greeks and Romans have been operating cause.

In spite of the introduction of sheep tended by men which gave them great wealth, the Navajo have remained matrilineal. Among the Crow and Hidatsa, also wealthy matrilineal people, certain kinds of property are transmitted from father to son without any change of descent. It is true, however, that when property goes through the male and descent through the female, the tendency of the social organization is to be unstable in the direction of patrilineal descent.

Although specific changes in the social organization of primitive peoples cannot be correlated with changes in economic organization, Morgan was correct in so far as he stressed the determining effect of the economic organization upon the other forms of social organization. One cannot well understand other aspects of the culture of any primitive people, without knowing their economic life and activity. A change of economic conditions, acting upon the existing institutions in their historical setting, fundamentally modifies the cultural pattern. This is clearly brought out in noting the effect of the introduction of the reindeer on the social organization of the reindeer Chukchi as compared to the maritime Chukchi, and by the far reaching effect of the introduction of the horse on the life of the Plains Indians.

Morgan believed, as did Henry Maine, that primitive society differed fundamentally from and is distinguished from civilized society in that it dealt with an individual as a member of a kinship group and lacked political organization which affected the individual through his territorial relations. But as Lowie has shown local contiguity is one of the factors determining social solidity independently of kinship relationship even in very humble cultural levels. Such tribes as the Vedda, the Maida, Shasta and Thompson River Indians show decided jealousy regarding territorial rights. Furthermore, the transition to a political state did not imply a disrupting of the ties of kinship as Morgan inferred, for there always existed such associations as men's clubs, age classes, and secret organizations which could take on a political character.

Morgan was quite pugnacious in his insistence that democracy was the universal pattern among primitive peoples because he projected the conditions he found among the Iroquois into a comprehensive generalization. The salubrious effect of this belief which he defended with much vigor, upon the treatment of Mexican cultural history has already been considered. But before Morgan published *Ancient Society,* Albert Gatschet, the linguist, tried in vain to modify his idea of uniform democracy in a letter to him which declared that "many of the Southern Indians had far more aristocratical institutions that the northern—as the Natchez, Toltecs, Incas and Aztecs." It is now an established fact that the Natchez had a caste system, and all recent investigators of the northwest coast Indians are in agreement that the acquisition of rank is the dominant motive in the lives of the Indians of that section. Kroeber speaks of the avarice which pervades even the poor and rude tribes of Central California and maintains: "The chief, or rather the man of influence and position, is not a man of courage or record in war, but the man of property. A poor chief is as unthinkable to the Indian of California as to him of Puget Sound or Queen Charlotte Island." Margaret Mead testifies as to the all importance of rank among the Samoans. Nor did slavery commence, as Morgan supposed, among the people who smelted iron, domesticated cattle and knew irrigation and stone architecture, for it is found among the neolithic Polynesians and the non-agricultural Nootka. Morgan would undoubtedly have modified his views had he known about the extremely monarchical social organization among the primitive African tribes. Furthermore, he was wrong in assuming that primitive peoples did not recognize differences in individual abilities, and that all *gens* and *clans* were of equal rank and importance among primitive tribes.

The limits of this article do not permit a more extensive analysis of Morgan's views as expressed in *Ancient Society* although there are many other hypotheses that merit consideration. Enough has been presented to indicate that he deserves a place of high rank among the early investigators of primitive life but that his views must be fundamentally revised in the light of contemporary ethnology and sociology. Morgan was not the "discoverer of the law of social progress" as he is boldly characterized on his commemorative tablet at Wells College in Aurora, New York. But he was an illustrious pioneer in the uncharted field of ethnology, who in spite of his limited scientific equipment and his very meager library was able to contribute much to the methodology and source material of that science.

From SOCIAL FORCES, Vol. VI, No. 3. (March, 1928), pp. 344–357.

Lewis Henry Morgan: An Appraisal of His Scientific Contributions

Lewis Henry Morgan is among the best-known social scientists in American history. His fame has not been confined to these shores, but is world wide. Many pioneer ethnographic field workers among the natives in Australia down under, in the Fiji Islands of the Pacific, among the natives of Siberia, in fact in all corners of the globe, have taken their point of departure from Morgan's researches. Even today the history of ancient Greece is being rewritten in the light of his views, as witness the recent volume on *Aeschylus and Athens* by George Thomson of the University of Birmingham. The British anthropologist A. C. Haddon in 1910 hailed Morgan as "undoubtedly the greatest sociologist of the past century"; and a host of sociologists in the United States long popularized his name and his findings in their classes and textbooks. Abroad, W. H. Rivers and Edwin S. Hartland in England, Heinrich Cunow in Germany, Elie Reclus and Charles Letourneau in France are only a few among the many scholars on the continent who have acknowledged Morgan's influence. A Hindu writer in far-off Calcutta few years ago acclaimed Morgan as "a colossus."

Morgan's fame has extended far beyond academic halls and beyond the covers of sociology textbooks and anthropological and historical monographs. His work evoked the warm admiration of Karl Marx, and on the basis of Marx's notes on Morgan's *Ancient Society*, Frederick Engels in 1884 wrote *The Origin of the Family, Private Property and the State* which bore the sub-title *In the Light of the Researches of Lewis H. Morgan*. In the preface to the fourth German edition of this book, published in 1891, Engels averred that Morgan's teaching "had the same significance for primitive history as Darwin's theory of evolution has for biology and Marx's theory of surplus value has for political economy."

There is no exaggerating the importance of this tribute in enhancing the reputation of Morgan among laymen the world over. Even before this preface had been written, Engels' book, in addition to having three large German editions, had been translated into Italian, Russian, and Danish, and a French translation was in the press. After his words of praise, editions multiplied in many other countries, making the name of Morgan a household word among persons who came into the orbit of socialist influence.

Some scholars have been annoyed at what they have regarded as the cult of Morgan in socialist circles, and have been more caustic in their criticism of Morgan than they might otherwise have been. By no means all of the sharp criticisms of Morgan have been so motivated, but this factor has undoubtedly been present, consciously or unconsciously, in many instances. On the other hand, Marx's and Engels' praise of Morgan has led to the enthusiastic reception of his work in the Soviet Union. There Morgan is now the best known and respected of all ethnologists. In 1936 the Academy of Science of the U.S.S.R. authorized me to make photostats and microfilms of all manuscripts of the books, articles, and letters of Morgan in this country to facilitate research in the Soviet Union in the preparation of an edition of his collected works. Some 17,000 prints and films were sent over, but pressing problems incident to World War II have interrupted the project.

In evaluating Morgan today it is, of course, erroneous to expect a pioneer to have the accumulated knowledge, insights, and techniques of later periods, or to expect his concepts to remain unmodified and unrefined by later researches. No science stands still. There are few of the specific postulates of Darwin's theory of evolution that remain unchanged, and yet no one would therefore challenge Darwin's contribution to biological thought. Morgan's ardent admirer, Engels, declared fourteen years after the appearance of *Ancient Society* that because of new findings "some of Morgan's hypotheses have been shaken, or have even become obsolete." As the years have passed, others have made similar judgments. But this should not be permitted to detract from Morgan's reputation, if the positive values of his basic teachings remain significant.

What should be our judgment on this point as we pick our way among the eddies of controversy? It may be truly said that Morgan's work has proved to be of more lasting worth to anthropology than that of most of his contemporaries and many of his later adversaries. As a field-worker Morgan has been shown to be accurate and honest with an "eye for essential fact." This is true not only of his classic *League of the Ho-de-no-sau-nee or Iroquois*, published in 1851, but of his observations of other tribes which he visited in his travels. Sometimes field investigators have thought that they had found errors, only to confess later that Morgan was right and they were wrong, as witness for example Lowie's work on the kinship system of the Crow Indians. Whenever and wherever Morgan gathered facts he was painstaking and exact. This judgment applies not only to his anthropological research, but likewise to his study of *The American Beaver and His Work*, which has served as a primary source of information about animal behavior.

Morgan's most important contribution to anthropology has been his collection of kinship terms acquired by his own tenacious field work and from correspondents in all parts of the world. His most severe American critic, Professor R. H. Lowie, acknowledges that, "In social organization and especially kinship terms, Morgan remains a towering figure. His work has been revised and amplified, but it cannot be ignored. . . . The distinction of Morgan is not simply that he heaped up vast stores of information on a subject of theoretical import, but that he immersed himself in this welter of fact and came to grips with it."

It was in coming to grips with this refractory data that Morgan formulated his evolutionary scheme that has proved to be a source of turbulent controversy. The storm has not cleared away. But as the years have passed, the tide has turned more in favor of Morgan. The permutations of the controversy and its many facets cannot be traced in this brief essay. But among the basic issues were whether kinship terminologies were to be explained on sociological lines; whether they corresponded to social reality; and whether they could be correlated to matrimonial institutions. On these points Morgan has been vindicated and his contemporary J. F. McLellan and a host of later critics have been shown to be in error. Evidence has also fully corroborated Morgan's contention that different elements of culture change at an uneven tempo, that certain elements lag, among them linguistic phenomena, which are very conservative.

Morgan's formulation of evolutionary stages of culture has aroused the most vigorous polemics. Here Morgan's views have often been oversimplified beyond recognition, and straw men have been set up and then demolished triumphantly. But apart from this, the underlying controversy has been over whether there can be general laws in history; whether there can be any synthesis of social data; and whether sociologists and anthropologists can go beyond the mere compilation of specific information and the study of the process of development of specific tribes. Many recent anthropologists have assumed as a basic premise that there can be no social laws, and so have never made the effort to formulate them. Morgan had no such misgivings. He took the hard way.

Morgan did not conceive his function to be that of the cultural historian who must trace specific historical events in their temporal reference in any one place. He was concerned primarily with classifying *types* of societies on the basis of certain distinguishing characteristics which peoples generally share in common at specific levels of culture, and with noting the sequences in the development of these types. Whatever inadequacies and crudities his particular evolutionary schemes may have had, this was a legitimate, though very difficult undertaking, and one that cannot be dismissed superciliously as has often been the case. Morgan's position was that "Progress has been found to be *substantially* the same in kind in tribes and nations inhabiting different and even disconnected continents, *while in the same status, with deviations from uniformity in particular instances produced by special causes.*" (Italics are mine.) He anticipated his critics by repeatedly recognizing that internal sequences within any culture are disturbed by borrowing from other cultures. He cautioned also that, "It is by no means easy to conceive of two peoples in disconnected areas living in conditions precisely similar," and noted differences in the cultural history of the Old World and the New World. But he declared nonetheless that "the experience of mankind has run in nearly uniform channels" and that "a thorough study of each successive stratum will develop whatever is special in its culture and characteristics and yield a definite conception of the whole, in their difference and in their relations." While this may be too general a principle to be of very great value as a research guide, it is unassailable.

This much can be said with certainty. The era of anti-evolutionism in social science has long passed its prime. Once more scientists are seeking, as Morgan sought, for evolutionary guides that will give them the requisite perspectives for the better understanding of local cultural variations, to facilitate their analysis of the direction of cultural change, and to implement their efforts to plan its future course.

Our appreciation of Morgan's contribution should not, however, lead us to slur over some basic errors. The most grievous of these is his belief that racial affinity explains tribal resemblances in their kinship systems, or as he once expressed it, "the custom of saluting by kin . . . (was) transmitted by the blood." Although his fundamental stress on the difference between what he called *societas*, in which a society is based on kinship, and *civitas*, in which other than kinship factors are primary determinants of human relationships was eminently correct, he erred in contending that the democracy of the *societas* prevailed in all American aboriginal tribes. In this way he misled Bandelier in his interpretation of ancient Mexican society. Morgan was also mistaken in assuming that the *gens* or unilateral kinship was once universal in America. But these and other errors do not dwarf Morgan's greatness. As a pioneer in paths untrodden, he cannot be expected to have invariably found the best way. His record of achievement does him great honor.

A final thought concerning Morgan's heritage to us: among the closing passages of his *Ancient Society* are found these oft-quoted and eloquent words, which show him to be imbued with a hopeful vision of a better future democratic society:

"The time will come when human intelligence will rise to the mastery over property, and define relations of the state to the property it protects, as well as the obligations and the limits of the rights of its owners. The interests of society are paramount to individual interests, and the two must be brought into just and harmonious relations. A mere property career is not the final destiny of mankind, if progress is to be the law of the future as it has been of the past. . . . The dissolution of society bids fair to become the termination of a career of which property is the end and aim; because such a career contains the elements of self-destruction. Democracy in government, brotherhood in society, equality in rights and privileges, and universal education, foreshadow the next higher plane of society to which experience, intelligence, and knowledge are steadily tending."

These words bear reiteration and serious contemplation today by the people of a nation that has just emerged from a conflict of devastating proportions, and has triumphed over a fascist foe who would have enslaved all humanity to acquire property and power for a few. We shall do well to ponder Morgan's words as we face the problems of the postwar world, the solution of which will determine the future of civilization.

From *Union Worthies: Lewis Henry Morgan.* Published by Union College as part of its sesquicentennial celebration, pp. 16–22.

A Note on Comte

Auguste Comte is variously known as the founder of positivism, the high priest of the "religion of humanity," and the first to give the name of sociology to the search for social laws. His plea for the extension of empirical methods in the social sciences, as contrasted with what he designated as theological and metaphysical methods, and his evolutionism, derived largely from Condorcet, have caused him to be characterized by many historians of social thought as a spearhead of enlightenment.

The influence of certain phases of Comte's thought among men and women of rationalist and humanitarian movements is indubitable. Harriet Martineau, in her introduction to her translation, gives the tone of the attitude with which his *Cours de philosophie positive* was welcomed in England:

> The theological world cannot but hate a book which treats theological belief as a transient state of the human mind. . . . As M. Comte treats of theology and metaphysics as destined to pass away, theologians and metaphysicians must necessarily abhor, dread and despise his work. . . . To those who have learned the difficult task of postponing dreams to realities till the beauty of reality is seen in its full disclosure, while that of dreams melts into darkness, the moral charm of this work will be as impressive as its intellectual satisfactions.[1]

Moreover, as indicative of the character and range of his influence, it is to be noted that among Comte's articulate disciples was Professor Edward Spencer Beesly, who was chairman of the

[1] *Cours de philosophie positive* (6 vols., Paris, 1830–42, 5th ed. 1892–94, tr. by Harriet Martineau, 3rd ed., New York, 1856), p. 9–10.

meeting in London at which the International Workingmen's Association (the First International) was founded.[2] The most socially minded of American pioneer sociologists, Lester F. Ward, did most to give Comte a noteworthy reputation in the United States, although Comte had had many earlier followers here. John Stuart Mill and Littré were likewise for a time disciples of Comte but later repudiated him.

There has repeatedly been a false identification of Comte with the liberalism and broad human sympathies of many of his disciples,[3] that has obscured the actual rôle played by Comte in the history of social thought, which this note will seek to elucidate briefly.

Comte's evolutionism, which is so often stressed, was in fact an insignificant phase of Comte's philosophy compared to his emphasis on order as a basic requisite for progress. Under the influence of Bonald and de Maistre, Catholic emigrés from the French Revolution, order in society became his chief concern. The French Revolution had seriously disturbed the tranquillity of the old régime, and Comte was among the many publicists of this post-revolutionary period interested in restoring its equilibrium.[4] In doing so, he became a philosopher of counter-revolution, a charge which I propose to document here through citations from his works.

Comte's conception of the function of sociology, in fact, originally stemmed from his belief in the urgent need for order in society. As early as 1822, in his pamphlet *Plan des travaux scientifiques nécessaires pour réorganiser la societé*, in which he first set forth his objectives in formulating social laws underlying human behavior, he argued that the discovery of such laws would

---

[2] Marx wrote to Kugelmann from London on December 13, 1870: "Professor Beesly is a Comtist and is as such obliged to support all sorts of crotchets, but for the rest a very capable and brave man." Marx, Karl, *Letters to Dr. Kugelmann* (New York, 1934), p. 114.

[3] See, for example, the adulation of Comte in F. J. Gould's *Auguste Comte* (London, 1920), and the many panegyrics of Frederic Harrison.

[4] Comte's objectives in this respect are recognized but not elaborated upon by Lucien Lévy-Bruhl in his *La philosophie d'Auguste Comte* (Paris, 1900; tr. New York, 1903), p. 2–4. American works on the history of sociological thought deal almost exclusively with Comte's evolutionary doctrines and his derived sociological concepts, to the neglect of this significant background.

enable man to circumvent revolutions, the violence of which he thought in a large part "due to ignorance of the natural laws which regulate the progress of civilization." He declared:

> It [political science] should exclusively employ itself in coordinating all the special facts relative to the progress of civilization and in reducing these to the smallest possible number of general facts, the connexion of which ought to manifest the general law of progress, leaving for a subsequent appreciation the various causes which can modify its rapidity. . . .
>
> A sound political system can never aim at impelling the human race, since this is moved by its proper impulse, in accordance with a law as necessary as, though more easily modified than, that of gravitation. But it does seek to facilitate human progress by enlightening it.
>
> . . . disturbances, of every sort, which arise in the body politic, may be in great part avoided, by adopting measures based on an exact knowledge of the changes which tend to produce themselves. . . .
>
> In other words, the essential aim of practical politics is, properly speaking, to avoid the violent revolutions which spring from obstacles opposed to the progress of civilization; and to reduce these to a simple moral movement, as regular as, though more intense than, that which gently urges society in ordinary periods. Now, in order to attain this end, it is manifestly indispensable that we should know, as precisely as possible, the actual tendency of civilization so as to bring our political conduct in harmony with it.[5]

Comte here conceives of man's directed efforts at change as futile before inexorable law, which had best be learned rather than ignored, or combatted by revolution. This leads him to disparage political action and hence to advocate the superiority of moral rather than political solutions of man's social and economic ills. He realized full well the objective results which would follow were this theoretical position accepted by the masses, for, already in his *Cours*, he outspokenly expressed his hopes of preventing,

[5] This article was republished by Comte to prove that his later views were consistent with his earlier ones, in refutation of the contention of John Stuart Mill, Littré and others that his *Système de politique positive* marked a change of front. It convincingly establishes the fact that his work is of one piece. *Système de politique positive* (4 vols., Paris, 1851–54, 3rd ed. 1890–95; tr. as *System of Positive Polity*, 4 vols., London, 1875–77), iv, p. 560.

by its promulgation, "collision with the governing classes" and danger to the institution of property:

> Even now, vast benefit would ensue if, in preparation for the system to come, positive knowledge and philosophy were sedulously brought within reach of the people. In the educational direction, the intellectual expansion would be much greater than is now easily believed: and the advantage in the other respect, in protecting them from collision with the governing classes, would be no less evident. The positive philosophy would teach them the real value of the political institutions from which they are apt to hope so much, and to convince them of the superiority of moral over political solutions. All evils and all pretexts derived from social disturbance would thus be obviated: quacks and dreamers would lose their vocation; and no excuse would be left for delay in social reform. When it is seen why wealth must chiefly abound among the industrial leaders, the positive philosophy will show that it is of small importance to popular interests in what hands capital is deposited, if its employment is duly useful to society at large: and that condition depends much more on moral than on political methods. No jealous legal provision against the selfish use of wealth, and no mischievous intervention, paralyzing social activity by political prohibition, can be nearly so effectual as general reprobation, grounded on an ascertained principle, under the reign of positive morality. The new philosophical action would either obviate or repress all the dangers which attend the institution of property, and correct popular tendencies by a wise analysis of social difficulties, and a salutary conversion of questions of right into questions of duty.[6]

As Comte's views matured, he stressed even more emphatically the need for moral reform prior to political change—a view which is antithetical to Marxism—and this became the cardinal feature of his positivism. In a letter to Senator Vieillard dated February 28, 1852, he characterized this outlook as the distinguishing feature of his program and boasted of its effectiveness in counteracting revolutionary philosophy:

> Positivists are the only men of the time who, putting the spiritual problem before the temporal investigation, would make an intel-

---

[6] *Cours de philosophie positive,* Martineau translation, p. 780.

lectual and moral renovation the basis of industrial reorganization. All other reformers, despite their innumerable divergences, agree in reversing this order, and would proceed to the temporal reorganization of society, without any previous discipline of opinions and customs. . . . In fact you rightly appreciated, in our pleasant interview of November 28, 1851, the admirable resolution of the *ci-devant* communists of Lyons recently converted to Positivism. In answer to the metaphysical sophisms of two representatives of their anarchical tour, they solemnly declared that *the moral regeneration of the people must precede their material enfranchisement.* [Comte's italics.]

Such a success allows, and even obliges the sound philosophy and the true religion to devote their chief social efforts henceforth to sincere conservatives. The two may now be able so to overcome their instinctive repugnance; since crucial experiences have demonstrated the inherent power of Positivism thoroughly to discipline the most ardent revolutionists, by obtaining from them the acceptance of order in the name of progress.[7]

Elsewhere he denounced, as useless and destructive, direct political efforts to change the social structure without previous spiritual reconstruction of mankind by the indirect method of education:

> Positivists find themselves at issue with all other progressive schools. They maintain that the organization of Industry must be based upon the organization of Education, whereas it is commonly supposed that both may be begun simultaneously or indeed that Labor may be organized irrespectively of Education. It may seem as if we are making too much of a mere question of arrangement; yet the difference is one which affects the whole character and method of social reconstruction. The plan usually followed is simply a revision of the old attempt to reconstruct politically, without waiting for spiritual reconstruction: in other words, to raise the social edifice before its intellectual and moral foundations have been laid. Hence the attempts made to satisfy popular requirements by measures of a purely political kind, because they appear to meet the evil directly; a course as useless as it is destructive. Positivism,

---

[7] Comte made public this letter in his preface to the second volume of *Système*. It was published in the fourth volume of the English translation, p. xlv–vi.

on the contrary, substitutes for such agencies an influence which is sure and peaceful, although it be gradual and indirect; the influence of a more enlightened morality, supported by a purer state of Public Opinion; such opinion being organized by competent minds, and diffused freely amongst the people.[8]

The argument here made, a familiar one in Comte's writings, is for gradualism of an extreme sort. In the interests of order, the most elementary organization of labor is to be deferred until man is enlightened morally through education.

Comte, for a few years in his youth, had been secretary and disciple of Saint-Simon, but his break with him and other radical groups of the period was incisive and complete. In the prefaces to the successive volumes of his *Système*, he repeatedly and sometimes with rancor disassociated himself from their views. Comte's famous letter of December 20, 1852 to Tsar Nicholas, in which he pleaded for the Tsar's endorsement of positivism, intensified the hostility between workers' groups and Comte. This letter exposed with a candor more complete than on any other occasion, Comte's orientation:

> The collective revolt of modern thinkers against all authorities of former times [he wrote to the Tsar] has gradually produced in each individual an habitual insurrection of the mind against the heart, tending to destroy all human discipline. The whole West is thus drifting towards a savage communism in which true liberty would be crushed under degrading Equality.[9]

Although he had on other occasions given grudging endorsement to the principle of the right of free inquiry, Comte here paid tribute to the Tsar for his "wise vigilance over the importation of Western books." He further expressed gratitude for what he designated as the "honorable distinction" accorded him by the

---

[8] *Système*, Eng. trans., I, p. 136.

[9] Comte published this letter in the preface to the third volume of his *Système*. See Eng. trans., III, p. xxv. Caird points out that Comte's condemnation of the individualistic theories of Rousseau is a parallel of the German idealists' attack upon the *Aufklärung*. René Caird, *The Social Philosophy and the Religion of Comte* (New York, 1885), p. 60.

fact that his books were not interfered with, and urged a more complete silencing of "an incompetent and subversive literature."

His interpretation of "subversive" embraced parliamentarism. "Universal suffrage," he declared in the same year, "extended to the proletariat even those intellectual and moral ravages which had hitherto been confined to the upper and middle classes." He regarded parliamentarism as peculiar to English political life and argued:

> ... its [parliamentarism's] official existence for one generation was more fatal to us [the French], than the tyranny of the empire; perverting as it did the intellect by accustoming it to constitutional sophisms, corrupting the heart by venal and anarchical habits, and degrading the character by growing familiarity with parliamentary tactics.[10]

It is in terms of this philosophy that Comte welcomed the *coup d'état* of Louis Bonaparte.[11] His insistent recourse to the symbol, order, was at one with the counter-revolutionary slogans of this critical period of French history. "The delusions of constitutionalism being finally set aside," he wrote, "the impossibility of terminating the revolution otherwise than by an effective alliance of Order and Progress is brought into full prominence."[12] How well this expressed the sentiments of the group which seized power, is seen by the similarity of the words which Baroche used on December 31, 1851, when he announced to Bonaparte the official results of the ballot that climaxed the *coup d'état:* "Restore the principle of authority in the country ... Wage unceasing war against those forces of anarchy that are attacking

[10] *Système*, Eng. trans., IV, p. xliii. He also declared that "Positivism rejects the metaphysical doctrine of the Sovereignty of the people. ... In the hands of the revolutionary party the doctrine is generally used to justify the right of insurrection," *ibid.*, I, p. 106.
[11] Comte hailed Louis Bonaparte as "the statesman who has just happily delivered us from the parliamentary regime," and spoke of the *coup d'état* as a "promising modification" destined to give new strength to positivism. He stated: "From its futile parliamentary commencement, fit only for the English transition, our republic passes by its own impetus to the dictatorial stage, the only one really suited to France, though equally suitable to the other Catholic populations, as may be seen in Spanish America." *Système*, Eng. trans., IV, p. xxxiv-vi.
[12] *Système*, Eng. trans., I, p. xxii.

the very basis of society ... Give back to the country ... order, stability and confidence."[13]

The contemporary political implications and consequences of this emphasis on order are clearly stated by Marx[14] in his *Eighteenth Brumaire of Louis Bonaparte:*

> During the June days, all other classes and parties united against the proletariat, styling themselves the Party of Order. The proletarians were stigmatized as the party of anarchy, socialism and communism. The Party of Order had "saved" society from the "enemies of society." It adopted the watchwords of the old society: Property, the Family, Religion, Order: and made these the passwords of its army. Under this sign you will conquer! said the Party to its counter-revolutionary crusaders. Thenceforward, whenever any one of the numerous parties which had marshalled themselves under that sign against the June insurgents, attempted a revolutionary struggle on behalf of its own class interests, it was defeated to the accompaniment of the cry: "Property, the Family, Religion, Order!". . . Every demand for the simplest kind of bourgeois financial reform, for the most everyday liberalism, for the most formal republicanism, for the most commonplace democracy, is punished as an "attack on society" and anathematized as "socialism."[15]

Comte opposed the end product, the hereditary Empire. But as one who had rationalized the *coup d'état* in the name of order, he helped prepare its path to victory over the Republic.

The role of Comte's ideas in this historical situation must certainly be regarded as an important framework of reference for

[13] René Arnaud, *La deuxième république et le second empire* (Paris, 1929; tr. by E. F. Buckley, London, 1930), p. 60.

[14] Marx, in letters, expressed himself specifically on Comte. On July 7, 1866, he wrote from London to Engels: "I am also studying Comte now as a sideline, because the English and the French make such a fuss about the fellow. What takes their fancy is the encyclopaedic touch, the synthesis. But this is miserable compared to Hegel. (Although Comte, as a professional mathematician and physicist, was superior to him, *i.e.*, superior in matters of detail, even here Hegel is infinitely greater as a whole.) And this positive rot appeared in 1832!" To Beesly he wrote on June 12, 1871: "And, by the way, you will allow me to observe that as a Party man I have always had a thoroughly hostile attitude towards Comte's philosophy, while as a scientific man I have a very poor opinion of it." K. Marx and F. Engels, *Correspondence, 1846–1895* (New York, 1935), p. 209, 313.

[15] Karl Marx, *The Eighteenth Brumaire of Louis Bonaparte* (New York, 1926), p. 33–34.

his sociological theories. The fact that it has been all but ignored is an item of further evidence of the need for Marxian studies in the field of history of social thought that will apply an institutional approach, alert to class forces, as contrasted with the current predominant practise of studying ideological traditions apart from their social settings.

The Liberal Views of Lester F. Ward

Grant Allen, the English publicist, once wrote aptly of Lester F. Ward, pioneer American sociologist, "Grasp is everything, and he grasps with an opposable thumb of no hesitation." It may truly be said of Ward that he exhibited none of the intellectual timidity that characterized many of his contemporaries. His work had an integrated purposefulness which gave it its stature. He was committed to the cause of intellectual freedom, and the diffusion of the results of that freedom, knowledge and social achievement, among the entire population. He did not hesitate to strike out at the forces which he conceived to be in the way of the "diffusion of knowledge among men." A friend in Washington, Frank Baker, editor of the *American Anthropologist*, wistfully replied to a rebuke by Ward in 1900, "I suppose I am a 'plastic' if by that you mean one who prefers to get along with people and things as we find them and make the best of a wicked world." Ward was intransigent in defense of his ideals, without being brash. He had convictions, and the unequivocating courage to defend them. In his moment of human history, this is perhaps the greatest lesson that a founder of sociology can transmit to his descendants.

The principles which he stoutly maintained should have met little opposition in terms of a functioning democracy. They arose out of his own experience in seeking to extricate himself from the poverty and ignorance that have ever been the lot of the common man. His youthful diary gives vivid documentation of the intensity of this struggle, and evidence that his experience was by no means unique. It is interesting in terms of the intellectual history of America, as yet unwritten, that his brother, C. Osborne Ward, who shared with him the failure in 1858 of the effort to make a living by manufacturing wagon hubs, chose a divergent road of intellectual and organizational expression. In 1869 Lester Ward, who was then employed as a government clerk in Washington, wrote the organizational call for the National Liberal Reform League, in which he appealed to

> ... all who favor the objects above set forth, under whatever name they prefer to be styled—Liberals, Skeptics, Infidels, Secularists, Utilitarians, Socialists, Positivists, Spiritualists, Deists, Theists, Pantheists, Atheists, Freethinkers, all who desire the mental emancipation of mankind from the trammels of superstition, and the dominion of priestcraft, to unite in this movement and join the National Liberal Reform League without delay *(Glimpses of the Cosmos.* New York: Putnam's, 1913, I, 40).

About the same time (1870) his brother wrote *The Great Labor Party.* Lester Ward, influenced by Comte, had stressed social change through education. C. Osborne Ward, who had read and met Marx, advocated social change through the organized power of the working class.

Comte set the evolutionary pattern of Ward's thinking, but Ward added to it the peculiar muscular quality that was his. The nature of his opinions on social evolution is best expressed in a passage in *Applied Sociology:*

> One after another the bulwarks of oppression—slavery, serfdom, feudalism, despotism, monarchy in its true sense, nobility and priestly rule—fell; the middle or business class, otherwise called *bourgeoisie* and third estate, gained the ascendant, which it still holds, and political freedom was attained.
>
> So all important did this issue seem that throughout the eighteenth century and down to near our own time it was confidently believed that, with the overthrow of political oppression and the attainment of political freedom, the world would enter upon the great millennium of universal prosperity, well-being, and happiness. But this was far from being the case. As sages predicted, events have proved that their remains another step to be taken. Another stage must be reached before any considerable degree of the hopes

that were entertained can be realized. This stage is that of *social freedom*. The world is to-day in the throes of this third struggle. Military and royal oppression have been overthrown. Slavery, serfdom, feudalism, have disappeared. The power of the nobility and the priesthood has been broken. The civilized world is democratic, no matter by what name its governments are called. The people rule themselves by their sovereign votes. And yet never in the history of the world was there manifested greater unrest or greater dissatisfaction with the state of things. National freedom and political freedom have been achieved. Social freedom remains to be achieved.[1]

Ward believed that this "social freedom" was to be achieved by enlightenment through education, and thought that it was the function of sociology to propound this fact. He contended that "Society has never and nowhere been so organized to transmit the products of its achievement to more than a fraction of its members"[2] and that

> Applied sociology differs from other applied sciences in embracing all men instead of a few. Most of the philosophy which claims to be scientific, if it is not actually pessimistic in denying the power of man to ameliorate his condition, is at least oligocentric in concentrating all effort on a few of the supposed elite of mankind and ignoring or despising the great mass that have not proved their inherent superiority . . . whatever may be the differences in their faculties, all men have an equal right to the exercise and enjoyment of the faculties that they have.[3]

This is clearly doctrine within the tradition of the Declaration of Independence. Yet, when Professor Edward L. Thorndike reviewed *Applied Sociology*, he attacked such views as "intellectual communism." They have since been repeatedly criticized as "equalitarian" and as ignoring individual differences. A careful reading of Ward would show at once the lack of validity of this criticism. When he argues that educational opportunity be given to submerged peoples Ward writes:

[1] *Applied Sociology*, New York, 1906, p. 27.
[2] *Ibid.*, p. 96.
[3] *Ibid.*, p. 7.

This does not at all imply that all men are equal intellectually. It only insists that intellectual inequality is common to all classes, and is as great among the members of the completely emerged tenth as it is between that class and the completely submerged tenth. . . . Class distinctions in society are wholly artificial, depend entirely on environing conditions, and are in no sense due to differences in native capacity. Differences in native capacity exist and are as great as they have ever been pictured, but they exist in all classes alike.[4]

Thorndike's criticism of Ward went further than an application of an epithet. He declared: "This semi-acceptance of the common philanthropic view of public education as the preventer of crime and crutch for the weak, as the direct helper of the many through changes in them rather than their indirect helper through changes in the few whose increased achievements have demonstrably brought immense social returns, is the one feature of Professor Ward's book which may do real harm."[5]

This controversy over the function of education is not of yesterday but of today and tomorrow. It is, in its most dramatic form, typified in the conflict between the fascist theory of the elite and the educational policy derived therefrom, and the democratic theory of education. It finds reflection in the eugenic controversy, in which Ward participated, and which has continued. Although the eugenists have been generally repudiated by the geneticists and have been practically routed from the scientific field, they still find expression in schools of education. The tempest over the constancy of the IQ, which tends to be low in groups of individuals deprived of educational opportunity, is blowing over with the tradition of Ward emerging triumphant, as evidence, in contrast with assertion, accumulates. Yet in this moment in history an asseveration in the educability of the common man and woman, and in the liberating influence of knowledge widely disseminated, is still a militant slogan, for democracy is still on the defensive against those who would abort its functioning.

[4] *Idem.*, p. 100.
[5] *The Bookman*, 1907, vol. 24, p. 291.

The critics of Ward from the left do not in any sense depreciate the value of education. In fact, a reading of Ward's correspondence will reveal the fact that the bulk of his support during his lifetime came from socialist groups.

Their criticism of Ward arises from the fact that they have felt that such educational objectives were impossible to realize under the existing class structure of society. One will search in vain through Ward's complete works to find any statement as to how his educational program was to be instituted, or how his substitute for socialism, "sociocracy" (defined as "the scientific control of the social forces by the collective mind of society for its advantage"), was to be established. In fact, he at times gives clear and vigorous expression to the uses of education by class interests, which might well have caused him to modify his view that education alone would suffice:

> After the formation of caste, the inequalities among men were greatly increased and it was easy for a few of the higher class to keep the mass of mankind in subjection. This was accomplished primarily of course by force, but forms of deception were also constantly resorted to. The idea of the essential inferiority of the subject class must be steadily kept in the minds of that class. The least suspicion that this was not true would greatly disturb the social state. It was therefore a settled policy to enforce this idea, and a great variety of subterfuges were adopted to this end. At later stages, and even at the present time, those artificial social inequalities which enable the prosperous classes to thrive at the expense of the proletariat, and of the less favored classes where no true proletariat exists, are chiefly maintained through the systematic deception of the latter. . . . Deception may almost be called the foundation of business. . . . In politics the practice of deception does not differ as much as is generally supposed from that of business. While principle is loudly proclaimed from the stump, interest lies behind it all. . . . Back of the politician and demagogue lie the "vested interests," and these it is that are "making public opinion." It is customary in these days to laud the newspaper, but, except for the little news that it contains, which is to its managers a secondary consideration, the newspaper is simply an organ of deception. Every prominent newspaper is the defender of some

interest and everything it says is directly or indirectly (and most effective when indirect) in support of that interest.[6]

Yet Ward never advocated, as have Marxists, a change in the ownership of the instruments of production that they might function in the interests of all of society instead of in the interests of a few, and thus permit education to function likewise for the benefit of all the people. His program always remained nebulous, however progressive, as in the final pages of *Pure Sociology*, when he declared:

> The question is being seriously considered why society as a whole, and all mankind from the highest to the lowest, should not profit by the brilliant achievements of the elite of mankind. Inventors and scientific discoverers are generous, and if they could dictate the policy of the world the results would be freely distributed and completely socialized. All they would ask would be a modest competency for themselves and their families and a decent legacy for their heirs. Alas! many of them never obtain even this. The results are taken up by the great economic world, as, indeed they should be and must be, if they are ever realized, and society only secures so much as cannot be prevented from filtering through the economic sieve which is often very fine. The great world movement of socialization is nothing else than the gradual recognition of this by society in its collective capacity, and the tardy, often fitful, inconsistent, and uneven, but yet sure and steady determination ultimately to claim and to have its full share in the achievement of the human race.[7]

Likewise the last part of *Applied Sociology*, which was supposed to be the culminating formulation of his program, is, by all odds, the most ineffectual writing of his career.

Already in 1892, E. A. Ross had made strictures of his educational program. In a letter dated February 22, 1892, he wrote to Ward: "We want less injustice, oppression, parasitism and this is secured by more education. Should there not, then, along with developing intelligence to give us command over natural and social forces, go increasingly a developing sympathy to prevent

[6] *Pure Sociology: A Treatise on the Origin and Spontaneous Development of Society.* [2nd ed.] New York, 1903, 486-7.
[7] *Ibid.*, pp. 571-2.

the (socially) costly pursuit of individual gain? It seems to me this education to stir and stimulate the dormant sympathies of individuals is something different from the education you plead for."[8]

Alfred Russell Wallace, too, had written him in 1898, in a letter dated October 12:

> What a terrible thing it is that under the present social system, the vast majority of the workers, however steady and well educated, have, and can have, no prospect but a life of toil and an old age of poverty or worse—and this when the work actually done, if properly organized, would provide not only necessaries but comforts for all, with ample leisure and a restful old age. Surely the coming century must see the end of the existing system of cutthroat competition, and wealth-production based on the misery and starvation of the millions![9]

Others, also, wrote in similar strain. But Ward to the end believed that not the private ownership of productive property but the inequality in the distribution of information and knowledge was the cause of the cleavage of society into an exploiting and an exploited class. Ward was on occasion emphatically critical of capitalism. In 1895, in an article entitled "Plutocracy and Paternalism,"[10] he wrote:

> Nothing is more obvious today than the signal inability of capital and private enterprise to take care of themselves unaided by the state; and while they are incessantly denouncing "paternalism"— by which they mean the claim of the defenseless laborer and artisan to a share in this lavish state protection, they are all the while besieging legislatures for relief from their own incompetency, and "pleading the baby act" through a trained body of lawyers and lobbyists. The dispensing of national pap to this class should rather be called "maternalism" to which a square, open and dignified paternalism would be infinitely preferable.

In the following year he wrote of himself to Ross: "No one is more anxious to throttle the money power." In *Pure Sociology*

[8] B. J. Stern, Ed. The Ward-Ross Correspondence, 1891–1896. *Amer. Sociol. Rev.*, 1938, vol. 3, [3], 362.
[9] B. J. Stern. Letters of Alfred Russell Wallace to Lester F. Ward. *Sci. Mon.*, 1935, vol. 40, 379.
[10] *Forum*, 1895, vol. 20, 200–210.

he declared that "there has never been a time when the laborer received a just share of the wealth produced."

But he remained, as did the utopian socialists, purely a negative critic of capitalism, and a friend of labor who believed that "nearly all the real amelioration, and it is considerable, that has taken place in the condition of the lower classes has been due to . . . disinterested sympathy on the part of members of the upper classes who have more to lose than to gain by it."[11]

Nevertheless, Lester Ward gave hope to many through his stress of the potentialities of achievement of the common man. He once wrote: "The true crown of a system of scientific philosophy is not an Ethics which seeks to restrain and circumscribe activity, but a Sociology which aims at the liberation of action through the directive agency of intelligence." For this orientation rather than for any specific theory Ward is remembered today.

[11] *Pure Sociology,* p. 93.

From *The Science Monthly* Vol. LXXI, No. 2, (August, 1950), pp. 102–104.

Franz Boas as Scientist and Citizen

When Franz Boas, the dean of American anthropologists, died at the age of eighty-four, on December 21, 1942, he was at lunch discussing race theory with Paul Rivet, noted French refugee anthropologist. This was a fitting climax to his life, for it is by his critical writings on race that Boas is best known internationally.

Physical anthropologists before Boas had talked glibly of races, and systematically classified the peoples of the earth on the basis of a few arbitrary measurements. Even now this practice has not by any means ceased. One of Boas' chief contributions lay in the fact that he revealed the basic hazards involved in this process.

Boas entered the arena of physical anthropology during his early work at Clark University, in association with G. Stanley Hall. He was interested in the influence of environment on growth, a subject which continued to occupy his attention throughout his life. He testifies that when he turned from the question of individual growth to a consideration of racial problems, he was shocked by the formalism of the work in this field. Nobody had tried to find the answer to the questions as to why certain measurements were taken, why they were considered significant, whether the traits they measured were subject to environmental influences or were exclusively hereditary. His interest remained focused on these problems, and until his death he made repeated rigidly critical studies, and wrote many monographs and articles, elucidating the need for more precise definitions, methods and generalizations in the field of race.

In this article, I shall not discuss the various significant individual studies in which he engaged, nor abstract their specific findings. I have instead sought to distill from these studies the important generalizations that, through Boas' persistent efforts, have now come to be part of the arsenal used by scholars in their refutations of the unscientific and socially deleterious judgments of the racialists. These propositions are presented here in categorical form without the wealth of data which Boas' researches have contributed to substantiate them. Such a presentation carries with it an air of dogmatism because the summary theoretical conclusions are abstracted from their supporting evidence. This is anything but characteristic of Boas' presentation, for he was cautious to the extreme in his conclusions.

The theoretical generalizations which emerge from Boas' work on race, I find to be as follows:

—When the term "race" is used scientifically, it applies exclusively to large groups of individuals with common genetic ancestry, and hence of a similar anatomical type.

—Anatomical types, languages and cultures of peoples are independent in their development and therefore classifications of mankind along each of these lines must necessarily differ from one another. There can be, for example, no "Aryan" race, for Aryan is a language classification, not an anatomical one; nor can there be a "Nordic culture."

—Heredity, environment and selection are the factors which stabilize or differentiate anatomical types.

—Similar types living in remote countries may be related genetically, may be the result of independent mutations, or of comparable response to comparable environments. Only knowledge of the history of each type can determine which is the correct answer.

—Negroes, Mongoloids and Whites became isolated in times sufficiently remote to permit the development of far-reaching differences in certain bodily traits.

—There is no scientific justification for classifying any one of these human types as more primitive on an evolutionary scale. They all represent specializations in different directions, with some features in each group closer, and others farther removed, from the anthropoid apes.

—The migration of peoples has played an important rôle in

determining the characteristics of anatomical types because it has influenced the degree of inbreeding or outbreeding.

—Race mixture is not harmful. On the basis of the anatomical features and the health record of mixed populations, there is no evidence to justify the assumption that there are unfavorable results either in the first or later generations of offspring.

—Man is a domesticated animal. He shares with other domesticated animals great variability of bodily traits, particularly of such traits as size, pigmentation and hair.

—The human organism is responsive in its development to environmental influences. Among the instable bodily traits are stature, weight, cephalic index and facial index, which are most frequently used as the basis of race classification, under the faulty assumption that they are fixed only by heredity.

—Social selection influences the nature of the anatomical type through cultural concepts of physical beauty and through traditions which determine mating and thereby help to preserve or stamp out certain types, e.g., red-heads and albinos.

—Social selection is also exercised by differential birth and mortality rates determined by social standards and religious codes.

—A racial type is based on averages and so has no actual reality. Individual variability is characteristic of all human types, with diversified ranges among different groups. No individual can be considered as representative of any existing group, because the members of all groups vary markedly among themselves.

—Even in the most rigidly inbred communities, considerable differences in family lines have been found. Heredity exists solely in the distinct family lines not in the racial group.

—Because of differences between family lines, and fraternal differences within families, there is no limit to the number of subtypes that can be distinguished within each of the major divisions of mankind, depending upon the criteria used.

—The criteria used to define types are selected arbitrarily. A type is an abstraction of striking peculiarities of the masses of individuals, which are assumed to be combined in a single individual. What the striking peculiarities are, depends upon the previous experience of the observer.

—Present knowledge of the manner in which bodily traits are transmitted by heredity, and of the effects of the environment on the development of the human organism, indicates that it is futile to attempt to segregate out the constituent elements of a population of mixed, but historically unknown, descent.

—Classifications made upon the basis of a selected number of traits describe how these traits are distributed statistically, but they do not give us the right to differentiate between racial strains, because of lack of information on the degree of fixity of the traits discussed.

—Similarity of a few traits of different peoples does not prove that they are descended from like stock because there are often other traits not so readily observed that may prove distinctness of origin.

—Human populations inhabiting adjoining territories overlap in regard to most features, so that it is not possible to assign with certainty any one individual to a definite group.

—Bodily forms and functions in each generation are dependent upon social habits which influence the organism, e.g., the position of the lower jaw, facial expression, gait and gesture.

—The physiological functioning of the human heart, endocrine glands, digestive and other organs vary according to different physical and cultural environments.

—The rates of sexual maturity and of the development of teeth vary, depending upon the cultural environment, the rate of the higher income groups being accelerated as compared to that of the poor.

—No convincing proof has been given that the observed differences in mental behavior of peoples are structurally determined, while on the other hand modifications of various aspects of personality of members of the same race who live under changed condition has been proved.

—Culture is a cumulative historical product, not a function of race. Cultural inferiority and superiority are therefore to be explained historically and not biologically.

Some of Boas' views here summarized have been accepted by many scientists who were at first reluctant to endorse them. Several have now become well-nigh axiomatic among scientists.

Others, however, are still ignored by anthropologists, sociologists and biologists, either because these writers have not been able to disentangle themselves from premature generalizations of the earlier geneticists, or because they yield to the insistent requests for facile race classifications, or because they identify themselves psychologically with the apologetics of race dominance. To the degree that the propositions here outlined become universally accepted, we shall have a firmer scientific foundation for political policy in relation to other races. They offer significant points of departure for further researches and valuable guides for governmental policy both during the war, and in working out the post-war peace.

The generalizations here summarized give a clear answer to those who criticize Boas for not presenting a cumulative book on the races of man, in the tradition of Deniker[1] and in the fashion of the recent book by Coon.[2] Boas clearly felt that such a work would inevitably be unscientific because of the lack of complete historical records to reconstruct the biological relationships of existing populations. His position was critical and destructive of the established facile categories of race classification. It might, however, have been possible for him to compile what he regarded as the authentic historical records of racial groups in so far as they were available, so that his approach would not be so negative.[3] But his was primarily an analytical, statistical method of the physical scientist, not that of the historian.

A more important criticism might be directed to the fact that although Boas worked on the materials of race for decades he never established a science of the systematics of man, comparable to the important work of the geneticist Mayr.[4] Boas' difficulties in synthesizing his findings, which he acknowledged to his stu-

[1] J. Deniker, *The Races of Man* (tr. from French, London, 1900).
[2] Carleton S. Coon, *The Races of Europe* (New York, 1939). See my critical review of this book in SCIENCE & SOCIETY v (Spring, 1941), p. 179–81, and of his discussion of the racial identity of the Jew, *ibid.*, vi (Fall, 1942), p. 389–90.
[3] His references to the migrations of peoples, for example, were based on the popular book of A. C. Haddon, *The Wanderings of People* (Cambridge, 1912) and not on any original compilation of data from historical records.
[4] Ernst Mayr, *Systematics and the Origin of Species* (New York, 1942).

dents, resulted in an emphasis upon the fallacies and rationalizations made by others on race, rather than upon positive constructive formulations.

It is erroneous, however, to suppose that Boas' position was entirely negative. He shied away from broad historical reconstructions of the development of modern human types, and when he presented them he did so with many qualifications. But it is possible to establish, from his writings, a broadly conceived racial history of modern man. In the following paragraphs I shall give the substance of his findings.

The Development of Modern Human Types

According to Boas, two fundamentally different forms developed early in man's history from an unknown common ancestor, the Negroid type and the Mongoloid type. The former spread all around the Indian Ocean. The latter found his habitat in Northern and Central Asia, and also reached Europe and the New World. The uniformity of these types ceased with their wide spread over the continents, and with their isolation in small communities. Some divergent developments of the Negroid type are the Bushmen, Negroes and Papuans. The Mongoloid type is represented by the American Indians, East Asiatics, Malays and Whites. The varieties in each group developed in similar ways. The Mongoloid type exhibited the tendency to loss of pigmentation of skin, eyes and hair; to a strong development of the nose, and a reduction of the size of face. Thus types like the Europeans, the Ainu of Japan and some Indian tribes of the Pacific coast exhibit striking similarities in form. This tendency to parallel modification of type indicates early relationship and furnishes the major support of the classification of the whites as a variation of the Mongoloid type.

The differences between the major types and also between the local subtypes became more marked during the periods of isolation that led to inbreeding. For example, in the long interim during which the aboriginal Americans were separated from their related groups in the Old World, independent development of types occurred. Family resemblances between Asiatics and American Indians persisted, but new lines of growth developed. As the

Indians spread over the two Americas there was a further sharp individualization of local types. As these types slowly increased in numbers they came in contact with one another, and through mixture and migration, a new distribution of distinct types and colors developed over the continent. The color of the skin varied from light to almost chocolate brown; the form of the head from rounded to elongated; the form of the face, from very wide to very narrow; the color of the hair from black to dark brown and even blond, from straight to wavy; the lips were on the whole moderately full; the nose varied from the eagle nose of the Mississippi Indian to the concave nose of some South American and northwest Americans. Each local area represented a fairly homogeneous picture, but above all the diversity, this continental type was distinguished from other continental types.[5]

This illustration of differentiation in the development of physical types on the American continent may be duplicated for other continents as well. In Europe, there were migrations from prehistoric times forward, which has made European types highly complex in origin. There were, however, intermittent periods of isolation of populations in different areas which led to differentiation of types. Boas often used the history of the Spanish population as illustrative. The earliest population known was the Iberian. These intermixed with Phoenician and Greek colonists. Then came the era of Celtic migration when these tribes entered Spain from France. Roman colonization was followed by the invasion of Germanic tribes some of which came from the regions of the Black Sea. Later there were migrations from North Africa, particularly during the period of the dominance of the Moors. Large numbers of Jews also settled in Spain and intermarried with other groups in the population. In medieval times, as the population became isolated and stable and as the Jews and the Moors were expelled, the physical type became relatively fixed. The Spanish people, however stable as they may now be, contain elements derived from practically all parts of Europe and from Northern Africa.

All other parts of Europe are similarly peopled by mixed groups

---

[5] "The History of the American Race," *Annals of the New York Academy of Sciences*, XXI (March, 1912), p. 177–83.

that develop specific types in isolation. In Germany, for example, where the racialist doctrine has been made the cornerstone of Nazi theory, local types are particularly diverse, in different regions. "The East German," wrote Boas, "is closer to his Polish neighbor than to the Frisian; the Tyrolese shows more similarity to the East Alpine Slav than to the North German, the Rhinelander more to the neighboring Frenchman than to the German in more distant parts."[6]

On all continents periods of relative stability led to the development of local types and these in turn mixed with other local types when they came into contact with them in periods of migration. Until the age of exploration in the sixteenth century and the period of the commercial and industrial revolutions which followed, continental developments continued to be distinct one from the other. Then the migrations were not only accelerated within continents but became intercontinental, and distinctly unrelated types that had long been isolated from one another came in contact and intermixed in different areas at varying rates.

A few generalizations emerge from these findings. In the first place the physical types that are now identified in the world population are products of inbreeding of formerly diversified stocks, during periods of relative stability. In northern and central Europe, this stability developed after individual hereditary landholding was substituted for the earlier forms of agricultural life, and with the attachment of the serf to the soil which he inhabited. During the earlier period in northern Europe when Celtic and Germanic tribes moved from place to place, mixture of types occurred. When feudal organization displaced tribal organization, those families of the population who were proprietors of the soil, or otherwise attached to the soil, became stable settlers and intermixture between peoples of distant parts of the continent was infrequent. Within a village where landed property was handed down from father to son, and where the wife was habitually selected from the same village, pronounced local types developed through inbreeding. The differences among the ancestors still made themselves felt, however, in the individuals composing each family, for the physical attributes of the body

[6] *Aryans and Non-Aryans* (New York, 1934), p. 8.

are not so closely bound together that they are inherited as a whole; the characteristics of one's long line of ancestors recur in ever new combinations.

The types which thus emerged derived their characteristics not only because of the inbreeding of closely related types over long periods of time. Their characteristics became defined in part also because of adaptation of the types to the physical and cultural environments. The characteristics of the environment have exerted significant influence upon bodily form and functions of man. This is contrary to the frequent assumption that the features of bodily development are absolutely stable and that modern human types are "permanent forms" which can be traced far back even to the beginning of the last geological period.

Boas propounded independently of Eugene Hahn, the theory of man as a domesticated animal. His view was that man domesticated himself about 50,000 years ago by inventing fire, weapons, tools and shelter. The use of fire enabled him to obtain a fairly regular and ample food supply by permitting the use of vegetable foods that would have been poisonous if eaten uncooked, and at the same time changed materially the demands made upon the digestive organs. Weapons enlarged man's power to get food while tools and shelter enabled him to protect himself against excessive cold and heat and so modified essentially the course of individual development and at the same time the conditions of propagation. The spiral hair of the Bushman and the smooth hair of the Mongol, the blond hair and blue eyes of the north European and the deep pigmentation of the Negro, the tallness of the Scotsman and the dwarfish stature of the pygmy, are variations paralleled among domesticated animals, while they are absent among wild animals. Since these traits are a result of domestication, they have developed independently in different areas. Therefore, when blondness is found among groups of people separated from one another geographically, it does not mean that these blond peoples are related to one another genetically as the Nazi racialists have argued, and as many anthropologists have taken for granted.

Boas also stressed the fact that in each generation the environment had pronounced effect upon the development of the human type. This recognition of environmental influences does not assume the inheritance of acquired characteristics for modification of the bodily form of the individual can take place without any modification of the germ plasm. In one of his best known studies, Boas compared immigrants born in Europe with their descendants born in New York City, and found that the latter types differed from their parents in head-form as in other traits.[7] He also compared the head-forms of city populations of Italy, and the rural population in the areas surrounding the cities, and found that the variability of head-form in each city was smaller than would be found in a population in which the constituent genetic types were present had there not been environmental modification.[8] Other researches by him revealed a change in the head-form of Puerto Ricans because of environmental conditions.[9] These findings upset the traditional classifications of races which had been formulated by many anthropologists on the assumption that head-form was stable and unaffected by environmental changes.[10] Boas stimulated many researches along these lines

[7] *Changes in Bodily Form of Descendants of Immigrants* (New York, 1912). See *Race, Language and Culture*, p. 60–75.
[8] Franz Boas and Helene M. Boas, "The Head-Forms of Italians as Influenced by Heredity and Environment." *American Anthropologist*, N.S., xv (1913), p. 163–188.
[9] Franz Boas, "New Evidence in Regard to the Instability of Human Types," *Proceedings of the National Academy of Sciences*, II (December, 1916), p. 713–17.
[10] Because of their effects upon race classification these studies were attacked but they have been repeatedly corroborated by independent investigations. Hrdlicka found the width of the face of Americans of the fourth generation—that is to say, of the descendants of Europeans who had no foreign born ancestor after the fourth generation back—was materially decreased as compared to the width of the face among European types. Shapiro's elaborate study of the Japanese in Hawaii, led him to conclude: "The assumption of stability in man's physical characters is no longer tenable without qualification. Indeed from the evidence of the Japanese in Hawaii man emerges as a dynamic organism which under certain circumstances is capable of very substantial changes within a single generation. Not only may migrant populations undergo modification when transposed to a sufficiently different environment, but physical changes may also occur in fixed populations if their environments alter in the course of time." H. L. Shapiro, *Migration and Environment: A Study of the Physical Characteristics of the Japanese Immigrants to Hawaii and the Effects of Environment on their Descendants* (London, 1939), p. 198 f.

among his students.[11] His notable "Report on an Anthropometric Investigation of the Population of the United States"[12] served as a storehouse of subjects for Ph.D. theses and for other researches.

It was his fundamental recognition of the instability of the human type, that led Boas to recognize the potent effects of the social environment. In academic circles and in popular literature, the influence of the biologists who stressed heredity had been extremely strong, and the eugenists had had for years almost a monopoly on books and articles dealing with the nature-nurture controversy. Such views have always served well as rationalizations for the prevailing stratifications in society. They have furnished apologetics for dominance and likewise arguments against social legislation that would improve standards of living. It must be credited in large measure to Boas and his students that a considerable modification of the thought of the nation has taken place in recent years in this important field of controversy.[13]

One of the crucial tests of the relative importance of nature and nurture is found in connection with the Negro's position in society. Boas repeatedly wrote to show that the status of the Negro was not to be taken as an index of his abilities. One of the most eloquent utterances on this subject was made six months before his death:

> What right have we to any judgment in regard to their [the Negroes'] ability or character when we first attempted to break their spirit in slavery and then continued oppression by economic discrimination and social ostracism? Anyone who is familiar with the history of Africa before its subjugation by the Europeans knows the industrial skill, the artistic genius, the political ability of the Negro. In every region from West Africa through the Sudan to South Africa we have proof of it. . . .

[11] Such studies as David Efron's *Gesture and Environment* (New York, 1941) and Otto Klineberg's *Negro Intelligence and Selective Migration* (New York, 1935) were written under Boas' direction. Ruth Benedict's *Race, Science and Politics* (New York, 1940), the book which I prepared with Alain Locke, *When Peoples Meet: A Study in Race and Culture Contact* (New York, 1942) and Melville J. Herskovits' works on the Negro are among the many books which took their point of departure from Boas' work.

[12] *Journal of the American Statistical Association*, XVIII (June, 1922), p. 181–209.

[13] See also p. 316 below.

However, we are more concerned with the present. How can we expect the Negro race to take its proper place in our culture as long as economic and social discrimination persist? We must demand equality, not equality on paper, but equal rights in life, equal opportunities for education, equal economic opportunities, and a breakdown of social barriers that oppress even those who in character and achievement are often infinitely superior to those who will not acknowledge for them the claim that is so often heralded as the basis of our society—the claim that all men are born with equal rights.[14]

Boas' teachings on race have thus provided a powerful ideological instrument for buttressing democratic sentiment on domestic issues. Similarly, in the war for the survival of democratic nations, they have offered scientific evidence to refute Nazi racialism and the cults of "Nordicism" and "Aryanism" which have served as battlecries for predatory destruction of the Jews and as incitements for territorial aggression. It was for this reason that the books of this distinguished scientist were destroyed by the Nazis in the book-burning of 1933 at Kiel, the very city whose University had granted him his Ph.D. degree in 1881, and had only a few years before Hitler's rise to power bestowed on him one of his many honorary degrees. This act only served to give a wider audience to Boas' views. From an author previously known primarily to scientists, his work on race now became of interest to the far wider circles of laymen united in a struggle against the irrationalities of fascism.

THE REJECTION OF GEOGRAPHIC DETERMINISM

Boas not only rejected the racialist interpretation of history and of human behavior, but also the doctrine of geographic determinism, which has had wide currency in the United States as well as in other countries. This is all the more significant because Boas' first contact with anthropology came about through geography. His first field trip was among the Central Eskimos around Cumberland Sound and Davis Strait in 1883–84. Then, under the influence of Ratzel, he had actually expected to demonstrate geographical determinism, but his field work convinced him

[14] "The Myth of Race," *New Masses* (July 29, 1941), p. 6.

otherwise. Boas pointed out that a variety of cultural forms occurs at various periods in the same physical environment and that therefore environment alone can not be said to determine specific cultural forms. He saw the geographic environment as a limiting rather than a creative force in the development of culture. He pointed out, for example, that the absence of wood on the steppes, of stone on coral islands, of fish in the desert, limit to some degree the cultural development in these areas. Fertility of the soil does not produce agriculture, but merely facilitates its development when the art has become known. The presence of domesticable animals does not necessarily mean their domestication, nor does the availability of iron ore mean the development of metallurgy. The occurrence of clay does not make pottery inevitable. Boas' position on geographic determinism is that the environment can only act upon a culture and the result of environmental influences is dependent upon the culture upon which it acts.

The impact of geographic factors upon cultures is nevertheless recognized to be important. The periodicity of the seasons, the habits of the animals, the configuration of the country all exert their influence on periods of activity and of leisure, on the location of villages, on the movements of tribes, on types of transportation. The size of the community is affected by the food supply, when food products are not imported, and so exerts an indirect influence over social and political organization. The environment also affects the content of traditional tales, religious beliefs and practices, e.g., the festivals connected with first fish and the harvest. The degree of geographical isolation of a people also facilitates or retards cultural contact and the diffusion of ideas and inventions. As man's knowledge increases, Boas points out, he is increasingly capable of transcending the limitations of the physical environment and of manipulating it to his economic and social needs.

The Influences of the Economic Factors

In their rejection of racial and geographic determinism, Boas and the historical materialists are in complete accord. It is in his discussions of the interrelations of cultural elements, that his views and those of the Marxists tend to diverge in some aspects. In appraising the role of economic factors in culture, Boas' formulations vary. When he is dealing with an analysis of concrete situations his views parallel those of the historical materialists; but his theoretical formulations differ.

Boas' clearest and most specific presentation of the relations between economic factors and other aspects of culture was published in 1930, in his article "Anthropology" in the *Encyclopaedia of the Social Sciences*.[15] Because of their importance, I shall quote relevant passages in considerable detail.

He first shows the importance of man's occupations in determining other aspects of culture:

> The occupations by means of which man obtains his food and shelter determine the directions in which his discoveries and inventions develop.[16] The sea-hunting Eskimo has developed his boats and his weapons because his whole life is based on the procuring of sea mammals for food and for heat; not that the specific forms are determined by the economic occupation, but the concentration of attention upon this occupation gives the opportunity for new achievements. The cattle breeder and agriculturists acquire their experiences and make their technical inventions in those domains of human activity upon which their attention is concentrated.
>
> The amount of leisure depends upon economic conditions. The more easily food and shelter are secured the more ready is man to devote his time to play with hands, tools and mind. The complexity of cultural activities increases, therefore, with favorable economic conditions.[17]

[15] "Anthropology," *Encyclopaedia of the Social Sciences*, II p. 100 f.

[16] See also his statement that inventions "are all the result of acute observation and of practical experience," and that primitive man "is familiar with the habits of animals and with the life of plants, so far as his practical experience brings him in contact with them. The regular movements of the sun and moon are known and lead to calendar systems based on the celestial phenomena, but closely related to seasonal occupations. Measures of space and time are the more elaborate, the more extensive their use in technical occupations and in the regulation of daily occupations. Counting is the more elaborate the more important the number of equal objects in everyday life." *Ibid.*, p. 93.

[17] Earlier in the same article, Boas writes: "When the necessity of procuring food and shelter does not fill all the time of waking life, either

As he continues, he relates rank and other types of social differentiation, and the organization of the family to economic conditions:

> In a region of ample food supply in which the maintenance of life depends solely upon physical skill and in which a sparse population allows everyone to find a productive hunting ground, a differentiation according to rank or wealth is not likely to occur, except in so far as orphans, widows and old people may be thrown upon the mercy of their friends and relatives. When the produce of the country does not allow all to share equally, when specially favored spots are claimed as property, the equality is disturbed and economic and social differentiations are found. Thus the development of property concepts, the organization of the family[18] and of occupations, the occurrence of societies with social and religious functions are all intimately related to economic conditions. The forms of organization cannot be explained as due to economic necessity, but their development may be favored or hindered by economic needs while they themselves always influence economic life.

Ritualistic behavior and intertribal relations are likewise strongly influenced by economic considerations:

> Whenever the transfer of property involves future obligations on the part of the recipient, the transaction is public and gives opportunity for the development of ritualistic behavior. African marriages,

---

because the food supply is plentiful and easily obtained, or because the ample supply of one season is laid up and man lives in the intervening season on accumulated stores, the leisure time is spent in a variety of occupations. The total amount of tangible property that constitutes the possession of a household depends largely on leisure time, on the permanence of the abode, and in migratory tribes, upon facilities of transportation. The variety of household goods increases with the amount of leisure time. Besides this, time becomes available for activities that do not serve the immediate needs of life, and complications of technique, social gatherings and religious rites of various kinds have opportunity to develop," *ibid.*, p. 89.

[18] Boas illustrates this in his interpretation of the sororate and levirate: "Since marriage is always accompanied by a transfer of property rights, often by exchanges between two families, or presents or payments made by the groom's family to the wife's family, the relationship between the husband and the wife is involved in these transactions. In case of payments made by the groom's family, the deceased wife's sister may be claimed as a substitute; or after the death of the husband his brother or son from another unrelated wife may claim the widow. In other cases the deceased husband's brother may be claimed as a substitute by the widow's family," *ibid.*, p. 87.

the potlatch of Northwest America, and the elaborate Kula Ring of the Trobriands are examples.

War is often a means to the acquisition of necessary or desired property. Peaceful contact is commonly based on mutual economic interest, on the regulated exchange of produce which may lead to the establishment of regular markets, as in Africa or on the islands in Bering Strait where Asiatic and American tribes meet for barter.

The nature of the economy is likewise seen to have decisive effect upon the density of the population, which in turn influences the development of the culture: [19]

> An Eskimo tribe that relies upon sea hunting, or a California tribe that lives on acorns, cannot increase permanently beyond the limit that can be sustained in the most unfavorable years. These limits are higher when agriculture or herding occur. When the food supply is ample, the density of a population may increase, provided there are no other checks like war, infanticide, or disease. If, at the same time, the food supply is seasonal or so easily secured that time for leisure remains, the total number of individuals who can devote their time to occupations other than the mere obtaining of food and shelter increases, and opportunities for the development of new cultural traits may be observed. Political organization depends upon the size of social units and upon the density of population.

Similarly the nature of the economy precluded or permitted the development of graphic or plastic arts, while music and literature are possible under all economies: [20]

> The conditions for the development of music and literature are different from those of the graphic or plastic arts, because they require a different kind of leisure. While hunting and food gathering, man cannot work with his hands. The time for technical occupation is when he is at rest. On the other hand, the imagination from which sprang music and poetry is at work at all times when attention is not concentrated on a particular object. For this reason even those tribes that are poor in industrial and art products like the Bushmen, have a large body of music, poetry and prose tradition.

[19] *Ibid.*, p. 99 f.
[20] *Ibid.*, p. 90.

In his theoretical formulations, Boas makes statements that are inconsistent with these findings. The historical materialist does not disagree with him when he dissociates himself repeatedly from "economic determinism." Boas might have felt that in so doing he was likewise dissociating himself from Marxism, and there is little doubt that some of his students interpreted his formulations in this light. There is, in fact, no evidence that Boas ever made an effort to determine, from the sources, what the Marxian position is. This is not surprising, however, for Boas never manifested interest in economic, sociological, philosophical or historical literature not directly related to anthropological research. He regarded himself as a technician, not as a social philosopher, and in spite of his extracurricular interest in social movements, and his known sensitiveness as a citizen to current political developments, he was indifferent to the theoretical writings of other social scientists and did not cite them in his lectures or books.

His rejection of economic determinism takes several forms. In the first place he states that "it would be an error to claim that all manifestations of cultural life are determined by economic conditions"; the simplest cultural forms, he asserts, prove this.[21] He also states: "It seems impossible to reduce the fundamental beliefs of mankind to an economic source,"[22] and "It is not possible to explain every feature of cultural life as determined by economic status. We do not see how art styles, the form of ritual or the special form of religious belief could possibly be derived from economic forces."[23]

From this repudiation of the economic factor as the *sole* creative force and as the determinant of cultural forms, Boas goes on to deny the *primary* importance of economic conditions: "There

---

[21] *Anthropology and Modern Life* (New York, 1928), p. 232.
[22] *Ibid.*, p. 234.
[23] "The Aims of Anthropological Research," Address as President of the American Association for the Advancement of Science, Atlantic City, December, 1932. *Science*, N.S., LXXVI (1932), p. 605–613. Reprinted in *Race, Language and Culture* (New York, 1940), p. 256. See also "Social Problems of Methodology in the Social Sciences" in *The New Social Science*, ed. by Leonard D. White (Chicago, 1930), p. 84–98. Reprinted in *Race, Language and Culture*, p. 267.

is no reason to call other phases of culture a superstructure on an economic basis," he writes, "for economic conditions always act on a pre-existing culture and are themselves dependent upon all other aspects of culture. It is no more justifiable to say that social structure is determined by economic forms than to claim the reverse, for a pre-existing social structure will influence economic conditions and *vice-versa,* and a people have never been observed that has no social structure and that is not subject to economic conditions. The claim that economic stresses preceded every other manifestation of cultural life and exerted their influences on a group without any cultural traits cannot be maintained."[24]

The specific singling out of the term "superstructure" by Boas is undoubtedly directed at the use of the term by some of his students influenced by Marxism. Yet it is difficult to see how his description of the fundamental importance of economic life, as described in his *Encyclopaedia of Social Sciences* article previously quoted, can be gainsaid, and nowhere does he give comparable evidence of the influence of non-economic factors on the economic. No Marxian scholar who uses the term "superstructure" implies that the specific forms of institutions other than the economic are moulded by economic factors alone. Even the most casual observer of comparative cultures would be aware that all fishing peoples had not the same customs, and that the same might be said of all hunting peoples, all pastoral peoples and all agricultural peoples. That there exist varieties of culture under each type of economy has never been questioned by Marxists. They have never assumed the static correspondence of specific societies because their economies were similar, but they have been concerned with the historical processes of change within the same culture. Nor has the reciprocal influence of other aspects of culture upon the economic been denied; in fact, it has been emphatically affirmed.[25] To recognize reverse relations does

---

[24] *Mind of Primitive Man* (2nd ed., New York, 1938), p. 193. This passage is not found in the first edition published in 1911.
[25] Engels wrote in 1890: "According to the materialist conception of history the determining element in history is *ultimately* the production and reproduction in real life. More than this neither Marx nor I ever asserted. If

not mean, however, that such influences are of equal importance. The fundamental question is whether changes in other aspects of culture had and do have as pronounced effects upon the entire pattern of human behavior as have changes in the economic. This Boas seems to infer, but does not substantiate.

Historical materialists do not try to reduce intricate social forms, religious ideas, or art styles to economic needs. What they do contend is that the forms of human associations established in the process of getting food and shelter, are the nucleus of social life, and that myths, rituals, religious ideas and political ideas, function to sanction and to strengthen and perpetuate these forms. When economies change, the forms of behavior and ideological sanctions adapted to the earlier economy tend to persist and create disparities between the superstructure and the needs of the new economy.

The Problem of Social Evolution

There is little doubt that Boas was the primary source of the negativistic critique of the social evolutionists that has been characteristic of American anthropology. His significant article on the "Limitations of the Comparative Method in Anthropology"[26] published in 1896, served as the opening gun of a battle against the classical anthropologists which was taken up by his

---

therefore somebody twists this into the statement that the economic element is the *only* determining one, he transforms it into a meaningless, abstract and absurd phrase." Letter to J. Bloch, September 21, 1890, in Marx-Engels, *Selected Correspondence* (New York, 1935), p. 475. In the same year he also wrote "ideological conception reacts in its turn upon the economic basis and may, within certain limits, modify it." Letter to Conrad Schmidt, October 27, 1890, *ibid.*, p. 482.

[26] "Limitations of the Comparative Method of Anthropology," *Science*, N.S. IV (1896), p. 901–08. Reprinted in *Race, Language and Culture*, p. 270–80. There is an interesting change of the text from the original article, as it is reprinted. The original reads: "This method of starting with a hypothesis is infinitely inferior to the one in which by truly inductive processes the actual history of definite phenomena is derived." In the reprinting this is changed to read: "Forcing phenomena into the strait jacket of a theory is opposed to the inductive process by which the actual relations of definite phenomena may be derived." In the intervening period he had come to realize that he too had started with an hypothesis, and that his rival method becomes in contrast "strait jacketing."

students, particularly Lowie,[27] with the militance of crusaders. An evaluation of the thesis of this article today gives important perspectives on Boas' views. Its major objection to the comparative method lay in the argument that anthropological research which compares similar cultural phenomena from various parts of the world, in order to discover the uniform history of their development, makes the assumption that the same ethnological phenomenon has everywhere developed in the same manner. The article was a plea that comparisons be restricted to those phenomena which research has proved to be the effects of the same causes and that, before extended comparisons could be made, the comparability of the material had to be proved. Generalizing on this basis, Boas declares: "Therefore we must also consider all the ingenious attempts at constructions of a grand system of the evolution of society as of very doubtful value."[28]

It was in this article that Boas set forth his program for anthropological research. We may thus use the objectives there expressed as criteria for the appraisal of his work. We may well ask: Were his objectives ever realized? How fruitful were they as guides to anthropological research?

Boas set as his goal the formulation of laws of the processes of the development of culture. He wrote:

> . . . Certain laws exist which govern the growth of human culture and it is our endeavor to discover these laws. The object of our investigation is to find the *processes* by which certain stages of culture have developed. The customs and beliefs themselves are not the ultimate objects of research. We desire to learn the reasons why such customs and beliefs exist . . . in other words, we wish to discover the history of their development. . . .

These laws were to be formulated on the basis of a detailed study of customs in their bearings on the total culture of the tribe practicing them and in connection with an investigation of their geographical distribution among neighboring tribes in order to obtain knowledge of historical causes and psychological processes at work in their development.

Recording the history of the cultures of diverse local tribes was

[27] R. H. Lowie, *Primitive Society* (New York, 1920).
[28] *Op. cit.*

regarded, however, as but the first indispensable step toward the ultimate objective of the formulation of general laws:

> I fully agree with those anthropologists [Boas wrote] who claim that this [the description of local cultures] is not the ultimate aim of our science, because the general laws, although implied in such a description, cannot be clearly formulated nor their relative value appreciated without a thorough comparison of the manner in which they assert themselves in different cultures. But I insist that the application of this method is the indispensable condition of sound progress. . . . When we have cleared up the history of a single culture and understand the effects of environment, and the psychological conditions that are reflected in it, we have made a step forward, as we can then investigate in how far the same causes or other causes were at work in the development of other cultures. *Thus by comparing histories of growth general laws may be found.* [Italics mine.—B.J.S.]

To what extent has this ideal so boldly stated been attained as a program of research by Boas? It must be said that one will search his writings in vain for general laws that have emerged from his many years of work in anthropology. After four decades of research, he comments, "I am far from claiming that no general laws relating to the growth of culture exist. Whatever they may be, they are in every particular case overlaid by a mass of accidents that were probably much more potent in actual happenings than the general laws."[29]

Boas even despaired of making a complete and adequate study of one culture. In 1930 he wrote: "The complexity of cultural development is so great, and the conditions that determine the course of historical happenings are logically so entirely unrelated, that the attempt to give an adequate explanation of the history of any individual society in regard to biological type, language

---

[29] *Anthropology and Modern Life,* p. 209–11. The single "definite causally determined relation" which he ventures to formulate is that between economic conditions of a people and the density of population. Of the effort to apply the results of anthropological studies to the problems of modern life, he says "we must not expect results parallel to those obtained by controlled experiments. The conditions are so complex that it is doubtful whether any significant laws can be discovered." The definition of cultural laws in terms of controlled experiment bears out the judgment that Boas remained to the end a physical scientist studying the forms of human behavior.

and culture seems hopeless."[30] For this reason he never published a complete monograph of any tribe, even of the Kwakiutl on whom he collected data for many years. His nearest approach to the application of his method even to a segment of culture was his analysis of Tsimshian myths[31] and in his discussion of primitive art.[32] The generalizations that emerge from these studies are, however, extremely scant.

In view of the fact that Boas has been attacked as a diffusionist by some writers defending social evolution and as a social evolutionist by writers defending diffusion it is pertinent to point out that he demanded, in this programmatic article, and always elsewhere as well, that each instance of cultural change be studied on its own merits. It is clearly apparent that he saw both processes at work: the internal development of culture through the creative manipulation by individuals of the transmitted material and the borrowing of culture from contacts with other cultures. The latter process brought in elements outside the normal line of development of the culture and so changed the direction of its growth. However, the foreign elements were selected and adapted in terms of a pattern of culture characteristic of the borrowing culture.[33] In this way aspects of culture, as they diffused, took on different meanings and served different functions in the cultures into which they were incorporated.

The study of the process of such diffusions was the preoccupation of students under Boas' direction for a considerable period. It consisted of breaking up the diffusing culture into its component parts and observing its diversified values in the cultures in which it was observed. This led to a mechanistic shattering of cultural institutions into their component elements. Goldenweiser's analysis of totemism[34] was the most notable of such

[30] *Encyclopaedia of the Social Sciences*, II, p. 109.
[31] *Tsimshian Mythology* (Washington, 1916), Thirty-first Annual Report of the Bureau of American Ethnology, Smithsonian Institution.
[32] *Primitive Art* (Oslo, 1927).
[33] This aspect of cultural patterning was elaborated upon by Ruth Benedict in *Patterns of Culture* (Boston, 1934) and in the several books of Margaret Mead.
[34] Alexander Goldenweiser, *Totemism, An Analytical Study* (1910). Republished in his *History, Psychology and Culture* (New York, 1932), p. 213–332.

studies. It revealed the inadequacy of the previous comparative studies such as the four-volume work of Frazer,[35] for it showed that what was called totemism had different historical and psychological origins in different areas. Features which had been regarded as inherent in totemism—exogamy, taboo, religious regard, totemic names, descent from the totem—were not invariably associated with it. In this monograph and in successive articles, he was intent to prove that totemism was not always associated with exogamy, or with clans or gens. But the rigid application of the analytical method atomized totemism to such a degree that there was nothing left of it. "As a result," wrote Goldenweiser in 1932, in his "final" note on the subject, "the concept 'totemism' loses its univocal character, and the very term seems to become futile. In view of the mass of descriptive facts, so well known to students, this outlook seems eminently foolish. . . . Sib systems [i.e., clans or gens] constitute an important phase in the history of primitive institutions. It is to this phase of society or of culture that totemism attaches itself as a congenial and therefore regular, though not invariable companion."[36] Thus after years of research and controversy, the results of the analytical method in this field admittedly add up to practically nothing.

Some results of Boas' analytical method were valuable. Columbia field workers under his guidance stressed the importance of texts in the native languages, so that there could be verification of the generalizations made about specific cultures, and the tests could serve as well as source materials for work on native languages. But there was an unfortunate tendency on the part of some of the investigators to equate the sum total of these texts with the culture of a people, and their monographs failed to give readers an integrated picture of the economic and social life of the people observed. There has been considerable activity collecting and translating texts as if they were ends in themselves, rather than the raw materials with which the ethnologist works. As a result, few of the studies of American Indian cultures convey a well-rounded portrait of the throbbing realities of people in action, solving economic and social problems, meeting crises and

[35] J. G. Frazer, *Totemism and Exogamy* (London, 1910).
[36] *History, Psychology and Culture* (New York, 1932), p. 356.

transcending them in the course of the cycle of the seasons and the cycle of their personal development. Instead the monographs are assemblages of static data on various segments of the culture.

Boas recognized the force of this criticism and found an explanation for it beyond that of the technical difficulties of ethnographic description. He wrote:

> The complaint has been made often and by every earnest student that the stereotyped ethnographical description provides us only with disconnected fragments of the living culture. If the old method is still being pursued, this is due rather to technical difficulties that often cannot be easily overcome than to a lack of recognition of the fact that a penetrating investigation would bring to light much that is important and new. However, it is not justifiable to conclude from the defects of the available descriptions which do not reveal a unity of culture, that the whole culture must be a compact unit, that contradictions within a culture are impossible, and that all features must be parts of a system. We should rather ask in how far so-called primitive cultures possess a unity that covers all aspects of cultural life. Have we not reason to expect that here as well as in more complicated cultures, sex, generation, age, individuality, and social organization will give rise to the most manifold contradictions?[37]

Boas was of course cognizant that the primitive peoples were humans, not automatons.[38] But his physical science method of collecting data long prevented this significant fact from becoming apparent, for the monographs dealt with "culture traits" and "culture elements," rather than with vital human beings in interaction. The correction of this tendency came late in Boas' career, when he stimulated his students to undertake acculturation studies.

Another product of the Boas method was the concept of culture area. This concept was originally conceived by Boas in his museum work with pottery and potsherds, when he found that forms of pottery could be distributed systematically by areas, with the marginal regions between the areas of specific styles having mixed types. The same system of classification came to

[37] Review of G. W. Locher's "The Serpent in Kwakiutl Religion" in *The Journal of American Folklore*, XLVI, p. 418.

[38] See in particular his introduction to *Primitive Art* (Oslo, 1927).

be applied to aspects of culture that did not have the same material form as pottery. Researchers shattered culture into various unit traits, working under the doubtful assumption that a marriage custom could be treated as a unit in much the same manner as a pot. Distribution charts in the manner of ecologists became the practice. There then followed a charting of aboriginal cultures into areas. While there is little doubt that these distribution charts have been helpful in a rough sort of way in the preliminary identification of cultures, yet the boundaries of the various culture areas were very subjective, and the criteria which determined the limits of each area rather ill defined. Moreover, the boundaries of the area for tribal cultures as a whole, and of specific institutions and traits of the culture, were found to vary, so that there was no end of overlappings in a carefully charted region. Moreover, in such studies the "marginal areas" tend to be slurred over as unimportant and regarded as mixed forms when they may not be so in fact.

Among the unsolved theoretical questions that emerged from the use of the culture area are whether the extent of distribution of a "culture trait" is an evidence of its age, and whether the place in which the trait has its fullest development is the place of its origin. Some anthropologists clearly make these assumptions, and yet they are unwarranted, as is evident in the case of tobacco, Indian corn and the banana.[39] If these assumptions are not granted, the culture area method is merely a crude descriptive technique and contributes little to an understanding of the historical development of culture. It therefore did not emerge as the valid substitute for the outmoded comparative method of the classical anthropologists, sought by Boas in his programmatic article.

In his general criticism of Morgan and of the other social evolutionists Boas overstated his case. He so formulated the position of the social evolutionists that he attacked a straw man. He concluded: ". . . it does not seem to be certain that every people in an advanced stage of civilization must have passed through all

[39] *Mind of Primitive Man* (2nd ed.), p. 167–171. Boas was critical of the use of the culture area concept as used particularly by Clark Wissler and repeatedly stressed its limitations.

the stages of development, which we may gather by an investigation of all the types of culture which occur all over the world."[40] It is questionable whether any of the social evolutionary writers ever made such sweeping claims. Morgan, whom he includes in his criticism, certainly did not. Morgan's catalogue of successive cultures does have obvious limitations in terms of our larger and more precise stock of ethnographic knowledge.[41] But his theory was not the extreme one that Boas was attacking. His position was that "progress has been found to be *substantially* the same in kind in tribes and nations inhabiting different and even disconnected continents, *while in the same status, with deviations from uniformity in particular instances produced by special causes.*"[42] Morgan recognized that internal sequences are disturbed by borrowing, although he did not discuss this problem in detail. He declared: ". . . whenever a continental connection existed all the tribes must have shared in some measure in each other's progress. All great inventions and discoveries propagate themselves. . . ."

Boas expressed doubt, on occasion, as to whether some types of culture may be identified as belonging to an earlier period and others as recent. One of his criticisms of this procedure applies to the manner in which evolutionists discussed the relationship between agriculture and herding. He pointed out that there is no plausible connection between the chronological development of these two occupations. The activities leading to the domestication of animals have nothing in common with those dealing with the cultivation of plants, because while herding is the occupation of men, agriculture is the occupation of women. This criticism is unassailable. He indicates, however, that the *cultivation* of plants wherever it is found is subsequent to the *gathering* of wild plants. Evolutionary classification of cultures into pre-agricultural and agricultural is therefore valid. Inasmuch as the discovery of agriculture has significant influence upon the

[40] *Ibid.*, p. 182.
[41] For an appraisal of Morgan's work see Bernhard J. Stern, *Lewis Henry Morgan: Social Evolutionist* (Chicago, University of Chicago Press, 1931).
[42] *Ancient Society*, Kerr edition, p. 18. The italics are mine. Boas never extended his studies into the origins of the modern state as Engels did in *The Origin of the Family, Private Property and the State.*

degree of stability and density of the population, and hence upon the development of the arts and social and political organization, this evolutionary classification is of some importance.

Boas further criticizes such evolutionists as Spencer who assume that because the history of industrial development is that of increasing complexity, that the rule of development from simplicity to complexity applies to all aspects of culture. He shows that in language "the grammatical categories of Latin and still more those of modern English seem crude when compared to the complexity of psychological or logical forms which primitive languages recognize but which in our speech are disregarded. On the whole, the development of languages seems to be such that the nicer distinctions are eliminated, and that it begins with the complex and ends with the simpler forms, although it must be acknowledged that opposite tendencies are by no means absent."[43] In primitive music as well as in decorative design there is a complex rhythmic structure unequaled in the popular art of today. In the social organization of primitive societies there is often a system of social obligations in relation to one's relatives far more complex than that prevailing in our society. A rigid universal principle of evolutionary development from the simple to the complex obviously does not hold. Yet Boas, after stressing these exceptions, finally granted they were exceptions and conceded that the evolutionary anthropologists "observed correctly the increasing complexity of cultural forms, the progress of knowledge, and the elimination of antiquated forms."[44]

It was not until 1938 that Boas took the opportunity to present in detail any but this negativistic approach to the problem of evolution in culture. At that time he went so far as to say that ". . . the increasing intellectual achievements as expressed in thought, in inventions, in devices in gaining greater security of existence and in relief from the ever-pressing necessity of obtaining food and shelter, bring about differentiations in the activities of the community that give life a more varied, richer tone. In

[43] *Ibid.*, p. 172.
[44] *Encyclopaedia of the Social Sciences*, II, p. 102.

this sense we may accept the term, 'advance of culture.' "[45] He does not, however, accept the corollary definition of primitive peoples as "those whose activities are little diversified, whose forms of life are simple and uniform, and the contents and form of whose culture are meager and intellectually inconsistent." This is because, he argues, there is no close correlation between all aspects of ethnic life. In this connection he remarks further: "There are people like the Australians, whose material culture is quite poor, but who have a highly complex social organization. Others like the Indians of California, produce excellent technical and artistic work, but show no corresponding complexity in other aspects of their lives." Elsewhere, however, he finds sufficient correlations between all aspects of culture to say: ". . . at the end of the glacial period, the Madeleine Culture has a highly developed industry and art which may be compared with that of modern tribes of similar achievement. It seems justifiable to assume that *the cultural level of tribes so similar in their technical culture may have been alike also in other respects.*"[46]

In grappling with the criteria of progress, Boas indicates that it is inadequate to rank cultures in terms of the presence or absence of specific inventions. He asks and answers negatively: "Should we rank a pastoral people as richer in inventions than an agricultural tribe? Are the poor tribes of the Okhotsk Sea less primitive than the artistic Northwest Americans because they have pottery? Is the ancient Mexican more primitive than the poor Negro tribe that happens to possess the art of smelting iron?"

Boas' judgment is in more general terms of efficiency. "We value a culture the higher," he writes, "the less the effort required for obtaining the necessities of life and the greater the technical achievements that do not serve the indispensable daily needs. . . . The more varied the play with techniques that furnish the amenities of life the higher we estimate a culture. Wherever spinning, weaving, basketry, carving on wood or bone, artistic stone work, architecture, pottery, metal work occur we do not

---
[45] *Mind of Primitive Man* (2nd ed.), p. 197.
[46] *Ibid.*, p. 207. The italics are mine.

doubt that an advance over the simplest primitive conditions has been made."

Food collectors (hunters and fishers) are too pressed by the urgent demands of obtaining an adequate food supply to develop these technologies, except in a limited number of tropical areas with a wealth of vegetable products and in regions the waters of which swarm with fish. Since there is no opportunity for invention and other intellectual work until a plentiful supply of food is secured, a general advance in culture depends in most regions on the artificial increase of the natural food supply by agriculture or herding. Between herding and agriculture, the latter offers more fruitful soil for the development of advanced culture because it makes possible large populations in a stable habitat, engaged in the same occupation thus permitting specialization and division of labor which are requisites of progress. With resulting increased leisure comes increased intellectual work. Of this Boas writes: "Intellectual work leads partly to the elimination of error and partly to a systematization of experience." Similarly he points out that decorative art does not exist when people lack the fullest control of their technique and time to play with it. Technique, intellectual pursuits and decorative art are thus shown to be dependent upon the mode of production —the fundamental thesis of historical materialism.

While Boas concedes the existence of objective criteria for the evaluation of cultures in the field of techniques, he hesitates to speak of progress in other fields. He considers "the evaluation of intellectual coordination of experience, of ethical concepts, artistic form, religious feeling . . . so subjective in character that an increment of cultural values cannot readily be defined."[47] The human code of ethics for the closed social group he considered universal. The differences he found to lie in the size of the social group to which the obligations are felt, and the clearer discernment of suffering. It is an interesting reflection of his rationalistic approach to human behavior that he found these dependent upon an increase in knowledge.

Boas found it even more difficult to define progress in social

[47] *Op. cit.*, p. 205.

organization. He follows the same argument as does Lowie[48] that "the extreme individualist considers anarchy as his ideal, while others believe in voluntary regimentation.... Progress can be defined only in regard to the special ideal we have in mind. There is no absolute progress."[49] This formulation ignores the fact that neither "anarchy" nor "voluntary regimentation" or other political ideals are to be regarded as ends in themselves. They are formulated as ideals in terms of their potential achievements. The standard of achievement of any form of social organization, as in other aspects of human behavior, is the degree to which it succeeds in fulfilling human needs, and in enlarging the scope of man's power over his environment. Progress in social organization in this sense can be evaluated in objective terms.

Boas' Social Outlook

In his social views Boas shows as little Marxist influence as in his anthropological writings. Yet there are in the latter a few passages written as if he had a theory of social classes. This is illustrated, for example, in *Anthropology and Modern Life*, where he declared that ... "it is perfectly safe to say that no amount of eugenic selection will overcome those social conditions that have raised a poverty- and disease-ridden proletariat which will be reborn from even the best stock, so long as the social conditions persist that remorselessly push human beings into helpless and hopeless misery."[50]

Similarly, he states in *The Mind of Primitive Man* that in advanced cultures with differentiated occupations members of certain classes are poorer in culture than primitive peoples because all their energy is required for the satisfaction of their basic economic needs.[51]

A careful analysis of his writings shows clearly, however, that he never consistently defined social classes in economic terms, that is, in terms of their role in the productive process. In the last article he wrote before his death, under the title "Class

[48] Robert H. Lowie, *Primitive Society* (New York, 1920), p. 438.
[49] *Mind of Primitive Man* (2nd ed.), p. 206.
[50] P. 115.
[51] P. 205.

Consciousness and Race Prejudice,"[52] "class" is used as if it were synonymous with any social group which differs from other groups in custom because it is dominant or submerged. The point made in the article is that the contempt with which submerged racial and religious groups are treated is primarily social, and "only accidentally emphasized by difference in bodily form, and that the conclusion that the inferior group belongs to an inferior race is merely a rationalization of our behavior." This is unassailable and worthy of repeated reiteration. But neither in this article nor elsewhere does he deal systematically with the contemporary causes of class stratification, and the resulting prejudices toward the exploited groups.

Boas' social outlook was organized around a theory of democratic individualism, not on a theory of social classes. In 1937 he wrote:

> Democracy is founded on the value of the individual who out of his free will fits himself into the social structure in which we live, who contributes in his way to its growth and development. Class consciousness of whatever kind it may be, has no room in our country. It is the task of education to teach that every individual should be appraised according to his personality and not be rejected or accepted because he is assigned to a class with which he himself may have nothing in common.[53]

Here again the term "class" was used as synonymous with an in-group and was not used in the Marxian sense. Boas never grappled with the larger problem of how capitalism in our country has led to the development of economic social classes, and the effects of this development on race prejudice.

His interest in democracy, however, was never formalistic but

---

[52] Published posthumously in *The Christian Register*, CXXII (January, 1943), p. 5 f. This use of the term "class" is characteristic of Boas. See, for example, the passage in an article in 1939: "An insidious tendency has induced men at all times to consider individuals not as individuals but rather as members of a class, racial, denominational, educational, or economic, bearing all the imaginary mental and moral characteristics of the class." *New Masses* (February 14, 1939), p. 17.

[53] Franz Boas, "Race and Race Prejudice," *Jewish Social Service Quarterly*, XIV (no. 2, December, 1937), p. 232.

was vital and all-pervasive. It was based on faith in the common man. He once wrote:

> I should always be inclined to accept, in regard to fundamental human problems, the judgment of the masses rather than the judgment of the intellectuals, which is much more certain to be warped by conscious control of traditional ideas. I do not mean to say that the judgment of the masses would be acceptable in regard to every problem of human life, because there are many which by their technical nature are beyond their understanding; nor do I believe that the details of the right solution can always be found by the masses; but I feel strongly that the problem itself, as felt by them, and the ideal they want to see realized is a safer guide for our conduct than the ideal of the intellectual group that stand under the ban of an historical tradition that dulls their feeling for the needs of the day.[54]

It is this sustaining faith that gave him insights which many other intellectuals missed. Throughout his life, Boas was an obdurate and valiant fighter for human liberty, but it was especially in his latter years that he became associated with mass organizations in this struggle. In the early days of the rise of fascism to power in Germany, Boas, along with many other liberals took the position that Nazism was comparable to an epidemic of hysteria, like the hysterias of the Middle Ages, and that it would pass over. In an address in 1934 he declared: "It is little use trying to fight such hysteria while it is at its height. It is a fire that must burn itself out."[55] Boas in this period was torn by the conflict between his cherished views on free speech and the need to do something to prevent the Nazis from attacking democracy and inciting anti-Semitism through such meetings as were organized by the Christian Front groups in New York and elsewhere.

Early in 1938, he resolved this conflict by taking the lead in organizing the intellectuals of the United States toward an awareness of the dangers that faced them. He formulated and

---

[54] *Anthropology and Modern Life*, p. 195–96.
[55] *Aryan and Semite*. An address delivered before The Judeans and The Jewish Academy of Arts and Sciences, March 4, 1934, in New York (Cincinnati, B'nai B'rith, 1934), p. 32.

circularized a manifesto signed by over 1,500 American scientists which read in part:

> We firmly believe that in the present historical epoch democracy alone can preserve intellectual freedom. Any attack upon freedom of thought in one sphere, even a non-political one, is in effect an attack on democracy itself. Scientists must be defended in their right to speak the truth as they understand it. If we American scientists wish to avoid a similar fate [that of intellectual life under fascism], if we wish to see the world continue to progress and prosper, we must bend our efforts to that end now.

In publicizing this manifesto, Boas went one step further. He declared: "Expressions of opinion are useful, but they are not enough; they must be followed by action. The standpoint of the scientist must be impressed again and again upon the people."[56] There followed Lincoln's Birthday meetings in New York, Boston, Philadelphia, Washington and in western cities organized to protest against racial and religious prejudice, and after these meetings the American Committee for Democracy and Intellectual Freedom was established. Under the leadership of Boas, this Committee took bold and unequivocal stands against manifestations of fascism in the life of the United States and all over the world. As a result it was a target of attack of the reactionary forces of the country. It was similarly assailed by individuals and groups who sought to influence Boas to attack the Soviet Union along with the fascists. This Boas emphatically refused to do, in spite of the fact that one of the agencies which aided the Committee's work withdrew its financial support as a result. The Committee was attacked by the Dies and Coudert Committees, but Boas unwaveringly stood his ground.

Boas also not merely lent the prestige of his great name but gave of his time and strength to other progressive causes. He organized intellectuals in defense of Loyalist Spain; supported the National Federation for Constitutional Liberties and numerous other committees protecting the rights of working men and women; he signed the petition to release Earl Browder

---

[56] "Franz Boas on Intellectual Freedom," *New Masses* (February 14, 1939), p. 17.

from prison and took part in other unpopular movements which he realized, with a vision shared by few scientists, to be the bone and marrow of America's fight against fascism. Hence, when the move was begun to destroy the American Federation of Teachers, by ousting progressive unions, Boas saw the significance of the step, and, in public protest, he joined the College Teachers Union and he remained a member until his death. The correctness of his judgments and his acts has already been demonstrated by history. As a result of them, he will be remembered not only as a scientist pre-eminent in his field, but as one who courageously identified himself with the common man in the struggle for a better society.[57]

[57] As this article goes to press, and therefore too late to be discussed here, a memorial volume on the life and work of Franz Boas has appeared which also contains a complete bibliography of his writings. See A. L. Kroeber, Ruth Benedict, Melville Herskovits, Gladys A. Reichard, and J. Alden Mason, "Franz Boas, 1858–1942," Memoir Series of the American Anthropological Association, no. 61, *American Anthropologist*, N.S., XLV, no. 3, Part 2.

From *Science and Society*, Vol. VII, No. 4 (Fall 1943), pp. 289–320.

Alternative Proposals to Democracy:
The Pattern of Fascism

Events of [early 1941] have shown that fascism respects no boundaries, that it is neither associated exclusively with any state or nation, nor is it a peculiar manifestation of the psychology of any one or two peoples, nor the product of the personality of specific leaders. Fascism is instituted in each country in a distinctive manner in terms of the historical backgrounds and political structure of that country, but its basic pattern is the same and its processes are similar. It must be faced as a potential alternative in the United States, not through the danger of foreign conquest, which is remote, nor primarily through imported propaganda which would fall on barren soil were democracy functioning adequately. Its threat comes from the fact that the socio-economic and political situation in the United States parallels in many respects that which led to fascism in Italy and in Germany.

Fascism represents the coordination of the ways and means by which business magnates and agricultural landlords have extended their class control and have institutionalized it through the seizure of political power. The outlook and method of fascism are neither new nor fundamentally different from those common to monopoly-orientated business enterprise. It is an extension into the realm of politics of authoritarian approaches to the common man. Whenever dominant economic groups have been in danger of losing control over government by being forced to yield to the demands of organized democratic expression of industrial unions and workers' and farmers' parties (a threat which is characterized as the danger of Communism), they have been willing to scrap the use of the liberal-democratic state or the

ALTERNATIVE PROPOSALS TO DEMOCRACY

constitutional dictatorship and to institute fascism. Fascist-minded industrialists and their collaborators, the agricultural landlords, of all countries have long believed that "democracy is a lie, equality of opportunity a juvenile illusion, liberalism no more than polite bolshevism, representative government subterfuge, truth a delusion of the naïve, science a tool for the strong, life the practice of man preying on man."[1] Fascism permits them to act upon these premises by the removal of the restraining mechanics of democratic action. Whatever fears, prejudices, discontents and tensions they exploit, whatever insecurities they play upon, whatever symbols and rhetorics they utilize to secure mass support, their fundamental objective is the maintenance and extension of their class control. The suppression of political parties and of trade unions, the extinction of freedom of the press, speech and assemblage, the terrorization of the populace by vigilante action and by murder and mass imprisonment of the opposition has been the fascist method of acquiring class hegemony and of maintaining it.

Fascist ideologies are incidental to their objectives and are flexible and elastic to the demands of class rule, with the result that there has been no stability or continuity in fascist thought. The proponents of fascism will manipulate national pride, develop romantic conceptions of racial and national destiny, incite hatreds towards minority groups, promote militarism, direct cruelty and despair into channels of destruction of the political opposition. They will build up through expert utilization of publicity techniques and of the mechanics of personal adulation the leader who serves as an instrument to crystallize and symbolize the struggle for power. They will take advantage of frustrations due to unemployment and low living standards to offer illusory hopes that will give an exhilarating thrill of achievement, even though their victories mean death and destruction to men and to values that have been vehicles of emancipation. But the specific formulations of fascism are dictated by the requirements of the dominant economic groups and are modified according to the need of the occasion and period and for the enticement of the

[1] Robert A. Brady, "The Fascist Threat to Democracy," in *Science and Society*, 2:165, Spring, 1938.

group whose mass support is being sought. The demagogy of fascism is for this reason shot through with contradictions. The consistency of fascism lies exclusively in the effort of the dominant economic groups to create a political form to perpetuate their power which can only be done through destruction of all democratic rights and through a military economy.

One can arrive at an understanding of the nature of the fascist alternative by tracing its course and its product in Italy and in Germany. America has reached a different level in its capitalist development, its configuration of class forces is diverse, its tradition of democratic political action more webbed in the fabric of its culture, its educational institutions somewhat less authoritarian than in pre-fascist Italy and Germany. But as one observes the march of fascism, the setting of its conquest of power, and its structure and spirit as it matured in Italy and Germany, one can construct the form it presents as an alternative of democracy in the United States.

The Fascist Alternative as Seen from the Experience of Italy

Fascism came into power in Italy through the connivance of industrial monopolists and landed aristocracy. As Mussolini declared in 1933, there had been an end of free competition in the industrial life of Italy long before World War I, and an era of pools, syndicates and trusts had superseded it. Competitive tactics in the control of markets had been displaced by monopolistic devices developed through trade associations, cartels and governmental agencies.[2] As a result of World War I, Italy's economy was completely dislocated. It had been excluded from its share of the spoils of the war which went to its allies, France and England, and its world markets were thereby considerably restricted. As monopoly capital sought to maintain and even expand its power at the expense of the already low standards of the workers, it was resisted by the dramatic strike wave of 1919–20. At the same time a virile peasant movement developed which threatened the power of the large landowners under the slogan of "Land to

[2] Carl T. Schmidt, *The Corporate State in Action*. New York: Oxford University Press, 1939, p. 21.

the Peasants." Rather than yield to these surging democratic forces, the government armed the Blackshirts and gave them freedom of action. It was later admitted by Volpe, the Italian finance minister, that "fascism did not lack certain indulgence from above." It was not communism that they were fighting, but democracy. Mussolini had declared in 1921 that communism was dead in Italy. Yet in its demagogic appeal to farmers, shopkeepers and bureaucrats, fascism made use of the fictitious bogey of the imminence of communism. And later when American capitalists came to the support of Italian fascism, they made much capital of the threat of communism to the world and sanctioned the establishment of fascism to check it.[3]

The General Confederation of Industry, Italy's organization of big business men, rushed to the support of the fascist regime immediately after the "March on Rome." The fascist government was on the verge of collapse in 1925 when American capitalists came to its aid through substantial loans. George Whitney, a partner of J. P. Morgan and Company, testified before a Senate committee investigating stock exchange practices that his company had loaned the Italian fascist government $100,000,000.[4] Dillon Read and Company also loaned the city of Milan $30,000,000. As recently as March, 1939, J. P. Morgan and Company was still the financial agent for the Italian Credit Consortium for Public Works, the Kingdom of Italy, and the City of Rome (to which it had loaned $30,000,000 in 1925), and Thomas W. Lamont, a Morgan partner, was a trustee of the Italy-American Society.[5]

Mussolini paid his debt to the industrialists with a precipitous haste. Three weeks after he acquired power the commission investigating war profiteering that had scandalized the country was dissolved and the publication of its findings prohibited. In-

[3] Cf. Thomas W. Lamont in *Survey*, March 1, 1927.
[4] Hearings before the Senate Committee on Banking and Currency, 73rd Congress, 1st Session, on S. Res. 84, Part 1, May 23–25, 1933, pp. 194–195.
[5] Hearings before the Temporary National Economic Committee, 76th Congress, 2nd Session, Public Res. No. 113, Part 23, pp. 12300–12301, 12325. For a compilation of the utterances of American supporters of Italian fascism see George Seldes, *You Can't Do That,* New York: Modern Age Books, 1940, pp. 187–191.

heritance taxes were drastically lowered. The sole authority of the state to issue insurance was abrogated. The tax on invested capital was eliminated. The salaries of workers employed by the state were taxed. Wage cuts up to thirty per cent were allowed, and exemptions were permitted to the eight-hour day.[6]

Benefits also accrued to the landlords and rich farmers with comparable dispatch. Within three months after the "March on Rome" with its accompanying terror, various decrees providing for cession of land to cooperatives were repealed, and steps were taken to oust the peasants from estates that they had occupied; the proposed law for the division of the *latifundi* was withdrawn and measures limiting rises in land rents and eviction of tenants were revoked.

It was not long before the demands of financing its military program and of maintaining its bureaucracy led the fascist government to establish "state controls," to engage in regulation of production and distribution in all phases of Italian economic life. But this intervention has been directed in the interests of landed property, commercialized agriculture and finance capital. As Carl Schmidt wrote after a study in Italy under a grant from the Social Science Research Council:

> Fascist intervention means subordination to the propertied. It is the big industrialists, landlords and commercial agriculturalists who find consistent championship in the actions—if not in the speeches of the Fascists. It is they who have been maintained and even strengthened by encouragement of monopolistic practices and special subventions. And the only socialization has been that of business losses.[7]

That the policy of Italian fascism has worked toward the interest of monopoly is seen by the increase in the number of mergers under fascism. While between July, 1917, and July, 1927, there had been only 160 business mergers and combinations

---

[6] Stephen Raushenbush, *The March of Fascism*, New Haven: Yale University Press, 1939, p. 199.
[7] Carl T. Schmidt, "Agricultural Property and Enterprise under Italian Fascism," *Science and Society*, 1:331–32, 348–49, Spring, 1937. Cf. *idem, The Plow and the Sword*, New York: Columbia University Press, 1938.

in Italy, the number increased to 221 mergers of 878 firms between 1927 and 1929 and an additional 244 mergers of 364 firms between 1930 and 1932. By the end of 1929 one-fourth of Italian stock companies controlled 86 per cent of the total corporate capital and by 1935 about 95 per cent of that capital.[8] The contentions of many writers, therefore, that fascism is divorced from the control of big private business and works contrary to its interests is contradicted by this evidence. Irrespective of the protective anti-capitalist dramaturgics, for purposes of mass consumption, fascism has been the medium by which monopoly capitalism has tightened its grip upon the economic life of Italy and debased the standard of living of its people. Article 8 of the Italy Labor Charter of 1926 states that "the corporate state considers that private enterprise in the sphere of production is the most effective instrument in the interest of the nation."[9] Mussolini's policies have never deviated from this principle.

THE FASCIST ALTERNATIVE AS SEEN FROM THE EXPERIENCE OF GERMANY

The story of the support given the rise of German fascism by the industrialists in the West and the landlords in the East, assisted by other industrialists in Europe and America, is a familiar one. Ambassador Dodd's diary has two interesting entries which illuminate this fact. Under the date of February 28, 1936, he writes:

> I received a report today from Cologne of a long conversation with Fritz Thyssen, the greatest manufacturer of arms after the Krupps. Thyssen said that he had given a great part of his fortune to help Hitler win his long struggle for dictatorship.

And light is thrown on the attitude of American industrialists by his entry of December 5, 1935, in which he wrote:

---

[8] Carl T. Schmidt, *The Corporate State in Action*. New York: Oxford University Press, 1939, p. 121.
[9] Benito Mussolini, *Fascism: Doctrine and Institutions*, Rome: Ardita, 1935, p. 135.

Colonel Edward A. Deeds of Akron, Ohio, and New York City, president or director of twenty great American industrial concerns including the National Cash Register and the National City Bank, came to lunch today with a score of others, Americans and Germans, including James Hazen Hyde. Deeds had negotiated a deal with a German corporation for sending over our airplane patents so that the German company could manufacture and sell a hundred planes to Italy, the American company to share the profits.[10]

The best known of American industrialists who have received medals from Hitler as "distinguished foreigners who have deserved well of the Reich" are Henry Ford, James D. Mooney of General Motors, and Thomas J. Watson, president of the International Business Machines Corporation and chairman of the International Chamber of Commerce.

The many books on fascism which stress the middle-class response to German fascism's vitriolic attacks on communism obscured the role of those who instigated the attacks for their own ends. It has become increasingly apparent as time has passed that the middle-class officials, small shopkeepers and artisans, have fared badly under fascism along with the working class. The extent of cartelization, which wiped out the small industrialists, is shown by the report of the German Institute for Business Research which estimated that in 1936 all domestically produced industrial raw materials and semi-finished goods, and at least half of the production of industrial finished goods, were cartelized.[11] In 1938, Otto D. Tolischus, the New York *Times* correspondent, could write that "the list of German millionaires, reduced by the economic crisis, is lengthening again."[12] A director of I. G. Farbenindustrie, the chemical trust, declared in January, 1938, that "one-third of the German export business

---

[10] William E. Dodd, Jr., and Martha Dodd, Editors, *Ambassador Dodd's Diary*. New York: Harcourt Brace and Company, 1941, pp. 313–314, 283. For a discussion of British corporate interests who have worked closely with fascism see Simon Haxey, *England's Money Lords*. New York: Harrison Hilton, 1939, pp. 194–233.

[11] Temporary National Economic Committee, *Regulation of Economic Activities in Foreign Countries* (Monograph No. 40). Washington: U.S. Government Printing Office, 1941, p. 66.

[12] The New York *Times*, May 19, 1938.

is in the hands of only twenty firms."[13] It was in this year that William F. Knudsen, in an interview upon his return from Germany, declared it to be "the miracle of the twentieth century."[14]

From the very beginning of fascism in Germany private ownership of the means of production was upheld by National Socialists both in principle and in fact. Only Jewish property was attacked. The controlling shares in the steel industry and in some of the biggest banks which had been owned by the pre-fascist German government were returned to private corporations and owners. Large department stores and banks which the Nazis had denounced continued to flourish. A higher court decision in the fascist-controlled German courts in 1936 declared that "the proprietor of a monopoly has the right to exploit his monopolist position. The monopolist position has not been misused if it supplies one business man with and excludes another business man from the supply of monopolist articles."[15]

There are encroachments of the fascist government upon private property necessitated by its war program, by the control of foreign trade and capital export, by investment control, by stock exchange control, by limitations on the distribution of dividends, by decommercialization of a considerable area of landed property, by control of prices and consumption, and by taxation. But all these have affected the small and middle capitalist entrepreneurs more than the bigger ones. Some monopolists have recently increased their complaints against the restrictions imposed upon private property because of the war, and some, such as Thyssen, have been cast out by the political machine which they created to destroy militant workers and to wipe out their competitors. Brady aptly characterized the nature of the complaints of the monopolists when he points out that "the more clearly business men control machinery, the more uniformly will they complain of any incidence on themselves of the burdens their playing rules may at any time impose."[16]

---

[13] Guenther Riemann, *The Vampire Economy*. New York: The Vanguard Press, 1939, p. 47.
[14] *The New York Times*, October 26, 1938.
[15] Reimann, *op. cit.*, pp. 33-34.
[16] Robert Brady, *op. cit.*, p. 164.

All evidence points, however, to the fact that monopolists, particularly those engaged in the production of war materials, are still the controlling forces in the Nazi state.[17] They must share their power with the bureaucracy of the Nazi state and party in different degrees in different sections of the country, but always at a profit.

The main onslaught of fascism in Germany, as in Italy, has been against the working class. With their trade unions destroyed and their leaders killed or placed in concentration camps, the workers have been powerless to resist the ever-tightening controls over their freedom. A decree of June, 1938, provided for labor conscription, in case of need, in respect to any man or woman resident in Germany not of foreign nationality, without regard to age or profession. A decree of April 22, 1939, required that all workers, whether dependent or independent, have employment books containing a record of the working career of the owner. Decrees issued in September, 1939, forbade all workers and employees to leave their jobs without the consent of the local labor office and lifted all restrictions on hours of work for adult men. They also abolished prohibition on night work for women, and empowered the authorities to remove all limitations governing the employment of women and children under 18. Because the detrimental effects of these decrees became manifest upon the physique and morale of the populace, a new decree of December 12, 1939, limited the working day to 10 hours or with special permission to 12 hours, and night work for women and children was again prohibited.[18]

As in the case of Italian fascism, in spite of its promises before coming into power, the Nazi government did not abolish the big agricultural estates of those who helped finance, or did not oppose, their advent to rulership. In 1935 some 412 large landowners owned 2,600,000 hectares, as much as 1,000,000 small farmers. Six-tenths of one per cent of all private landowners owned 23.8 per cent of all arable land and forest land. Some

[17] Ernst Fraenkel, *The Dual State: A Contribution to the Theory of Dictatorship*. New York: Oxford University Press, 1941, pp. 171–187.
[18] Temporary National Economic Committee, *op. cit.*, pp. 78–79.

3,600,000 small farmers must live on an average of 3.2 hectares, which corresponds to 7.9 acres of land.[19]

THE FASCIST WORLD VIEW

When fascism came into power in Italy, it was a terroristic anti-democratic movement. Mussolini has frankly stated, "I had no doctrinal attitude in my mind." Only later did fascism seek to rationalize its conquest with theory of a corporate state. In Germany, *Mein Kampf* furnished the texts for battle, but it may hardly be regarded as a systematic political tract. Efforts to bring a semblance of coherence into Nazi doctrine were undertaken by Nazi academic theoreticians. There has developed a fantastic array of apologetics which it would serve little purpose to analyze in this article.[20]

In spite of the contradictions of fascist thought already remarked upon, there emerge, however, from the behavior and writings of the fascists several approaches to life and culture which might well be recapitulated in considering fascism as an alternative to democracy. As will be noted, the attitudes now regnant in fascist countries have a long history which go back to pre-fascist sources. They are, moreover, not confined to these countries, but are the common property of significant groups of landed aristocrats and business magnates in all countries.

The principal elements of the fascist view on life may be summarized for purposes of brief discussion under the headings of the theory of the élite, the doctrine of the totalitarian state, the glorification of militarism, the intensification of nationalism and racial chauvinism, the emphasis upon "idealism" as opposed to "materialism," and the retreat from reason. These doctrines have all an economic and political function.[21] The doctrine of the élite disparages the ability of the common man and thus rationalizes economic inequality. As interpreted by innumerable fascist writers, the concept bears little resemblance to that which would

---

[19] Stephen Raushenbush, *op. cit.*, p. 63.
[20] Cf. Samuel Rosenberg, "Three Concepts in Nazi Political Theory," *Science and Society*, 1:221–230, Winter 1937.
[21] Cf. Melvin Rader, *No Compromise*. New York: Macmillan, 1939, pp. 12–19.

give an important place to skill and knowledge in rulership. It has become in their hands an unabashed justification of the existing economic stratification of social classes as immutable and divinely ordained. Darré, the Nazi Minister of Agriculture, declares that "the order of society rests upon the inequality which cannot be abolished. . . . Inequality is as unchangeable as mathematical truths and as eternal as the laws which govern the movements of our planetary system." From this rises the corollary that some few are born to command and the many must obey, hence the business man is the worker's "natural leader."[22] The hierarchy of the army is transposed into the state and into economic life. As Brady writes: "It becomes, in short, as natural for business leadership to ally itself with the military as it has long been for the landed aristocrat to visualize himself in the story books as a knight in shining armor. The internal economy of the patronal estate, the hierarchy of command and subordination within the far-flung business empire, the ordered gradation of duties and responsibilities in the army are at one in structure and point of view."[23]

This concept of the élite dispenses with the need for democratic political or economic action on the part of the people, and as a result parliamentary government is condemned as pernicious and the annihilation of minority political parties, trade unions and farmers' organizations is declared to be justified. The state is declared to be totalitarian in the sense that it embraces all activities of persons under its sovereignty. Not only are agencies guarding the economic and political interests of workers and farmers destroyed but such groups as the Rotary and the Masons are similarly abolished. Religious bodies too are made subservient to the state.

A cycle can be observed in the extension of the rule of fascism.

---

[22] Brady shows how this is a common concept in business circles by a quotation from the proceedings of the National Manufacturers' Association in 1936 which reads, "From time immemorial the common people have followed the leadership of somebody and they will continue to do so. Some of the working people of this country follow their natural leaders, the owners and managers of industry." Quoted in *Science and Society*, 2:162, Spring, 1938.

[23] Brady, *op. cit.*, p. 163.

The first line of fascist attack has been invariably against communists. Social Democratic and liberal groups have permitted this infringement on democracy and have even joined in the attack, only to find that they were the next victims along with the trade unions of even the most conservative type and independent religious leaders of all denominations. It has been the experience of the history of fascism that once the attacks on minority parties such as communists are sanctioned, the floodgates of persecution are opened against all others, and they too are finally overwhelmed.

The fascist state as a product of capitalism in crisis seeking to survive against democratic forces within, and against imperialist rivals without, is inevitably militaristic. Its entire economy comes to be geared to the war machine. The production of materials for war is the primary source of profits for business and employment for workers. The authoritarian discipline of the war apparatus is superimposed upon and intensifies the "principle of leadership" in business. The brutality, insensitivity, and hysteria associated with war permeate all phases of the body politic. Intense nationalism is generated, a nationalism that eschews as pernicious all forms of internationalism and of tolerance of diversities of culture. Identification with the nation is offered as a form of compensation for economic insecurity. In order to heighten nationalism, special groups within the fascist state are attacked as alien, and intense racial chauvinism is incited. Jews are attacked with special ferocity as a counter-race. They are fictitiously portrayed as the source of both international finance and international communism. There is no scruple against using discredited racial doctrine and forged documents against them. Scientific evidence contrary to racialism is rejected as the product of rationalism and materialism, both of which are condemned. Democracy as well as communism is denounced as materialistic because it regards as important the economic welfare of the common man. Science and reason are rejected in so far as these impinge upon politics, and a cult of irrationality is fostered. The world view of fascism both in its total configuration and in its separate categories reflects an economy and a culture in decay.

The Fascist Alternative as Seen from the Experience of the United States

The 43 monographs and the 32 volumes of hearings of the Temporary National Economic Committee have further corroborated the fact, immediately relevant to a discussion of the fascist alternative, that the economic controls of American life are becoming increasingly concentrated. The extent of this concentration is now overwhelming and embraces all phases of American economy. It is impossible in the scope of this article to summarize the dramatic import of these studies. For our purposes it is sufficient to indicate that three family groups—the DuPonts, Mellons and Rockefellers—have shareholdings which directly or indirectly give control over 15 of the 200 largest nonfinancial corporations with aggregate assets of over $8,000,-000,000, or more than 11 per cent of their total assets. These 200 corporations comprise all of the major manufacturing industries of the country and also its electric, gas, and water utilities, its railroads, and large sections of its retail distribution and its service industries. In about 40 per cent of these 200 largest corporations one family or a small number of families exercise either absolute control by virtue of ownership of a majority of voting securities, or a working control through ownership of a substantial minority of the voting stock. About sixty corporations, or an additional 30 per cent, are controlled by one, or more, other corporations. Moreover the ownership of stock of all American corporations is highly concentrated, with 10,000 persons (0.008 per cent of the population) owning one-fourth, and 75,000 (0.06 per cent of the population) owning fully one-half, of all the corporate stock held by individuals in this country.[24] Similar concentration prevails in the control exercised by the financial corporations. Thirty banks together hold 34.3 per cent of the banking assets of the country outside of the Federal Reserve

[24] Raymond W. Goldsmith and others, *The Distribution of Ownership in the 200 Largest Non-Financial Corporations.* (Temporary National Economic Committee, Monograph 29.) Washington: U.S. Government Printing Office, 1941, pp. xvi–xvii.

ALTERNATIVE PROPOSALS TO DEMOCRACY 255

Banks, while 17 life insurance companies account for over 81.5 per cent of the assets of all life insurance companies.[25]

The control which these corporations exercise over the economic life of this country is prodigious. Smaller industrial and distributive enterprises are being pushed out of the field by their inability to obtain credit and to compete with the large corporations because of the latters' control of the market through patents and restricting licenses and through manipulation of prices. The age of free competitive enterprise in the United States has passed.[26] At the same time the problems of unemployment and of the agricultural crisis remain acute.

Political power goes hand in hand with economic power. The mighty influence which giant wealth has exercised on the political life of America is too well known to require documentation.[27] In recent years it has been able first to obstruct and then to defy social legislation passed to meet the exigencies which arose out of the economic crisis. The sixty-five volumes of the hearings of the Senate committee to investigate violations of the right of free speech and assembly and interference with the right of labor to organize and bargain collectively present vivid testimony of the anti-democratic attitudes and practices of corporate wealth both against industrial and agricultural workers. Because of space limitations one illustration will have to suffice. In his recent report to the Senate, on the investigations of this committee, Senator La Follette declared:

> The Iron and Steel Institute, which is the trade association of the [steel] industry, and the National Association of Manufac-

[25] National Resources Committee, *The Structure of the American Economy.* Washington: U.S. Government Printing Office, 1939, p. 103.
[26] Cf. John H. Cover and others, *Problems of Small Business.* (Monograph No. 17, Temporary National Economic Committee.) Washington: U.S. Government Printing Office, 1941; George Perazick and Philip M. Field, *Industrial Research and Changing Technology.* Philadelphia: W.P.A. National Research Project, 1940; Walter Hamilton and others, *Patent and Free Enterprise.* (Temporary National Economic Committee, Monograph 31.) Washton: U.S. Government Printing Office, 1941; Kemper Simpson, *Big Business Efficiency and Fascism.* New York: Harper and Brother, 1941.
[27] Cf. Donald C. Blaisdell, *Economic Power and Political Pressures.* (Temporary National Economic Committee, Monograph No. 26.) Washingington: U.S. Government Printing Office, 1941.

turers, of which "Little Steel" companies are heavy contributing members, adopted and publicized an anti-union policy. . . . To break the strikes of 1937, "Little Steel" resorted to the traditional practices of espionage, the "rough shadowing" of union organizers and men, the arming and deputizing of private persons, and coercion of local law enforcement officers. The strike of 1937, however, was more ominous than the others since in it the companies sought to incite a spirit of vigilantism in the citizens and to subvert the community to strike-breaking activities. Their conduct in arming private persons and in coercing the duly constituted law-enforcement agencies exceeded legal limitations and must be considered reprehensible.[28]

The hearings show that the same tactics were used by the Associated Farmers on the Pacific Coast and in other areas as well. The activities of Father Charles Coughlin, William Dudley Pelley, James True, Joseph McWilliams, John B. Trevor and other advocates of vigilantism against labor, and of anti-Semitism, are merely incidental to a much wider program of attack upon democracy.

War Intensifies the Danger of Fascism

The manner in which contracts for war materials are granted is intensifying the concentration of economic power in the United States and is simultaneously increasing the political power of the monopolist groups making way for fascism. Of the eleven and one-half billions in prime contracts awarded between June 13, 1940, and February 15, 1941, between one-fifth and one-quarter had gone to two groups of companies of closely interconnected ownership. Between 40 and 45 per cent had gone to six closely interconnected groups and a total of 80 per cent had gone to 62 companies or interrelated groups of companies.[29]

As Donald C. Blaisdell, Economic Expert of the Temporary National Economic Committee, declares:

[28] Senate Committee on Education and Labor, *Labor Policies of Employers Associations*. Part IV, "The 'Little Steel' Strike and Citizens Committees," 77th Cong., 1st Sess., Senate Report No. 151, March 31, 1941, p. 330.
[29] Temporary National Economic Committee, Final Report and Recommendations, Investigation of Concentration of Economic Power, 77th Congress, 1st Session, Senate Document No. 35, March 31, 1941, Appendix 3.

Business refuses to work except on terms which it dictates. It controls the natural resources, the liquid assets, the strategic position in the nation's economic structure, and its technical equipment and its knowledge of processes. The experience of the World War, now apparently being repeated, indicates that business will use this control only if it is "paid properly."[30]

It is not merely that the industrial monopolists determine the rate of profits. They are simultaneously waging an assault upon, and seeking exemption from, all legislation protecting the rights of workers to organize and to strike. In this attempt they have secured the overt collaboration of many of the important government agencies. The war situation is providing the social and psychological setting by which fascism can be instituted. It is a mark of the strength of the organized labor movement that it has thus far been able to resist these encroachments and so to perpetuate democracy in this country.

Fascism in the United States is not coming by one dramatic act of conquest, but by a step by step attenuation of democratic rights. Nor will it come through those who advocate fascism under that slogan, which is now discredited because of the rôle of Italy and Germany in World War II. As Huey Long, who knew fascist techniques well, declared: "Fascism in America will arrive on an anti-Fascist platform." It is for this reason that various recent steps of government policy must be understood as retreats in democracy and thus as steps in the development of fascism. State after state is suppressing minority parties, which attack the encroachment of industrial and financial privilege upon America's politics and culture.[31] The passage of the Alien Registration Act, which establishes a domestic passport system in the United States, has been a signal for intensified discrimination against foreign-born, citizens as well as non-citizens, particularly in the economic field, and has engendered new prejudices and hates in terms of an exclusive definition of an American. The federal sponsorship of new state criminal syndicalism laws, which are so drawn that organized labor has protested their

---

[30] Donald C. Blaisdell, *op. cit.*, pp. 172–173.
[31] Cf. Labor Research Association, *Labor Fact Book: 5.* New York: International Publishers, 1941, pp. 195–197.

potential use against trade unions; the enforcement, with new interpretations against communists, of the syndicalism laws of World War I; the use of Congressional committees, such as the Dies Committee, to incite public sentiment against legitimate strikes, trade union organization drives, and peace activity on the part of workers' groups; the attack upon education and freedom of teaching by such state committees as the Rapp-Coudert Committee of New York State—these and other governmental activities of a like nature, signify that the onrush of fascism is accelerated by a war situation. Still, it is not inevitable, for the democratic forces in America are yet powerful and can stem and reverse the current.

Relevance to the Negro

To a Negro American, fascist theory and practice cannot but appear comparable to that which he already experiences within our unfulfilled democracy. He may ask whether fascism is really an alternative for him or merely another word for the prevailing system. The caste concept of the élite has long functioned to submerge him. Racial chauvinism oppresses him in all his social and economic relationships. The coercive control of the large landowners and of the owners of mills, mines, and factories over the lives and destinies of Negro farmers and workers is a familiar story. The single political parties of the fascist states differ little in end-result from the single-party system in the South. The violence of the lynch-mob and the coercions of terror that mark white-Negro relations in some areas of this country are of the same piece with fascist vigilantism. Whenever the Bill of Rights and the Constitution are ignored and violated, as is well nigh universal in connection with the Negro in the United States, democracy is only a metaphor, and not a reality.

The Negro American has much to lose, nonetheless, by the extension of fascism to this country. For fascism will mean the extinction of those organizations, Negro and white, which have been in the forefront of the struggle for the improvement of the status of the Negro. With the champions of the cause of Negro equality out of the way, all the gains which the Negro has acquired through years of strife will be annulled. The rights of

Negro and white masses are clearly indivisible, and if trade unions are destroyed and liberal opinion suppressed, the impact upon the lives of all Negroes as well as whites will be overwhelmingly deleterious.

Democracy and fascism are still alternatives in the United States; for how long will depend upon activity based on awareness of the true nature of the fascist threat.

part four

THE FAMILY

The Family and Cultural Change*

From the beginnings of culture there has been an intimate web of interrelationships between the family and other institutions because the persons who make up the family are also participants in the economic, religious, and other social activities of a community. Never has the family lived alone. The family as an isolated institution is as unrealistic as the individual economic man of the classical economists and the abstract ego of the Freudian man.

The exigencies of the struggle for survival from primitive to contemporary societies have required not only that individuals have the additional security which economic and psychological participation in the family life affords but also that several families cooperate in economic activities. Moreover, families have always commingled on ceremonial occasions, whether religious or political, and have combined into larger groups in feuds and warfare. The family members, therefore, bring to the family group the social attitudes, the patterns of behavior and the knowledge of technologies that reside in the larger community. Within the family there is, in varying degrees, not only a merging and funding of joint property but also of attitudes and experiences through the reciprocal intercommunion of family members. The impact of personality upon personality through common residence, and the intimacy between family members rooted in affectional relations, give fertile soil for a relatively cohesive family tradition which is a composite of cultural aspects

* Read before the Family Section of the American Sociological Society, Detroit Michigan, Dec. 28, 1938.

derived from the larger community. The family, in turn, while functioning as an agency for joint economic activity or for joint sharing of products of labor earned outside the home, and for the transmission of property, has served also as the unit through which the larger community inculcates attitudes of authority and of loyalty to traditional ideas and ideals.

One effective method of studying the impact of culture on the family is through an analysis of how cultural change affects the status and role of woman as wife and mother and, consequently, how it affects family form and function. Woman, by her ability to bear and nurture children and by definition in our culture, is the nucleus of family life. Historically, cultural changes, and in particular economic changes, have had decisive effect upon women's place in society and in the family. Women's rights have been inextricably bound up with the broader problem of human rights, and improvements in the status of the masses, through changes in productive relations, have had repercussions on the status of women. When the dominant ideology of an era has been humanitarian and rationalistic and geared to the enlargement of freedom and the release of human potentialities, woman's status has advanced, if not always formally through legislation, none the less in practice. On the other hand, in periods of cultural retrogression, as under fascism, when human rights are curtailed, the earlier institutionalized restrictions which sanctioned and enforced the subordinate status of women are revived and intensified.[1] The relative freedom accorded woman in economic and political life and in other forms of social activities has immediate and decisive influence on intrafamilial relationships, on the husband-wife roles, and on parent-child authority. I shall illustrate this for modern times in brief historical perspective.

In western society, the patriarchal social organization prevailed for centuries. Although there had been permutations in degrees of dominance, women unquestionably had been sub-

---

[1] I have documented this thesis more fully and from a different angle in "Women, Position of, in Historical Societies," *Encyc. Soc. Sci.*, 15: 442–450, and in my book, *The Family: Past and Present*, New York, 1938.

ordinate to men within the family throughout the ancient[2] and medieval[3] world. When in early modern times the bourgeoisie began to develop its attitudes, the subjection of women was accepted by both the Church and aristocracy. The exalted formalism and passionate eroticism of romantic chivalry were merely veneer that did not interfere with the application of corporal punishment to wives as permitted by canon law. It was a manifestation of woman's changing relations when, beginning with the thirteenth century, the bourgeoisie began to exhibit in some respects more regard for the personality of the woman than did either the aristocracy or the Church. The wives of the bourgeoisie had entered into trade, both independently and as shopmanagers and assistants, and also the wives of artisans were admitted to some guilds on an equal footing with men. As a result, borough regulations permitted them to go to law and provided that their husbands were not to be held responsible for their debts. The middle class and artisan husband was, moreover, dependent upon his wife's assistance in these days of family and domestic industry. Neither husband nor wife could prosper without each other's help and it was to his interest that she be trained in some skill which would make her economically proficient. Traditional attitudes were tenacious but by the sixteenth century the cloistered life of woman of feudal days had begun to disappear.

These changes in outlook towards women cannot be ascribed to the Reformation, although it liberalized the canonical view of divorce. Luther still regarded marriage as "a physic against incontinence" and declared that women "should remain at home, sit still, keep house, and bear and bring up children."[4]

That women's prestige had not been greatly heightened among the clergy in England, is illustrated by Bishop Aylmer's characterization of them in a sermon before Queen Elizabeth:

---

[2] L. T. Hobhouse, *Morals in Evolution*, chap. 5, New York, 1916; F. Warre Cornish, "The Position of Women," in Leonard Whibley, ed., *A Companion of Greek Studies*, Cambridge, 1905.

[3] Eileen Power, "The Position of Women," in C. G. Grump and E. E. Jacobs, eds., *The Legacy of the Middle Ages*, Oxford, 1926; C. G. Coulton, *Medieval Panorama*, 614–628, New York, 1938.

[4] Martin Luther, *Table Talk* 298 ff. (1566), trans. by William Hazlitt, London, 1857.

Women are of two sorts; some of them are wiser, better learned, discreeter, and more constant than a number of men; but another and a worse sort of them, and the most part, are fond, foolish, wanton flibbergibs, tattlers, triflers, wavering, witless, without counsel, feeble, careless, rash, proud, dainty, nice, tale-bearers, eavesdroppers, rumor-raisers, evil-tongued, worse-minded, and in every wise doltified with the dregs of the devil's dunghill."[5]

The improved position of women in the family that came with the rise of the middle class resulted in a large part from the desire of the thrifty citizen to make his life a success according to mercantile ideals. As Wright declares of this citizen:

Like all true believers in the divine right of property, he was aware of the positive service rendered by so important a functional unit as the home to the organization of that society which made his goods safe and gave his accumulated possessions continuity. Hence, he was seriously concerned to maintain a code fostering ideals useful in the efficient conduct of the household, so that the home might make the greatest possible contribution to the happiness of its component parts, without friction and waste, either material or emotional. In this middle class code of domestic relations, the husband was recognized as the primary earner of wealth while upon the wife devolved the duty of the thrifty utilization of the income for the comfort of her household. Therefore the wife became, acknowledged or unacknowledged, the factor determining the success of the individual home. If the wife were a railing shrew, a slattern, an extravagant, gossipy, or faithless creature, the domestic efficiency and happiness so earnestly desired by every worthy husband would be jeopardized."[6]

The Elizabethan tradesman considered it his duty to be well informed on the domestic relations that might lead to the stability of the home. There arose a vast literature of handbooks and printed guides which gave advice to the middle class on family happiness and crystallized attitudes independent of the tradition of the aristocracy.[7] In these manuals, a gradual improvement in

[5] Daniel Neal, *The History of the Puritans*, 1:218, London, 1843–44.
[6] Louis B. Wright, *Middle Class Culture in Elizabethan England*, 201, Chapel Hill, N.C., 1935.
[7] Chilton L. Powell, *English Domestic Relations, 1487–1653*, New York, 1917.

women's position is discernible. They repeatedly insist that the woman must be treated as the lieutenant of her husband, sharing his confidence and trust, and not as his chattel and slave. The husband retained his powers of discipline and his authority, but there was an increased emphasis on woman's rights. Family industry and domestic economy, however, by its very nature offered a limited horizon to women and perpetuated men's dominance in all essential respects.

With the introduction in England of industrial capitalism which broke away from the family system and dealt directly with individuals, husbands were freed to some extent from whatever economic dependence they had had on their wives. The ideal of the subjection of women to their husbands could be put into practice without the husband fearing the consequent danger of his wife's inefficiency. Women no longer were given specialized training with the result that one of the first fruits of capitalist individualism was their exclusion from the journeymen's associations. Excluded from the skilled trades, the wives of the men who became capitalists withdrew from productive activity and became economically dependent and to a large degree parasitic. The wives of journeymen either were obliged to confine themselves to domestic work, or to enter the labor market as individuals in competition with their male relations. The competition which had previously existed only between families in which labor and capital had been united within the family group, was now introduced into the capitalist labor market where men and women struggled with each other to secure work and wages. Capitalist organization tended to deprive women of opportunities for sharing in the more profitable forms of production and confined them as wage workers to the trades where they were obliged to accept lower wages than men and thus to depress labor standards.[8]

As a reflection of the development of capitalist economic life, the political theories of the seventeenth century regarded the state as an organization of individual men only, or of groups of men, not as a commonwealth of families. Consequently, edu-

[8] Alice Clark, *Working Life of Women in the Seventeenth Century*, London, 1919.

cational, scientific, economic, and political associations formed for public purposes did not include women as members, which underscored their postulated inferiority and made their functioning in the larger community difficult.

It is erroneous to overestimate the rapidity with which domestic industry and the family life which centered around it disintegrated. As late as the mid-eighteenth century, the population of England remained mainly rural and women continued to be engaged in productive work in their homes and in some form of domestic industry, but from that time forward, agrarian and industrial changes deprived them of their employment. There was great distress and unemployment among women as well as men at the turn of the century. The laborer's wage remained below the level of family subsistence, and women and children were urgently obliged to work to supplement the father's income. In rural areas, a new class of women day laborers developed in agriculture, and the infamous Gang System for the exploitation of women and children developed. As urbanization was accelerated concomitant with the introduction of power-driven machinery of the industrial revolution, women came to the cities in increasing number to sell their labor power as factory workers.[9] The conditions under which they were obliged to work aroused the shocked indignation of the Victorian writers who became nostalgic for a return to the feudal family.[10] It is to the credit of Marx and Engels that they anticipated the advances in family life that these technological changes implied, identifying the distress occasioned by factory employment to the exploitive nature of capitalism rather than to the use of machines.[11]

Development of the family in the United States paralleled in many respects that of the Old World. With the culture of colonial New England dominated by the Puritan clergy, the patriarchal regime of Biblical tradition prevailed. Women's status is clearly defined by a seventeenth century document:

[9] Ivy Pinchbeck, *Women Workers and the Industrial Revolution, 1750–1850*, London, 1930.
[10] Wanda F. Neff, *Victorian Working Women*, New York, 1929.
[11] Karl Marx, *Capital*, 527–529, trans. from 4th ed. by Eden and Cedar Paul, New York, 1929; and Frederick Engels, *The Origin of the Family*, 196, Eng. trans., Chicago, 1902.

The dutie of the husband is to travel abroad to seeke living: and the wives dutie is to keepe the house. The dutie of the husband is to get money and provision; and the wives, not vainly to spend it. The dutie of the husband is to deale with many men: and of the wives, to talke with few. The dutie of the husband is, to be entermedling: and of the wife, to be solitarie and withdrawne. The dutie of the man is, to be skilfull in talke: and of the wife, to boast of silence. The dutie of the husband is, to be a giver: and of the wife, to be a saver . . . Now where the husband and wife performeth the duties in their house we may call it College of Qyietness: the house wherein they are neglected we may term it a hell.[12]

According to Calhoun, for nearly 150 years after the landing of the Pilgrims there were practically no women wage earners in New England outside of domestic service. Later, however, theory and practice did not always coincide, for some women of the poor classes went outside of the home to work and others of the middle class engaged in independent enterprise. An analysis of advertisements from 1720 to 1800 reveals that women were teachers, embroiderers, jellymakers, cooks, wax workers, japanners, mantua makers, and dealers in crockery, musical instruments, hardware, farm products, groceries, drugs, wines and spirits. Hawthorne noted one colonial woman who ran a blacksmith shop, and Peter Faneuil's account books show deals with many Boston tradeswomen.[13] Mrs. Spruill has recently shown that the same situation prevailed in the southern colonies where women's function was likewise conceived as being limited to that of childbearing and serving as housekeeper.[14]

Whatever distinctive characteristics the American family assumed were derived from the fact that the frontier areas of the United States were settled by individual families rather than by groups as in the agricultural villages of Europe. Their relative

---

[12] Quoted by Katherine DuPre Lumpkin, *The Family: A Study of Member Roles*, xiv-xv, Chapel Hill, N. C., 1933.
[13] A. W. Calhoun, "The Early American Family," *Amer. Acad. Pol. and Soc. Sci.*, March 1932, 155: 7–12, also A. W. Calhoun, *A Social History of the American Family from Colonial Times to the Present*, Vol. I, Cleveland, 1917.
[14] J. C. Spruill, *Women's Life and Work in the Southern Colonies*, Chapel Hill, N. C., 1938.

isolation tended to develop, therefore, a pronounced functional ingrown economic and affectional pattern. In the United States, moreover, diverse family forms were constantly being brought to these shores by different immigrant groups. These persisted as long as ethnic communities retained their strength but gave way, as their communities gave way, to the standardizing effects of industrial society. The adaptation of the second and third generation immigrants to the dominant family pattern repeatedly developed frictions in intrafamily relations based on divergent outlooks between parents and children. The clash of national family traditions merely intensified the conflicts that arose in native families from the fact of the existence of alternative patterns of behavior in a complex society undergoing rapid economic and political transitions.

The ferment created by the discussion of human rights that accompanied the American revolution penetrated into the home. Abigail Adams asked her husband that he see to it that the new government should not "put such unlimited powers into the hands of the Husbands." In John Adams' jesting response there was recognition of the fact that the problem of woman's rights was but a part of the larger problem of minority rights. He expressed surprise that the British ministry, after stirring up "Tories, land-jobbers, trimmers, bigots, Canadians, Indians, negroes, Hanoverians, Hessians, Russians, Irish, Roman Catholics, Scotch renegadoes," had also stimulated women to demand new privileges.[15] It is significant that the organized woman's rights movement in the 1840's was associated with the antislavery movement, which was women's recognition of the fact that their own inferior status had sociological implications comparable to the oppression of the Negro people. The campaign for the removal of woman's disabilities in the home as well as in the state became a part of a broader program for the extension of democratic rights.

As in Europe, it was the factory system that accelerated changes in the functions of the family by bringing women from the household into the larger industrial world, for the majority of

[15] Charles Francis Adams, ed., *Familiar Letters of John Adams and his Wife Abigail Adams During the Revolution*, 155, New York, 1876.

the employees of early American factories were women. The basis was thus laid for a changed status of woman in the family derived from the fact that she contributed to the family income, and in some instances was the major source of family support. While the process tended to disintegrate the patriarchal family which yielded slowly but surely to industrial trends, the shifting of production from the home to the factory formed the basis of a new type of family.

As technological changes have proceeded apace, there has been no turning back to the preindustrial patriarchal family here or abroad. The accompaniments of industrialism have made this impossible. Concentration of production has led to the increase of urban communities which have permitted wider social contacts for men and women, offering greater variety of possibilities for the manifestations of an individual's potentialities. Centralization of wealth in cities has increased educational opportunities, decreased illiteracy, and provided recreational opportunities outside of the home. Modernization of housing and the mechanization of the home have tended to lighten the drudgeries which thwart and frustrate the housewife.[16] Advances in public health and sanitation and the control of epidemic diseases have to some degree lessened the anxieties of family life.[17]

There is no intention here to suggest that advances have been uniformly distributed over the entire population. Divergences are so pronounced that to discuss adequately the nature of the family, it is imperative to differentiate between the forms and functions of the family as they are found in different social classes, and not merely to limit oneself, as has often been done, to the middle class. The family situation is markedly different among the 65 percent of the families in the United States whose annual incomes were less than $1,500 in 1935 from what it is among the 32 percent between $1,500 and $5,000 and the 3 per-

[16] William F. Ogburn and Clark Tibbitts, *Recent Social Trends in the United States*, vol. I, chap. 8, New York, 1933; William F. Ogburn, "The American Family Today: Its Trends," *The New York Times*, August 27, 1933.
[17] M. C. Buer, *Health, Wealth and Population in the Early Days of the Industrial Revolution*, 59–60, London, 1926.

cent above $5,000.[18] The findings of the President's Committee on Farm Tenancy,[19] of the National Emergency Committee on Conditions in the South,[20] of recent housing surveys,[21] and of the National Health Survey,[22] should dissipate the complacent assumption that modern science as utilized by capitalism has improved the living standards and lightened the burdens of the household so that the American family of the masses can feel secure. Family insecurity, never eliminated from the American scene, was even further intensified by the social changes concomitant with the recent economic crisis.[23]

Recent economic developments have not checked the increase in women's participation in industrial life. Contrary to the judgment of sociologists such as A. J. Todd, who predicted that reduced wage levels and a surplus labor force would check the economic tendency of women to enter industry,[24] the number of women workers has increased considerably since the crisis. The unemployment census revealed that between 1930 and 1937, 2,740,000 additional women workers had entered the country's labor market.[25] Women are not merely entering industry in larger

---

[18] National Resources Committee, *Consumers Income in the United States*, 18, Washington, D.C., 1938.

[19] National Resources Committee, *Farm Tenancy*, Washington, D.C., 1937.

[20] National Emergency Council, *Report on the Economic Conditions of the South*, Washington, D.C., 1938.

[21] E. E. Wood, *Slums and Blighted Areas in the United States*, Washington, D.C., 1935; L. W. Post, *The Challenge of Housing*, New York, 1938.

[22] U. S. Public Health Service, *The National Health Survey, 1935-36*, "Illness and Medical Care in Relation to Economic Status," Washington, D.C., 1938. See also Interdepartmental Committee to Coordinate Health and Welfare Activities, *The Need for a National Health Program*, Washington, D.C., 1938.

[23] Samuel A. Stouffer and Paul F. Lazarsfeld, *Research Memorandum on the Family in the Depression*, Social Science Research Council Bulletin 29, New York, 1938; R. S. Caven and K. H. Ranck, *The Family and the Depression*, Chicago, 1938; E. Franklin Frazier, "Some Effects of the Depression on the Negro in Northern Cities," *Science and Society*, Fall, 1938, 489-499; R. S. and H. M. Lynd, *Middletown in Transition*, chap. 5, New York, 1937.

[24] A. J. Todd, "Limits to the Changing American Family Functions," *Essays in Social Economics in Honor of Jessica Blanche Peixotto*, 314, Berkeley, Calif., 1935.

[25] *Census of Partial Employment, Unemployment and Occupations: 1937, Final Report*, Washington, D.C., 1938.

numbers than ever before, but more of them are remaining in industry permanently.[26] There is, as a result, an unprecedented approach of equality between the sexes and a less coercive discipline of the children. The participation of women in industry has, however, not resulted in actual equality for women in the United States because women have been at a disadvantage in their bargaining power with men and they have had the double burden of home and work. Traditionally, women have been paid less for their labor and have been obliged to combat historically derived attitudes that they are less capable than men of developing skills and attaining man's level of productivity. There have been many impediments to women's social equality both in law and in practice, and social services and legislation have been insufficient to cushion the effects upon the family of women's entrance into industry.

The reinterpretations of family roles which recent social changes have produced may perhaps best be illustrated by comparing Levy and Munroe's *The Happy Family* and *A Plan for Marriage* edited by Folsom, both contemporary guides to successful marriage for the middle classes of today, with their Elizabethan counterparts discussed earlier in this paper. There have been marked realignments of authority between the sexes to the advantages of wives, and a pronounced less doleful stress on duties of parents and children. Reciprocal responsibilities receive important attention, but the family is conceived as existing for the welfare of its members rather than they for the family. The family is not sacrificed to a strident individualism, but its very important function is as a training ground for personalities capable of adjustment to society. It soon becomes apparent that in the redefined family few of its earlier functions have been completely relinquished. The modern urban family is clearly no longer a productive unit, but that it has an economic function as a property sharing agency has been decisively underscored by the manner with which family members assumed mutual responsibilities during the last crisis even when not obliged to do so by

[26] M. E. Pigeon, "The Employed Woman Homemaker in the United States," U. S. Dept. of Labor, *Women's Bur. Bul. No. 148*, Washington, D.C., 1936.

law.[27] Although a child's formal education is as a rule acquired through public schools, the participation of the family in the educational process in conjunction with the school is decisive in the formation of personality and in the building of social attitudes. Recreational activities outside of the home have supplemented rather than replaced family gatherings, especially since the radio has brought the world into the home. The emphasis on the individuality and personality of the constituent members of the family has enhanced rather than minimized the difficult family function of giving emotional security and a sense of adequacy, through reciprocal affection, in order that the maturing child will be able to cope with the impact of a competitive society with its inevitable insecurities.[28]

For all of its limitations, this form of the modern family which few families as yet share, has undeniably superior values as compared to earlier forms. To the degree that it prevails, it has been made possible by the improvement in living standards and by the advances in the status of women. Its survival and extension is contingent upon these conditions, and whatever social and political conditions affect them affect the family.

The modern family is reinforced by developments in the Soviet Union, where industrialism and urbanism and the mechanization of collectivized rural areas are now involving women in all phases of economic, social, political, and cultural life. Women's equality is implemented by its legalization in the Soviet constitution and facilitated by a vast network of state social services that relieve tensions and anxieties that have been the traditional lot of the working woman. Through these services, the difficult problem is solved of how women can enter industry on a par with men and at the same time be the nucleus of satisfying family life. With economic security and improved living and working standards assured in an expanding collectivist economy, the basic cause of marital unhappiness is removed. The family is thus more firmly

[27] Howard M. Bell, *Youth Tell Their Story*, Washington, D.C., 1938, and citations in Note 23.
[28] For an excellent analysis of the difficulties which the family under capitalism has in fulfilling this important function, see Francis H. Bartlett, "The Limitations of Freud," *Science and Society*, Winter, 1939, 87–89.

established, with its cohesive force resting primarily on the affectional relations between parents as equals and parental authority over children derived not by force but by responsible guidance. These advances in the status of women, associated as they have always been historically with the extension of rights to other submerged groups, such as national minorities, are penetrating remote areas, although they involve drastic shifts in older institutionalized values.[29]

The threat of retrogression in the family comes from fascist countries, where monopoly capitalism in crisis has abolished democratic forms. There has been an outspoken and organized effort to subordinate women once more to an inferior status and to confine them to childbearing and domestic work under the indisputable authority of the male members of the family. In spite of its announced plan, it has not been able to eliminate women from industry, for in a highly industrialized country like Germany, women are required in economic life, but the fascist program has worked to their detriment. Employment of women in civil service, in the professions, and in skilled trades is barred. Men have displaced women at their lower wages with the result that the entire wage structure is depressed and insecurity is intensified. The patriarchal family is glorified, and family life, dominated by the husband and father, reinstitutes those qualities of coercion the elimination of which had been the achievement of centuries of progressive thinking. The regressive developments in women's role in the family and society are but a part of a larger picture which includes as well the denial of rights to minority peoples.[30]

At the present juncture of human history, sociologists and others interested in the preservation of the family, must therefore

---

[29] M. Fairchild and Susan Kingsbury, *The Family, Factory and Woman in the Soviet Union*, New York, 1935; M. Fairchild, "The Russian Family Today," *J. Amer. Assn. Univ. Women*, April, 1937, 142–148; S. and B. Webb, *Soviet Communism: A New Civilization?* 2: 812–838, New York, 1938; F. Halle, *Women in the Soviet East*, New York, 1938.

[30] Alfred Meusel, "National Socialism and the Family," *The Brit. Sociol. Rev.*, 1936, 182–184, 389–399; Clifford Kirkpatrick, *Nazi Germany: Its Women and Family Life*, New York, 1938. For evidence of the progress of women in Germany prior to the advent of Hitler, see H. W. Puckett, *Germany's Women Go Forward*, New York, 1930.

determine which form of family they wish to preserve. There are those in the United States who are finding hitherto unsuspected and eminently suspicious values in the families of the Ozark and Appalachian mountaineers. Minimizing the pathology of such isolated rural families, well portrayed in Caldwell's *Tobacco Road* and for New England in O'Neill's *Desire Under the Elms*, these sociologists hanker after the stability of the mountaineer families as contrasted with the more loosely knit modern family.[31] There are, moreover, powerful forces in the United States which would eliminate from our culture those democratic rights that give sustenance to the modern family, and in particular, resent the rights which women have acquired. Civilized family living is in the balance. Its future rests with the preservation and extension of democracy.

[31] C. C. Zimmerman and M. E. Frampton, *Family and Society*, New York, 1935. These writers get their inspiration from LePlay, whose work receives the plaudits as well of Nazi writers on the family. See C. Kirkpatrick, *op. cit.*, 101.

Engels on the Family

I

The major work in Marxian literature on the family, Engels' *Origin of the Family, Private Property and the State*,[1] appeared thirty-six years after the *Communist Manifesto*. There are several anticipations of its points of view, however, in the *Manifesto* and in other writings of Marx and Engels prior to it, which throw light on the genesis and development of their later judgments.

The discussion of the family in the *Communist Manifesto* is not extensive. In developing the theme that the bourgeoisie cannot exist without constantly revolutionizing the instruments of production and thereby the relations of production and with them all social relations, it asserts that "the bourgeoisie has torn from the family its sentimental veil and has reduced the family relation to a mere money relation."[2] On the other hand, because "the proletarian is without property, his relation with his wife and

[1] Frederick Engels, *Der Ursprung der Familie, des Privateigenthums und des Staats. Im Anschluss an Lewis H. Morgan's Forschungen* (1st ed. Zurich, 1884; 5th ed., Stuttgart, 1892). Between the appearance of the first and fifth editions, the book had been translated into Italian, Roumanian, and Danish and it has since been published in many languages. The most recent English translation is *The Origin of the Family, Private Property and the State. In the Light of the Researches of Lewis H. Morgan*. (New York, International Publishers, 1942). All references to the book in this article will be to this edition. August Bebel's *Die Frau in der Vergangenheit, Gegenwart und Zukunft* (Zurich, 1884), later editions of which were published under the title, *Die Frau und der Sozialismus*, was also translated into many languages and did much to extend the influence of Engels' book.

[2] Karl Marx and Frederick Engels, "The Communist Manifesto," *Selected Works*, 2 vols. (New York, 1935), I, p. 208.

children has no longer anything in common with bourgeoisie family relations."[3]

The *Manifesto* pours scorn upon those who contend that Communists advocate the abolition of the family. Its authors plead guilty only to the charge that they seek the end of the form of the family founded on private gain, that they aim to prevent the exploitation of children by their parents, that they advocate the substitution of social education for home education which their opponents then declared was "a destruction of the most hallowed of relations." Marx and Engels stated vigorously that "Bourgeois claptrap about the family and education, about the hallowed correlation of parent and child, becomes all the more disgusting, the more by the action of modern industry, all family ties among the proletarians are torn asunder, and their children transformed into simple articles of commerce and instruments of labor." To the charge that Communists want to make women common property they retort angrily that "The bourgeois sees in his wife a mere instrument of production. He hears that the instruments of production are to be exploited in common, and naturally, can come to no other conclusion than that the lot of being common to all will likewise fall to the women. He has not even a suspicion that the real point aimed at is to do away with the status of women as mere instruments of production."[4] Marx and Engels argued that the false charge of "communization of women" against the Communists comes with ill grace from a class that maintains public prostitution, and among which the seduction of the wives of others is not infrequent. They predicted that the abolition of the present system of production would lead to the disappearance of both public and private prostitution.

The comments on the family in the *Communist Manifesto* had had their antecedents in the earlier writings of Marx and Engels. Marx in 1845 had warned against considering the family abstractly, apart from its specific historical setting. In his criticism of the anarchist Max Stirner he wrote: "We make a mistake when we speak of 'the' family without qualification. Historically, the bourgeoisie endows the family with the characteristics of the

---

[3] *Ibid.*, p. 216.
[4] Citations *ibid.*, p. 223–25.

bourgeois family, whose ties are boredom and money." Marx then contended that in the eighteenth century the family had already been in the process of dissolution:

> The inner ties of the family, the individual parts out of which the concept of family life is made up, such as obedience, affection, conjugal fidelity, etc., had vanished; but the real body of the family, property relations, an exclusive attitude towards other families, an enforced life in common—the conditions that were determined by the existence of children, by the structure of modern towns, by the development of capital, etc.—these persisted, despite considerable modifications.[5]

In *The Holy Family*, written in 1845, Marx and Engels first made the observation that the degree of the emancipation of woman could be used as a standard by which to measure general emancipation. This was restated by Marx in 1868 in a letter to the surgeon, Dr. L. Kugelmann, in which he wrote: "Social progress can be measured exactly by the social position of the fair sex," and then added banteringly, "(the ugly ones included)."[6]

The impact of the technological changes of the industrial revolution on the family was also discussed at some length by Engels prior to the appearance of the *Communist Manifesto* in his *The Conditions of the Working Class in England*, published in 1845.[7] The significance of his findings on this subject and also those of Marx who discussed the same problem further in *Capital*[8] will be analyzed later in this article.

II

Most of the recent discussion in the United States of Engels' *Origin of the Family, Private Property and the State* has focused upon criticism of Morgan's data on the evolution of the family upon which Engels based his work and which later anthro-

[5] Quoted in D. Ryazanoff, ed., *The Communist Manifesto of Karl Marx and Friedrich Engels* (New York, 1930), p. 162.
[6] Karl Marx, *Letters to Dr. Kugelmann* (New York, 1934), p. 83.
[7] Frederick Engels, *Die Lage der Arbeitenden Klasse in England* (Leipzig, 1845), English translation, *The Condition of the Working Class in England in 1844* (London, 1892).
[8] Karl Marx, *Capital*, translated from 4th ed. by Eden and Cedar Paul (New York, 1929), p. 527–29.

pologists have found to be invalid. What has not been noted is the productive use to which Morgan's findings were put by Engels in what is without doubt one of the most influential documents on behalf of the emancipation of women in the world's literature.

Engels' discussion of the position of women under a supposititious group marriage, and his reconstruction of the rise of monogamy, are merely prefatory to his major thesis of the subjection of women in modern capitalist society. The book transcends the limitations of the anthropological materials utilized. Morgan's work is but a springboard for a bold and trenchant indictment of male dominance over women, marked by biting satire and sophisticated humor. Engels has written a humanistic tract that uses the mature scholarship of many fields to pour scorn upon conventional hypocrisies that debase women in modern society. Its barbs are most stinging on subjects that were then, and still are to a large extent, tabu. As a document aimed at freedom for womankind, it is vigorously frank and plain spoken. It is more than popular polemics, however. It abounds in insights and establishes many fundamental principles of sociological analysis of the family that are of great value.

The number of positive and valid general propositions that emerge from Engels' work is impressive. Not always formulated explicitly by Engels, they lay the basis of his approach to the family, and determine his method of analysis. They are presented here in categorical form without the corroborating data and supporting argument given in the book:

> The family is a dynamic, ever changing cultural historical product, not a divinely ordained natural institution;
>
> Its forms and functions vary widely from period to period, from country to country, and from class to class, and tend to respond to the demands which each society places upon it. It must not therefore be studied apart from its social content, but rather in its economic, technological, legal and religious settings;
>
> Changes in methods of production lead to changes in the relations of production and consequently they modify the totality of social relations, including the family;
>
> Patterns of family relationships are tenacious, and there are lags

in the adjustment of attitudes and practices to changing productive relations, with customs of previous periods persisting and influencing behavior;

Division of labor between the sexes in the family has been characteristic of all societies;

Authority, power and property relationships between the sexes in the family are determined by the role which men and women play in the productive process, which is in turn determined by the nature and ownership of the instruments of production;

When in simpler societies women's work is socially as important as that of men, there is an approximate equality between the sexes;

The patriarchal family which developed in Old World societies involving exclusive supremacy of the men was an outgrowth of the domestication of animals and the breeding of herds. This innovation developed a hitherto unsuspected source of wealth and created new social relations. Because of the division of labor within the family, the men became the owners of the new source of subsistence, the cattle, and later of the new instruments of labor, the slaves. This greatly enhanced men's position in the family and subordinated the women;

Individual sex love, in the modern sense of the word, played little part in the rise of the patriarchal monogamy, which was based primarily upon the economic purpose of making man supreme in the family, and of propagating as future heirs to his wealth, children indisputably his own;

Polygyny and polyandry are only exceptional "historical luxury products";

Under the patriarchal family, woman's exclusion from "social production," that is from employment outside the home, has been not merely to her economic disadvantage but has involved social and sexual discrimination as well. Prostitution, adultery and the principle of the indissolubility of marriage are by-products of such discrimination;

Under these circumstances, co-existent with monogamous marriage, there has been "hetaerism," i.e., sexual intercourse between men and women outside of marriage, which sometimes develops into open prostitution. There also has developed the neglected wife, hence the wife's attendant lover and the cuckold husband;

Sexual (i.e., romantic) love between mates is a modern concept depending for its realization upon the degree of equality of rights of the sexes. Such love can only develop fully when marriage is no longer a marriage of convenience, for the preservation and inheritance of property;

Family law is a reflection of past and present property relations;

The legal concept of freedom of contract under Protestant capitalism affected the family through the introduction of the right of choice of mates on the basis of mutual love, but property relations rendered this right largely theoretical since they still left power in the hands of the parents to choose mates for their children;

The lady of civilization surrounded by false homage and estranged from all real work, has an infinitely lower status than the hard-working woman of primitive societies;

The emancipation of women is possible only when women take part in production outside the home on a large scale, and work in the household no longer claims anything but an insignificant amount of their time. This has become feasible because modern large-scale industry not merely permits the extensive employment of female labor but demands it, while it also tends toward ending private domestic labor by the development of service industries;

Under capitalism, however, if the wife carries out her family duties, she is denied the opportunity to engage in production outside of the home and is unable to earn; while if she wants to earn independently by outside work, she cannot carry out family duties. For this reason, the individual family in capitalist society is in Engels' words "founded on the open or concealed domestic slavery of the wife, and modern society is a mass composed of these individual families as its molecules";

When the family ceases to be the major economic unit of society through the introduction of large-scale production and social ownership, the care and education of the children become increasingly a social responsibility, relieving the wife, now socially employed, of oppressive home burdens and permitting real affectional relations to develop;

The socialization of the means of production, Engels predicted, would make freedom to choose a mate a reality by reducing to a minimum the anxiety about bequesting and inheriting; it would negate male supremacy, established for the preservation and inheritance of property, and would make love rather than money the basis of choice of mate;

Marriage based on sexual love is by its nature exclusive and thus individual, so that if economic conditions disappear which make women put up with the habitual infidelity of their husbands (i.e., the concern for their own means of livelihood and that of their children), the equality of women will tend to make men really monogamous rather than to make women polyandrous.

This list of generalizations is imposing because of the many fertile ideas it contains. Many of them anticipated by years and even decades the research findings of later social scientists. Later studies on the family might have profited considerably if they had followed some of these leads instead of disdainfully repudiating Engels' total contribution on the basis of some of his book's manifest weaknesses in the use of data on primitive societies.

III

Engels' relation to Morgan in the discussion of the family in primitive societies merits brief treatment. Morgan's views were hailed by him as far in advance of those prevalent among his contemporaries in the infant science of anthropology. Engels cited Morgan's data and theories profusely, and based many of his own judgments upon them. Yet Engels cautioned as to the tentative nature of Morgan's scientific generalizations and of his own conclusions. In the preface to the fourth edition of the *Origin of the Family,* he wrote in 1891: "The fourteen years which have elapsed since the publication of his (Morgan's) chief work have greatly enriched the material available for the study of the history of primitive societies. . . . As a result some of Morgan's minor hypotheses have been shaken or even disproved. But not one of the great leading ideas of his work has been ousted by this new material."[9] Since Engels wrote these words, anthropological research has made significant strides and it can now no longer be said that anthropology sustains all of Morgan's basic generalizations on the family, although it is recognized that they compare favorably with the views of Morgan's contemporaries.[10]

[9] Engels, *Origin of the Family,* p. 17 f.
[10] For a critical approach of Morgan's work see Bernhard J. Stern, *Lewis Henry Morgan, Social Evolutionist* (Chicago, University of Chicago Press, 1931). This book was written when the attack upon the weaknesses of early social evolutionism was at its height. It contains what I now recognize to be some errors of fact and interpretation. The position taken in the book on Morgan's views on the family, however, remain essentially correct. See also

Today anthropologists do not support the hypothesis, for example, that group marriage was the earliest form of family relationship, a view upon which Engels relied heavily. Engels himself was not uncritical of Morgan's discussion of group marriage and declared that "here lies a newly discovered field of research which is almost completely unexplored."[11] He stated:

> At the time Morgan wrote his book, our knowledge of group marriage was still limited. . . . The punaluan family [Morgan's term for the Hawaiian family, which he designated a group marriage] provided, on the one hand, the complete explanation of the system of consanguinity in force among the American Indians, which had been the starting point of all Morgan's researches; on the other hand, the origin of the matriarchal gens could be derived directly from the punaluan family; further the punaluan family represented a much higher stage than the Australian classificatory system. It is therefore comprehensible that Morgan should have regarded it as the necessary stage of development before pairing marriage and should believe it to have been general in earlier times. Since then we have become acquainted with a number of other forms of group marriage, and we know now that Morgan here went too far."[12]

Engels then goes on, however, to claim as evidence of "a cruder form of group marriage" the exogamous classes or moieties described by Lorimer Fison and A. W. Howitt for Australia. Their data, however, and the later descriptions of Australian marital relationships do not support the contention that a functioning

---

Bernhard J. Stern, "Lewis Henry Morgan Today," SCIENCE AND SOCIETY, X (1946), p. 172–76, and Melville Jacobs and Bernhard J. Stern, *Outline of Anthropology* (New York, 1947), p. 146–72.

Engels' statement in the preface to the first edition written in 1884, that in the period preceding civilization, the social structure is determined not only by the production of material goods but also by the family as the producer of human beings, has recently been sharply criticized in the Soviet Union. See L. A. Leontiev and others, "Political Economy in the Soviet Union," SCIENCE AND SOCIETY, VIII (1944), p. 115 f. An attempt to recast Morgan's general evolutionary stages has been made by C. P. Tolstoi, "On the Question of the Periodization of the History of Primitive Society," *Sovetskaia Etnografia*, 1 (1946), p. 25 f. Marx's original notes on Morgan's *Ancient Society* which, Engels asserts, stimulated him to prepare the *Origin of the Family* have recently been published in his *Collected Works* in Russian.

[11] Engels, *op. cit.*, p. 40.
[12] *Ibid.*, p. 37 f.

and stable marital union of a group of males with a group of females ever existed.[13] In fact, Engels nowhere states that such a stable group family prevailed, although he is often so interpreted because of his ambiguity. He declares:

> Group marriage which in these instances from Australia is still marriage of sections, mass marriage of an entire section of men, often scattered over the whole continent, with an equally widely distributed section of women—this group marriage, seen close at hand, does not look quite so terrible as the philistines, whose minds cannot get beyond brothels, imagine it to be. . . . The Australian aborigine, wandering hundreds of miles from his home among people whose language he does not understand, nevertheless often finds in every camp and every tribe women who give themselves to him without resistance and without resentment; . . . the man with several wives gives one up for the night to his guest.[14]

These passages merely define the nature of the sexual prerogatives found in this area, and do not describe a stable marriage relationship of a group of men with a group of women.

In an article he published in *Die neue Zeit* in 1892,[15] Engels indicates how loosely he applied the term "group marriage." He here designates as evidence for "a newly discovered case of group marriage," Sternberg's findings among the Gilyaks on the island of Sakhalin. Sternberg had reported that:

> The Gilyak addresses as father, not only his own natural father, but also all the brothers of his father; all the wives of these brothers, as well as all the sisters of his mother, he addresses as his mothers; the children of all these "fathers" and "mothers" he addresses as his brothers and sisters. . . . Every Gilyak has the rights of a husband in regard to the wives of his brothers and to the sisters of his wife; at any rate the exercise of these rights is not regarded as unpermissible.[16]

---

[13] The letters of Lorimer Fison and A. W. Howitt to Lewis Henry Morgan throw light on this controversy. See "Selections from the Letters of Lorimer Fison and A. W. Howitt to Lewis H. Morgan," edited by Bernhard J. Stern, *American Anthropologist*, XXXII (1930), p. 257–79 and 419–53. See also Stern, *Lewis Henry Morgan: Social Evolutionist*, p. 158–69.

[14] Engels, *op. cit.*, p. 39.

[15] *Die neue Zeit*, XI (1892), p. 373–75. This article has been translated and published as an Appendix to Engels, *op. cit.*, p. 164–67.

[16] Engels, *ibid.*, p. 165.

In his deductions from this, Engels seems to confuse the kinship terms of the clan system and the potential rights subsumed under them with actual functional family relationships. He seems to sense how tenuous such evidence is, for in the same passage he comments: "this form of marriage, at least in the instances still known to occur today, differs in practice from a loose pairing marriage or from polygamy only in the fact that custom permits sexual intercourse in a number of cases where otherwise it would be severely punished. That the actual exercise of these rights is actually dying out only proves that this form of marriage is itself destined to die out which is further confirmed by its infrequency."

The primary error underlying Engels' entire discussion of this problem is the assumption that clan terminology and the customs of levirate and sororate could be explained only by postulating an earlier form of group marriage of which they are thought to be survivals. Such an explanation is, however, unnecessary, for they are explicable in terms of their social function.[17] Such of Engels' generalizations as are dependent upon the premise of an initial group marriage in primitive societies, as for example, that the incest tabu came late in human history, need to be revaluated in terms of present knowledge of anthropology. For it is now recognized that bilateral families, usually but not always monogamous, are found among simple hunting, food-gathering societies such as the Andamanese, the Fuegians, the Bushman and the Semang as well as among the simpler tribes of North America. In these primitive societies, as in our own, kinship is reckoned both through the father and the mother, and upon marriage the newly formed social unit of man and wife tends to have somewhat greater autonomy than is characteristic of societies where the clan is the important unit. In simple food-gathering societies the size of the groups is so small that few have clans, the possible exception being the clan-like divisions of the Australians. In the advanced hunting and food-gathering societies of the Northwest Coast of the United States, clans are found in some communities and not in others. Clan societies are most characteristic of agricultural and pastoral areas. While it is not known how early clans

[17] See below, p. 290.

developed in human history, it now appears quite certain, contrary to Morgan, that the small family unit, the extended bilateral family, the work party of either sex, the band and the small community or village, developed much earlier than did the clan. The development of clan institutions, either matrilineal or patrilineal, does not mean a catastrophic change in social organization. Clans represent a formal naming and classification of kin groups which everywhere previously functioned in the economic sphere even though unformalized.[18] After the clan has been formalized, the bilateral family relationship, though weakened considerably, does not entirely disappear. Secondary distinctions are usually made, for example, between actual brothers and sisters and cousins although they may be classified by one kinship term. Engels in his discussion of group marriage and elsewhere is often obscure in his differentiation between the family and the clan. This is readily explicable, for the relationship between them had not been defined by the scientists of his day. It was not understood for decades afterward, and there is no unanimity on the subject today.

IV

A fruitful approach to an analysis of the changes in relations between the family and the clan in primitive societies is to be found through the application of one of Engels' important generalizations that changes in the instruments of production influence the division of labor between the sexes and determine property surpluses which, in turn, lead to marked changes in the position of women in society and in the family. The division of labor between the sexes was a necessary condition of survival among hunting and food-gathering peoples. While women's occupations were different from those of men, they were of equal importance. Because the bearing and nursing of children impeded their movements in the hunting of animals, women usually performed the more sedentary but none the less essential and arduous tasks. There were significant exceptions, but generally

[18] See Julian H. Steward, "The Economic and Social Basis of Primitive Bands," in *Essays in Anthropology Presented to A. L. Kroeber* (Berkeley, Cal., 1936), p. 331–47.

men occupied themselves with the chase of large and swift animals, while women gathered vegetable products and slow-moving animals such as grubs, shellfish and small fish that were within the reach of the camp. Fish traps and fish hooks were often tended by women, but such fishing as required continuous labor and prolonged movement was man's work. Men usually prepared the utensils for the chase, and since the principal materials utilized by the hunter were made of stone and wood, he used the hammer, knife and drill as he manufactured the required tools. Normally in these societies women worked on meat, skins and fibres; they cooked, preserved food, prepared skins, sewed and weaved baskets and cloth. Since the welfare of the community depended equally upon the labor of both sexes, there was a rough and ready equality between them. Engels was thus right, and helped correct a widespread misapprehension, when he wrote: "One of the most absurd notions taken over from eighteenth-century enlightenment is that in the beginning of society, woman was the slave of man."[19]

The relationship of the families to one another is also determined by the nature of the economy. Because of the limitations of food supply, simple hunting and fishing communities were sparsely populated. They usually consisted of bands of less than forty and not more than eighty persons. Individual families never lived alone. Their members went out on food-collecting parties in season. During the winter months, they assembled for ceremonies that bound various families together socially and politically and served the purpose of mutual defense and joint sharing of meager food supplies. Because of the absence of surpluses, there was no significant exchange possible and hence no chance for individual, family or other group specialization along lines of specific skills and interests. These developed along with other changes in the structure of society, whenever property surpluses developed, whether in advanced hunting, food-gathering societies (as in the case of the salmon-fishing peoples of the Northwest Coast of the United States), or in agricultural and agricultural-pastoral societies.

The decisive factor which determined the structure and func-

[19] Engels, *op. cit.*, p. 42.

tioning of the family was, in Engels' opinion, the manner in which property was inherited. He rightly observed that there was a difference in the rules of inheritance of property in primitive societies and in class societies. His formulation of these differences must, however, be modified in terms of what is now known. Recent studies have shown that one must distinguish between the right to the *use* of property which the members of a family share, and the right to *control* of property over time, that is inheritance.[20] In primitive societies, with few exceptions, spouses have a common domicile, and their children remain with them for various periods. Food, shelter and household paraphernalia are therefore shared in common. Within the family, both parents generally contribute to their mutual support and to that of the children without consideration of the value of the goods. In general, when exchanging goods and making presents to outsiders, individual ownership manifests itself. If and when the family breaks up, the man and woman claim the property each has collected or made. There is in other words common use of property within the family, but individual property rights are maintained.

In contrast to our society, the right to shared property in the family does not extend to inheritance. Among us, both spouses may legally inherit from their separate family estates, and the property of both spouses legally descends to their children or to the living spouse, although each has the right to will the property as desired. In our society, in other words, the members of the family have prior claims to property which any one member holds individually during his lifetime, and this priority overrides any right of the dead spouse's consanguinal kin (i.e., father, mother, brothers, sisters) to claim this property. That is, the members of the marital group now possess a joint right to economic goods and the family derives property by inheritance from both spouses.

Such recognition of the duality of parenthood in relation to permanence of property rights is not found in primitive societies. It is absent both from primitive societies organized into small

[20] Ruth Benedict, "Marital Property Rights in Bilateral Society," *American Anthropologist*, xxxviii (1936), p. 368–73.

family groups (those which trace kinship bilaterally) and from those societies organized unilaterally (i.e., in patrilineal or matrilineal clans). Except for a few special cases, the small family in primitive societies does not constitute the legal unit for the pooling of permanent rights over economic goods. This means that the husband does not inherit from the wife nor the wife from the husband, nor do the children have prior rights to property drawn from the father's and the mother's line. In such bilateral primitive societies just as in those that have a formal clan system, property is transmitted to the consanguinal relatives excluding the spouse. Commonly none of the children are given priority, but instead property goes to the brothers of the deceased. The wife and the children have no claims, and are left destitute as far as the economic goods of the husband and father are concerned. The functional significance of the widespread practice of the levirate (the marriage of the deceased husband's brother by the widow) is clarified in the light of this rule of inheritance, for in this way the widow and her children continue to have use of the deceased's property which his brother takes over. If the widow returns to her kin, the children have no claim on the property whatsoever. In the matrilineal and patrilineal clan societies, unilateral inheritance of the property receives greater emphasis.

In simple food-gathering societies, authority in the men's sphere of activity centers around the father and in the women's sphere around the mother. If authority tends to be superficially patriarchal in character, this may be attributed to the relative backwardness of women's knowledge and skills as compared to those of men, and hence their lesser economic importance. The elaboration of mother-right seems to be a development especially characteristic of agricultural peoples. The domestication of plants was a product of women's work, an outgrowth of their food-gathering activities. As a consequence of women's development of agriculture, economic power and hence social importance shifted relatively in favor of women, so that many, although not all, agricultural peoples are matrilineal. The domestication of animals was achieved by men as an outgrowth of their hunting activities. When domestication of animals was combined with agriculture by the use of the animal-drawn plow, and in some areas with pastoralism as well, even larger surpluses were possible. Woman's economic importance then receded relative to man's, and patrilineal descent became predominant.

Clans developed from the earlier bilateral family because of rules of residence and inheritance of property. Newly married couples reside either with the husband's or wife's parents, and patrilocal residence tends to develop into patrilineal lineage, matrilocal residence into matrilineal lineage. The inheritance of property unilaterally increases the importance of the clan grouping as property surpluses develop. This is because there is a continuity in the clan that does not exist for the family. The family is inevitably a loose unit, not only because of the possibility of divorce, separation or death of either of the spouses but because, as the children grow up, they leave to found new families. Even in the case of the extended families in the agricultural communities of the Old World, composed of blood brothers with their wives and descendants, the girls leave the family upon marriage. The clan, however, operates on the principle that once a member always a member, and so it is capable of providing a greater sense of security to its members.

While it appears clear that both matrilineal and patrilineal clans can be direct offshoots of prior bilateral families, there has been acrimonious controversy over whether or not the matrilineal clan was prior to the patrilineal. Engels felt this to be Morgan's great contribution and declared: "The rediscovery of the primitive matriarchal gens as the earlier stage of the patriarchal gens of civilized peoples has the same importance for anthropology as Darwin's theory of evolution has for biology and Marx's theory of surplus value has for political economy."[21] Engels laid much stress on the fact that the domestication of cattle was the crucial factor in modifying the balance of power between the sexes in favor of man by creating significant surpluses through men's work. V. Gordon Childe recently supported this hypothesis when he declared:

> Among the pure cultivators, owing to the role of the women's contributions to the collective economy, kinship is naturally reck-

[21] Engels, *op. cit.*, p. 16.

oned in the female line, and the system of "mother right" prevails. With stockbreeding, on the contrary, economic and social influence passes to the males and kinship is patrilineal.[22]

American anthropologists, particularly Swanton,[23] Lowie,[24] and Kroeber,[25] emphatically assailed the generalization that the matrilineal clan preceded the patrilineal and contended for the priority of the patrilineate. Murdock's careful appraisal of the evidence[26] shows the conclusion to be inescapable that the simpler cultures tend to be matrilineal and the more advanced ones patrilineal. There is not, however, universal matrilineal priority. The type of clan organization that prevails is found to be directly correlated with economic aspects of culture, as Engels had contended. Murdock concluded that

> the patrilineate and matrilineate represent adjustments to special elaborations respectively in the male and female realms of economic activity. . . . Social organization under primitive conditions tends to be matrilineal only partially and in an incipient sense, and is elaborated into a full-fledged and consistent matrilineal system only after cultural advances favorable to the retention and the expansion of the principle, e.g., the adoption of agriculture. Typical motherright, or the full matrilineal complex, would then be, not primitive, but a special adjustment to a somewhat exceptional set of social and economic circumstances on a relatively advanced level of cultural development.

---

[22] V. Gordon Childe, *What Happened in History* (New York, 1946), p. 58 f.

[23] J. R. Swanton, "A Reconstruction of the Theory of Social Organization," *Boas Anniversary Volume* (New York, 1906), p. 166–178; also his "The Social Organization of American Tribes," *American Anthropologist*, n.s., VII (1905), p. 663–73.

[24] R. H. Lowie, "Social Organization," *American Journal of Sociology* XX (1914), p. 72 f.; *Primitive Society* (New York, 1920), p. 148–58, 177, 182. In the latter work Lowie declared: "I am not aware of a single student in this field who has failed to accept his [Swanton's] position" (p. 150).

[25] Alfred Kroeber, *Anthropology* (New York, 1923), p. 355–57.

[26] George Peter Murdock, "Correlations of Matrilineal and Patrilineal Institutions," *Studies in the Science of Society* (New Haven, 1937), p. 445–70. This has been substantiated by the studies in comparative cultures made by Leo W. Simmons, *The Role of the Aged in Primitive Society* (New Haven, 1945), p. 207–16.

"Patrilineal forms," he further declares, "show an especially high correlation with animal domestication, metal-working and general occupational specialization, all of which fall mainly within the masculine sphere of economic activity."[27] Linton makes a comparable generalization: "There does seem to be a very rough and general correlation between the line of descent selected by a particular group and the sex which is of preponderant economic importance. Male-supported societies tend to be patrilineal, female supported ones matrilineal."[28] Thus while Morgan erred in conceiving the matrilineal clan to be the earliest form of social organization, he was more nearly correct than were his later American critics when he contended that the matrilineal clan preceded the patrilineal.

In historical times, the bilateral family superseded the clan as the primary unit for the inheritance of property, and both family and clan became subordinate to the state. This development is associated with economies in which surplus commodities are exchanged with the intermediacy of money. In such societies there are families which engage in what may be called industrial food production, that is, they produce enough food to feed not merely their own members, but also families which are engaged in industry other than food production. When such industrial production, with its large surpluses, develops, then urban culture becomes possible. With it comes an emphasis on private property and exchange, with consequent differences in wealth among persons; also the possibility of utilizing the labor of others, and hence the basis of the development of classes. In the course of time, the society based on kinship groups is broken up. Control is exercised through the state, the subordinate units of which are not unilateral kinship groups but local territorial associations. Such cultures arose in the Mediterranean area, in the ancient world. In Greece, for example, the importance of the patrilineal clan or gens was undermined by the edict of Cleisthenes in 508 B.C., which reorganized the society into demes or township communities along territorial lines in order to break up the power of the kinship groups. Within the territorial group the bilateral

---

[27] Murdock, loc. cit., p. 468 f.
[28] Ralph Linton, The Study of Man (New York, 1936), p. 169.

family remains to take on different forms and to serve diverse functions in different periods and classes.

V

The impact of a change in the methods of production upon the family is effectively illustrated in the case of the shift from locally self-sufficient agricultural economies with domestic handicraft production to large-scale factory production under commercial and industrial capitalism. In this process the home became separated from the place of work and joint labor by family members gave way to the sale of individual labor to employers who owned the instruments of production and utilized them for profit. Men and women, husbands and wives, often competed for the same jobs as individuals on the labor market.[29] Engels and Marx were not alone in stressing the revolutionary significance of the resulting transformation that occurred not only in the economic functions of the family, but in the authority relationships between husband and wife and parents and children. The Victorian reformers in novels with social themes,[30] the aristocratic critics of rising capitalism,[31] and many others who upheld

[29] There has been considerable literature on the effects of these changes in England. See, for example, Ivy Pinchbeck, *Women Workers and the Industrial Revolution* (London, 1930); J. B. and Barbara Hammond, *The Rise of Modern Industry* (London, 1926), and *The Town Laborer 1760-1832* (London, 1925); E. Lipson, *The History of the Woolen and Worsted Industries* (London, 1921); G. W. Morris and L. S. Wood, *The Golden Fleece* (Oxford, 1922); Paul Mantoux, *The Industrial Revolution in the Eighteenth Century* (New York, 1927). Comparable effects in the United States are discussed in selections by Arthur W. Calhoun, Willystine Goodsell, Katherine D. Lumpkin and Dorothy W. Douglas, William F. Ogburn and Lawrence K. Frank published in Bernhard J. Stern, *The Family: Past and Present* (New York, 1938), p. 212-29 and 243-55, and in Andrew G. Truxal and Francis E. Merrill, *The Family in American Culture* (New York, 1947), p. 325-47. For China see Olga Lang, *Chinese Family and Society* (New Haven, 1946), p. 102-17, 333-41.

[30] These are discussed in Wanda F. Neff, *Victorian Working Women* (New York, 1929).

[31] Engels says of the philanthropic Tories who had constituted themselves a group called "Young England": "The hope of Young England is the restoration of the old 'Merry England' with its brilliant features and romantic feudalism. This hope is of course unattainable and ridiculous, a satire upon all historic development; but the good intention, the courage to resist the existing state of things and prevalent prejudices, and to recognize the vile-

rural values against urban values, all decried the changes in the family occasioned by the employment of women and children as factory wage earners.

Official government reports laid bare not only the exploitation of women and children in the factories but the changing moral standards and family disruption.[32] Engels made full use of these official documents in his *Condition of the Working Class in England* (first published in German in 1845), as Marx did later in *Capital*. In his early work Engels, like other contemporary writers, stressed primarily the disintegration of the family brought about by capitalism. While describing the distressing working and living conditions prevailing in factory towns, he declared:

> The employment of the wife dissolves the family utterly and of necessity, and this dissolution, in our present society, which is based upon the family, brings the most demoralizing consequences for parents as well as children. A mother who has no time to trouble herself about her child, to perform the most ordinary loving services for it during its first year, who scarcely indeed sees it, can be no real mother to the child, must inevitably grow indifferent to it, treat it unlovingly like a stranger. The children who grow up under such conditions are utterly ruined for later family life, can never feel at home in the family which they themselves found, because they have always been accustomed to isolation, and they contribute therefore to the already general undermining of the family in the working-class. A similar dissolution of the family is

---

ness of our present condition, is worth something anyhow." See Engels, *Condition of the Working Class in England in 1844*, p. 294, footnote. Marx later wrote: "There is an old English proverb to the effect that when thieves fall out, honest men come to their own. In actual fact, the clamorous and passionate dispute between the two sections of the ruling classes as to which of them was exploiting the workers most shamefully, helped on either side, to bring the truth to light, Lord Shaftesbury, at that time Lord Ashley, was commander-in-chief in the aristocratic campaign against the factory owners," *Capital*, translated from the 4th ed. by Eden and Cedar Paul (New York, 1929), p. 747. The role of Lord Shaftesbury as a reformer is described in J. L. and Barbara Hammond, *Lord Shaftesbury* (London, 1932).

[32] See especially the Reports of the Inspectors of Factories, and data in Great Britain, *Commissioners for Inquiring into the State of Large Towns and Populous Districts* (London, 1844–45). A summary of official records is given in Charles Wing, *Evils of the Factory System Demonstrated by Parliamentary Evidence* (London, 1837).

brought about by the employment of the children . . . the children emancipate themselves, and regard the paternal dwelling as a lodging-house, which they often exchange for another, as suits them.

In many cases the family is not wholly dissolved by the employment of the wife, but turned upside down. The wife supports the family, the husband sits at home, tends the children, sweeps the room and cooks. . . . It is easy to imagine the wrath aroused among the working-men by this reversal of all relations within the family, while the other social conditions remain unchanged.[33]

Engels then also expressed strong views on the consequences of continuous factory employment of children and unmarried women upon preparation for marriage:

It is self-evident that a girl who has worked in a mill from her ninth year is in no position to understand domestic work, whence it follows that female operatives prove wholly inexperienced and unfit as housekeepers. They cannot knit or sew, cook or wash, are unacquainted with the most ordinary duties of a housekeeper, and when they have young children to take care of, have not the vaguest idea how to set about it.[34]

Engels does not in this book indicate his belief that the disintegration of the feudal family was laying the basis for a higher form of the family. Not that he or Marx ever glorified the feudal family, as has been erroneously charged.[35] For example, after he described the results of the situation then frequently found, in which the women became the sole providers because of male unemployment, he wrote:

If the wife can now base her supremacy upon the fact that she supplies the greater part, nay, the whole of the common possession, the necessary inference is that this community of possession is no true and rational one, since one member of the family boasts offensively of contributing the greater share. If the family of our present society is being thus dissolved, this dissolution merely

---

[33] Engels, *Condition of the Working Class in England in 1844*, p. 144.
[34] *Ibid.*, p. 147.
[35] John Ise, for example, took a passage of the *Manifesto* out of context and declared that "his (Marx's) discussion of the beauties of medieval religion, family and chivalry verges on utopian sentimentalism," *American Economic Review*, xxviii (1938), p. 19.

shows that, at bottom, the binding tie of this family was not family affection, but private interest lurking under the cloak of a pretended community of possessions.[36]

Yet Engel's account of the influence of women's employment in factory production is here wholly negativistic. It does not explicitly indicate positive trends actual or potential in the new situation.[37]

In his *Capital* (published in 1867) Marx corrected this emphasis without weakening the indictment of capitalism's use of the new technology. He wrote in the chapter on "Machinery and Large Scale Industry";

> However terrible, however repulsive, the breakup of the old family system within the organism of capitalist society may seem; none the less, large-scale industry by assigning to women, and to young persons and children of both sexes, a decisive role in the socially organized process of production, and a role which has to be fulfilled outside the home, is building the new economic foundations for a higher form of the family and the relations between the sexes. I need hardly say that it is just as stupid to regard the Christo-Teutonic form of the family as absolute, as it is to take the same view of the classical Roman form, or of the classical Greek form, or of the Oriental form—which by the way constitute a historically interconnected developmental series. It is plain, moreover, that the composition of the combined labor personnel out of the individuals of both sexes and various ages—although in its spontaneously developed and brutal form (wherein the worker exists for the process of production instead of the process of production existing for the worker) is a pestilential source of corruption and slavery—under suitable conditions cannot fail to be transformed into a source of human progress.[38]

Engels later took a like position in the *Origin of the Family*.[39]

[36] Engels, *op. cit.*, p. 146.
[37] Engels in 1892 indicated that he was aware of the limitations of many of the interpretations of this early work. He wrote in the preface to the British publication of the English edition: "It will be hardly necessary to point out that the general theoretical standpoint of the book—philosophical, economical, and political—does not exactly coincide with my standpoint today." Engels, *Condition of the Working Class*, p. x.
[38] Karl Marx, *Capital*, Paul transl., p. 528 f.
[39] See especially Engels, *Origin of the Family*, p. 148.

When Marx and Engels stressed the constructive consequences of industrialism, they dissociated themselves from the feudal critics of the changing family. They differentiated sharply between technological changes and their use for profit under capitalism. They noted the beneficent effects of women's employment outside the home, of their escape from the insularity of the restricted environment of the home with its limited social contacts, and from the dependence upon the earnings of their husbands. They observed that outside employment afforded women means for the fulfillment of their personalities, and the attainment of full economic, psychological, cultural and legal equality with their spouses. These potentialities they declared could not be fulfilled under capitalism. Marx and Engels understood fully the dilemmas with which women were confronted under capitalism, and the difficulties of women who carry the double responsibilities of being workers and wives.

Marx and Engels visualized the full solution of this problem only under socialism. They did not underestimate, however, the important role played by trade unionism and political activity under capitalism for the improvement of working and living conditions, as a means to permit more effective participation of women in economic affairs and in civic life. Collective bargaining, the struggle for legislation for the shorter work day and for more healthful factory environments, and the women's rights movement have achieved significant results although constant vigilance has been necessary to sustain gains. Historically, the position of women in society and in the home has generally reflected prevailing attitudes toward human rights. As the rights of the masses have been extended and their conditions improved, women have benefited directly and indirectly. On the other hand, in periods of reaction and counter-revolution, restrictions against women in economic life and their disabilities in the home have been intensified.[40] Yet even in recent periods of reaction, as under the Nazi government in Germany, where there were insistent and organized efforts to subordinate women and to

[40] Bernhard J. Stern, "Women: Position in Society," *Encyclopaedia of the Social Sciences* (New York, 1930–35) xv, p. 442–46; *idem*, "The Family and Cultural Change," *American Sociological Review*, IV (1939), p. 199–208.

confine them to childbearing and domestic work under the indisputable authority of the male members of the family, women could not be completely restored to their feudal status. Modern capitalist productive techniques demand the employment of women, as Engels noted, and in spite of its announced program, the Nazi regime was unable to eliminate women from industry.[41] The Nazis were, however, able to prevent the employment of women in civil service, in the professions and in skilled trades, to institute lower wage scales for women than for men, and to reinstitute many of the coercive customs of the patriarchal family that had been eliminated in previous decades.[42]

In the United States there are sociologists who contrast favorably what they regard as the stability of the families of the Ozark and Appalachian mountaineers with the looser structure of the modern family.[43] One of the authors, who attacks modern progressive trends in the family, gloomily predicts that "unless some unforeseen renaissance occurs, the family system will continue headlong its present trend toward nihilism." To prevent this, he advocates that powerful educational and propaganda agencies be used "to bring about a revision and more or less permanent reinstatement of familism," and to "make it extremely uncomfortable for the agents provocateurs of atomism," which is his designation for progressive writers on the family.[44] Such views as these find support from those Freudian analysts who would have women "accept their feminity," a position that has recently been promulgated in its most blatant form in Lundberg and Farnham's recent work,[45] which glorifies medieval values.

[41] Alfred Meusel, "National Socialism and the Family," *British Sociological Review*, XXVIII (1936), p. 182–84, 389–99.
[42] For the advances in women's status in Germany prior to the advent of Hitler, see H. W. Puckett, *Germany's Women Go Forward* (New York, 1930).
[43] C. C. Zimmerman and M. E. Frampton, *Family and Society* (New York, 1935).
[44] C. C. Zimmerman, *Family and Civilization* (New York, 1947), p. 808 f.
[45] Ferdinand Lundberg and M. F. Farnham, *Modern Women: The Lost Sex* (New York, 1947). That this position is not that of progressive analysts is well shown in Judson T. Stone, "The Theory and Practice of Psychoanalysis" SCIENCE AND SOCIETY, X (1946), p. 54–79. The fallacies of the book have been ably exposed by Mildred Burgum, *ibid.*, XV (1947), p. 382–88.

Recent developments in the United States, however, have all encouraged family trends in the opposite direction from those advocated by these writers. Technological advances in the sources of motive power, in manufacturing processes and in new materials have increased rather than checked the possibilities of women's participation in industrial life. The marked expansion in the employment of women during World War II was an acceleration of an historic trend. Since 1870, the number of women employed has mounted along with the increase in urbanization and apartment dwelling, with the decline in the birth rate, with the increase in consumers' goods and the rise of living standards, with the greater availability of housekeeping conveniences and of canned and processed foods, with better educational opportunities for women, and with the growth of the women's rights movement and other liberal and trade union movements which have improved the social, economic and political status of women in American life. The extent of the recent increase in employment of women is seen by the fact that the total number of non-agricultural employed women rose from 10,730,000 in March, 1940 to over 16,000,000 in 1944 and 1945. Contrary to the predictions of many authorities, it did not recede to the pre-war level after V-J day. By the end of January, 1946, the total was 14,750,000.[46] Since that time the number of non-agricultural employed women has fluctuated but the figure has risen again to about 16,000,000.[47] That the number of women in factory production increased by 1,000,000 from the fall of 1939 to September, 1946 when it totalled 3,750,000,[48] is particularly significant.

The proportion of married women in the labor force has been considerable and has grown appreciably from 35.5 percent in 1940 to 44.3 percent in 1946.[49] In 1946, both the husbands and

[46] U. S. Department of Labor, Women's Bureau, *Employment of Women in the Early Postwar Period* (Washington, 1946), p. 2, Table 1.
[47] U. S. Department of Labor, Women's Bureau, *Facts on Women Workers*, August 31, 1947.
[48] U. S. Department of Labor, Women's Bureau, *Facts on Women Workers*, Jan. 31, 1947.
[49] U. S. Department of Labor, Women's Bureau, *Employment of Women in the Early Postwar Period*, p. 11, Table 7, *Facts on Women Workers*, Aug. 31, 1947, p. 2.

wives in over 5,000,00 families (almost a fifth of all families with both husband and wife present) were in the labor force, an increase of about 2,000,000 over 1940.[50] In February, 1946, 15 percent of wives in normal families with one or more children worked, compared with nine percent in 1940.[51] Of the married women working in 1946, 890,000 were wives or the heads of families in which there were children under six years of age.[52]

These developments have had important effects upon the allocation of authority in the American family, as Marx and Engels anticipated. They have increased women's demands, and have given them greater bargaining power for the attainment of equality of rights and duties with their husbands, including sexual as well as economic and intellectual rights. To assist women to carry on the double task of home and work, husbands have come to take a more active share in household duties, and the ideal of mutuality of interests and sharing of difficulties of husbands and wives has to that extent been strengthened. Governmental provisions for educational and recreational services for children while their mothers are at work, have become imperative, but these services, which were provided reluctantly by economy-minded legislators during World War II are now being curtailed. Although there has been considerable progress, the participation of women in industry has by no means resulted in actual equality for women with men in the United States. Conventional attitudes on women's responsibilities in the home are still tenacious. There remain marked sex distinctions in civil and in political laws which discriminate against women.[53] Traditionally, women have been paid less than men for performing the same labor and have had to combat historically derived attitudes, used to advantage by employers, that they are less capable than men in developing skills and attaining men's level of productivity. Thus in our society there have been many impediments to women's social equality both in law and in practice,

[50] U. S. Department of Labor, *Labor Information Bulletin*, June 1947.
[51] U. S. Department of Labor, Women's Bureau, *Facts on Women Workers*, June 30, 1947.
[52] U. S. Department of Labor, *Labor Information Bulletin*, June 1947.
[53] U. S. Department of Labor, Women's Bureau, *The Legal Status of Women in the United States of America* (Washington, 1941).

and social services and legislation have been insufficient to cushion the effects upon the family of women's entrance into industry. The emancipatory effects of technological change have not been fully realized because of the restraining effects of the class structure of society and the conservative attitudes and customs it nurtures.

Marx and Engels gave valuable perspectives for an evaluation of the contemporary situation. They were not concerned merely with formal, material equality of women with men. Economic emancipation of women they regarded as a prerequisite, the foundation stone, for the emancipation of women in family relations. But they were also alert to the need for equality in all aspects of human relationships, including sex relations. Engels, for example, discussed the fact that the sanctions of monogamy have historically only been applied to women, and contended that both enjoyments and restrictions in sex relations should be shared equally by both parties.[54] He set forth an ideal of a monogamic family of equals in which both spouses would find personality fulfillment through stimulating companionship and mutually satisfying sex enjoyment. He envisioned a relationship devoid of male coercion and condescension; a family which was stable, not because religious sanctions and laws made divorce difficult, but because it was cemented by reciprocal love. The family was above all, in his mind, an agency to give a sense of personal security to its members through the affection of the spouses for one another, and through rewarding devotion of offspring and parents. He advocated governmental services and technological innovations to facilitate the fruition of the family based on affection, by relieving women of drudgery associated with household tasks.[55] He thus enriched the ideal of the family

[54] Engels, *Origin of the Family*, p. 56.
[55] Lenin, in the tradition of Marx and Engels, declared in 1919 that "Not a single democratic party in the world, not even in any of the most advanced bourgeois republics, has done in this sphere [abolition of restrictions against the rights of women] in ten years a hundredth part of what we did in the very first year we [the Soviets] were in power," and went on to say: "Notwithstanding all the liberating laws that have been passed, woman continues to be a *domestic slave*, because *petty housework* crushes, strangles, stultifies and degrades her, chains her to the kitchen and to the nursery, and wastes her labor on barbarously unproductive, petty, nerve-racking, stultifying and

and offered designs for living for the development of free and emotionally mature persons. It is for the complete attainment of these enlightened goals of family and personal living, that Marx and Engels in the *Communist Manifesto* called for the end of class exploitation and the establishment of socialism.

---

crushing drudgery. . . . Public dining rooms, crêches, kindergartens—there are examples of the shoots, the simple everyday means, which assume nothing pompous, grandiloquent or solemn, but which can *in fact emancipate women,* which can in fact lessen and abolish their inferiority to men in regard to their role in social production and in social life." V. I. Lenin, *Women and Society* (New York, 1938), p. 13 f. For the methods by which this principle was implemented under the socialist society in the Soviet Union, see Susan M. Kingsbury and Mildred Fairchild, *Factory, Family and Women in the Soviet Union* (New York, 1935). Discussions of the Soviet family and women by Beatrice King and Ralph Parker, and Soviet laws for the protection of women are published in Bernhard J. Stern and Samuel Smith, *Understanding the Russians* (New York, 1946), p. 151–58 and 235–38.

From *Science and Society*, Vol. XII, No. 1 (Winter, 1948), pp. 42–64.

part five

HEREDITY AND ENVIRONMENT

The Relationship of the Social Sciences to the Biological Sciences from the Point of View of the Sociologist

Some inquiring minds may well have questioned the immediate relevance of the topic, "The Relationship of the Social Sciences to the Biological Sciences," to the major theme of a conference on planning to meet human needs in the post-war period. Yet, in my judgment, it may well be said that the destiny of our nation and of the world lies in the types of answers one gives to this question. Major political issues of democracy as compared to fascism, of the future of the colored and other minority peoples of the world; problems of the value of education, of the efficacy of extending medical care to all the people, and of the advisability for social security programs are but a few of the issues that in the last analysis are resolved in terms of certain basic theoretical principles which emerge from a fruitful discussion of this topic. This paper can do no more than suggest why this is so. It will chart out recent important developments in the field and note their implications for the present and the future.

The last hundred years has been a period of marked activity in biology. The original interest of the century in human biology was primarily in classification and in origins. Following Darwin, eminent authorities made systematic classifications of human races and traced their relationship with other species through the use of anthropometric measurements that became more refined as the years passed. Geneticists like T. H. Morgan made significant advances in their understanding of the nature of the genes and chromosomes as agencies of heredity, and eugenists wrote boldly of human heredity while the science was still in its infancy. The techniques of controlled laboratory investigation were improved and the experiments with rats, guinea pigs, and fruit flies were used to generalize about the behavior of human beings. In medicine, progress was made in clinical diagnosis, and then after Pasteur and Koch, so many discoveries were made of specific microorganisms responsible for communicable diseases, that many came to think of all medicine in terms of infection. In psychology, a surging flood of tests inundated the schools, and pedagogues reduced qualities such as intelligence to quantitative units, and achieved a reckless sense of certainty in evaluating individual differences by the use of the concept of the I.Q. or intelligence quotient. Psychiatrists also achieved an illusory sense of power by designating the mentally disordered with the names suggested by the classification of Kraepelin. Criminologists for a time got a similar sense of satisfaction as the devotees of the biological determinism of Lombroso, who unhesitatingly defined a criminal biological type. At the same time, social-Darwinians, recruited for the most part from the ranks of biologists, explained individual and group success or failure in our competitive society as the survival of the fit in the struggle for existence. Deterministic biology was then in its heyday of triumph.

It is interesting to trace how this carefully reared structure crumbled as biologists went beyond their controlled laboratory experiments, and began to grapple along with social scientists with real problems of human beings in interaction with the physical and social environment. One after another of their basic assumptions had to be revised as evidence accumulated, as concepts became more sophisticated and as research methods improved. I shall touch hastily on a few of the retreats from biological determinism by the leading scientists as they recognized the inadequacy of the intellectual defenses of this position, particularly as they applied to human beings in society.

In view of the pernicious influence of racialism in contemporary America, aggravated by the spread of fascist doctrine, it is appropriate to note first that the elaborate classifications of races built up by early authorities in human biology and physical anthropology have been found to have little validity.

It was discovered, for example, that many of the traits upon the measurements of which the classifications were made, on the assumption that they were fixed by heredity (such traits, for example, as stature, head form, and face form), were unstable and subject to environmental influences. Bodily forms and functions in each generation are found to be dependent upon socially derived habits which influence the development of the organism. The physiological functioning of the human heart, the endocrine glands, the digestive and other organs, for example, vary depending upon the physiographic and cultural environment in which the individual matures. The rates of sexual maturity and the development of the teeth also were found to depend upon the cultural environment. As more and more attention was paid to the study of individual growth, and more comparisons were made of human groups in the perspective of generations in different cultural environments, the former purely descriptive classifications of races were recognized as utterly inadequate. The grandiose generalizations based on these early racial studies remained only as myths and apologetics of dominance of vested interest groups.

Similarly, studies of the growth of organisms under diverse environments shattered the doctrine of unit characters prematurely propounded by eugenists, and incorporated in high school and college textbooks in the egregiously specious accounts of the Jukes and Kallikaks, and the distorted interpretations of the genealogy of Jonathan Edwards. It is a grave reflection on the lag between scientific progress and its diffusion through educational channels that many textbooks still retain these illustrations of human heredity repudiated by every geneticist and social scientist of rank in this country.

Progress in medicine has focused attention even more strikingly on the influence of the social as well as physical environment on the growth of the organism. Control of the pathogenic microorganisms involved in communicable diseases had necessitated attention to sanitation, food inspection and other public health measures as an element in human survival irrespective of heredity. But when the significance of deficiency diseases was appreciated by medical men, a very marked step forward was made in the recognition of the fact that heredity could not be understood without taking into consideration the cultural media in which the organism matures. Knowledge of vitamins led to findings on the importance of diet in diseases such as pellagra, which then turned the spotlight on the relation of income to health and on the importance of food customs. Knowledge of endocrine function has likewise enhanced the understanding of the process of human growth in its environmental setting so that the mechanistic biological determinism of earlier decades has been left far behind.

In psychology, too, through the influence of social scientists, the so-called intelligence tests came to be recognized as achievement tests. It has been conceded, often reluctantly, that they could give no insight into pristine native ability, and that the achievement measured by the tests was dependent upon social opportunity. Comparative tests of urban as compared to rural populations, of northern Negroes as compared to southern Negroes, of Negroes and of immigrants classified according to the length of residence in an urban community relatively free from cultural and educational discriminations, all underscored the fact that the tests measured cultural attainments rather than biological capacities. These tests, as well as other educational experiments proved, moreover, the plasticity of human personality. They invalidated the assumption that the present differences in the mental behavior of individuals and peoples are structurally determined by heredity and thus immutable. The rapid transformations of the culture of the peoples of the world during the last fifty years gave added supporting evidence to the sociological hypothesis that cultural inferiority and superiority of any people at any specific time must be explained historically and not biologically, from the point of view of social tradition and not of individual inheritance.

A more sociologically orientated approach to human behavior has come from other sources as well. Students of child development have begun to stress the fact that individual behavior inevitably occurs in a socio-cultural setting, in the matrix of human relations, where the impact of social values as well as of physical environmental factors condition the person from infancy to death. Child psychologists now use such key concepts as the "total personality," and talk in terms of "functionally important situations," of socially derived "security," and "frustration." Functional studies of interpersonal relations have been substituted for the static measurements of isolated factors in individual behavior.

Vast strides have been made in psychiatry, too, since it has abandoned its fatalism, born of scientific inadequacy, and with new socially orientated concepts has gone beyond mere classification into therapy. Its major milestone was when it began to distinguish between functional and organic disorders, that is, when it began to study psychological disorders in their own terms, rather than seeking to explain them in biological terms. The entire mental hygiene movement rests upon the valid supposition that social situations determine personality patterns, and that the prevention of personality disorders is possible if given the proper social environment. A new era in the psychological sciences is in the offing, as studies go forward not merely of the socially derived tensions, the conflicts, and the insecurities of psycho-pathological persons, but of normal personalities. But I leave the prognoses in this field to the competent hands of Dr. Overholser.

In criminology there has been a major change of emphasis. Although there have been occasional clamorous assertions of Neo-Lombrosians that there are criminal biological types, their statistical evidence and scientific reasoning has been overwhelmingly assailed by the vast body of contemporary social scientists. The reason can be stated simply. Terms like "a crime" and "a criminal" are not natural, that is, biological concepts, but social concepts. There can be no crime, and hence no criminal unless a cultural norm is considered to have been violated to such an extent that society moves to impose penal sanctions against the offender. Over time and over space in different societies there has been, and there are wide fluctuations in the range of the definitions of crime and its manifestations. The laws of a society are prescribed by the varying standards and values and social structure of a society, all of which are historically derived, and not by any inherent characters of man. Since crime is a breach of social convention, criminal motivations and criminal behavior cannot be successfully studied from a biological point of view, but must be approached from the point of view of sociology and social psychology. Not the individual criminal but the social situation that breeds crime and patterns the criminal personality is the correct focus of study.

There remains for consideration the doctrine of social-Darwinism. This doctrine represented, as noted previously, an effort to project into the sphere of human relationships the struggle for existence found among lower animals. Sociologists have pointed out that this negates the all important distinction between man and the lower animals, that is, man's possession of a social tradition. Man's relation to his environment is primarily one of adjustment, through cumulative knowledge and skills, and not through biological adaptation as among the lower animals. To illustrate: man has invented fire, steam, electricity to cope with cold climate; he has not through natural selection grown heavy protective furs; he has invented the digging stick, the plow, the tractor to dig the soil and has not developed longer claws with which to dig. Man's inventions are not inherited through the germ plasm, through biological heredity. Rather he learns to utilize them and to improve them as a participant in society, and the extent of his participation depends on opportunities primarily related to the historical period in which he lives and to his class status.

But in applying the theory of natural selection to the social scene, the social Darwinians have ignored all this. They have used their theory to justify imperialist policy toward colonial peoples, to rationalize white man's dominance over the darker peoples, to commend exploitation of man by man in our competitive society. They propose that the lower economic classes and submerged peoples are inferior biological stocks, that the wealthy and dominant peoples are biologically superior, and that, in fact, through natural selection, there is a positive correlation between wealth and power and biological aptitude, that is, a "survival of the fittest."

Some have sought to explain the existing differential mortality and morbidity rates between upper and lower income groups as occasioned by the functioning of these laws of natural selection. This completely ignores the basic effects of diversity in the social and economic environment, the inferior nutrition and medical care of the poor, and the lack of availability of knowledge of health and preventive medicine occasioned by poverty. Ample experience has shown that life can be extended and sickness rates can be lowered for the members of any class or race, if existing resources of medical care be made available to them and the social environment be improved. Moreover, it has been one of the great achievements of democracy that when the potentialities of the common man are permitted expression, great creative energies are released for the common good of all members of society.

It is not difficult to see the bearing of this controversy on post-war policy. If one accepts a social-Darwinian outlook, one will advocate "free enterprise" to the exclusion of any governmental controls in the interests of all the people. Programs for the expansion of educational institutions to bring out the potentialities of the common men and women in our democracy, and to equip them with the intellectual and technical tools for attaining a fuller life, risk being scrapped as wasteful because of the lack of faith in the potential intellectual growth of those now underprivileged. A careful reading of educational literature, and a scanning of recent trends in the allocation of money for education in the state legislatures because of the pressure of lobbyists permits some cause for alarm. America has been proud of her policy of free universal education and it will be disastrous if it is curtailed in the future. There is every indication from the results of the findings of selective service on illiteracy in the United States and of census data on the inadequacy of schools in many areas, that educational expenditures should not be contracted but expanded.

Even more threatening is the attack of the proponents of social-Darwinism upon the social security programs as "coddling the poor" and "perpetuating the incompetents." Should such ruthless anti-social views, now expressed by more than a few articulate publicists and politicians, become public policy there would be an end to those social services which prevented the economic collapse and maintained the psychological morale of America during the difficult years of the last decade. These are dire forebodings. Good sense, knowledge of past history, and elementary foresightedness on the part of business groups should deter them from supporting such a policy which may yield immediate class advantage but has in it the elements of social disaster. The men and women in our armed forces who are fighting and those on the home-front who are sacrificing for an early victory have solemn aspiration for the future that cannot be ignored. They want the opportunity to work usefully and creatively during their productive years under good working conditions, to receive incomes sufficient to provide the necessities of life, which include adequate and nutritious food, necessary clothing, wholesome housing, effective education, satisfying leisure and recreation and adequate medical care. These aspirations demand an extension of social security programs not their curtailment. Our allies see the force of this demand of their people. The British have recognized it in the Beveridge plan; the Soviet government has barely pushed the Nazi invaders from their land before it has announced vast plans for social services. America with its vast resources, which have grown prodigiously during the war, cannot repudiate the program of social security to which it is now committed without danger to its very democracy.

The biological sciences have made tremendous contributions to our understanding of the structure and functioning of the human organism, which have great power to contribute to the health and welfare of mankind. They have, moreover, through enlarging our knowledge of stock raising and by making vast strides in scientific agriculture made it possible to banish famine and want from the earth. But social scientists underscore the fact that the use of this knowledge depends upon the structure of the economy and the functioning of social institutions. It depends upon the patterning of our governmental policy in terms of the welfare of all the people. The decision as to whether we are to permit the frustration and non-utilization of this vast body of scientific knowledge rests with us as citizens.

It is worthy of the concern of the participants in this conference on planning to meet human needs in the post-war world.

Address delivered at Boston University Founders' Day, March 11, 1944. Reprinted from *Bostonia*, Vol. XVII, No. 1 (April, 1944), pp. 31-33.

Human Heredity and Environment

At the mid-century it is appropriate to consider the shifting ground of the perennial heredity-environment controversy in the perspective of the last fifty years. Attention will be devoted here to limited segments of that controversy: those which apply to the changing relations between human genetics and eugenics, to the meaning of intelligence test scores, to the anthropological evidence of the instability of the human type, and to the part played by culture in differentiating man's adjustment to the environment from the adaptation of other animals.

The twentieth century began with the rediscovery of Mendel's work and the concomitant strident pronouncements by biologists that knowledge of human heredity had reached the level at which it was competent to determine public policy. Karl Pearson set the tone and established the pattern of this outlook. In his *National Life from the Standpoint of Science*, published in 1901, he contended that: "The form of a man's head, his stature, his eye color, his temper, the very length of his life . . . these and other things are all inherited and in approximately the same manner"; and he urged that "if we once realize that this law of inheritance is as inevitable as the law of gravity, we shall cease to struggle against it." He spoke glibly and ominously of bad stock, presumed the superiority of the white race and wrote of the Kaffir and the Negro: "Educate and nurture them as you will, I do not believe you will succeed in modifying the stock." He equated class status with biological ability, bemoaned decreased fertility among the "superior stocks," and large families among what he called the "reckless and improvident." His attitude toward social legislation was epitomized in the contention that "social sympathy and state aid must not be carried so far within the community that the intellectually and physically weaker stocks multiply at the same rate as the better stocks."[1]

At this time, however, an opposing position was taken by various sociological, anthropological and Marxist writers such as Lester F. Ward, Edward B. Tylor and the socialists. There were alternatives to choose from. Nevertheless genetics was born and nurtured in the soil of social Darwinian doctrine and in turn fertilized it. The doctrines of the continuity of the germ plasm, the theory of unit characters, and the penchant of geneticists to publish over-simplified genealogical charts illustrating Mendelian principles, all contributed to a distortion and exaggeration of the importance of the role of heredity. Moreover, whatever geneticists may have privately felt, or whatever misgivings they may have confided to friends, a long time unfortunately passed before geneticists of prominence publicly disassociated themselves and their science from the exaggerated claims of eugenics, and denounced the manner in which eugenics had latched itself on to genetics. The Carnegie Institution of Genetics at Cold Spring Harbor long continued to finance and publish widely quoted documents abetting eugenic doctrine.

A trend against eugenics became evident in the late 1920's.[2] As late as 1935, Muller declared in the preface to a book based on several of his earlier lectures:

> Eugenics in the sense that most of us are accustomed to thinking of it, has become a hopelessly perverted movement. Beyond imposing some slight limitation on the numbers of the grossly defective, it would be, with its present methods and outlook, powerless to work any positive changes for the good. On the other hand, it does incalculable harm by lending a false appearance of scientific basis to advocates of race and class prejudice, defenders of vested interests of church and state, Fascists, Hitlerites and reactionaries generally. Even the least unreasonable of the professional spokesmen of this

---

[1] Pearson, Karl, *National Life from the Standpoint of Science*. (London, 1901) p. 15–54.

[2] E.g., H. S. Jennings, *Prometheus, or Biology and the Advancement of Man* (New York, 1927).

modern Eugenics have taken no clear stand against the atrocities recently proposed and carried out in its name.[3]

Muller's vigorous rejection of eugenics[4] was itself restricted to its gross manifestations. He offered in its place a romantic proposal that after the social and material environment had been favorable for the development of the latent powers of men in general, it would be possible by artificial insemination to breed "comradeliness" and "intelligence" which "when active and well organized, issue in the 'co-operation' and 'knowledge' by which mankind has advanced." Acknowledgement was made that "each of these two traits is of course the resultant of a complex system of more elementary factors, and the development of each is simply responsive to environmental influences as well as affected by genes." But Muller contended that after the weight of economic and social oppression had been removed there would be "fair means of recognizing most of the individuals in whom an exceptional concentration of such desirable genes lies."[5]

Any contemporary linking of genetics and eugenics might, perhaps, be thought of as unwarranted stirring up of dead issues belonging to the early, groping neo-Mendelism of the past. Genetics has repudiated its early blunder of the concept of unit characters, and recognized the complexity of inheritance in man. There is much frank criticism of its previous position as "crude and naive."[6] The role of selective agents in causing genetic changes in human heredity is now known to be small. Genetics at present holds that "no statement about genetic difference has any scientific meaning unless it includes or implies a specification

[3] H. J. Muller, *Out of the Night: A Biologist's View of the Future* (New York 1935), p. ix f.
[4] It is noteworthy that this utterance was not hailed at the time nor given the support by geneticists and others accorded his more recent polemics against Lysenko. The review of *Out of the Night* in the *Journal of Heredity*, xxvii (1936), which was captioned "Communist Eugenics" and was largely an abstract of the book's contents, declared in its opening paragraph that "some parts may be read with safety even by a man with a weak heart." Popenoe and Johnson's *Applied Eugenics* had received a favorable, uncritical review in the previous volume.
[5] Muller, *op. cit.*, p. 118–20.
[6] H. J. Muller, C. C. Little and L. H. Snyder, *Genetics, Medicine and Man* (Ithaca, N. Y., 1947), p. 20.

of the environment in which it manifests itself in a particular manner."[7] Jennings' 1935 formulation is now generally accepted that "characteristics do not fall into two classes, one exclusively hereditary (or dependent on genes), the other exclusively environmental; that every characteristic is affected both by the materials of which the organism is composed, and by the effects of the environmental conditions on these materials, and that some characteristics are more readily altered by these conditions than others."[8] There is little left of the former assurance that geneticists know enough to dictate public policy, for they are busy restructuring the very foundations of their concepts of the nature of the gene, and its relation to hereditary and growth processes.

Yet because of the reluctance of geneticists to relinquish entirely the hope for human genetic engineering the linkage of genetics to eugenics is still a real one. Some widely used college genetics textbooks continue to publish chapters on eugenics repeating traditional eugenic doctrines with minor qualifications.[9]

The most recent evidence that the issue is not a dead one, and that eugenics has a tenacious and pernicious hold on genetics, is given in Curt Stern's *Principles of Human Genetics*,[10] published in 1949. The chapter on "Selection and Eugenics," was widely circulated, in preliminary and slightly contracted form, in *Science*.[11] This wide currency, and the author's influence as a geneticist of recognized stature, make necessary a refutation of his erroneous formulations. He has, to be sure, incorporated in his analysis some of the well-established criticisms of eugenics. But as he presents the eugenicists' thesis that the intellectual genetic endowment of Western populations is in danger of decreasing because of differential fertility along class lines, he manifests conventional biases, pitching the authority of his science on the side

---

[7] Lancelot Hogben, *Nature and Nurture* (London, 1933), p. 14.
[8] H. S. Jennings, *Genetics* (New York, 1935), p. 232–65.
[9] E.g., L. H. Snyder, *Principles of Heredity*, 3rd ed. (Boston, 1946); E. C. Colin, *Elements of Genetics*, 2nd ed. (Philadelphia, 1946).
[10] Curt Stern, *Principles of Human Genetics* (San Francisco, 1949), p. 506–41.
[11] Curt Stern, "Selection and Eugenics," *Science*, cx (1949), p. 201–08.

of eugenic doctrine. He begins by acknowledging that "it is not possible, at the present time, to state with certainty whether different socioeconomic groups are genetically differentiated" (p. 514). However, when interpreting the divergent I.Q. scores of "own" and foster children grouped by occupational categories, he nevertheless contends that "it is hard to avoid the conclusion ... that there *are* mean differences in the genetic endowment of the different socioeconomic groups" (p. 515; italics in the original). Curt Stern makes repeated qualifications as he proceeds, but his discussion concludes that "it is likely that the present differential fertility of the different socioeconomic groups has a dysgenic effect in regard to intelligence" (p. 520).

This is a crucially important judgment. If accepted, it may well have profound influence upon social and educational policy. Hence the author is under an obligation, before pronouncing it, to utilize only the most reliable data. Yet the very contrary is true. Curt Stern has selected Leahy's 1935 study of the comparison of I.Q.'s of "own" and foster children in homes of different occupational categories, from among other like studies analyzed in Osborn's *Preface to Eugenics* (1940), but he ignores Osborn's recognition that the study has limited applicability "in view of the small number of persons included in the present studies and the many weaknesses of the studies themselves."[12] Similarly, the table presenting the findings of Goodenough's study in 1928 of the I.Q.'s of 380 preschool children correlated with the occupation of their fathers is a fragment of a larger table derived from Osborn, but Curt Stern has paid no attention to the footnote warning in Osborn's table that testing for preschool children "is not so valid as for the school years."[13] He evidently felt that his case would be stronger if he showed that his generalization applied to the Soviet Union as well as to the United States. In his preliminary publication of the chapter in *Science* he used data derived from intelligence tests given in Kharkov in 1929.[14] However, in the book he abandoned these data as unsatisfactory and used in their place a table showing correlation coefficients be-

[12] Frederick Osborn, *Preface to Eugenics* (New York, 1940), p. 66.
[13] Osborn, *op. cit.*, p. 82.
[14] Stern, *Science, loc. cit.*, p. 203.

tween mental test scores of infants, and the earnings of fathers in Kazan in 1938,[15] not realizing that infant mental tests used at that time were in the experimental stage and were of doubtful value. This is the sum total of his proof for the likelihood that the present differential fertility of different socioeconomic groups "has a dysgenic effect in regard to intelligence."

There is a basic error involved here, and one that is frequently made by many geneticists. It is the credence given to intelligence tests modeled after the Binet tests as instruments for establishing genetic differences. Curt Stern does not do enough to protect himself from this error when he makes qualifying comments such as this: "Psychological tests which measure mental differences are imperfect indicators of the genetic nature of such differences, since psychologists have not yet fully succeeded in devising tests which are equally intelligible to individuals who have grown up in different social surroundings (p. 151)." For he then proceeds to declare: "Yet even with these imperfections of the tests in mind, the results . . . strongly suggest hereditary influence." This might have been excusable in 1940 when Osborn wrote *Preface to Eugenics*, although such a contention is debatable. But recent detailed investigation on what is measured by intelligence tests in use by Davis, Havighurst and their co-workers[16] have proved unequivocally that the differential scores of persons when classified according to the occupations of their parents are explicable entirely in terms of the nature of the tests themselves. These studies render spurious any surmises about genes of intelligence determining the scores of conventional intelligence tests. Hence, I.Q. scores should no longer be used as evidence by geneticists as Curt Stern and many others have done.[17] Recent studies by Davis and Havighurst go beyond the earlier ones which had already cast doubt upon the value of such tests in measuring innate abilities. It had already been demonstrated that I.Q.'s among races

[15] Stern, *Principles of Human Genetics*, p. 55.
[16] W. Allison Davis, and Robert J. Havighurst, "The Measurement of Mental Systems (Can Intelligence Be Measured?)" *Scientific Monthly*, LXVI (April, 1948), p. 301–16. W. Allison Davis, *Social Class Influence upon Learning* (Cambridge, Mass. 1948).
[17] See for example Lionel Penrose, *The Biology of the Mental Defect* (London, 1949), esp. ch. 6.

change under different socioeconomic environments. Thus when Negroes have superior economic and educational and other cultural opportunities in the North as compared to the South, the I.Q. results vary accordingly. So also do the I.Q.'s of rural and urban populations, and of members of upper and lower income groups within closely related peoples, and of identical twins raised apart. Davis and Havighurst have regarded it as the crux of their problem to discover just why the intelligence tests *have* proved to be more difficult for the lowest socioeconomic group.

Discrepancies in the scores were found to be caused by the preponderant use in tests of those words, situations, pictures, and experiences which are most familiar to individuals who have grown up in middle and upper socioeconomic groups. The conventional tests measure, therefore, not the real intelligence of the child or adult, but the cultural and economic opportunities which they have had. Davis and Havighurst have demonstrated experimentally that when the tests employing only such words, grammatical constructions, and situations which are about equally common in the environments of all socioeconomic groups, the differences in scores between socioeconomic groups disappear,[18] while differences between individuals in all groups remain.

It should be noted that while the assumption of psychological differences along class lines reiterated by Curt Stern is arrived at inferentially, the fact that environmental variables are significant in psychological growth has repeatedly been documented by cultural historians, psychologists and educators.[19] However, the biases that have assumed hereditary causes for divergent scores in intelligence tests along socioeconomic lines have led the schools to fail to recognize and to develop fully the potential mental ability of the children in this country who are from working-class families. The failure in America to take advantage

[18] W. Allison Davis, "Education for the Conservation of the Human Resources of the United States." Address delivered at a meeting of the American Association of School Administrators, February 21, 1949 (Multigraphed). See also Ernest A. Haggard, "Influence of Culture Background on Test Performance." Paper presented before conference on testing problems sponsored by the Educational Testing Service, October 29, 1949 (Multigraphed).

[19] See for example C. Kluckhohn and Henry A. Murray, *Personality in Nature, Society, and Culture* (New York, 1948).

of the abilities of the working-class population was strongly corroborated by the experience of the army psychologists during World War II working on the problem of the discovery, development and conservation of aptitudes. In the case of the large group of functional illiterates and slow learners it was demonstrated that their limitations could be greatly ameliorated through an educational program.[20] Even more important was the evidence that among more than three million men in the higher levels of learning ability, the army interviewers for personnel classification found that almost one million had not even completed a high school course, much less gone on to a technological institute, a college, or a professional school, largely because of insufficient economic resources.[21] If differential psychological potentialities are assumed to exist according to socioeconomic groupings, a heavy restraining hand is laid upon programs designed to enlarge the educational opportunities of lower income groups. Rather, separate educational programs along class lines, are encouraged giving inferior facilities to the poor because they are regarded as less satisfactory material, with the result that class stratification is made more rigid.

It seems to be incumbent upon geneticists to stress more than is generally done, the important principle that to define something as hereditary does not mean to negate the importance of environment, that both must be considered as reciprocally related to the process of growth. While there is a formal theoretical acceptance of the dynamic flexibility of the human organism, there does not seem to be a full recognition of the implications of this principle in genetics literature. The influences of environment in the growth of the human organism are often treated in a cavalier fashion, almost in the manner of granting concessions. Yet evidence from other fields for the pronounced significance of environmental influences on the human physique is mounting. The important findings of Boas in 1911, which showed the changing head-form, stature and weight of the American-born children

[20] Walter C. Bingham, "Military Psychology in War and Peace," *Science*, CVI (August 22, 1947), p. 156 f.
[21] Walter V. Bingham, "Inequalities in Adult Capacity from Military Data," *Science*, CIV (1949), p. 147-52.

of immigrants as compared to their parents,[22] are being corroborated by more recent investigators. For example, Spier has found differences between the growth of Japanese children born in America and in Japan,[23] Goldstein between Mexican parents and their offspring born in Mexico and in the United States,[24] Lasker between immigrant and American-born Chinese,[25] and Shapiro for the Japanese in Hawaii.[26] These cumulative data support the hypothesis that man is capable of very substantial changes in physical characteristics long regarded as stable, within a single generation, if radical changes in environment occur. Proof about the plasticity of the human organism is derived not only from studies of migrant populations and their offspring. Physical changes also occur in fixed human populations if their environments alter in the course of time. This was thoroughly documented in relation to the changing stature and weight and age of puberty of stable European populations during the nineteenth century, by data compiled by the League of Nations.[27] It was demonstrated in this country by the study of Bowles of the changing height and weight of fathers and sons of Harvard and mothers and daughters of women's colleges,[28] and by other studies.[29] Recent studies in New Haven and New York show

[22] Franz Boas, *Changes in the Bodily Form of Descendants of Immigrants*. Senate Document 208, 61st Congress, Second Session (Washington, 1911).

[23] Leslie Spier, *Growth of Japanese Children Born in America and Japan*. University of Washington Publication on Anthropology (Seattle, Washington, 1929).

[24] M. S. Goldstein, *Demographic and Bodily Changes in Descendants of Mexican Immigrants with Comparable Data on Parents and Children in Mexico*. Institute of Latin American Studies (Austin, Texas, 1943).

[25] G. W. Lasker, "Migration and Physical Differentiation. A Comparison of Immigrant with American Born Chinese," *American Journal of Physical Anthropology*, N. S., IV (1946), p. 273–310.

[26] H. I. Shapiro, *Migration and Environment* (London, 1939).

[27] C. Wrcynski, "Physics and Health," *Quarterly Bulletin of the Health Organization of the League of Nations*, VI (1937), p. 594–601. See also Mixed Committee of the League of Nations, Final Report on the Relation of Nutrition to Health, Agriculture, and Economic Policy (Geneva, 1936).

[28] G. T. Bowles, *New Types of Old Americans at Harvard* (Cambridge, Mass., 1932).

[29] William Deegan, "A Fifty-Nine Year Survey of Yale Reveals Freshmen Are Becoming Younger, Heavier, and Taller," *The Research Quarterly*, XII (December, 1941), p. 707–11; L. B. Chenoweth, "Increase in Height and

increases in the height and weight of Negro children under improved nutrition and living conditions.[30]

In the case of human, as in other organisms, some characteristics have a wider range of variability in their response to environmental influences than do others. Dobzhansky has declared: "Heredity determines the responses, the norm of reaction to the environment."[31] However, the "norm" can only be ascertained after exposure to varied environments, and the number of environments observed never represents the full gamut of possibilities.

In disease as in health, hereditary and environmental approaches go hand in hand. There is no contradiction between the recognition of an external agent whose presence, as in tuberculosis or syphilis, or absence, as in vitamin deficiency, leads to a disease and the recognition that different heredity might make different individuals more or less susceptible to attacks by microorganisms or to nutritional deficiencies. Repeatedly however, differential morbidity and death rates of different races and diseases have been erroneously interpreted as reflecting differential inherited susceptibility, when later evidence (based on decline in rates after living conditions have improved) showed rather that they could be more correctly ascribed to differences in environmental conditions and in the availability of public health and medical services.

It has been common practice for many geneticists to project the principle of natural selection, postulating the survival of the genetically superior from the lower animals into human society. This ignores the unique characteristics of man, the possession of culture. Dobzhansky and Ashley Montagu have noted that "the

---

Weight and Decrease in Age of College Freshmen," *Journal of the American Medical Association*, CVIII (January 30, 1937), p. 354–58; T. D. Stewart, "Food and Physique," *Annals of the American Academy of Political and Social Science*, CCXXV (January, 1943), p. 22–28.

[30] Benjamin Pasamanick, "A Comparative Study of the Behavioral Development of Negro Infants," *Journal of Genetic Psychology*, LXIX (1946), p. 3–44. Nicholas Michelson, "Studies in the Physical Development of Negroes. II. Weight." *American Journal of Physical Anthropology*, N. S., I (September, 1943), p. 289–300.

[31] T. Dobzhansky, "What Is Heredity?" *Science*, C (November 3, 1944), p. 406.

possession of the gene system, which conditions educability rather than behavioral fixity, is a common property of all living mankind."[32] This is an important but not the decisive difference between man and the lower animals. Man's relation to his environment goes beyond biological adaptation characteristic of other animals. It is one of adjustment through cumulative knowledge and skills defined as culture. To meet the impact of inclement weather man has not, through natural selection, grown heavy furs or depended alone upon physiological changes; he has invented fire and the use of steam and electricity and has transmitted knowledge of these to his offspring by means of education through the use of articulate language, not through hereditary processes. To acquire food more effectively, man has not, through natural selection, developed longer claws with which to dig; he has invented the digging stick, the plow, the tractor. In all phases of his behavior, there is interposed between man and his physical environment a cultural heritage independent of his genetic inheritance. Man does not acquire this cultural heritage through the germ plasm; he learns to utilize it through his conditioning as a member of society, and to improve it through creative manipulation. Granted normality, the extent of participation of individuals or groups in this funded knowledge depends predominantly not on their biological equipment but upon the cultural epoch and pattern in which they live and their class status within that culture.

Man is not committed by his biological constitution to any particular variety of human behavior. The great diversity of solutions he has worked out in different cultures in regard to the acquisition of food, to marriage, to house building, to art expression and other cultural activities, have all been equally possible on the basis of this hereditary endowment. Culture is not a biologically transmitted complex, nor can we anticipate the range of potential hereditary responses to cultural tradition. When Dobzhansky says: "We do not know whether or not the populations which inhabit different portions of the earth's surface differ greatly in the incidence of not only genes for the blood groups,

[32] T. Dobzhansky and M. F. Ashley Montagu, "Natural Selection and the Mental Capacities of Mankind," *Science*, cv (1947), p. 589.

head shape, and skin color but also in that of genes which influence intellectual and moral qualities,"[33] he has no justification for implying that any such unproven differences, if they exist, make it impossible on genetic grounds for members of any race to share in, to manipulate creatively and to transmit any known human culture. The differential responses of peoples to cultural patterns are explicable in terms of their prior cultural conditioning without reference to variations in their genetic makeup.

I find it especially difficult to conceive of the genetic influence on moral qualities postulated in the passage just quoted. The human organism responds to cultural institutions as manifestations of stimuli of physical energy. The symbolic meaning and value judgments of culture are derived, not through the organic responses made possible by heredity, but through cultural contexts which are independent of organic processes. While cultural developments may possibly have limits, as yet unknown, determined by the ability of the human organism to respond to the stimuli evoked by them, no cultural institutions, including moralities, can be considered anticipated by specific genes or combinations of genes.[34] It is time for geneticists to abandon unreservedly and definitively this type of determinism.

[33] T. Dobzhansky, "Genetics and Human Affairs." *The Teaching Biologist*, XII (April, 1943), p. 106.

[34] It is the realization of the importance of the distinction between man's cultural heritage and his biological inheritance which led the Praesidium of the Academy of Sciences, U.S.S.R., to declare, in its reply to the resignation of H. S. Muller, that "Soviet scholars categorically reject the attempts to apply biological laws to social life, including the conclusions of Michurin biology. The development of society is subject not to biological but to higher social laws." (See *Pravda*, December 14, 1948.) For further discussion of the nature of culture, see Bernhard J. Stern, "Concerning the Distinction Between the Social and the Cultural," *Social Forces*, VIII (1929), p. 264–71; also "Some Aspects of Historical Materialism," in *Philosophy for the Future*, edited by Roy Wood Sellars, V. J. McGill and Marvin Farber (New York, 1949), p. 340–56.

Address delivered before the joint meeting of Philosophy of Science Association, American Philosophical Association, and Section L, American Association for the Advancement of Science, Hotel New Yorker, December 30, 1949. Reprinted from *Science and Society*, Vol. XIV, No. 2 (Spring, 1950), pp. 122–133.

Genetics Teaching and Lysenko

In the current discussion of Lysenko's criticism of genetics, the important question has arisen as to whether he is justified in assailing contemporary genetics in terms of the doctrines of Weismann concerning the continuity of the germ plasm and its independence of the soma. This is of special interest to American readers, because in the course of the debate, Lysenko cites in verification of this tie-up, an article by T. H. Morgan on "Heredity" and one by W. E. Castle on "Genetics" in the 1947 edition of the *Encyclopedia Americana*. Here, he declares, "We, naturally, may expect to find the quintessence of the question under discussion."[1]

Upon closer examination, however, it turns out that these articles in the 1947 edition have been reprinted by the editors of the *Encyclopedia Americana*, without change from the 1919 edition. They were therefore written about 1917 or 1918, and reflect genetic doctrine of thirty years ago rather than of today. One cannot, of course, justly chide Lysenko for the irresponsibility shown by the editors of a commercial encyclopedia, who save the expense of paying for new articles by assuming that science has not changed in three decades. One may question, however, his recourse to such encyclopedia articles as the most authentic sources of information on the current status of genetics. If some Soviet geneticists still support the views expressed in these articles, they are in fact advocating the genetic science of an earlier generation, not contemporary American theories. Lysenko directs much of his attack against these two encyclo-

[1] T. Lysenko, *The Science of Biology Today* (New York, 1948), p. 19 f.

pedia articles as representing the science of genetics in general. Since they are out of date, the whole question must be reconsidered. The present article will be limited to this aspect of the discussion.

If one were to judge by popular books on heredity and by some widely used college textbooks there would appear to be grounds for Lysenko's criticism. A best-selling book on heredity, published in 1939, in which a geneticist is listed as scientific consultant, and which is used in high school and some college undergraduate biology classes, declares:

> Regardless of the differences in their process of formation *the sperms or eggs receive chromosomes which are replicas of those which the parents themselves received when they were conceived.* Nothing that happened to the *body cells* of the parents throughout their lives could have been communicated to their germ cells as to alter the genes, or hereditary factors, which their child would receive. The chromosomes in our germ cells are not affected by any change that takes place within our body cells.[2]

Several recent textbooks perpetuate Weismann's doctrine unchanged, as Lysenko's critique implies. The fourth edition of the textbook of A. F. Shull, Professor of Zoology at the University of Michigan, published in 1948, states:

> The germ cells of animals give rise in every generation to somatic cells, as well as to more germ cells. But the somatic cells do not produce germ cells, or do so very rarely, in animals. The germ cells thus constitute a reserve out of which the genetic continuity of the germ cells and the repetition of the production of bodies in each generation are maintained. This sharp distinction between the two classes of cells has very important consequences in the theory of heredity.[3]

Sturtevant and Beadle's text[4] describes Weismann's germ plasm theory sympathetically as "laying emphasis on the germ line as the conservative element in heredity, the successive individuals

---

[2] A. Scheinfeld and Morton D. Schweitzer, *You and Heredity* (Philadelphia, 1939), p. 15–17. (Italics in the original.)
[3] A. F. Shull, *Heredity*, 4th ed. (New York, 1948), p. 13.
[4] A. H. Sturtevant and G. W. Beadle, *An Introduction to Genetics* (Philadelphia, 1939), p. 359.

being produced by it, but not themselves modifying it," without suggesting in any way that the theory had undergone changes. Colin's text, used in Columbia University genetics classes for premedical students, likewise presents an abstracted statement of the theory in historical context without comment as to its validity.[5]

In contrast, in the second and third editions of Sinnott and Dunn's text published in 1932 and 1939, there is a direct statement disassociating the authors from Weismann in these terms:

> This distinction [between the germ plasm and the soma] had great influence in focusing attention on the nuclear material of the gametes as the seat both of heredity and heritable variations; but since the distinction between germ plasm and somatoplasm does not seem to exist in plants, in which the processes of heredity and variation are similar to those in animals, it cannot be considered as of fundamental or of universal importance.[6]

This is particularly relevant to our discussion since Lysenko refers to this text critically by name. He appears, however, to have based his comment on the Russian translation of its first edition published here in 1925, which edition does not contain the important passage just cited.[7]

It is noteworthy that while Weismann's influence on American genetics has undoubtedly been great, and vestiges of it are still current, his views met strong opposition among biologists in this country when they were first propounded. Lester F. Ward, for example, who was a government botanist as well as a pioneer sociologist, engaged in vigorous polemics with Weismann along lines comparable to those which Lysenko now uses. In a review of Weismann's book *The Germ-Plasm*, he wrote in 1894:

> Like produces like, and if we cannot explain why, it is because we have not solved the problem of heredity. The elaborate theory offered by Prof. Weismann in his Germ-Plasm, plausible as it sometimes seems, true as it doubtless is in many of its details, utterly

---

[5] L. C. Colin, *Elements of Genetics*, 2nd ed. (Philadelphia, 1947), p. 98.
[6] E. W. Sinnott and L. C. Dunn, *Principles of Genetics*, 2nd ed. (New York, 1932); 3rd ed. (1939), p. 10.
[7] T. Lysenko, *The Science of Biology Today* (New York, 1948), p. 24. The edition is not identified in the footnote.

fails to solve this problem. It is altogether too rigid, too mechanical, to explain such subtle phenomena. Nature is more flexible, more self-adjusting, more delicate than his system contemplates, and is constantly doing just those things which he insists cannot be done.[8]

Sharp of Cornell University summed up the judgments of the advanced geneticists on Weismann in the 1920's when he wrote:

> In their conception of the nature of the units of inheritance, geneticists have departed rather widely from Weismann. The gene of today . . . stands neither for a complete organism nor for any constituent part thereof; it is conceived rather as a mass of some chemical substance which acts together with other genes in affecting many processes and hence characters in various parts of the organism. Genes are not simply the "determiners" of characters, but are rather constitutional factors influencing the course of the developmental processes, which are also affected in various degrees by environmental agencies.[9]

This critical judgment of Weismann has recently been reiterated in even more emphatic terms by S. J. Holmes, emeritus professor of zoology of the University of California.[10] He characterizes Weismann as a "mechanistically minded person" and declares:

> This [Weismann's doctrine] is a purely formalistic explanation [of nuclear division] based on assumptions that are antecedently improbable and which created difficulties that proved very troublesome to meet. The theory evoked a formidable volume of adverse criticism and was quite completely wrecked by the results of discoveries that were made in the newly born science of experimental embryology. Its basic error lay in the theory of qualitative nuclear division as a means of explaining the assumed mosaic character of embryonic development. . . .

[8] Lester F. Ward, "Weismann's Concessions," *Popular Science Monthly*, XLV (1894), p. 184. Reprinted in *Glimpses of the Cosmos* (New York, 1917), v, p. 127.
[9] Lester W. Sharp, *An Introduction to Cytology*, 2nd ed. (New York, 1926), p. 486.
[10] S. J. Holmes, "Micromerism in Biological Theory," *Isis*, XXXIX (August, 1948), p. 145-58.

Most geneticists would protest vigorously against identifying genes with Weismann's determinants, and they undoubtedly stand for somewhat different conceptions, although in a literate sense both are looked upon as essential to the determination of the particulate nature of the inheritance. Weismann looked upon determinants as standing to the parts of the organism in much the same relation that seed bears to a plant. Although in the early days of Mendelism a gene may frequently have been looked upon in the same way, it is now regarded as merely one of the many genetic factors that determine the part in question. All the cells are regarded as containing the same complement of genes however greatly their functional activity may come to differ in different parts of the organism. This complement of genes, together with cytoplasmic factors which in many instances have been shown to be controlled by antecedent gene action, is therefore the presumable basis for the preformation required in the development of an organism.[11]

This statement, which could hardly be regarded as an endorsement of Weismann, reflects the views of most outstanding American geneticists. Lysenko's effort to link them directly with Weismann, and to criticize them on the basis of his views, appears to be unjustified.

In an appraisal of Lysenko's attack upon "Mendelism-Morganism" one must also distinguish between the many textbooks, which reach thousands of students and laymen, and the periodical and monograph literature, which has a much more limited circulation. Although the third edition of the Sinnott and Dunn text, for example, rejects Weismann's views, it may justifiably be criticized along with the majority of other American texts in genetics for the formalism with which it persists in expounding Mendelian principles.[12] From these texts the students get an over-schematized, simplified picture of the hereditary and developmental processes, with hardly an inkling of the problems that occupy advanced geneticists in their researches. The texts as a rule adopt a static, purely statistical approach to genetics, as opposed to a dynamic approach.

Students derive from the texts a feeling of dogmatic certitude

[11] *Ibid.*, p. 155 f.
[12] A new edition of the Sinnott and Dunn book is in press which, it is hoped, will break from this tradition.

as to the finding of genetics that is not merited, and that leading geneticists themselves disclaim in their monographs. When Lysenko speaks disparagingly of "the neat chromosome theory of heredity," he is characterizing aptly the mechanistic manner in which genetics is presented in these texts. As Waddington has noted, the various types of "biological cobblers" have in the past stuck too closely to their lasts, and geneticists have often failed to take into consideration the close connection between their field and the study of cytology and embryology, the study of evolution and of the biochemical nature of the cell constituents.[13] As long as they were so restricted in their horizons, their findings were necessarily formalistic. Waddington wrote in 1947:

> The technique by which genes were originally discovered was that of crossing individuals and counting the categories of offspring. This method served to identify genes, but failed altogether to elucidate the relation between the genes it discovered and the characters by which they were recognized. In a very similar way the original atomic theory of chemistry was derived from a study of combining weights of substances and failed, until the recent development of quantum mechanics, to account for the fact that certain atoms constitute a metal, others the forms characteristic of sulphur or carbon, and so on. The genetical theory of genes, dealing with their behavior during inheritance, has only a tenuous connection with the rest of biology until it can be supplemented by an epigenetic theory, which will deal with their behavior in the developmental processes by which the fertilized egg becomes the adult with which most biological investigations are concerned.[14]

It is their failure to deal adequately with processes of development that has made most genetic textbooks so conspicuously inadequate. When Goldschmidt published his text on physiological genetics in 1938[15] he mentioned how dynamic genetics "was practically banned from advanced treatises and textbooks of ge-

[13] C. H. Waddington, *An Introduction to Modern Genetics* (London, 1939), p. 8.
[14] *Idem*, "The Genetic Control of Development," *Growth, in Relation to Differentiation and Morphogenesis*, Symposia of the Society for Experimental Biology, NO. 2 (New York, 1948), p. 152.
[15] Richard Goldschmidt, *Physiological Genetics* (New York, 1938), p. 2.

netics, and the opinion has developed and has even been voiced that it is not worth while to mention a field in which nothing is known with certainty." There has been but little advance in textbook writing since that time.

When one leaves the textbooks and turns to periodical literature and monographs, however, there is the frankest acknowledgment by American and British geneticists that "the manifestations of Mendel's principle have been shown to be vastly more complex than their pioneers of Mendelism could have surmised";[16] that many very basic questions in the field remain to be solved, that the theory of the gene is still to be worked out, and that in this healthy exploratory process the entire science is being transformed. Holmes' list of some of the problems that occupy the attention of workers in genetics reveals how much the subject is in flux at present.[17]

> Genes obviously multiply, but do they divide by fission as has been described in several small plastids? Is a gene a complex molecule? Is it an aggregation of smaller self-perpetuating entities, the so-called genomeres of sub-genes? Is it an autcatalytic enzyme or a group of possibly many such? What is its relation to a virus and to the various self-perpetuating bodies found in many kinds of cells? Do genes pass into the cytoplasm or stay put in the chromosome and carry on their functions *in situ*? What is the relation of gene mutation to chromosome breaks with whose location they are so frequently associated? What is the mechanism of the so-called position effect that goes along with different juxtapositions of genes in the chromosomes? . . .

The same ambiguity as to the nature of the gene is found in the recent writings of other geneticists. Two examples may be culled from papers delivered at the Symposium on the Genes and the Cytoplasm held during the 1948 meetings of the American Association for the Advancement of Science. Curt Stern of University of California then declared: "What the gene consists of, or what distinguishes it from other genes at other loci, remains

[16] Lancelot Hogben, *Genetic Principles in Medicine and Social Science* (New York, 1932), p. 148.
[17] Holmes, *op. cit.*, p. 156.

an unsolved problem."[18] David M. Bonner, similarly, in discussing genes as determiners of cellular biochemistry, said:

> The mechanism whereby genes can control specific morphological traits, *i.e.* the mechanism of gene action, is not well understood, and we know less still concerning the process that enables a gene to make exact replicas of itself at each cell division. . . .
>
> Single genes are known to control single biochemical reactions, and this control is probably exerted through control of enzyme production. The nature of the relationship existing between gene and enzyme remains a major biological enigma.[19]

Such characteristic statements clearly reveal how far research geneticists have left behind them the "neat chromosome theory of heredity."

The laboratory researches of geneticists have in general been narrowly confined to the task of searching for the answers to specific specialized questions which they pose for themselves. They have recently made considerable progress in answering, through such experiments, some of their long standing inquiries, and they have validated some of their presuppositions. It was announced, for example, in January of 1949 that chromosomes and genes had actually been seen under the electron microscope.[20] In the same month, Arthur E. Mirsky made public the results of his experiments that had proven that genes are nucleo-proteins, that one of their constituents is desoxyribonucleic acid, and that the amount of the acid varies with each species. The account of his findings stated that

> the amount of protein and the amount of cytoplasm associated with each chromosome group could be varied by dietary regime, by the physical state of the living animal, and by many other external considerations. *When the varying factors were eliminated in recent laboratory tests,* the amount of desoxyribonucleic acid present proved to be exactly the same for all cells of any one creature,

[18] Curt Stern, "The Effects of Changes in Quantity, Combination and Position of Genes," *Science,* CVIII (December 3, 1948), p. 615.
[19] David M. Bonner, "Genes as Determiners of Cellular Biochemistry," *Science* CVIII (December 31, 1948), p. 735, 738.
[20] Daniel C. Pease and Richard F. Baker, "Preliminary Investigations of Chromosomes and Genes with the Electron Microscope," *Science,* CIX (January 7, 1949), p. 8–10 and 22.

regardless of the organ or tissue from which the cell came. Further tests with a variety of living creatures revealed that the constant acid content of the living cell was in each case peculiar to the species.[21]

I have italicized the significant phrase, "when the varying factors were eliminated in recent laboratory tests," for it underscores the inevitable requirement of controlled laboratory experimentation, namely that part of a problem be isolated from its larger context; that reality be arbitrarily segmentalized. It had been an unfortunate failing of many of the earlier geneticists and especially of their popularizers, that in making their generalizations concerning heredity, they neglected the importance of the fact that controlled experiments had rigidly excluded the variables of the cytoplasmic and other environments. Having excluded them as factors for purposes of experimentation, some went so far as categorically to deny their importance. The fallacy of this approach has long been acknowledged, and most texts now contain a discussion of the influence of environment. Unfortunately such discussion often has little relation conceptually to the other chapters of the texts, but seems rather to be included as an afterthought.

There has been, on the other hand, an actual effort of some geneticists to take theoretical account of the fact that the environment is important in defining the nature of the gene and its development.

The late H. S. Jennings, noted biologist of the Johns Hopkins University, in a popular work in 1927,[22] and more academically in 1935,[23] stressed the fallacy involved in the assumption that if one shows a characteristic to be hereditary, one proves that it is not altered by environment. In his book *Genetics*, he wrote:

> Just what the gene shall produce in development is always dependent both on the nature of the genes that are at work, and on the conditions in which they find themselves. . . .

[21] Arthur E. Mirsky, address before the American Chemical Society reported in the New York *Times*, January 23, 1949. (Italics added.)
[22] H. S. Jennings, *Prometheus, or Biology and the Advancement of Man* (New York, 1927).
[23] H. S. Jennings, *Genetics* (New York, 1935), p. 232–65.

Many of the same features that can be altered by changing the genes can likewise be altered by appropriate changes in the environment. Characteristics do not fall into two classes, one exclusively hereditary (or dependent on genes), the other exclusively environmental; but any characteristic is affected both by the materials of which the organism is composed, and by the action of the conditions on these materials.

Yet, as we shall see, in practice some characteristics are more readily altered by environmental conditions than are others. Certain characteristics owe most of their peculiarities to diversities among genes. Others are readily affected both by genes and by environment. Still others depend mainly on environmental conditions.[24]

Lancelot Hogben has argued similarly, that "no statement about a genetic difference has any scientific meaning unless it includes or implies a specification of the environment in which it manifests itself in a particular manner."[25]

Elsewhere Hogben wrote:

Every character is the end product of an immensely complicated series of reactions between external agencies and the hereditary materials of the living cells. Differences can be described as determined predominantly by hereditary or predominantly by environmental agencies if, and only if, the conditions of development are specified. Three kinds of variability may thus be distinguished. The first is variability which depends upon hereditary differences for which the appropriate external differences are present in almost any environment in which the organism will live and reproduce. The "unit characters" like coat color or plumage, to which Mendel's method was first applied, belong to this group. A second type of variability includes differences brought about by environment acting on the same genetic material. This group includes all those modifications of the normal course of development and growth produced by the experimental embryologist and the animal physiologist. The third is a class of variability which is less familiar in the laboratory because it is more difficult to handle. It arises from the combination of a particular hereditary constitution with a particular kind of environment. The geneticist can only study this kind of variability

[24] *Ibid.*, p. 236 and 241.
[25] Lancelot Hogben, *Nature and Nurture* (London, 1933), p. 14.

with precision when he is able to specify the appropriate external conditions.[26]

He distinguishes between differences that are due primarily to genes and differences due primarily to environment by an example from animal genetics:

> If chickens are fed on yellow corn or given green food, we can distinguish between some varieties which breed true for yellow shanks and others which breed true for colorless shanks. This is a *genetic difference*. Crosses between such varieties, when all the progeny are fed on yellow corn or given green food, yield numerical ratios of the two types in conformity with Mendel's principle. If chicks of the variety with yellow shanks are fed exclusively on white corn, they grow up with colorless shanks. The difference between a fowl of the yellow variety fed on yellow corn and a fowl of the same variety fed on white corn is a *difference due to environment*. If we crossed fowls of the yellow variety with fowls of other varieties, giving some of the progeny yellow corn and others, white corn, we could not expect to obtain constant numerical ratios such as Mendel's principle predicts. If two poultry farms, both using yellow corn for food, specialized respectively on birds with black plumage and yellow shanks and birds with barred plumage and white shanks, we should call both differences genetic differences. If both farms decided to use white corn, we should only be able to recognize the plumage difference as a genetic difference. If both farms varied their procedure quite promiscuously, we should not be able to tell whether the difference between one bird with yellow shanks and another bird with colorless shanks was a genetic difference or a difference due to environment.[27]

Muller has repeatedly stressed the importance of environment. In 1947 he wrote:

> A given gene, however, is never to be thought of as literally being a gene for this or that character, but only as a gene with given *possibilities of reaction*, affording the potentialities for the development of certain characters *provided* external conditions as well as the assemblage of other genes present with it are suitable.

[26] *Idem, Genetic Principles in Medicine and Social Science* (New York, 1932), p. 98.
[27] Lancelot Hogben, *Nature and Nurture*, p. 11 f.

There can be no greater blunders in genetics than those so rife in the early years of science of confusing the gene itself with the character caused by it, and of assuming a fixed one-to-one relationship between them. Of the various fallacies which this crude and naive point of view led to, the most objectionable of all were the beliefs that if a certain trait is hereditary it cannot also be influenced by the environment and, conversely, that if it is influenced by the environment it cannot at the same time be hereditary.[28]

The way in which the environment is taken into consideration in recent genetic work is further illustrated by a quotation from Bonner:

> If genes do control enzyme production, it is possible that various alterations of a given gene might lead to enzymes of various types or to an enzyme entirely lacking specificity for its customary substrate. On the other hand, a less drastic gene alteration might give rise to an enzyme possessing specificity under certain environmental conditions and lacking it under others. There are, for example, mutant strains of *Neurospora* which are different from the wild type only under certain conditions of temperature or pH, while allelic strains also occur which are mutant in phenotype under all conditions of temperature and pH. Many other sorts of alleles could probably be found if suitable methods were available for detecting them, e.g. forms showing altered efficiencies, forms converting the substrate to different end products.[29]

Perhaps some such process is meant by Lysenko when he states vaguely and without elaboration that "A living body builds itself from the conditions of the external environment, and changes itself thereby."[30] It may be said also that while Lysenko criticizes the work of the geneticists he does not deny the functions of the chromosomes. He says in this regard:

> Naturally, what has been said above does not imply that we deny the biological role and significance of chromosomes in the develop-

[28] H. J. Muller, C. C. Little and L. H. Snyder, *Genetics, Medicine and Man* (Ithaca, N. Y., 1947), p. 20.
[29] Bonner, *op. cit.*, p. 739.
[30] T. D. Lysenko, *Heredity and Its Variability* (New York, 1946), p. 65.

ment of the cells and of the organism. But it is not at all the role which the Morganists attribute to the chromosomes.[31]

We await clarification as to just what role it is conceived that they play, if as Lysenko contends "Any living particle possesses the property of heredity."[32]

The latter contention—that any living particle possesses the property of heredity—brings to the fore the question of the relation of the gene to the cytoplasm. In this connection we may cite the findings of Tracy Sonneborn of Indiana University, presented at the American Association for the Advancement of Science, referred to previously. In the published abstract of the paper Sonneborn declared:

> It is well known that the cytoplasm protects the genes, nourishes them, is the site of activity of their products, and manifests the results of their activity. May the cytoplasm also play a part, comparable to that of the genes, in controlling hereditary traits?
>
> The existence of hereditary differences among genetically identical cells and organisms is demonstrated by a number of examples in microorganisms, higher plants, and higher animals. In these examples the hereditary differences are cytoplasmically controlled. Though often ignored, this should be recognized as one of the capital facts of biology. . . .
>
> Regardless of what hypothesis of cytoplasmic control turns out to be correct, the primary fact remains established: the control of hereditary cellular traits is in these cases cytoplasmic and self-perpetuating. The cytoplasm, as well as the genes, plays a decisive role in determining hereditary traits.[33]

A similar conclusion was reached by Spiegelman through experimental studies. He concluded that the mechanism of gene control over enzymatic constitution, far from being rigid, is extremely flexible, and that genes merely determine the potentiality of enzyme formation, but whether or not the enzyme is *actually* formed in the cytoplasm is apparently mediated by other factors of which substrate is obviously one. It is his judgment

---

[31] Lysenko, *The Science of Biology Today*, p. 21.
[32] Idem, *Heredity and Its Variability*, p. 32.
[33] Tracy M. Sonneborn, "Genes and Cytoplasm in Cellular Heredity," *Science*, cviii (November 26, 1948), p. 580.

that "differentiation *can* consists of a *purely cytoplasmic* modification of its proteins and enzymes."[34]

Caspari, who has recently prepared an extensive analysis of the present state of knowledge of cytoplasmic inheritance, concludes that the evidence establishes the fact that the transmission of cytoplasmic characters actually exists. He reviews the cases of "dauermodifications," the environmentally induced cytoplasmic changes which are transmitted maternally through a number of successive generations in animals and plants. Also discussed are cytoplasmic inheritance due to the plastids of plants, to plasmgenes and to viruses. "It may therefore be concluded," he writes, "that a plasmon, *i.e.* certain transmissible characteristics of the cytoplasm, exists which is more or less stable under the influence of foreign genes and can be reproduced through several generations independently of the genes present in the organism."[35]

The relation of dauermodifications and other types of cytoplasmic inheritance are as yet unclear. On this point, Caspari writes:

> Dauermodifications, which have been defined above as cytoplasmic changes, are induced by an environmental factor which decrease in penetrance and expressivity in succeeding generations in the absence of the inducing stimulus. There has been some discussion as to whether dauermodifications and plasmon effects are essentially the same phenomenon or not. . . . It seems preferable to distinguish the two effects for the time being, keeping in mind, that they will probably turn out to be connected in some way.[36]

He suggests that "the number of cases of cytoplasmic inheritance described, though not large, is now large enough to suggest a normal phenomenon is actually involved which is not as easily detected as Mendelian inheritance."[37] The long time and the amount of work involved in establishing cytoplasmic differences beyond doubt may have caused failure to observe many cases.

---

[34] S. Spiegelman, "Differentiation as the Controlled Production of Unique Enzymatic Patterns," Society for Experimental Biology, *Growth in Relation to Differentiation and Morphogenesis* (New York, 1948), p. 295.

[35] Ernst Caspari, "Cytoplasmic Inheritance," *Advanced Genetics*, edited by M. Demerec (New York, 1948), II, p. 20.

[36] *Ibid.*, p. 55.

[37] *Ibid.*, p. 27 f.

"This may explain," declares Caspari, "why in the last ten years, after genetic techniques have become more refined, a relatively large number of new cases of cytoplasmic effects have been described." At the same time he contends that "the existence of a plasmon does not conflict with the well founded views on gene behavior."[38]

The foregoing evidence seems to indicate that in Lysenko's polemical addresses available in this country, one of which represents his important policy-influencing speech before the Soviet Academy of Sciences, he has not done justice to the present theoretical position of genetic scientists in the United States and England. However meritorious his positive practical achievements are, his critical analysis of genetic theory represents an attack upon positions long since abandoned by the vanguard of geneticists in this country and in England. This may be attributed in part to the notorious lag in the teaching of advanced views in some textbooks and in popular works. Not only is Weismannism no longer accepted by American geneticists; it is further clear that the views of Mendel and Morgan are constantly being revised as scientific investigations, particularly in relation to developmental processes, show need for their modification. Thus it becomes clear that the gap between Lysenko and geneticists does not appear to be absolute, and may be further narrowed as reliable evidence becomes more readily available to both groups.

[38] *Ibid.*, p. 60.

part six

SOCIOLOGY OF MEDICINE

Resistances to Medical Change

Resistance to innovations in medicine may be said to be the rule rather than the exception. This is not peculiar to medicine among the sciences, for a study of the history of science and technology reveals striking resistances to the adoption of important discoveries. But there are specific features of medicine which create a situation conducive to delay in acceptance of innovations. The first lies in the relation between physician and patient. The physician, in the tradition of the ethical vow of the Hippocratic code, feels a strong sense of responsibility not to harm the patient by undue experimentation. The inhibiting effect of this responsibility is intensified by the chagrin he has experienced through past failures when he has prematurely tried a new drug or therapeutic procedure. "Once bitten, twice shy," has special relevance in medicine where traditional failures tend to be accepted sadly, but somewhat fatalistically, while failures arising out of the use of new methods give the physician a searing sense of personal defeat and the disesteem of having been taken in. Having met frequent disillusionment, the physician becomes very cautious. Garrison has remarked, "A physician of sound sense, once buncoed by commercialized drugs, the confusable status of medical doctrine, or the senseless proliferation of inferior medical literature, is apt to follow Davy Crockett's sage precept (i.e., 'First know you are right. Then go ahead.') or the *méfiez-vous* (μέμνησο ἀπιστεῖν) of the Greek philosopher, or the *Nichevo* of the Russians."[1]

[1] Fielding H. Garrison, "Review of Bernhard J. Stern, *Social Factors in Medical Progress*," *American Historical Review*, vol. XXXIII, No. 1 (October 1927), p. 90.

There are many complex factors involved in each bedside situation, with each patient offering distinctive problems. At the same time, in spite of extraordinary progress, exact scientific data in medicine are meager compared to those which are purely empirical or derived from traditional authority. As science advances, increasing certainty takes the place of guesswork which involves capricious personal judgment. But medicine in the past has been largely uncharted, and this is true even at its present stage. A special responsibility is thus imposed on the physician. In many instances, he cannot act according to fixed rules, but has a multitude of variant choices to make, any one of which may be crucial to the outcome of a case. He has, moreover, neither the time nor the competence to investigate adequately the value of the many conflicting opinions as to the etiology and treatment of all the diseases he is treating, or to get beneath the enticingly advertised claims of the prodigious number of new drug and serum products. As a consequence he may take recourse in authority, which means, in fact, that he proceeds in the traditional, supposedly well-established methods imbibed from his teachers in medical school or set forth by textbook writers. There is the dread of being unfaithful to his professional trust, of being classed among the "quacks" or "faddists," both of which groups he abhors. He assumes the characteristic pride of the conservative in being able to stand out against the influence of mass suggestion, which is particularly strong in medicine because of the public's desperate yearning for cures.

This caution is often excessive and not altogether commendable or excusable. Garrison's mordant comment is sadly true that "Even the greatest physicians may turn bigots on occasion, sometimes from 'inadequate ideas' (Spinoza), sometimes from subconscious professional jealousy ('catch me advertising him'), sometimes from settled aversion to change." He might have added, sometimes from economic interests and other reasons for resistance to change.[2]

[2] *Ibid.* For an analysis of factors involved in resistance to change see Bernhard J. Stern, "Resistance to the Adoption of Technological Innovations," National Resources Committee, *Technological Trends and National Policy* (Washington, D.C.: U.S. Government Printing Office, 1937), pp. 39–

Roux, the noted French scientist, once spoke of "the tyranny of medical education," because it contributed so much to the authoritarian attitude of physicians. There is an old adage that it takes ten years to get a medical discovery into a medical textbook and at least ten years more to get it out after it has been superseded. Particularly in a rapidly changing scientific situation, medical education has tended to lag behind the advanced practice of specialists. Efforts to introduce new and important courses based on recent findings meet the objection of an already overcrowded curriculum. Medical education has, moreover, not yet made up its mind as to its objectives—whether it wishes to develop men with specialized medical skills or students whose basic training in scientific methods, as well as in the content of science, will develop competence in the evaluation and use of changes as they occur.

Recourse to traditional authority is, to a large degree, determined by the extent to which the physician has acquired the competence to evaluate data by an understanding of the value of experimental proof. Historically, it was first necessary to establish the efficacy of the experimental method itself. This was done in the face of very strenuous opposition, most dramatically illustrated by the opposition to dissection and the resistance to Harvey's theory of the circulation of the blood. The resistances in both of these instances involve a composite of psychological and institutional factors which deserve extended analysis.

The Church played an important role in delaying the practice of dissection.[3] The bull, *De sepulturis*, issued by Boniface VIII in 1300, which forbade the dismemberment and boiling of dead crusaders for the purpose of more easily transporting their bodies to their native land, was enforced against dissection. This is shown in a passage in Mondino's writings; and in the intro-

---

66; *idem*, "Frustration of Technology," *Science and Society*, vol. II (1937), pp. 1-28; *idem*, "Restraints upon the Utilization of Inventions," *Freedom of Inquiry and Expression*, ed. Edward P. Cheyney (Philadelphia, 1938), *Annals of the Academy of Political and Social Science*, vol. CC (November 1938). [The latter two essays are included in this volume.]

[3] See Bernhard J. Stern, *Social Factors in Medical Progress* (New York: Columbia University Press, 1927), pp. 34-7.

duction to his anatomical textbook,[4] Guido da Vigevano also reported that the Church prohibited dissection.

The attitudes of the popes of the later centuries were not consistently antagonistic, but permission to dissect had to be obtained as an indulgence.[5] In 1519, Pope Leo X denied Leonardo da Vinci admission to the hospital at Rome where he wished to pursue anatomical studies because he had practised dissection.[6] The opposition of the Church served to reinforce the prevailing attitude toward the experimental method of research in anatomy. The authority of the Galenic tradition had acquired theological sanction, and to question it, as did some dissectors, was comparable to heresy. Charles Estienne (Stephanus), who dissected human bodies and published medical books, was persecuted, imprisoned for heresy, and finally died in prison in 1564.

It was in this atmosphere that Vesalius did his work. He did not receive a death sentence by the Inquisition when he criticized Galen, as is frequently contended, but attacks upon him were extremely violent.[7] Sylvius, his teacher at the University of Paris, called him "an impious madman whose breath poisoned Europe." The results of his research which ran counter to Galen, were obstinately rejected. There was an attempt to explain away the errors in Galen as text corruptions, or by the hypothesis that the human body had changed since Galen's time. The seven pieces of the sternum which Galen had described from apes and attributed to man were interpreted as indicating how much more developed the thorax was in Galen's time. The curvature of the thigh bones, not seen in man, was said to be their natural free condition before they were straightened out by the wearing of tight breeches.[8] The force of tradition is seen by the fact

[4] Charles Singer, *Evolution of Anatomy* (London: Kegan Paul, Trench Trubner, 1925), pp. 85 ff.

[5] George Sarton, *Introduction to the History of Science* (Baltimore: Williams & Wilkins, 1927), vol. II, pp. 783, 1081; Theodor Puschmann, *History of Medical Education*, tr. and ed. Evan H. Hare (London, 1891), p. 94.

[6] J. P. McMurrich, "Leonardo da Vinci and Vesalius," *Medical Library and Historical Journal*, vol. IX (1906), p. 344.

[7] Stern, *op. cit.*, pp. 37–8; cf. Richard H. Shryock, "Freedom and Interference in Medicine," *Freedom of Inquiry and Expression*, ed. Edward P. Cheyney, Annals of Political and Social Science, vol. CC, pp. 32–59.

[8] W. H. Locy, *Biology and Its Makers* (New York: Holt, 1915), p. 35.

that as late as 1750, Zedler's *Universal Lexicon* did not recognize the epoch-making character of Vesalius's *De fabrica humani corporis* (1543), but, on the contrary, criticized it as having gone too far in criticism of Galen.[9]

The vested interest of organized medical groups also delayed the wider practice of dissection. In England the Company of Barber-Surgeons claimed exclusive monopoly rights on dissections. The following entry made in the Annals of the Company on May 21, 1573, illustrates this fact: "Here was John Deane and appoynted to brynge in his fyne xli for having an Anothomye in his howse contrary to an order in that behalf between this and mydsomer next."[10] In 1714, William Cheseldon, the operative surgeon at St. Thomas's Hospital, was called before the court of the Barbers-Surgeons' Company and publicly reprimanded for the fact that he "had often procured the bodies of malefactors and [did] privately dissect them at his own house . . . contrary to the Company's by law in that behalf." At late as 1745, a fine of ten pounds was imposed by the Company on any one dissecting outside of the Barber-Surgeons' Hall.[11]

The fact that governmental agencies refused to recognize sufficiently the value of experimental investigation as opposed to book authority has seriously impeded medical education, because they have failed to provide an adequate number of cadavers for dissection. The legislators have always been deterred by the prejudices of their lay constituencies against dissection, prejudices which have been expressed with various degrees of intensity in different periods. These antipathies are based on repugnances derived from social attitudes toward the "sanctity of the human body;" from the religious belief that it was impious to cut up a corpse "made in the image of God"; from beliefs in bodily resurrection and in the continued relation between the bodily remains of an individual and his "immortal spirit"; from religious reverence and emotional attachment to the deceased; and from tabus connected with the touching of dead bodies. They go back even

---

[9] Philip Shorr, *Science and Superstition in the Eighteenth Century* (New York: Columbia University Press, 1932), pp. 60–1.
[10] Sidney Young, *Annals of the Barber-Surgeons* (London, 1890), p. 317.
[11] *Ibid.*, p. 568.

to ancient Greek times, when Herophilis and Erasistratus encountered resistance to their dissection, because of the hostility of the Greeks toward any interference with the bodies of the dead as shown by their stringent laws of the sepulcher.

As Christianity has been the dominant religion in medieval and modern times, its influence has been decisive in stimulating these attitudes. Saint Augustine helped to set the tradition when he wrote disparagingly of dissection, declaring that "with a cruel zeal for science, some medical men who are called anatomists, have dissected the bodies of the dead, and sometimes even of sick persons who have died under their knives, and have inhumanly pried into the secrets of the human body in order to learn the nature of the disease and its exact seat and how it might be cured."[12]

There has been vast ignorance of the scientific purpose of dissection—a widespread belief that dissectors wantonly and unnecessarily have mutilated dead bodies and that they often dissect live bodies. On these gruesome grounds the opponents of dissection have been able to intensify the physiological revulsion which some people experience at the sight of a cadaver or even of a skeleton, and to incite violent antagonism to the dissector. Moreover, because the initial laws sanctioning dissection granted rights to the medical schools to use only the bodies of legally executed murderers, there arose the belief that dissection was a foul practice to be used only upon the bodies of the most degraded criminals.

The result of the lack of cadavers provided by law led to the practice of grave robbing, commonly called body snatching or "resurrectionism." This practice transformed the passive opposition into bitter hatred, for in the popular mind dissectors came to be identified with violators of graves. Wherever the laws provided adequate dissection material for anatomists, who were therefore not obliged to have recourse to grave robbing, opposition was negligible compared to intense resistance elsewhere. There were innumerable outbreaks and attacks against dissectors.

[12] Augustine, *The City of God*, Book XXII, chap xxiv, in *A Select Library of the Nicene and Post-Nicene Fathers of the Christian Church*, ed. Philip Schaff (New York: Scribners, 1903), vol. II, p. 503.

In 1629, when Rolfink at the University of Jena asked for cadavers of criminals for dissection, people were so wrought up that they hurled stones at him, and culprits before being executed implored that they be not "Rolfinked." Attacks of mobs on anatomists are reported to have occurred in Lyons and Berlin in the eighteenth century, incited particularly by the report that living men were being dissected.[13]

In the United States no dissection of the human body was made until 1751 when Thomas Cadwalader dissected in Philadelphia.[14] In 1765 riots repeatedly interrupted William Shippen's lectures on anatomy because of objections to his recourse to human dissection. A contemporary rhymester played upon the sentiments of mourners in his doggerel of a corpse protesting:[15]

> "The body snatchers they have come
> And made a snatch at me;
> It's very hard them kind of men
> Won't let a body be!
> Don't go to weep upon my grave
> And think that there I be;
> They haven't left an atom there
> Of my anatomy."

Even more violent expressions of public disapproval occurred in New York during the winter of 1788, where it is reported that the public was angered because medical students dug up bodies "not only of strangers and blacks . . . but the corpses of some respectable persons." What has been called the "Doctor's Mob" broke into the building where Wright Post was teaching a course in anatomy and destroyed a valuable collection of anatomical and pathological specimens. The militia had to be called out to prevent the threatened lynching of doctors imprisoned in jail for safekeeping, and three members of the crowd were killed.[16] About the same time outbreaks against dissection occurred in Baltimore.

[13] G. Fischer, *Chirurgie von 100 Jahren* (Leipzig, 1876), pp. 49, 95.
[14] Henry B. Shafer, *The American Medical Profession, 1783 to 1850* (New York: Columbia University Press, 1936), p. 56.
[15] James T. Flexner, *Doctors on Horseback* (New York: Viking, 1937), pp. 18–19.
[16] Shafer, *op. cit.*, pp. 56–62.

Other similar attacks occurred in the United States, and in 1844 the equipment of the college in St. Louis was destroyed.

Excitable opposition to dissection was especially prevalent in Great Britain, particularly after the shocking exposé of the work of the "resurrectionists." In 1714 the Quaker, John Bellers, wrote: "At present it's not easie for the Students to get a Body to dissect at Oxford, the Mob are so mutinous to prevent their having one."[17] In 1725 there was a public riot in Edinburgh directed against body snatching, which led the Incorporation of Chirurgeons to publish and distribute a statement deprecating and denying body snatching as a means of obtaining bodies for dissection. A reward was offered for information substantiating the "villainous report" that the country people and the servants in the town "are in danger of being attacked and seized by Chirurgeons' apprentices in order to be dissected."[18] In 1823 two Americans visiting an abbey in Edinburgh after nightfall were mistaken for resurrectionists and assaulted.[19] The discovery that a cadaver was about to be exported caused a tumult in the streets of Dublin in 1828 and led to the murder of a porter at the College of Surgeons.[20]

Popular opposition to dissection was intensified as a result of the revelations at the famous trial of William Burke and William Hare in December 1828. Burke, whose methods led to the creation of the word "to burke" as a synonym for to smother, and his collaborator, Hare, had killed sixteen patrons of their cheap boardinghouse and had sold their bodies to Robert Knox, an anatomist, for dissection purposes. A violent clamor against body snatching arose throughout Great Britain and particularly in Edinburgh, which led to repeated attacks upon the home and

[17] M. C. Buer, *Health, Wealth and Population in the Early Days of the Industrial Revolution* (London: Routledge, 1926), pp. 126–7.

[18] John B. Comrie, "Early Anatomical Instruction in Edinburgh," *Edinburgh Medical Journal*, vol. XXIX (1922), p. 278; John Struthers, *Historical Sketch of the Edinburgh Anatomical School* (Edinburgh, 1867), pp. 21 ff.; C. H. Creswell, "Anatomy in the Early Days," *Edinburgh Medical Journal*, vol. XII, p. 149.

[19] James B. Bailey, *The Diary of a Resurrectionist* (London, 1896), p. 69.

[20] C. A. Cameron, *History of the Royal College of Surgeons in Ireland* (Dublin: Fannin, 1916), p. 208.

lecture rooms of Knox.[21] The excitement created by the trial was so great that it finds reflection in the works of Walter Scott, DeQuincy, George Eliot, Mrs. Gaskell, Robert Louis Stevenson, Charles Dickens and Robert Southey. Another trial in London in 1831 proved that two body snatchers, Bishop and Williams, had, during twelve years, sold to the medical schools at least 500 bodies for dissection. Public animosity was kept at fever heat.[22]

These trials led to governmental investigation of the problem and to the passage of Warburton's Anatomy Act of 1832, the first of a series of laws in England which provided increasingly adequate material for scientific purposes.[23] In the United States Massachusetts had passed an anatomical act in 1831. Until similar legislation was eventually passed by the various states, after much difficulty, the problem of obtaining dissection material remained acute and the practice of body snatching was frequently used as an unfortunately necessary measure by some of America's leading anatomists.[24] The imperative need for scientific medical investigation by work directly with the human body through dissection is now recognized. Legislation is regularizing the supply, and illicit body snatching has therefore become unnecessary. As a result, public opposition has tended to subside, but it still influences legislative action, and is occasionally incited by press headlines such as that in a New York newspaper which read: "Chapman Grave is Hid Lest Ghouls Steal Skull for Scientist."[25]

While the populace was an important factor in the opposition to dissection, the resistance to Harvey's theory of the circulation of the blood remained largely a quarrel among scientists. As with Vesalius, the opposition arose from the fact that Harvey's views ran counter to the Galenic tradition. But it had broader

[21] Frank Packard, "Early British Resurrectionists," *Medical News*, July 12, 1902, pp. 64–73; A. C. Jacobson, "Robert Knox and the Resurrectionists," *Interstate Medical Journal*, vol. XXII (1915), pp. 162–72; Bailey, *op. cit.*; cf. James M. Ball, *The Sack-'Em Up Men* (London: Oliver & Boyd, 1928).

[22] Packard, *op. cit.*, p. 72.

[23] D. F. Harris, "History of Events which Led to the Passing of the Anatomy Act," *Canadian Medical Journal*, vol. X (1920), pp. 283–4.

[24] Alan F. Guttmacher, "Bootlegging Bodies," Society of Medical History of Chicago, *Bulletin*, vol. IV (1935), p. 401.

[25] *New York Evening Journal*, April 7, 1926.

implications. Seventeenth century England was astir with the conflict between experimental science and traditional authority. This is reflected in the attack of Henry Stubbe on what he calls the *Bacon-faced* generation:[26]

> Tis *malapertness* in this *Bacon-faced* generation to oppose Galenical physic. Old books and not the *Novum Organum* nor the writings of modern experimenters will qualify a man for medicine . . . those *foundations* are most *sure*, which are laid by the Most Men, if they be *judicious* and *observing*, and have endured the test of *more ages* and *tryals* [The followers of Bacon are more like] Cobblers, or *day-labourers*, than *Practitioners in Physic* . . . [He bewails the sorry plight of medicine when] the reading of two or three *Books*, a *Comical Wit*, a *Bacon-face*, a *contempt of Antiquity*, and a *pretence to novel Experiment* [which are *meer* excuses for *Ignorance* and *Indiscretion*] are sufficient Qualifications" [for a doctor].

To this George Thomson replied in defense of the "intelligent virtuosi of the Royal Society":[27]

> Tis *Works*, not *Words: Things*, not *Thinking: Pyrotechnic*, not *Philology; Operation*, not meerly *Speculation*, must justifie us Physicians. Forbear then hereafter to be so wrongfully Satyrical against our Noble Experimentators, who questionless are entred into the right of detecting the Truth of things."

Active in opposition to the new experimentalism were churchmen who felt that the theological foundations for their beliefs were being undermined by scientific investigations. Royalists after the Restoration joined in impugning science, and particularly the work of the Royal Society, because of the close connection between its members and Baconianism and Puritanism.[28]

---

[26] Henry Stubbe, *An Epistolary Discourse Concerning Phlebotomy. In Opposition to G. Thomson Pseudo-Chymist, a Pretended Disciple of the Lord Verulam* (London, 1671), quoted by Richard F. Jones, *Ancients and Moderns*, Washington University Studies (St. Louis, 1936), p. 269.

[27] *Misochymias Elenchos: Or, a Check given to the insolent Garrulity of Henry Stubbe; in Vindication of My Lord Bacon, and the Author; With an Assertion of Experimental Philosophy: Also Some Practical Observations exhibited for the Credit of the true Chymical Science* (London, 1671), pp. 9, 40, quoted by Jones, *op. cit.*, p. 272.

[28] R. K. Merton, "Science, Technology and Society in Seventeenth Century England," *Osiris*, vol. IV, part II, pp. 443–4.

It was in this climate of opinion that Harvey worked. In 1559 John Geynes had been cited before the College of Physicians because he challenged the infallibility of Galen and he was obliged to sign a recantation of his error.[29] Harvey's predecessor, Fracastorius, had held that the motion of the heart was to be comprehended only by God.[30] Harvey, cognizant of the bold novelty of his innovation, delayed the publication of his views twelve years, just as Copernicus had waited thirty years, Newton twenty, and Bacon twelve, before they published the works that made them immortal. Scientific workers in that period were subject to surveillance and persecution. The primary suppression was in the field of religion, as illustrated by the fact that in 1637 the Star Chamber enacted the penalty of imprisonment and whipping for the publisher of any book opposing the authority of the Church of England.[31] But the scientist likewise did not feel secure. In Harvey's dedication of *De Motu Cordis* to Argent, the president of the College of Physicians in London, he states the reason for his hesitance and his justification for experimental research:[32]

As this book alone declares the blood to course and revolve by a new route, very different from the ancient and beaten pathway trodden for so many ages, and illustrated by such a host of learned and distinguished men, I was afraid lest I might be charged with presumption . . . unless . . . I had confirmed its conclusions by ocular demonstrations in your presence . . . For true philosophers, who are only eager for truth and knowledge, never regard themselves as already so thoroughly informed, but that they welcome further information from whomsoever and from whencesoever it may come, nor are they so narrow-minded as to imagine any of the arts or sciences transmitted to us by the ancients, in such a state of forwardness and completion that nothing is left for the ingenuity and industry of others. . . . I profess both to learn and to teach anatomy, not from books but from dissections; not from the positions of the philosophers but from the fabric of nature.

[29] Arthur Newsholme, *Evolution of Preventive Medicine* (Baltimore: Williams & Wilkins, 1927), p. 34.
[30] Robert Willis, *Works of William Harvey* (London, 1847), p. 19.
[61] Newsholme, *op. cit.*, p. 23.
[32] Willis, *op. cit.*, pp. 2–7.

When he reached the discussion of the circulation of the blood, he prefaced his account with a correct anticipation of the opposition his views would encounter:

> But what remains to be said about the quantity and source of the blood which thus passes, is of so novel and unheard-of-character, that I not only fear injury to myself from the envy of a few, but I tremble lest I should have mankind at large for my enemies, so much doth wont and custom, that become as another nature, and doctrine once sown and that hath struck deep root, and respect for antiquity influence all men.[33]

Harvey's contemporaries recognized that the storm of criticism directed against him was one stemming from the struggle of ancient tradition against truth derived from experiment. George Ent, in his defense of Harvey, inveighed against those who believed that antiquity was the only source of truth and declared:[34]

> It is considered impious to wish to deprive them [the ancients] of this absolute sway. Thus modernity is shackled to antiquity and those who would revolt are vilified. If a new discovery is put forth, buttressed with demonstrations, then envy declares that it had been discovered by the ancients or poorly demonstrated.

James DeBack declared that "by setting down the circulatory motion of the blood innumerable axioms of ancient writers were overturned; whence it comes that all the order of teaching is troubled,"[35] and Zachary Wood, a physician in Rotterdam, came to his defense in this eloquent passage:[36]

> Truly a bold man indeed.
> O disturber of the quiet of Physicians!
> O seditious citizen of the Physical Commonwealth!

---

[33] *Ibid.*, p. 45.
[34] Quoted by Jones, *Ancients and Moderns*, p. 166.
[35] *The Discourse of James DeBack, physician in ordinary to the town of Rotterdam in which he handles the nullity of spirits, Sanguification, the heat of living things. There is premised a speech to the Reader and annexed an addition in defense of Harvey's Circulation* (London, 1673), quoted by Stern, *Social Factors in Medical Progress*, p. 45.
[36] Zachary Wood, *Preface to Harvey's Anatomical Exercises* (London, 1673), pp. 2–3.

who first of all durst oppose an opinion confirmed for so many ages by the consent of all, and delivered up to monuments of so many Physicians, and as it were given from hand to hand to posterity, as if no man had been wise in all ages past. Indeed they do so very decently who worship antiquity as becomes them; but it is a thing unworthy in wise men who do ascribe wisdom to antiquity, with no little wrong to posterity. Therefore, since to be wise, that is to say to search after truth is form with all men, they take away all wisdom from themselves who without any judgment approve of their forefathers' inventions and are by them led like cattle and do brag rashly that they see those things in them that they do not see.

That Harvey needed defense is seen by a passage in his letter to John Riolan:[37]

Scarce a day, scarce an hour, has passed since the birthday of the circulation of the blood that I have not heard something for good or evil said of this discovery. Some abuse it as a feeble infant, and yet unworthy to have seen the light; others again think the bantling deserves to be cherished and cared for; these oppose it with much ado, those patronise it with abundant commendation; one party holds I have completely demonstrated the circulation of the blood by experiment, observation and ocular inspection, against all force and array of argument; another thinks it scarcely yet sufficiently illustrated—not yet cleared of all objections. There are some, too, who say I have shown a vainglorious love of vivisections, and who scoff and deride the introduction of frogs and serpents, flies and others of the lower animals upon the scene, as a piece of puerile levity, not even refraining from opprobrious epithets . . . Detractors, mummers and writers defiled with abuse, as I resolved with myself never to read them, satisfied that nothing solid or excellent, nothing but foul terms was to be expected from them, so I have held them still less worthy of an answer. . . . The authority of Galen is of such weight with all that I have seen several hesitate greatly with that experiment before them.

Harvey claimed that no man over forty was found to adopt the doctrine of the circulation of the blood.[38] He was especially

[37] Willis, *op. cit.*, pp. 109–10.
[38] *Ibid.*, p. xlvii.

disturbed by the attitude of Casper Hoffmann, professor of medicine at Nuremberg, who had been a fellow student at Padua.[39] Hoffmann, who had himself rejected Galen, refused dogmatically to perform the demonstration and accused Harvey of having "impeached and condemned Nature of folly and error." To this charge Harvey retorted that he was willing to perform the experiment in his presence but "if you either decline this, or care not by dissection to investigate the subject for yourself, let me beseech you, I say, not to vilipend the industry of others, nor charge it to them as a crime; do not derogate from the faith of an honest man, not altogether foolish or insane, who has had experience in such matters for a long series of years."

The tradition is that Harvey gave the demonstration which convinced everyone present but Hoffmann, whose persistent objections led Harvey to throw down his knife and leave the operating theatre.[40] One is here reminded of the letter of Galileo to Kepler in 1610:[41]

> What do you think of the foremost philosophers of the University? In spite of my oft-repeated efforts and invitations, they have refused, with the obstinancy of a glutted adder, to look at the planets or the moon or my telescope! . . . Kindest Kepler, what peals of laughter you would give forth if you heard with what arguments the foremost philosopher of the University opposed me, in the presence of the Grand Duke, at Pisa, laboring with his logic chopping argumentations as though they were magical incantations wherewith to banish and spirit away the new planets [the satellites of Jupiter] out of the sky.

It was this dogmatic unyielding spirit that led one of Harvey's loyal supporters to write with some heat in 1652:[42]

[39] *Ibid.*, p. xliii.
[40] D'Arcy Power, "A Revised Chapter in the Life of Dr. William Harvey, 1636," *Selected Writings, 1877–1930* (Oxford: Clarendon Press, 1931), pp. 147–8; Willis, *op. cit.*, p. 596.
[41] Cited by B. Hessen, "The Social and Economic Roots of Newton's Principia," *Science at the Crossroads* (London, 1931), p. 18.
[42] Henry Power, *Circulatio Sanguinis* (1652), quoted by Humphrey Rolleston, "The Reception of Harvey's Doctrine of Circulation of the Blood in England as Exhibited in the Writings of Two Contemporaries," *Essays on the History of Medicine Present to Karl Sudhoff*, ed. Charles Singer and Henry E. Sigerist (London: Oxford University Press, 1924), pp. 248–9.

Amongst all the rabble of his [Harvey's] antagonists, we see not one that attempts to fight him at his own weapon, that is by sensible and anatomical evictions to confute that which he has by sense and autopsy so vigorously confirm'd. And therefore we cannot but looke upon such skepticall and Tyrrhonian Authors as Disciples to Anaxagoras that in defiance to the noblest of his senses would needs maintain the snow was black and shall only confute them as the walking Philosopher did the Stoick, that peremptorily asserted there was no such thing in the world as motion.

Thomas Hobbes wrote of his friend Harvey as "the only man I know, that conquering envy, hath established a new doctrine in his lifetime."[43] But this is, in fact, an over-statement. Although Harvey was Bacon's physician, he is nowhere mentioned by Bacon, perhaps because he knew that Harvey had said of him, "He writes philosophy like a Lord Chancellor."[44]

While Descartes admitted Harvey's views on the greater circulation, he rejected what Harvey insisted to be the keystone of his whole argument, the propulsion of the blood by the contraction of the heart, and held on to the Galenic doctrine of the expansion of the heart by its innate heat.[45] Thomas Winston, whose term of anatomy lectureships paralleled Harvey's, made no mention of the latter's work in his book published after his death in 1651, although he refers to Galen, Columbus and Riolan.[46] Sir William Temple paired the work of Copernicus and Harvey and said, "These two great discoveries have made no change in the conclusions of Astronomy nor in the practice of Physic, and so have been but little use to the world, though perhaps of much honor to the authors."[47] The works of his contemporary, Thomas Sydenham, do not contain any reference to Harvey or

[43] *The English Works of Thomas Hobbes of Malmesbury,* ed. William Molisworth (London, 1839), p. viii.

[44] John Aubrey, *Brief Lives,* ed. Andrew Clark (Oxford, 1898), vol. I, p. 299; William Hale-White, "Bacon, Gilbert and Harvey" (London: Bale Sons & Danielson, 1927).

[45] Michael Foster, *Lectures on the History of Physiology During the Sixteenth, Seventeenth and Eighteenth Centuries* (Cambridge, Eng.: Cambridge University Press, 1924), pp. 57–9.

[46] William Osler, *An Alabama Student* (New York: Oxford University Press, 1908), p. 321.

[47] Quoted by Osler, *op. cit.,* p. 323.

show any conception of the significance of his discovery.[48] Even as late as 1781, Cullen made no mention of Harvey's work in his chapters on physiology.[49]

The most vigorous opposition was from the medical school of the University of Paris, where the son of John Riolan perpetuated the prejudices of his father. There, too, Guy Patin regarded the new doctrine as ridiculous and called the partisans of it *circulateurs* in allusion to the Latin word *circulator* which means charlatan. In 1652 he wrote that the question as to whether the blood passes through the septum of the heart or through the lungs was still unsolved. As late as 1670, twelve years after Harvey's death, Patin decided in the negative when, at a bachelor's examination, the circulation of the blood was discussed. The official recognition of the doctrine did not come in France until 1673.[50]

While the criticisms of Harvey were by scientists, they had repercussions among laymen, and Harvey suffered from the discriminations traditionally the lot of the innovator. He is reported to have said that after his book appeared, "it was believed by the vulgar that he was crackbrained and all the physicians were against him" with the result that "he fell mightily in his practice."[51]

Following Harvey there continued to be a lag in appreciation of the value of experimental investigations. Malpighi, who discovered the capillaries, was opposed by his associates in Bologna. Haller and Morgagni were both ignored by their contemporaries.

There was long delay in an understanding of the significance of Auenbrugger's theory of percussion. In the preface to his book, published in 1761, he wrote:[52]

---

[48] Rolleston, *op. cit.*, p. 250.
[49] T. Clifford Allbutt, *Greek Medicine in Rome* (London: Macmillan, 1921), p. 531.
[50] Osler, *op. cit.*, pp. 324–7.
[51] Willis, *Works of William Harvey*, p. xxiv. For a fuller analysis of opposition to Harvey see H. P. Bayon, "William Harvey, Physician and Biologist: His Precursors, Opponents and Successors," *Annals of Science*, vol. III (1938), pp. 84–118.
[52] Leopold Auenbrugger, *Inventum Novum*, tr. in Charles N. Camac, *Epoch Making Contributions to Medicine, Surgery and Allied Sciences* (Philadelphia: Saunders, 1909), p. 123.

In making public my discoveries respecting this matter I have been actuated neither by an itch for writing, nor a fondness for speculation, but by the desire of submitting to my brethren the fruits of seven years' observation and reflection. In doing so, I have not been unconscious of the dangers I must encounter; since it has always been the fate of those who have illustrated or improved the arts and sciences by their discoveries to be beset by envy, malice, hatred, detraction, and calumny.

He met the treatment he anticipated at the hands of his contemporaries, and his work was ignored and remained practically unknown until Corvisart secured its recognition in 1808. Even as late as 1840, Wolff in Berlin conducted a clinic in which neither percussion nor auscultation was used.[53]

Laennec had first invented his stethoscope for mediate auscultation in 1819. It made slow progress at first and as late as 1829, John Elliotson, who was the first in England to use the stethoscope, was still obliged to defend its use.[54] Sir Henry Halford, who had the reputation of being an excellent diagnostician, refused to the end of his life to have anything to do with the stethoscope.[55] Oliver Wendell Holmes comments on its reception in the United States:[56] "It is perfectly natural that they [the old practitioners] should look with suspicion upon this introduction of medical machinery among the old, hard-working operatives; that they should for a while smile at its pretensions, and when its use began to creep in among them, that they should observe and signalize all the errors and defects which happened in its practical application." The first mention of the stethoscope, in the catalog of the Harvard Medical School, was in 1868-69.[57]

[53] Fielding H. Garrison, *An Introduction to the History of Medicine* (4th ed.; Philadelphia: Saunders, 1929), p. 778.
[54] Max Neuburger, *Essays in the History of Medicine*, tr. and ed. Fielding H. Garrison (New York: Medical Life Press, 1930), p. 195; George Rosen, "John Elliotson, Physician and Hypnotist," *Bulletin of the Institute of the History of Medicine*, vol. IV, NO. 7 (July 1936), p. 601; idem, "A Note on the Reception of the Stethoscope in England," *Bulletin of the History of Medicine*, vol. VII, NO. 1 (January 1939), pp. 93-4.
[55] Arnold Chaplin, *Medicine in England during the Reign of George III* (London: Kingston, 1919), p. 46.
[56] Quoted by Osler, *op. cit.*, pp. 59-60
[57] Abraham Flexner, *Medical Education in the United States and Canada* (New York: Carnegie Foundation, 1910), pp. 8-9.

Centuries were required to overcome the inertia which met the idea of asepsis. The authoritarian belief of Galen that suppuration in wounds was a natural condition, and that it was the physiological process leading to cicatrization, was already boldly challenged by Theodoric in the thirteenth century, who argued that it was a complication that could be avoided by appropriate measures. He urged that the wounds should be cleared of foreign bodies, that the edges of the wounds be sutured, and that pads and pledgets soaked in wine be used to foment the sutured wound and the neighboring parts. Neither he nor Henri de Mondeville, who perfected the method, suspected that wounds could be contaminated by dirty hands or instruments, nor did they have an inkling of the role of microbes. But their advocacy of cleanliness and simplicity in surgery raised the fury of opposition that Holmes and Semmelweis later encountered in their campaign against puerperal fever, and also that which greeted the advocates of antisepsis and asepsis. De Mondeville, who dared to say that "God did not exhaust all his creative power when he made Galen," wrote bitterly in 1312 of the manner in which this innovation, which would have reduced death by suppuration six hundred years earlier, was received by the surgeons of his day:[58]

> It is very dangerous for any surgeon to operate except in accordance with the practice of other surgeons. . . . We have indeed suffered great contempt, and the most insulting epithets from the public, and many threats and menaces from our own colleagues. From certain persons, and even from doctors, every day and at each new dressing, we have put up with discussions and violent expostulations. And, half overcome and discouraged by so much opposition, we have even considered the abandonment of the treatment, and we should have completely given it up without the support of the most serene Count of Valois. But this prince has come to our assistance, as also have some others, who have seen the care of wounds by this wonderful method in the field. Moreover, we have been sustained by truth. But if we had not been firm in

[58] G. D. Hindley, "Aseptic Surgery in the Fourteenth Century," *Nineteenth Century and After*, xcviii (October 1925), p. 586.

our faith, we should have been forced to give up our new method of treatment.

After De Mondeville died the method passed out of use and Guy de Chauliac, the noted surgeon of the next generation, rejected his theory of suppuration and his method with contempt.

The same treatment was accorded Oliver Wendell Holmes in the United States and Ignaz Semmelweis in Vienna when, independently, they charged that physicians were the vehicles by which puerperal fever was transmitted. Holmes first published his views in 1843, and little attention was paid to them until 1852 and 1854, when they were attacked by Hodge, professor of obstetrics at the University of Pennsylvania, and by C. L. Meigs, professor of midwifery at the Jefferson Medical College, Philadelphia. Hodge begged his students to divest their minds of the dread that they could ever carry the dreadful virus. Meigs scorned Holmes's deductions as characteristic of the "jejune and fizzenless vaporings of sophomore writers" and added that he preferred to attribute the deaths to "accident, or providence, of which I can form a conception, rather than to a contagion of which I cannot form any clear idea, at least as to this particular malady."[59]

In 1855 Holmes answered these attacks vigorously. He was concerned that the medical students might be misled by their professors and poured scorn on the latter's inadequacy: "They [the students] naturally have faith in their instructors, turning to them for truth and taking what they may choose to give them; babies in knowledge, not yet able to tell the breast from the bottle, pumping away for the milk of truth at all that offers, were it nothing better than a professor's shrivelled forefinger."[60]

He then made his eloquent plea that rather than being apathetic in the face of the death of mothers, physicians should make serious investigations into his claims:[61]

> The teachings of the two professors in the great schools of Philadelphia are sure to be listened to, not only by their immediate pupils, but by the profession at large. I am too much in earnest for

[59] Oliver Wendell Holmes, *Medical Essays (1842–1882)* (Boston, 1891), p. 103.
[60] *ibid.*, p. 108.
[61] *ibid.*, pp. 127–8.

either humility or vanity, but I do entreat those who hold the keys of life and death to listen to me also for this once . . . this is no subject to be smoothed over by nicely adjusted phrases of half assent and half censure divided between the parties. The balance must be struck boldly and the result declared plainly. . . . If the doctrine I have maintained is a mournful truth; if to disbelieve it, and to practise on this disbelief, and to teach others so to disbelieve and practise, is to carry desolation and to charter others to carry it into confiding families, let it be proclaimed as plainly what is to be thought of the teachings of those who sneer at the alleged dangers and scout the very idea of precaution. Let it be remembered that persons are nothing in this matter; better that twenty pamphleteers should be silenced, or as many professors unseated, than that one mother's life should be taken. There is no quarrel here between men, but there is deadly incompatibility and exterminating warfare between doctrines . . . if I am right, let doctrines which lead to professional homicide be no longer taught from the chairs of those two great institutions. Indifference will not do here; our journalists and committees have no right to take up their pages with minute anatomy and tediously detailed cases while it is a question whether or not the 'black death' of childbed is to be scattered broadcast by the agency of the mother's friend and adviser.

The opposition to Holmes was due to inertia and to the injured vanity of the profession at being called carriers of death. The acrimonious assault on Semmelweis, who, independently of Holmes arrived at the same discovery, was based on these factors and many more. It was regarded as an insult by his colleagues that he should declare their traditional theories of atmospheric, telluric and cosmic influences to be in error, and they thought silly his belief that a simple piece of chloride lime could arrest an outbreak of the disease. Personality conflicts and rivalries enlivened the debate and muddied the issues. Semmelweis did not have the social standing and the literary poise that Holmes possessed, and his defense of his position was denounced as "irascible, impatient, tactless." His republican sympathies in the revolution of 1848, when he joined the "academic legion," led his reactionary superior to refuse to reappoint him. His successor in the hospital repeatedly referred to the doctrine of his predecessor as all "humbug."

Yet Semmelweis had reduced the death rate of mothers in his hospital ward by the simple requirement that physicians wash their hands in chloride solutions prior to their entry. He succeeded in doing this in spite of the fact that the authorities once went so far as to refuse to purchase new sheets on the ground that several accouchements could very well be performed without a change of sheets. As soon as Semmelweis was dismissed from the hospital, maternal mortality began to rise again. But his explanation of the causes of this rise was not accepted.[62]

His views were ignored or ridiculed with rare exceptions. Virchow, whose authority carried tremendous weight, treated them with disdainful silence while teaching the conflicting views, and Semmelweis was denounced for his temerity when he challenged him. When Skoda advocated Semmelweis's views he aroused the opposition of Scanzoni of Prague, who considered his remarks to be a personal affront. At the latter's suggestion a commission of which Hamernik was a member was appointed to investigate the whole question of puerperal fever, but eleven years later it had not yet made a report. Although Semmelweis, in 1850, emphatically denied that he believed cadaveric poison to be the sole cause of puerperal fever, he was denounced as "the apostle of cadaveric poison, the preacher of a one-sided creed." Surgeons referred to him sarcastically as a physician who expressed opinions on surgical questions which were outside of his province. When Weigert attempted to make Semmelweis's work known in France, his article was published in the *Union Medicale* under the heading of "doubtful anecdotes." As a result of all this hostile disparagement and apathy, Semmelweis finally died in an insane asylum. When Lister visited the continent in 1883 the name of Semmelweis was not even mentioned.[63]

Lister, too, had his difficulties, and strenuous ones they were. Pasteur's theory that "microbes must have parents," had not been readily accepted in England and on the continent, and the belief in the spontaneous origin of disease persisted among many medical men long after Pasteur's notable experiments of 1862–66.

---

[62] William Sinclair, *Semmelweis, His Life and His Doctrine* (Manchester: Manchester University Press, 1909).

[63] Stern, *Social Factors in Medical Progress*, pp. 67–9.

Vallery-Radot, Pasteur's biographer, says that "the theory of germs, the doctrine of virus ferments, all this was considered as a complete reversal of acquired notions, a heresy which had to be suppressed."[64]

Since Lister's method was based on Pasteur's theory, opposition to both developed simultaneously. Nunnely, in an address on surgery at the 1869 meeting of the British Medical Association, declared that "the theory and reasoning by which the antiseptic treatment of wounds is supported appear to overlook facts open to all the world, to disregard observations familiar to every person through all ages from the earliest period to the present day. . . . We may probably with safety deny the existence of germs in the number and universality maintained by Pasteur and Lister."[65] A letter concerning Lister's treatment in the *Lancet* in 1870, by a Glasgow surgeon, argued that "Pasteur's theory in regard to the existence of certain spores or germs in the air" had not been satisfactorily proved.[66] Robert Lawson Tait, noted English ovariotomist, refused to see any relation between bacteria and disease.[67] That resistance to the theory was strong in England is evidenced by Cheyne's comment[68] that "the non-Listerians looked on the others as crazy believers in vain things like germs, rash to a degree, blinded by their enthusiasms . . . and as they said . . . that their wounds did not suppurate while those of the other side did, liars of the first water."

In France, LeFort maintained that the germ theory was "absolutely unacceptable" in its applications to clinical surgery, and continued,[69] "I believe in the *interiority* of the principle of purulent infection in certain patients; that is why I oppose the extension to surgery of the germ theory which proclaims the constant *exteriority* of that principle." That these views were representative is seen by the fact that Champonniére, the advocate of

[64] René Vallery-Radot, *The Life of Pasteur*, tr. R. L. Devonshire (New York: Doubleday, Page, 1923, p. 83.
[65] G. T. Wrench, *Lord Lister* (London: Unwin, 1914), p. 193.
[66] Rickman J. Godlee, *Lord Lister* (London: Macmillan, 1917), pp. 250–1.
[67] Garrison, *An Introduction to the History of Medicine*, p. 649.
[68] Watson Cheyne, *Lister and His Achievement* (London: Longmans Green, 1925), p. 25.
[69] Vallery-Radot, *op. cit.*, pp. 270 ff.

Lister's method in France, declared later: "I was subject to a sort of persecution on the part of those whose scientific repose I was violently upsetting."[70] Theodore Billroth in Vienna followed Leibig in denying that microorganisms caused decomposition and wrote to Volkmann in 1874, "If you were not so energetic a supporter of this [the antiseptic method] I should say the whole thing was a swindle."[71]

In Germany, Von Nussbaum reported in retrospect in 1887:[72]

> Ten years ago, many distinguished surgeons called Lister's treatment humbug and considered it an unpardonable attack on surgical freedom to assert that no surgeon has any right to be ignorant of the antiseptic treatment.
>
> In 1880, I said in a clinical lecture that in medico-legal cases a surgeon could be called to account if he completely ignored antiseptics and lost a patient from pyemia.
>
> For this I was reproached in a most violent manner both verbally and in print. A distinguished medical jurist wrote a letter about me in which he called me a fanatic and said that no medical jurist alive would reproach a practical surgeon who acted faithfully according to the teaching of the text books recommended at the University because a practical surgeon could neither buy all new books, nor ought he to allow his principles to be shaken by every new discovery.

In the United States, Robert Weir asserted in 1878 that the most weighty objection to Lister's method was the positive manner in which it explained the process of decomposition in the secretions of a wound in terms of the germ theory.[73] Stephen Smith comments that when he introduced Lister's method into the wards of Bellevue Hospital many of his colleagues who believed in "laudable pus" were outraged and refused even to visit the wards when the patients were under treatment to observe the effectiveness of the method.[74]

[70] Godlee, *op. cit.*, p. 353.
[71] *ibid.*, p. 349.
[72] *ibid.*, p. 340.
[73] Robert E. Weir, *On the Antiseptic Treatment of Wounds* (New York, 1878).
[74] Stephen Smith, "Reminiscences of Two Epochs, Anaesthesia and Asepsis," Johns Hopkins Hospital, *Bulletin*, vol. XXX (1919), p. 276.

Apart from the opposition to the germ theory there were elements in Lister's innovation that were a legitimate basis of controversy.[75] An editorial in the *Lancet* argued:[76] "The germ theory may be perfectly well founded but nine out of ten surgeons do not much care whether it is or not, so long as they cure their cases and reduce their mortality to the lowest possible degree." Failure to understand the germ theory led to a careless and mechanical application of Lister's method with negative results that tended to discredit it, to the extent that even those who were receptive began to discard it. There were other rival methods of avoiding suppuration that were reporting more favorable results, and the evidence was very conflicting because of the inadequacy of Lister's statistical proof of his successes.

Vigorous opposition by James Simpson, the famous English surgeon, was influential in the disparagement of Lister. Simpson was acquainted with the difficulties of the innovator. When he had introduced anesthetics in surgery and obstetrics he was denounced by clergymen, both from the pulpit and in pamphlets, on the grounds that anesthetics were decoys of Satan. In reply he had written a paper entitled, "Answers to the Religious Objections Against Employment of Anesthetic Agents in Midwifery and Surgery," in which he defended the practice by ingenious exegesis of the opening chapters of Genesis. But his own experience did not prevent him from attacking Lister, first in terms of the charge that he had been antedated by Lemaire in his use of carbolic acid and then on the grounds that Lister displayed the most culpable ignorance of medical literature. It was, however, primarily Simpson's vested interest in his own method of "acupressure" which led him to attack Lister.[77] This was supplemented by his antagonism to John Symes, Lister's father-in-law and chief, and perhaps too, as Garrison suggests, by the fact that Lister did not live on Harley Street.[78]

Some of the opposition to Lister's method was well grounded, particularly the insistence of Lister and his followers on the value

[75] Stern, *Social Factors in Medical Progress*, pp. 80–92.
[76] *Lancet*, October 23, 1875, p. 597.
[77] Wrench, *Lord Lister*, pp. 141–2; Godlee, *Lord Lister*, pp. 199 ff.
[78] Fielding H. Garrison, "Review of Social Factors in Medical Progress," *American Historical Review*, vol. XXXIII, No. 1 (October 1927), p. 90.

of the antiseptic spray machine in creating an antiseptic atmosphere around the wound. The spray created important hazards both to the surgeon and to the patient. Yet despite repeated evidence of its disutility, summarized in 1880 by Bruns in his paper, "*Fort mit dem Spray*," Lister and many of his followers continued to employ it until 1887. In 1890 Lister confessed his error before the International Medical Congress in Berlin, saying, "I feel ashamed that I should ever have recommended it [the spray] for the purpose of destroying the microbes of the air." Yet it was this recommendation that had been crucial in abetting the opposition to the theory of germ infection. It had offered a legitimate basis of criticism of Lister's method that had led to condemnation of the entire procedure and theory behind it. Laymen joined the fray, and groups in England hostile to scientific medicine spoke of "lunatic Listerism which tried to kill imaginary germs by directing carbolic spray on the wounds on the operating table."[79]

The economic and psychological interests of administrators of institutions were involved by some of Lister's criticisms of prevailing hospital practices, and by what they regarded as his unfounded assertions of his own successes. The reputations of their hospitals were being destroyed, they thought, by one they charged with seeking to glorify himself at the expense of their reputations and those of his fellow surgeons.[80] This intense indignation sometimes expressed itself in print as in 1877, after Lister had been reported to have said that the teaching of surgery in Edinburgh was much superior to that pursued in London, the *Lancet* fulminated editorially:[81]

> Like a man who in the excitement of enthusiasm raves at the false creations of his heat-oppressed brain, Mr. Lister fancied he saw his profession confreres in London only unsubstantial shades and showy shams. . . . In many quarters, Mr. Lister has acquired the reputation of a thoughtful, painstaking surgeon and has done some service to practical surgery by insisting on the importance of cleanliness in the treatment of wounds, although this has been

[79] Stern, *op. cit.*, pp. 85–6.
[80] Godlee, *op. cit.*, pp. 246–51.
[81] *Lancet*, March 10, 1877, p. 361.

done by the glorification of an idea which is neither original nor universally accepted, but even these circumstances do not warrant him in arrogating to himself the right to sit in judgment on his fellows and publicly denounce as imposters those who have the misfortune to differ from him.

This editorial accounts in part for the fact that Lister was apathetically received when he first came to London. Because their examiners were hostile to Lister, students avoided his courses.[82] The vanity of some surgeons was also piqued by the fact that consultants were forbidden to see their own patients in Lister's surgical clinics.

The financial costs of carbolic acid dressings as compared to water dressings retarded the use of the antiseptic method. The governing board of the Edinburgh Infirmary complained about the expense involved, and in Munich Von Nussbaum was obliged to meet the argument of excessive costs.[83]

Antisepsis must be regarded historically as merely a transition stage to the more efficacious methods of asepsis. These were introduced by von Bergmann and developed by Schimmelbusch, beginning in 1892. The role of the Listerians in the process of change to the improved method affords an interesting illustration of how innovators can become conservative when the innovation for which they have struggled is superseded. They had attached such a vehement emotional tone to their practice, and had such a vested interest in it that they resented improvements which made their methods antiquated. Adaptation to asepsis was more difficult for them than for other surgeons. Although Lister was not as vehement as some of his disciples, he expressed himself against asepsis, "It has grieved me to learn that many surgeons have been led to substitute needlessly protracted and complicated measures for means so simple and efficient [as the antiseptic]."[84]

Cameron, Lister's friend, stated in 1907 that Lister deplored the complications which he said he knew from his own experience to be wholly superfluous. Voicing the opposition of many

[82] Cuthbert Dukes, *Lord Lister* (London: Parsons, 1924), p. 155.
[83] Stern, *op. cit.*, p. 88.
[84] J. B. Lister, *Collected Papers* (Oxford, 1908), vol. III, p. 370.

physicians, he complained that, because of the technical arrangements necessary to secure for asepsis the amount of skilled assistance required, and because of the necessary use of masks, gloves and other expensive accessories, ordinary surgical practice was being eliminated, that surgery was being confined to the well-equipped hospital. Champonniére, who upset the scientific repose of others when advocating Lister's methods, was now himself upset, and denounced asepsis in 1902:[85]

> This surgery is nothing more than laboratory work. . . . Never before have the architects been more indispensable. The least defect in the condition of an operating room manifests itself by disasters. If the surgeon does not surround himself with impracticable precautions—masks, gloves, etc.—the safety of the patient is imperilled. The old surgical world protested against the easygoing and regular precautions which Lister took. Modern surgeons, instead of moderating these precautions which might be moderated, introduce new and incredible precautions incompatible with regular practice. And yet, have they altered the results of surgery? Certainly they have caused it to lose its safety.

He was outdone in his vehemence by Wrench, another Listerian, who voiced the scorn of the many physicians who were impatient with the demands of the aseptic method, and were annoyed by the personal inconvenience it involved. Asepsis also seemed greatly to enlarge the role of hospitals in medical services:[86]

> Lister did not use the nailbrush, which he regarded as superfluous. He did not scrub his hands for so many minutes by the watch nor soak them in several lotions. He did not use boiled gloves, boiled robes, boiled cap, boiled mask or boiled muzzle. He remained an ordinary human being to the eye of the spectator. He was not attired like a mummer at a carnival. He never adopted all these 'improvements' because he had faith in his own observations of the power that carbolic acid possessed of rendering and keeping organic matter aseptic. . . . The avoidance of septic disaster—quite apart from surgical skill—instead of being represented as a reward of faithful adherence to Listerism, is shown to the

[85] Quoted by Wrench, *op. cit.*, pp. 326 ff.
[86] *Ibid.*, pp. 331–3.

student to be dependent—and even then it is not assured—upon an enormous and expensive equipment of various forms of sterilizers, autoclaves, mosaic floors, tiled walls, sterilized water, air filterers, highly trained assistants, boiled robes boiling a short time to rag, boiled gloves soon becoming rotten, boiled instruments soon becoming blunt, architectural rotundities and mechanical specialties, which can only be enjoyed at hospitals by the charity of the public, and at nursing homes by the largeness of the fees, by quite a limited number of surgeons. The certain benefits of Lister which could have been spread through the land in cottage as well as in palace, have been converted into a ring and a fetish. The student walking the hospital instead of being taught the beautiful simplicity and mastery of Lister, is like an acolyte instructed in mysteries; but should he not join the ranks of the peculiar priesthood he eventually finds himself turned out upon the world, dubious and incompetent, because he has not at his beck and call the elaborate paraphernalia of a palatial modern hospital. Surgery, in a word, has been not only rendered unsafe but it has been made an expensive monopoly of the surgeons who get attached to the public hospitals. Not only does the student and future practitioner suffer gravely from this rapid departure from the simplicity of Lister, but the ever-increasing cost to the public is enormous. "The need of asepsis," says a writer upon the London Hospital and its construction and outfit which he admires, "has led to an enormous expenditure which becomes a fixed and permanent expenditure."

Many improvements in hospital technique proposed to guard patients from infection have met a measure of indifference and open hostility similar to that accorded the initial innovations of asepsis. These are now customary and routine and therefore acceptable, while new measures require readjustments in habitual practices that stimulate resentment. The resentment provides a ground for rationalization, for evasion, and for justification of neglect. When the innovation disturbs economic interests, or pricks personal vanity it leads not merely to passive opposition but to open hostility.

The germ theory which was at the basis of antisepsis and asepsis led, of course, to a transformation of medical practice in other ways as well. The entire battle against epidemics had a new start and a new rationale. Preventive inoculation which had

RESISTANCES TO MEDICAL CHANGE 373

been merely empirical came to be understood in scientific terms, and the century-old opposition to vaccination could be combated on new grounds. The antivaccinationists realized this, as is seen by the violent temper of their denunciations of Pasteur of which the following are typical: [87]

> There are no limits to credulity, any craze is possible; but audacity may be too audacious. Miraculous claims advanced in Pasteur's name have already passed into the category of illusions. We have not forgotten the abortive insurance company to make good the losses of stock under M. Pasteur's inoculation. There is evidently an active financial spirit associated with the savant and if only a furore can be excited over the cure of rabies by inoculation, the project of the Mansion House subscription will be revived. . . . Much of the praise lavished on Pasteur is inspired by the hope that he will yet redeem vaccination from the discredit that is gathering around it. . . . We renew our conviction that either M. Pasteur does not know what constitutes valid evidence or that he is deliberately practising on public credulity for the sake of gain. His parade of cases of hydrophobia taken as cured, when he must know that the majority had nothing of hydrophobia about them, leaves him under the most odious imputation.

The attack upon Pasteur as a vivisectionist initiated the antivivisectionist campaign that has done much to harass medical research workers in many countries. He was denounced as the "murderer of innocent animals," a "vile, murderous, rascally fiend" and other scurrilous epithets that identified him and other medical workers with cruelty. An extreme diatribe written in 1911 pleads: [88]

> Extinguish Jennerism and Pasteurism and relieve the national and local treasuries of the burden of the parasites now foisted upon them by the Jennerian and Pasteurian cults, prohibit the cruelties to children, to adults and to our humble animal brethren and friends

[87] *Vaccination Inquirer*, vol. VII, p. 155; vol. VIII, p. 114.
[88] Montague R. Leverson, *Pasteur the Plagiarist* (London, 1911), p. 16; J. J. Garth Wilkinson, *Pasteur and Jenner, An Example and a Warning* (London, 1883). For an analysis of opposition to vivisection see Shryock, "Freedom and Interference in Medicine," *Freedom of Inquiry and Expression*, Annals of Political and Social Science, vol. CC, pp. 4–6; Stern, *Social Factors in Medical Progress*, p. 77, note 2.

which Jenner, Pasteur and their ignorant and dishonest followers daily commit.

The antivaccination campaign, which has led to legislation impeding medical progress, began within the medical profession, when Jenner advocated vaccination in 1798. It can be traced to the variolationists, whose entire income was derived through the specialized practice of inoculating with the smallpox virus. A study of early antivaccination tracts has shown that the large majority of them were written by these specialists. Their financial interests were threatened by Jenner's advocacy of vaccination, which could be performed by anyone.[89] Motivated as they were by their economic interests, they attacked the new practice in terms of a propaganda appeal rather than with facts. They were out to discredit vaccination and sought to do so, not merely on the basis of possibly valid criticism of the original overenthusiastic statements of its effectiveness, but by exploiting the medical ignorance of the masses, and creating fear, repulsion and aversion to the innovation.

One may well doubt whether Rowley and Moseley, two of the most active of the physicians opposing vaccination, really believed that cowpox inoculation brought with it the horrible diseases they described as being the result of "the bestial humour." One cannot be sure, because knowledge of the causes of epidemic diseases and immunity was entirely lacking at that time. Even John Sims, the president of the London Medical Society, who later became an advocate of vaccination, at first questioned whether the "infection by an inoculation of a variety of acrid animal poisons" would not introduce new diseases. The limitation of Moseley's scientific knowledge is shown by the fact that he believed the phases of the moon to be a causal factor in hemorrhage of the lungs. Engravings were used to show that children who had been vaccinated were developing cow's faces. Rowley wrote of "Cow Pox Mange," "Cow Pox Ulcers," "Cow Pox Evil or Abscess" and "Cow Pox Mortification." Moseley described "Facies Bovilla" or "Cow Pox Face," "Scabies Bovilla or

[89] The discussion of opposition to vaccination is based on Bernhard J. Stern, *Should We Be Vaccinated: A Study of the Controversy in Its Historical and Scientific Aspects* (New York: Harper, 1927).

Cow Pox Itch or Mange," "Tinea Bovilla or Cow Pox Scaldhead," and "Elephantiasis Bovilla or Cow Pox Farcy." These characterizations have the appearance not of ignorant, mistaken judgments, but of unscrupulous attempts to make people abhor and dread vaccination.

They not only exploited fear, ignorance and disgust effectively as do most opponents to innovations in medicine, but played upon envy and medical rivalries. Jenner and other vaccinationists were pictured as making fortunes on a worthless procedure learned from milkmaids and were ridiculed as being victims of "cow-mania." It was argued that if vaccination were really a prophylactic against smallpox, physicians would not adopt it because they make money on the ills of people and their income would therefore be lowered, which is also a familiar theme to detractors of the medical profession. After vaccination had proved its efficacy among the profession by statistical evidence, the arguments of the early antivaccinationists within the profession were taken up by many patent medicine manufacturers, osteopaths, chiropractors, hydropaths, Christian Scientists, naturopaths and other medical sects which have exploited the antivaccination movement for their own ends. John Simon characterized their work aptly:

> Quacks with their touters have often found it convenient to hitch themselves on the skirts of a discussion in which the public has been interested, ready for any chance of reviling the science which condemns their wretched arts, but above all, eager to assure their dupes that while vaccination is so worthless a precaution, life may be prolonged and youth made perpetual by one incomparable pill or elixir.

In spite of the early attacks, the theory of vaccination was accepted enthusiastically in England because of desperate fear of smallpox and because of the active work of Jenner, Pearson, Woodville, and Ring, with the effective support of Lettsom. In the United States, however, Benjamin Waterhouse in Boston met "chilling apathy and repellent suspicion." Seaman in New York, Rush, Cox, Oliver and Currie in Philadelphia, and James Smith in Baltimore, all refer to the initial antagonism to vaccination which they encountered. In Germany, Strohmeyer of Hanover stated in 1800 that "most of our physicians here exclaim against the vaccine inoculation," and Stuve of Gorlits wrote in 1802 that "calumniators were not wanting who vented their spleen against me as a vaccinator; for many persons were my enemies on that account and almost everyone was envious." Yet in spite of loud and clamorous opposition, the practice spread rapidly.

There was wide disillusionment when it was found that vaccination offered immunity only for a limited period, a fact that the proponents of vaccination were not, at first, ready to accept so that they opposed periodic revaccination as unnecessary. There were controversies among the friends of vaccination over revaccination. Among its proponents there were personal rivalries, particularly those which arose over Jenner's unjustifiably jealous attempts to detract from the work of Pearson and Woodville, whose corroboratory evidence had established the practice. These differences were exploited to full advantage by the opponents. Rare cases of serious complications after vaccination have been given lurid publicity so that uninformed people would be deterred through fear. Religious prejudices have repeatedly been utilized on the ground that vaccination was "sinful and doubting of providence," and that to be immunized was to interfere with "the plans of God."

Questions as to how to cope with smallpox and other epidemic diseases provoked conflicts between governmental public health agencies and medical men, and raised questions of authority and sphere of control that are also involved in the contemporary controversy on the distribution of medical services. Physicians argued then as now that they were the only ones able to determine and meet medical needs. But epidemics, such as smallpox, went beyond the personal relation between the individual doctor and the individual patient. They could be checked only by plans which involved stringent control, not only over laymen but over physicians as well. During the Black Death in the fourteenth century, Italian cities, and, in the sixteenth century, English cities, began to recognize the need for quarantine regulations and to isolate plague victims. Quarantine regulations and isolation procedures from then on have consistently been opposed by commercial interests who have resented the closing of markets and interference with trade.

Many religious groups defied isolation. As a writer during the epidemics that swept England in the sixteenth century declared:[90] "Some believe that one ought not to shun another Christian that is infected, and as a result, unless God unnaturally interferes, this infection is spread, and some who did this are dead and all their household." By the General Orders of 1592, clergymen were forbidden to preach if they published the doctrine "that it is a vaine thing to forbeare to resort to the infected, or that it is not charitable to forbid the same, pretending that no person shall die but at their time prefixed." Laymen who argued in this manner were sent to prison. Yet in 1603, a book appeared which defied this injunction and preached the doctrine that the plague was but the arrow of God flying through the air.[91] Comparable religious views received wide currency in combating public health regulations throughout the following centuries. Economic and religious objections were augmented by individualistic views of political liberty which affected laymen and physicians alike.

With these powerful pressures opposed to public health regulations, medical men, while on the whole cooperative, were often lax about enforcement and resented the rigid surveillance which brought them to task. As epidemiology advanced, the reporting of cases of epidemic and contagious diseases added extra burdens to overworked physicians who sometimes did not fully comprehend the need for such routines and attributed them to bureaucratic interference with doctor-patient relationships. A proposal made in Baltimore in 1820 to make smallpox cases reportable was successfully opposed by physicians, and this procedure, now recognized as obviously reasonable, was delayed until 1882. It is interesting to note that there is no allusion in the Baltimore health department reports to efforts to control diph-

---

[90] Quoted by J. H. Thomas, *Town Government in the Sixteenth Century* (London: Allen & Unwin, 1933), pp. 150–1.

[91] F. P. Wilson, *The Plague in Shakespeare's London* (Oxford: Clarendon Press, 1927), pp. 70–1.

theria, scarlet fever, measles, whooping cough and typhoid fever by isolation, hospitalization, or otherwise until late in the nineteenth century. In 1838 medical opinion held that "scarlet fever and measles occur under no fixed laws, and both seem inclined to abide with us." By the 1880's, however, the influence of William Farr and his followers in England, of Lemuel Shattuck of Boston, and of Jones and Frick of Baltimore, had been able to convince the medical profession that statistical methods were a determining force in the study of individual diseases and in the entire field of public health inquiry and administration.[92]

Although in England and Scotland compulsory notification of febrile diseases had been enforced in a few urban districts in 1876, it was not widely adopted before 1882, and not until 1889 in London, at which time it still remained optional elsewhere. Later laws added other diseases to the reportable list, but each time over the opposition of some medical men who regarded such actions as unnecessary. These medical men are often merely uninformed or are unwilling to take on a personal inconvenience, but sometimes they reflect the attitudes of economic interests that do not want an accurate statement of the epidemic conditions in their communities, but instead prefer that any discussion of the nature and extent of an epidemic should be tabu.

A typical instance of such a reaction even before the days of epidemic statistics is the bitter and violent attack on Benjamin Rush in 1794 for his honest report on the existence of yellow fever in Philadelphia and his warning that it was contagious. It was charged that his report would "not only render multitudes uneasy, and interrupt the usual course of business, but injure the interest and reputation of the city in several respects," and the press and the population were asked to ignore it.[93] This secretiveness on the extent of epidemics, and failure to give publicity to the precautions necessary, have had serious consequences. Some physicians have at times consented to such se-

---

[92] William T. Howard, Jr., *Public Health Administration and the Natural History of Diseases in Baltimore, Maryland, 1797–1920* (Washington, D. C.: Carnegie Institution, 1924), pp. 149, 294.
[93] Nathan G. Goodman, *Benjamin Rush, Physician and Citizen, 1746–1813* (Philadelphia: University of Pennsylvania Press, 1934), p. 198.

cretiveness because they have had little faith in the public's ability to understand matters relating to health.

For perspectives on today's controversies it is interesting to recall the types of opposition to the public health movement which Shattuck, over ninety years ago, regarded seriously enough to seek to refute at some length in his pioneer report on, "A General Plan for the Promotion of Public and Personal Health" presented to the Massachusetts Legislature. "It may be said," the report declared, that "this measure will interfere with private rights. If I own an estate haven't I a right to do with it as I please? To build upon it any kind of house, or to occupy it in any way, without the public interference? Haven't I a right to create or continue a nuisance—to allow disease of any kind on my own premises, without accountability to others?"[94]

There is no doubt that many property owners in all countries have acted upon the assumption that these questions should be answered in the affirmative, and that the most difficult task of the public health officer has been to combat this individualism that puts rent and profits above human welfare. Simon well characterized this behavior in the 1850's in England:[95]

> When your orders are addressed to some owner of objectionable property—of some property which is a constant source of nuisance, or disease, or death; when you would force one person to refrain from tainting the general atmosphere with results of an offensive occupation; when you would oblige another to see that his tenantry are better housed than cattle, and that, while he takes rent for lodging he shall not give fever as an equivalent—amid these proceedings you will be reminded of the "rights of property" and of "an Englishman's inviolable claim to do as he will with his own."

This spirit was not and is not confined to England. Each extension of preventive medicine has met the same opposition, and as improvements in public health control have involved an increase in expenditures, property interests as taxpayers have often

---
[94] Massachusetts Sanitary Commission, *Report of a General Plan for the Promotion of Public and Personal Health* (Boston: Dutton & Wentworth, 1850), p. 236.
[95] Quoted in Henry Jephson, *The Sanitary Evolution of London* (Brooklyn: Wessels, 1907), p. 61.

stood in the way of improvement on grounds of economy. Many an advocate of preventive medicine has felt chagrin comparable to that which Playfair manifested when in 1845 he charged the authorities of Liverpool with neglect of health to the extent that more than one-half of the children born there died before they reached the age of five.[96] "With strange pertinacity," he wrote, "they have refused to give credence to the authentic accounts of the unhealthiness of the town and with an ingenuity worthy of a better cause, have endeavored to escape the force of the returns presented to them."

Shattuck listed another familiar form of opposition, one that has found response among some medical men.[97] "If you diffuse information on these [health] matters generally among the people, will you not make every person his own physician? Will you not increase and not suppress quackery, and thus magnify and not diminish the sanitary evils which it is your purpose to prevent?" It has repeatedly been necessary to prove that a preventive health program does not usurp or interfere with the interests of the medical profession by creating an informed public alert to the need of treating diseases at their early stages; that it has given prestige to the medical man by destroying the fatalistic concepts that nothing can be done to prevent and to cure diseases. Some physicians, however, have looked upon public health workers as meddling reformers, who are arrogating to themselves functions which should belong exclusively to the medical practitioner. They have insisted on control by the medical profession of all ventures in the field of health and disease, even when they have been out of sympathy with them at times, and when the tasks have been administrative in character.

Antagonisms between government public health officers and the medical profession first manifested themselves sharply in England. These controversies had wide repercussions which served to develop traditional attitudes of conflict between the two groups. The shocking revelations of the health conditions

[96] Lyon Playfair, *Report on the Sanitary Conditions of the Large Towns in Lancastershire,* Second Report of the Commissioners, vol. I, (London, 1845), p. 398.
[97] Massachusetts Sanitary Commission, *op. cit.,* p. 290.

in Great Britain had been exposed by the nonmedical sanitarian, Edwin Chadwick, with the help of a few physicians, and the passive non-cooperation of others. His exposures, however, were interpreted as a reflection upon the achievements of the profession, and he was accused of having little faith in medical science. When, through his efforts, the first national health board was established in 1848 with no physicians appointed as members, the editor of the *Lancet* denounced it as an insult to the medical profession. The later appointment of Dr. T. Southwood Smith did not ease the opposition which argued as if sanitation and other public health work negated the importance of medical science and of the personal services of the medical practitioner.[98] Physicians had allies in their attacks upon the national health board, as is revealed in the vigorous defense of the board in 1853 by Lord Shaftesbury, one of its members: [99]

> We roused all the Dissenters by our Burial Bill, which, after all, failed. The parliamentary agents are our sworn enemies, because we have reduced expenses, and, consequently, their fees, within reasonable limits. The civil engineers also, because we have selected able men, who have carried into effect new principles, and at a less salary. The College of Physicians, and all its dependencies, because of our independent action and singular success in dealing with the cholera, when we maintained and proved that many a Poor Law medical officer knew more than all the flash and fashionable doctors of London. All the Boards of Guardians, for we exposed their selfishness, their cruelty, their reluctance to meet and relieve the suffering poor, in the days of the epidemic. The Treasury besides (for the subalterns there hated Chadwick; it was an ancient grudge, and paid when occasion served). Then come the water companies, whom we laid bare, and devised a method of supply, which altogether superseded them. The Commissioners of Sewers, for our plans and principles were the reserve of theirs; they hated us with a perfect hatred.

It was in this setting that the controversy broke out on the contagious nature of cholera. Although writers in the late eighteenth

---

[98] Richard H. Shryock, *The Development of Modern Medicine* (Philadelphia: University of Pennsylvania Press, 1926), p. 238.
[99] J. L. and Barbara Hammond, *Lord Shaftesbury* (London: Constable, 1923), p. 168.

and nearly nineteenth centuries had attached great importance to proper quarantine regulations during epidemics, the stress laid on sanitation led to a disparagement of these methods. Epidemic diseases had come to be explained in terms of the miasmatic theory of Hippocrates, which ascribed these diseases to offending smells such as sewer gas, decomposing filth, and even to the accumulation of garbage. Chadwick, T. Southwood Smith and others of the early sanitary leaders, in their general campaign to improve conditions of the towns, were "anticontagionist" in their views.

When in 1848–49, Dr. Snow promulgated the view that cholera was spread by poison contained in the evacuations of infected persons and by the subsequent contamination of drinking water, his theory was not accepted by the sanitarians or by the College of Physicians, because it ran counter to the accepted views of the nature of contagion. In 1855 Snow addressed a letter to the president of the general board of health in which he referred to the attacks made upon him in medical and other journals. He was being denounced for contending that certain offensive trades "do not cause, or in any way promote, the prevalence and mortality of cholera, fever and other diseases, which are communicated from person to person." He went on to point out that scabies was not ascribed to gases given off by decomposing matter, although it is found especially among the poor who dwell in dirty unsanitary districts. Its parasitic nature was well known.[100] Snow struck here at the vital cause for the delay in the understanding of contagion.

The theory of contagion, as it was held up to 1880, could not explain all the facts with which the physicians and sanitarians were familiar. They knew that in diseases like plague and cholera and typhoid fever, direct exposure to personal contact often failed to produce infection, while cases frequently rose without such contact. For this reason, Sydenham did not recognize the communicability of any acute febrile disease except the plague, not even the communicability of smallpox. It remained for Pasteur

---

[100] Buer, *Health, Wealth and Population in the Early Days of the Industrial Revolution*, pp. 229–30; Newsholme, *Evolution of Preventive Medicine*, p. 136.

and Koch and their successors to isolate the specific causative agents of many diseases, before the long conflict between the contagionists and anticontagionists was closed by scientific knowledge. The germ theory was, however, not readily accepted, as has already been shown in the discussion of Pasteur. Koch, too, encountered difficulties. Ziegler, Recklinghausen and other authorities did not grasp his methods, nor were they quite open to his new view. Even Virchow opposed his theories on toxin and antitoxins.[101]

As the germ theory became proved scientific doctrine, public health work became ever more important. The sanitarians had laid the ground work by their general campaigns for cleanliness, which improved living conditions and the water supply. At times they had gone too far in assuming the adequacy of sanitation, as when they opposed compulsory vaccination on the grounds that general sanitation was ignored by the advocates of vaccination, and when they failed to respond at once to the evidence that cholera and typhoid were water-borne diseases due to specific infections. But once the theory of contagion was grasped, their preventive work became ever more important, for then the study and control of disease extended beyond the patient into the environmental situation, beyond the doctor-patient relationship into society.

Campaigns against smallpox, cholera, typhoid fever, yellow fever, tuberculosis, diphtheria and, during the last few years, syphilis, became crusades for the saving of lives and the reduction of the illness rate in which philanthropic and state agencies have taken the leading role. Individual doctors have done important work and given notable leadership, but the profession as a whole has usually lagged behind. The reforming zeal which motivated and sustained these drives has often been looked upon with distrust, even with open hostility at times, by some members of the medical profession. As scientists, these medical men have given zealous and effective services to individual patients in the application of the new knowledge and skills which the

[101] Shryock, *op. cit.*, pp. 294–5; William H. Welch, "The History of Pathology," *Bulletin of the Institute of the History of Medicine*, vol. III, No. 1 (January 1935), p. 13.

germ theory initiated. But many doctors have been consistently suspicious of public or semi-public agencies and the efforts of these agencies toward preventive medicine, and through their inactivity, if not through open disparagement, they have impeded the activities of these agencies.

These health campaigns have met vigorous resistance on the part of nonmedical groups whose immediate, although not long-run, economic interests have been endangered. It is a common experience for health officers to encounter the opposition of real estate owners and commercial interests when health regulations to control epidemics threaten to interfere with established profitable business relationships.[102] Sometimes, as in the case of syphilis, the opposition is not primarily economic. Traditional concepts of sin and of moral sanctions regarding sex relations are in this instance so persuasive that until recently there has been an aversion even to a discussion of the disease. The tabu on the mention of the word "syphilis" has taken extreme forms. Until a few years ago when the campaign for the control of syphilis began in earnest, no reputable newspaper in the United States would mention syphilis or gonorrhea by name. As late as 1938 speakers were refused permission to discuss syphilis on the radio. While the populace no longer accepts the diagnosis given in the fifteenth century edict of Emperor Maximilian, which defines syphilis as punishment for the prevailing blasphemy of God, there remains a widespread belief that venereal diseases are divine punishment for licentious living, and a prejudice has thus persisted toward coping with the disease in the same frank, open manner as one might deal with smallpox.[103]

Resistance to the application of medical knowledge continues to take organized form. For example, opponents of the use of diphtheria toxin-antitoxin in Chicago have recently published a

[102] See Robert S. and Helen M. Lynd, *Middletown* (New York: Harcourt Brace, 1929), p. 447.

[103] 75 Cong.: on S.B. 3290, *Investigation and Control of Venereal Diseases, Hearings before a subcommittee of the Committee on Commerce*, U. S. Senate (Washington, D. C.: U. S. Government Printing Office, 1938): Thomas Parran, "The Next Great Plague to Go," *Survey Graphic*, vol. XXV (July 1936), p. 407; Harvey J. Locke, "Changing Attitudes toward Venereal Diseases," *American Sociological Review*, vol. IV, No. 6 (December 1939), pp. 836–43.

circular under the bold caption of "Slaughter of the Innocents." This circular, characteristic of propaganda against the medical profession, plays upon ignorance and fear and upon economic interest as well. Signed by the "Taxpayers' and Voters' League of Illinois," it asks:

> Has the Health Department the right to squander millions of the taxpayers' money to promote the sale of serums and vaccines, or work up business for the Allopathic Cult through fraudulent, misleading advertising, by exploiting the children of our public schools for mercenary motives only? Do you as a taxpayer approve of having millions of dollars of your money used in promoting publicity campaigns for the medical trust and serum manufacturers?
>
> As a taxpayer you are now paying advertising bills to promote business for the Allopathic Cult, who are acting as publicity puppets and salespeople for the serum and vaccine manufacturers.

While the appeal of this type of attack on the medical profession cannot be underestimated, since the educational campaign for preventive medicine and for the public diffusion of health knowledge is still in its infancy, these recent drives have never achieved the success of the antivaccination campaign. The chief reason for this is that the scientific attainments of the profession during the last few decades have made it less vulnerable to such attacks. But the prestige of the medical profession is a recent phenomenon. There always remains the possibility of a change in sentiment, irrespective of scientific achievement. Public sympathy may still be alienated if the medical needs of society are not met in a more adequate manner, through the broader application of this knowledge.[104]

[104] The findings of the National Health Survey that medical care varies markedly with income and also with the size of the city for the same income group are given in Rollo H. Britten, "The National Health Survey: Receipt of Medical Services in Different Urban Population Groups," *Public Health Reports*, vol. 55 (November 29, 1940), pp. 2199–2224 (Reprint No. 2213).

From *Society and Medical Progress*, ch. 9, Princeton University Press, 1941.

The Health of Towns and the Early Public Health Movement

The rapid growth of cities during the Industrial Revolution was not alone responsible for the distressing filth, the polluted water supplies and the congested housing conditions that made life so miserable and so short for the people of the early nineteenth century. Most European communities during the period prior to the rise of industrial civilization were likewise insanitary and overcrowded. When Jonathan Swift (1667-1745) wrote these oft-quoted verses on the consequences of a city rainfall, his allusions might have been applicable to any community in Great Britain:

> Now from all parts the swelling kennels flow,
>   And bear their trophies with them as they go;
> Filth of all hues and odors seems to tell
>   What street they sailed from by the sight and smell;
> Sweepings from the butchers' stalls, dung, guts and blood,
>   Drowned puppies, stinking sprats, all drenched in mud,
> Dead cats and turnip-top come tumbling down the flood.

Throughout European history, epidemics had decimated the population at frequent intervals and had disrupted trade and commerce. Infant mortality was very high, and the men and women who survived their first few years lived their lives harassed by "fevers," by diseases of malnutrition, and a host of other ill-defined disabling diseases.

Prior to the nineteenth century there had been repeated efforts to cope with public health problems by community action and by legislative decree. The strong centralized government of the Tudors in sixteenth century England had sought to control epidemics, and also to eradicate some of the fundamental factors responsible for the cause and spread of disease. Housing plans had been proposed to relieve the overcrowding of cities, some pure food laws had been passed, rules had been made to keep the streets clean, and a commission had been appointed to regulate the disposal of sewage. Some of these regulations were carried out, as is shown, for example, in Shakespeare's *The Merry Wives of Windsor*, where Falstaff is represented as being thrown into the Thames "like a barrow of butcher's offal." Sanitation regulations were, however, by no means universally applied and were widely ignored. Streets continued to be used as receptacles for all kinds of garbage and rubbish, and as a result Shakespeare's London was a "city of kites and crows." When the recommendation had been made in 1603 that the London slaughterhouses be "placed in some remote and convenient place neere to the river of the Thames, to the end that the bloud and garbige of the beasts that are killed may be washed away with the tide," the proposal was not accepted.

Between the sixteenth and the nineteenth centuries the philosophy of *laissez faire* became triumphant, and most of the previous efforts at sanitary regulations were abandoned. Permanent boards of health were not established in English towns until almost the end of the eighteenth century and by that time the general authorities had lost interest in the enforcement of such statutes as then existed. While in the sixteenth century it had been at least regarded as an offense to throw rubbish in the streets, in the middle of the nineteenth century such a procedure was the accepted method of disposal. No matter how vile the filth, it remained in the streets until the accumulation induced someone to cart it away for profit. The sixteenth century "scavenger" who cleared away the deposits in his cart for use as fertilizer could not function in the nineteenth century for the filth had become private property.

As time passed, the development of large industrial urban centers gave a sense of urgency to the need for public health services. Cholera, typhus fever, typhoid fever, smallpox and tuberculosis took a heavy toll. The misery and degradation of the slums with their high death and sickness rates became glaringly apparent, in contrast with earlier periods when the population was scattered, and misery and ill health had been hidden in the recesses of the countryside. The poorer classes and their sympathizers tended to become more articulate in the expression of their dissatisfaction. Moreover, newer developments in technology required a more ordered flow of materials and services during the productive process, and the owners of the instruments of production stood to profit from a healthier, disciplined labor supply, from better pavements to permit more effective transportation, and from the absence of disruptive epidemics. Unfortunately, however, at first the owners of industry and the landlords were oblivious to the truth of Benjamin Franklin's dictum that "public health is public wealth."

Factory production, at which workers in the cities were employed, was not *per se* any more unhealthy than domestic production in crowded, dingy, one-room cottages. But the factory owner's lack of concern for anything but production led to degrading working and housing conditions among the workers of the industrial areas that could not fail to affect sickness and death rates. It appeared as if the cities, fed by immigrants from the countryside, were devouring their inhabitants.

It is this fact which determined the characteristic tenor of the early public health movement. In contrast with the narrower focus of public health work after the modern science of bacteriology had developed, the objectives of the pioneers of public health included demands for better housing conditions, nutritious food, unpolluted water, cleaner streets and improved working conditions. These men anticipated the fundamental truth of modern preventive medicine, that the health of the individual is intimately and indivisibly tied up with the social as well as the physical environment in which he resides.

Public health was then but one phase of the larger movement for social reform in which interested physicians as well as laymen participated. Thomas Percival, M.D., in his *Observations on the State of the Population in Manchester* (Manchester, 1773), and in his four-volume *The Works of T. P., Literary, Moral and Medical* (London, 1807), exposed the virulence of the fever epidemics among factory children at Manchester and advocated better working conditions. He noted the serious limitations of private voluntary efforts at public health control and favored public health laws and factory legislation enforced by paid officials. Robert Owen's humanitarian innovations in Scotland took account of Percival's criticisms of prevailing factory conditions. Similarly, Percival's colleague in the establishment of the Manchester House of Recovery or Fever Hospital, John Ferriar, in his *Medical Histories and Reflections* (Manchester 1792–1798, 2nd ed., London, 1810–13), advocated such modern innovations as the abolition of night work, and the inspection and licensing of common lodging houses and their compulsory whitewashing. John Howard's *The State of the Prisons in England and Wales* (Warrington, 1777–80) helped to abolish typhus fever from prisons and John Roberton's *Medical Police: or The Causes of Disease with the Means of Prevention* (2 vol., 2nd ed., London, 1812) helped to heighten the consciousness of the relation of urban industrialism to social misery.

After an absence of active public health agitation for over a decade, a series of important documents appeared that showed the close correlation of ill health and poverty and laid the basis for public health reforms. Louis René Villermé's report in 1828 for a committee of the French Royal Academy of Medicine, which showed statistically that morbidity and mortality rates in Paris were related to the living conditions of the different social classes, was widely quoted in England. Charles T. Thackrah's *The Effects of Arts, Trades and Professions and of Civic States and Habits of Living on Health and Longevity* (London, 1831), revealed that the deplorable working and living conditions prevailing in the industrial city of Leeds were responsible for the fact that the illness and death rates were higher than those of the surrounding country. Striking statistics were given by Dr. T. Southwood Smith, physician to the London Fever Hospital, in his *Report on the physical causes of Sickness and Mortality, to which the Poor are particularly exposed, and which are capable of Prevention by Sanitary Measures* (London, 1837).

The most epoch-making of all the early English investigations on this subject, in that it led to administrative action, was Edwin Chadwick's *Report on the Sanitary Conditions of the Labouring*

Population of Great Britain (London, 1842). This report to the Poor Law Board was based upon the findings of all the English poor law physicians on the disease conditions in their respective areas. In his summary, Edwin Chadwick declared: "We have seen that there are whole streets of houses, composing some of the wynds of Glasgow and Edinburgh, and great numbers of the courts in London, and the older towns in England, in which the condition of every inhabited room, and the physical condition of the inmates, is even more horrible than the worst of the dungeons that Howard ever visited."

The Chadwick report led to an official government inquiry by a Sanitary Commission that laid bare for all who would see the appalling conditions prevailing. (Great Britain, Commissioners for Inquiring into the State of Large Towns and Populous Districts, Report. 2 vols., London, 1844–45.) Among the physicians who testified before the inquiry was William A. Guy, professor of forensic medicine at Kings College, who introduced evidence of the disabling effect of occupational hazards. When Parliament failed to respond to the startling revelations of the report, Dr. T. Southwood Smith, in 1847, in his "Address to the Working Classes" called upon the English people, stirred at that time by Chartism, to demand action, declaring that "for every one of the lives of these 15,000 persons who have thus perished during the last quarter, and who might have been saved . . . those are responsible whose proper office is to interfere and endeavor to stay the calamity—who have the power to save but who will not use it. But their apathy is an additional reason why you should arouse yourselves. . . . Let a voice come from your streets, lanes, alleys . . . that will startle the ear of the public and command the attention of the legislature."

In 1848, the Board of Health which had been recommended in the Sanitary Commission report, was established and Chadwick, Lord Shaftesbury and Southwood Smith were named as its commissioners. The Act setting up the Board limited its trial duration to five years. The Board encountered the opposition of vested interests from the beginning even to its elementary proposals for the improvement of the water supplies and drainage and the better administration of health services under the Poor

Law. John Simon, in his *Report on the Sanitary Condition of the City of London* (London, 1849), showed how the health officers dedicated themselves with crusading zeal:

> Ignorant men [he wrote] "may sneer at the pretentions of sanitary science; weak and timorous men may hesitate to commit themselves to its principles, so large in their application; selfish men may shrink from the labor of change which its recognition must entail; and wicked men may turn indifferently from considering that which concerns the health and happiness of millions of their fellow creatures but in the great objects which it proposes to itself, in the immense amelioration which it proffers to the physical, social and, indirectly, to the moral condition of the immense majority of our fellow creatures, it transcends the importance of all other sciences; and in its beneficent operation, seems to embody the spirit, and to fulfill the intentions, of practical Christianity.

In spite of the efforts of the Commissioners, Parliament in 1854 refused a Government proposal to renew the Act, and the first Board of Health came to an end. The reasons for the defeat of the Act are clearly suggested by Lord Shaftesbury:

> The parliamentary agents are our sworn enemies, because we have reduced expenses, and, consequently, their fees, within reasonable limits. The civil engineers also, because we have selected able men, who have carried into effect new principles, and at a less salary. The College of Physicians, and all its dependencies, because of our independent action and singular success in dealing with the Cholera, when we maintained and proved that many a Poor Law medical officer knew more than all the flash and fashionable doctors of London. All the Boards of Guardians, for we exposed their selfishness, their cruelty, their reluctance to meet and relieve the suffering poor, in the days of the epidemic. The Treasury besides (for the subalterns there hated Chadwick; it was an ancient grudge, and paid when occasion served). Then come the water companies, whom we laid bare, and devised a method of supply, which altogether superseded them. The Commissioners of Sewers, for our plans and principles were the reverse of theirs; they hated us with a perfect hatred.

In consequence of this defeat, it was not until the *Public Health Act of 1875* that public health legislation in England was consolidated. Prior to that time, however, according to John Simon, "The grammar of English Public Health Legislation acquired the novel virtue of the imperative mood," through the Sanitary Act passed in 1866.

In the 1830's to 1860's, there was parallel interest in public health in the United States where the effects of urbanization concomitant with industrialism made the need for public health services more apparent and urgent than in previous periods of American history. In spite of the fact that the United States did not have the burden of medieval misery, city life was sordid and unhealthy. An observer wrote in 1861 that "Narrow and crooked streets, want of proper sewage and ventilation, absence of forethought in providing open spaces for recreation of the people, allowance for intramural burials and of fetid nuisances, such as slaughter houses, and manufacturers of offensive stuffs, have converted cities into pestilential inclosures."

As in England, the early public health movement was permeated with a spirit of social reform, and was conceived in its broadest aspects. Dr. Benjamin W. McCready, in his pioneer prize essay on industrial medicine, written in 1837 for the Medical Society of the State of New York, entitled *On the Influence of Trades, Professions and Occupations in the United States in the Production of Disease* reflected the influence of Thackrah. McCready was concerned not merely with working conditions in the shops and mills, but with the unwholesome living conditions of the workers. Noting the effects of bad housing on health, he declared: "Motives not only of mercy for the poor, but fear for ourselves, call for a reform; for infectious diseases when once fully developed do not always confine themselves to the localities in which they originate. The enactment and enforcement of a few wholesome laws, and the attention of capitalists to the erection of buildings for the poor, which would yield greater and as sure returns as more elegant dwellings, would render the city more healthy and prove of incalculable benefit to the laboring population."

McCready also wrote a letter to John H. Griscom on the relation of bad housing to typhus fever which the latter published in *The Sanitary Condition of the Laboring Population of New York with Suggestions for its Improvement* (New York, 1845). In this book Griscom declared of the slums:

> ... There is, as is well known to the physicians who move among these haunts of wretchedness, a silent agency continually at work, destroying annually the health and lives of hundreds of our fellow citizens and entirely within the power of the city government to control or subdue, but which by a strange neglect, appears to have been hitherto allowed to work out destruction unopposed. ... Disorders arising and fostered in these low places, will sometimes become as virulent as to extend among and jeopardize the lives of the better classes of citizens. ...

Griscom influenced T. Southwood Smith in England who quoted him in his testimony at Chadwick's inquiry. Among the first critical discussions of the baneful nature of urban slums in American cities are those of the Committee on Hygiene of the newly established American Medical Association in its reports of 1848 and 1849. (American Medical Association, *Transactions I*, 355 ff.; II, 431 ff. Philadelphia, 1848, 1849.)

The most famous of the early public health documents in the United States is that prepared by Lemuel Shattuck who is frequently referred to as the American Chadwick. This report, published by the Massachusetts Sanitary Commission, under the title of *Report of a General Plan for the Promotion of Public and Personal Health* (Boston, 1850), had literary as well as scientific merit. However, as Dr. Henry I. Bowditch later remarked, "It fell still-born from the State printer's hand." One of its major recommendations that a state board of health be established to cope with the distressing health conditions it exposed, was not heeded until nineteen years later.

In the meantime, several other investigations of urban health had exposed the gravity of the high mortality and sickness rates of cities and had recommended action. Among the effective documents is that prepared by Dr. Stephen Smith, Dr. Elisha Harris and others published under the title, *Report of the Council of Hygiene and Public Health of the Citizens' Association of New York Upon the Sanitary Conditions of the City* (New York, 1865). This report which led to a reorganization of the health department of New York City and initiated basic reforms in municipal sanitation in this country, contended "that it is an imperative demand of civilization and a duty to humanity to seek out and restrain the preventable sources of disease, debasement, and pauperism, which in the City of New York, are found closely allied." It also declared eloquently in words that have a very modern ring that:

> It is a maxim in the medical profession that it is far easier to *prevent* disease than to *cure* it, and it certainly is far more economical to do so. And when we remember that the great excess of mortality and of sickness in our city occurs among the *poorer classes* of our population, and that such excessive unhealthiness and mortality is a prolific source of physical and social want, demoralization and pauperism, the subject of needed sanitary reforms, in this crowded metropolis, assumes such important bearings and such vast magnitude as to demand the most serious consideration of all persons who regard the welfare of their fellow-beings, or the best interests of the community.

Not long after this document was issued, epoch-making advances in bacteriology initiated a new era in public health that sought to cope with communicable diseases through the control of their specific pathogenic microorganisms.

From the Ciba Symposium, 1948, pp. 870–876.

The Physician and Society

The role of the physician in contemporary society is a social-historical product. The entire web of scientific and social arrangements and attitudes which regulate his behavior to his fellow physicians, to his patients and to the larger society of which he is a part, is not a spontaneous development or a contrivance of the individual physician, but is rooted in historical traditions, and is basically conditioned by his socioeconomic environment.

Therefore, an understanding of the relation of medicine and society requires a delineation of the course of the changes in medical practice as American society developed from a locally agricultural economy with domestic handicraft production, to an urban industrial economy, primarily characterized by factory production with wage labor. This involved a study of the relation of changes in medical practice to urban living; to the development of corporate forms of business enterprise; to varying purchasing power; to the changing age composition of the population for which medical science is to a considerable degree responsible; to improved transportation and communication; to changes in standards (or levels) of living; to advancement in the educational standards of the American population; to the trends in the decline in local governmental authority and the increased role of the federal government in all aspects of American life.

The adjustment of medical practice to these new situations has, of course, been greatly influenced by changes that have occurred in the competence of the medical profession. This competence has been derived from theoretical understanding of the nature of health and disease, improved technics, higher licensing standards, advances in medical education on all levels and the significant influence of the hospital as the crucial center for medical practice, research and education.

Medical science has gradually gained increasing stature in the midst of social changes and with the help of developments in related fields of science. The social attitudes which have prevailed toward empirical science have affected medical change. Aristocratic attitudes towards working with one's hands, derived originally from a slave economy of the ancient world, had long helped to hold medical progress in check. Such attitudes set up a false antithesis between theory and practice that glorified scholasticism and condemned laboratory research. They served as a throttle upon the experimental science without which medicine could not advance.

The movement toward a realistic approach to the problems of medicine which recognizes the interrelated and joint role of theory and practice has not been even and regular. Periods such as the Renaissance and the seventeenth century in England, in which there has been an upsurge of experimental science, have been followed by times in which sterile schematization prevailed. These changes reflect the prevailing temper of intellectual life, which in the last analysis is related to social and economic developments within a society.

This can be illustrated by the work of Harvey; Harvey's achievement is clearly a part of the larger pattern of the seventeenth century, the age of Galileo and Newton, which surged with experimental science in all fields. This spurt in science was inspired largely by the new needs of the middle class for more adequate means of transportation and communication, especially in navigation. It manifested itself in part as a revolt against the scholastic tradition and carried with it a demand for experiments and quantitative records of their findings. The contemporary interest in technology, especially the mechanics of pumps for water-works and for the drainage of mines, seems to have led Harvey to think of the heart as a pump and to explain the circulation of the blood upon its functioning. Such a practical conception helped to nurture a scientific, as opposed to a mystic, attitude toward the human body and facilitated a more realistic understanding of the behavior of its parts.

Scientific medicine since Harvey has had no easy road to travel, and its future is by no means entirely certain. It is far more securely entrenched than in 1864, when the American medical profession could still be characterized as a bedlam of "allopaths in every class of allopathy; homeopaths of high and low dilutions; hydropaths mild and heroic; chronothermolists, Thomsonians, Mesmerists, herbalists, Indian doctors, clairvoyants, spiritualists with healing gifts and I know not what besides." The phenomenal growth of clinical medicine following the Paris school of clinicians and pathologists; the formulation of the cell doctrine; developments in medical bacteriology following Pasteur and Koch; in nutrition, in endocrinology, in biochemistry and in psychiatry all have heightened the effectiveness and hence the prestige of the medical scientist. These advances have been social as well as scientific products for they have depended upon the funded economic and institutional resources of society.

When one evaluates his present predicaments in historical perspective, it becomes clearly apparent that never before in the history of mankind has the medical man been held in such high esteem, for medicine has but recently matured as a science. The rise in prestige of the medical profession is necessarily correlated with the extension of its services to larger segments of the population. Correspondingly, to the extent that any segment of the population is excluded from the benefits of adequate medical care, the prestige of the profession is endangered.

This prestige of the medical profession is a recent phenomenon. There remains the serious possibility of a change in sentiment, irrespective of the scientific achievements of the profession. Public sympathy may still be alienated if the medical needs of society are not met in a more adequate manner through the more effective distribution of medical services. The ease with which the obscurantist press can mischievously stir up large numbers of people to protest against experimental vivisection is a dangerous symptom that the benefits of medical research and science are still not so well understood as is sometimes supposed by those who are complacent about the problems of the distribution of medical service.

The medical profession is beginning to face realistically the crucial fact that medical services have not kept pace with medical knowledge. Of this the public is keenly aware, and resentfully so. People are not concerned with advances in the abstract but only as they impinge upon them personally. Advances in therapy are of little significance if they are outside the range of their experience because they belong to low income groups or live in rural areas or are Negroes. It is to the self-interest of the profession that this situation be remedied, for when medical care is unavailable, patients and their relatives are likely, consciously or unconsciously, to hold the physicians accountable.

The primary social responsibility of the medical profession therefore is to provide a high quality of curative and preventive medical service to all the people, whether they belong to low or high income groups, whether they be rural or urban residents, whether they be Negro or white.

That this responsibility is not met has been abundantly proved by national, state and local studies. For example, statistical tables and charts prepared by the New York Tuberculosis and Health Association in cooperation with the Department of Health of the City of New York and Neighborhood Health Development, Inc. show wide disparities in the mortality rates between low and high income groups and between Negroes and whites.

The situation in New York City is paralleled in other communities and for the country as a whole. Infant mortality for the years 1938-40, for example, was approximately 66 percent higher for Negroes than for whites, and maternal mortality during the same period was 2.3 times as high for Negroes as compared to whites throughout the United States. Similar disparities are found among whites of different income groups and between rural and urban residents. In a study of the mortality records of rural areas of Ohio, published in 1940, it was found that the standardized death rate in the poor economic areas was about 10 percent higher than the corresponding rate in the good economic areas. As recently as 1931, infants in Denver families with an annual income of less than $500 died at about the same rate as average Massachusetts infants in 1880; whereas among the Denver families with incomes of $3,000 or more there were only 3 infant deaths for each 100 live births. The death rate for pulmonary tuberculosis among unskilled laborers was found to be seven times, and among skilled workers nearly three times the rate for professional men.

It is incumbent upon physicians to make frank and sincere appraisals of the evidence as to whether the present combination of fee-for-service medicine, charity medicine, and voluntary payment plans is capable of coping with this grievous situation. Their responsibility clearly extends beyond the expert care of the individual patient coming to them for treatment, to the health problems of the larger community.

It is not enough to point to the irrefutable fact that the disparities in the death rates that have been mentioned, are only partly to be accounted for by the variations in the amount and quality of medical care obtained by the residents of the different health districts. This is often in the nature of an evasion of responsibility, for the evidence is available that improvement in medical care, irrespective of other factors, can markedly influence the death and sickness rate advantageously. But more than that, since the health of the people depends upon an improvement in their housing, in their working and living conditions and in public health and sanitation, it would clearly appear to be incumbent upon the medical profession to take an active part in promoting progressive legislation in this field. The responsibility of the medical profession is not merely to relieve the distress and cure diseases of individual patients, and to lower the death rates. It is to prevent the occurrence of sickness and to promote health. It therefore becomes the responsibility of the physician as a professional man, as well as a citizen, actively to promote measures designed to provide social security which will make personal security possible.

The health problems of the people cannot be studied merely in terms of the local medical and social situation. In these days of extensive mobility of the labor force from one community to another, the health of one section of the country is intimately related to the health of every other. For this reason it becomes the further responsibility of organized medicine and of the citizens of every community to concern themselves with a national health program aimed to provide medical care of high quality for all the people. It is far too late to equivocate on this matter. Wishful thinking that constructive programs involving national health insurance can be exorcised by the use of denunciatory slogans such as "regimentation," "bureaucracy" and "socialism" is futile and harmful to the medical profession. An uninformed profession is ill-equipped to handle these crucial issues on which the status and public esteem of the profession rests. If physicians are to fulfill their responsibilities, they should be in the front ranks of those promoting measures to bring adequate medical care of high quality to all the people, and not engage in obstructive tactics.

It is to be hoped that the youth of the medical profession will see the urgency of the public need and will push beyond the horizons of the present into an area of enlarged service to mankind.

Socio-Economic Aspects of Heart Diseases

The noted physician, William Osler once said that "tuberculosis is a social disease with medical aspects." When this thought became a working principle of tuberculosis societies, they began their most satisfying work. Similarly the range and importance of the field of nutrition widened decisively when Goldberger and his collaborators showed the relation of pellagra and other deficiency diseases to socio-economic conditions. The time is ripe for a comparable underscoring of the importance of the socio-economic factors in the field of degenerative diseases, particularly cardiovascular diseases.

Medical educators are recognizing increasingly that medicine is a social science as well as a biological science. Yet, it cannot be said that this idea has percolated more than faintly into the curriculum of the schools and into medical practice. The successes of medical science in the control of external agents in communicable diseases have tended to detract attention from the study of the patient as a whole and, at the same time, from the prodigious social changes which have been taking place that have affected the living and working conditions and consequently the health of the populace.

The development of clinical medicine and pathology with its emphasis on checking symptoms against lesions focused attention on specific organs and militated against an approach to patients as members of families and of society. The importance of taking cognizance of the patient as a human being in a specific cultural setting has also been in danger of being neglected because of the formality in physician-patient relationships arising out of urbanization and medical specialization. The treatment of patients under hospital conditions tends to negate the importance of the effect of home and working conditions on the health of the patient who becomes an organism abstracted from his social environment. It is thus one of the incongruities of modern medicine that while developments in the field of deficiency and degenerative diseases and particularly in psychiatry and psychosomatic medicine have impelled consideration of patients in the context of their life histories and socio-economic and cultural environments, many specialists persist in ignoring as irrelevant anything but the particular matter under scrutiny and treatment.

In dealing with cardiovascular diseases, it is especially important to bear in mind that human development takes place in the course of human activity and so is dependent upon the concrete historical conditions of human life, i.e., the material and social relations in which human beings mature. This is more than saying that an individual with certain hereditary characteristics is affected by conditions of his environment. The person and his social environment are in fact indivisible. His existence and his development are part of a process of continuous, active relationship with his social and cultural situation. In this sense persons, sick or well, are not merely organisms fulfilling their life cycles. They are also socially defined by the role given them by the society in which they are participants, by the work they do, by the sanctions and restraints by which each society regulates their conduct. Sex for example is something more than differences in anatomy and hormones; it is socially defined by cultural dictates of anticipated and enforced behavior along sex lines, by sex division of labor and differential sex etiquette which vary widely in different communities Likewise differences in skin pigmentation, head form, facial features, and stature become important when, because of such differences, persons and groups are discriminated against or privileged in job and cultural opportunities and their full physical and emotional development are thwarted or take place under special conditions. Thus, sociological factors must be taken into consideration in the interpretation of differences in rates of cardiovascular diseases by sex and race, and these differences cannot be considered exclusively, or perhaps even primarily, in organic terms.

Mortality and morbidity statistics substantiate the importance of socio-economic environment in cardiovascular diseases. There are variations in accuracy of diagnosis and reporting; difficulties in isolating statistically the many factors involved in the etiology of cardiovascular diseases; and hazards in collating data originally collected and compiled for different purposes. Moreover changes in terminology over time complicate the analysis of the findings. Yet in spite of these difficulties substantial statistical evidence is available which is sufficient to corroborate the thesis that socio-economic factors play a significant role in cardiovascular diseases.

There are many general mortality and morbidity studies, which directly or indirectly demonstrate the relationship between the socio-economic environments and diseases designated statistically as chronic, degenerative, cardiovascular-renal and circulatory. They reveal differential rates by income levels, by social status, by extent of urbanization, by degrees of industrialization and by racial groups.

The role of economic factors, as measured by differences in income, is shown in a nation-wide study of the relationship between per capita income and mortality in 92 cities of 100,000 or more population.[1] The cities were arranged into three approximately equal groups on the basis of per capita buying power. It was found that in the case of the chronic diseases (which included intracranial lesions of vascular origin, all forms of heart disease, diseases of the coronary arteries and nephritis) the age-adjusted death rate per 100,000 population in 1939 and 1940 for the lowest income group was 514.9, for the middle group, 487.0 and for the highest income group 479.7. The mortality rates of these diseases thus decrease consistently from the lowest to the highest income groups with an especially significant difference between the mortality rates of the lowest and middle income groups.

These findings are substantiated by morbidity data derived from the National Health Survey, which was conducted by the U. S. Public Health Service in 1935–36, and based upon a house-

[1] Altenderfer, M. E., "Relationship Between Per Capita Income and Mortality in Cities of 100,000 or More Population," *Public Health Reports* 62: 1681–1691, 1947.

to-house canvass of some 800,000 families including 2,800,000 persons in 84 cities and 23 rural areas in 19 states. When the data are classified under the category of degenerative diseases the generalization that income affects disability emerges clearly. The annual per capita days of disability per person per year is, for the age group under 25 years, almost three times as high in families on relief, and twice as high for families with incomes under $1000 as for families with incomes of $5000 or over, and for the ages 26 to 64 years, it is over three and one half times as high for families on relief, and over twice as high for families with incomes under $1000 as for families over $5000.[2]

Local mortality studies in New Haven,[3] Chicago,[4] New York,[5] and Boston[6] corroborate the conclusions of the national studies. In England and Wales, the statistics of the Registrar-General show a steep rise in mortality for valvular heart disease and chronic endocarditis with a decline in social status associated with occupational differences not only for men[7] but for their wives.[8]

Recorded mortality for diseases of the heart in the United States in 1940 declined as the size of city decreased, with clearly marked urban-rural differences. The extent of industrialization and related factors such as income and availability of medical facilities and services are correlated with heart disease when the

[2] National Health Survey, 1935–36. Disability from Specific Causes in Relation to Economic Status. *Preliminary Reports,* Sickness and Medical Care Series, Bulletin No. 9, Washington, 1938.

[3] Sheps, J. H., Cecil and Watkins, "Mortality in the Socio-Economic Districts of New Haven," *Yale Journal of Biology and Medicine,* 20:51–80, 1947.

[4] Coombs, L. C., "Economic Differentials in Causes of Death," *Medical Care,* 1:246–255, 1941.

[5] Study of Health Needs—New York City, under the Joint Auspices of the Health Council of Greater New York and the New York Academy of Medicine (Manuscript).

[6] Hiscock, I. V. and Leavell, H. R., "Survey of the Social and Health Needs and Services of Greater Boston," Boston, 1949, p. 18 (Mimeographed).

[7] Registrar-General's Decennial Supplement, Part II. Occupational Mortality, Fertility and Infant Mortality, England and Wales, London. These reports have been analyzed by Morris, J. N. and Titmus, R. M., "Epidemiology of Juvenile Rheumatism," *Lancet* 2:59–63, 1942.

[8] Metropolitan Life Insurance Company, *Studies in Heart Disease,* New York, 1946, p. 7.

size of the city is held constant.[9] In the case of the major component, disease of the myocardium, the rural rate was only about two-thirds that of urban parts of the United States.[10] Deaths from diseases of the coronary arteries and from acute endocarditis showed similar differences between urban and rural rates. Both urban and rural mortality recorded for all diseases of the heart in 1940 was slightly higher in the North and in the eastern than in the South and central sections of the United States. The broad regional distribution of industrialization, as measured by the percentage employed in manufacture, generally corresponds to that of mortality from heart disease.[11]

Mott and Roemer, who also compared the crude and age-adjusted death rates of rural communities with those of towns and cities have concluded:[12]

> While the problem of heart disease is complex, and must be considered in relation to its different causes, it seems fair to assume that this differential is due mainly to the oft-described stresses and strains of urban life and occupations. Whatever may be the actual pathogenesis of arteriosclerotic or hypertensive heart disease, the most common types found, there is much evidence to point to a relationship with the nervous strains more typically a part of urban than of rural life.

Sex differentials in mortality from heart disease in 1940 strongly suggest socio-economic determinants. Seven of the eight specific forms of heart disease showed a higher mortality for men of all ages than for women, the exception being acute rheumatic fever where the rate was almost the same.[13] The greatest sex differential was noted in the case of syphilitic heart disease with the male rate nearly four times that for females. Death rate from diseases of the coronary arteries among males exceeded those of females by 141 percent. In urban areas the excess of male over female heart

---

[9] Gover, M., "Mortality from Heart Disease (all forms) Related to Geographic Section and Size of City," *Public Health Reports* 64:439–456, 1949.

[10] Gover, M. and Pennell, M. Y., "Mortality from Eight Specific Forms of Heart Disease among White Persons," *Public Health Reports* 65:824, 1950.

[11] Gover, *ibid.*

[12] Mott, F. D. and Roemer, M. I., *Rural Health and Medical Care.* New York, 1948, p. 58–60, 72.

[13] Gover and Pennell, *ibid.*, p. 822.

disease mortality was markedly higher than in rural areas with the exceptions of valvular heart disease and congenital heart disease.

The Census Bureau publication on "Vital Statistics Rates in the United States, 1900-1940" aptly declares, "An observed difference in mortality between races may in actuality be no more than a difference in mortality of different economic classes." This offers the clue to the understanding of the differential mortality rate for cardiovascular-renal diseases among non-whites and whites. A comparison of the crude and age-adjusted death rates per 100,000 for non-whites and whites for 1919–21, 1929–31, and 1939–41 for diseases of the heart, intracranial lesions of vascular origin and nephritis, shows that adjusted rates are consistently to the disadvantage of the non-white.[14]

Similar results are brought out by a comparative analysis of the mortality rates among industrial policy holders of the Metropolitan Life Insurance Company[15] for the years 1911–15 and 1940–44 which showed that the death rates for cardiovascular-renal diseases were consistently higher for all ages and at both periods for colored males and females as compared to whites. The death rate for colored males in the 45–54 age category, was in 1940–44, 747.9 per 100,000 as compared to 573.8 for the white, higher than the white rate was in 1911–15 (713.8). Similarly in the 55–64 age group the rate was 1801.5 per 100,000 for the colored males as compared to 1449.3 for the white males, also higher than the rate of the white group in 1911–15 (1782.14).

Further evidence of differential rates for Negroes and whites is shown by the fact that the incidence of defects from cardiovascular diseases among the first two million selectees in World War II, ranging in age from 21 to 36 years was found to be 46 per 1000 for Negroes and 27 per 1000 for whites.[16]

The high incidence of hypertension in the Negro at an earlier

[14] Gover, M., "Negro Mortality. III. Course of Mortality from Specific Causes, 1920–1944," *Public Health Reports* 63:201–213, 1948.

[15] Metropolitan Life Insurance Company, "Large Decline in Mortality from Degenerative Diseases," *Statistical Bulletin*, March 1946, p. 3.

[16] Rowntree, L. G., McGill, K. H. and Folk, O. H., "Health of Selective Service Registrants," *Journal American Medical Association*, 118:1223–1227, 1942.

age may be ascribed to the tensions involved in his adjustment to an unfavorable environment.[17] The high rate of syphilitic heart disease among Negroes, a sequel to the very high rate of syphilis, has been demonstrated statistically as being associated with the poverty of the Negro and with inadequate medical care.[18] Information on the comparative rates for coronary diseases among national groups in the United States is fragmentary and inconclusive.

There has long been considerable interest in the relation of coronary diseases to occupation. Physicians have generally followed the early judgment of Osler[19] that coronary artery disease occurs more frequently among persons in the business and professional groups than among persons in other occupations. This observation, which has been based largely on clinical impressions, may perhaps be derived in part from the fact that cardiologists engaged in consultation practice deal for the most part with patients among the well-to-do classes. Careful statistical studies are necessary before this judgment or the contrary judgment that the incidence is practically the same for all walks of life,[20] can be fully validated. Time does not permit a review of the conflicting conclusions of the published studies.

Answers to questions of the relation of occupation, social status, or social class to coronary occlusion are closely associated with judgments on the role of effort, trauma and work in the onset and

[17] Hunter, W. S., "Coronary Occlusion in Negroes," *Journal of the American Medical Association*, 131:12–14, 1946. Weiss, M. M. and Pruskmack, J. J., "Essential Hypertension in the Negro," *American Journal Medical Science*, 195:510–516, 1938. Orenstein, L. I., "Hypertension in Young Negroes," *War Medicine*, 4:422–424, 1943. Kesilman, M., "The Incidence of Essential Hypertension of White and Negro Males," *Medical Record*, 154:16–19, 1941. Schwab, E. H. and Schulze, V. E., "Heart Disease in the American Negro in the South," *American Heart Journal* 7:710–717, 1932.

[18] Usilton, L. J. and Ruhland, G. C., "Survey of Venereal Diseases in the District of Columbia," *Venereal Disease Information*, 21:244–254, 1940. Hazen, H. H., Syphilis in the Negro, U. S. Public Health Service, *Venereal Disease Information Supplement*, No. 15, Washington, 1942, p. 7.

[19] Osler, William, "Lumleian Lectures on Angina Pectoris," *Lancet* I:697–702, 839–844, 973–977, 1910.

[20] White, P. D., *Heart Disease*, New York, 1931, p. 414. Boas, E. P., and Donner, S., "Coronary Artery Disease in the Working Classes," *Journal American Medical Association*, 98:2186–2189, 1932.

subsequent course of coronary artery occlusion. Whether or not coronary occlusion can be precipitated by physical exertion has been a matter of considerable medical debate. The trend in medical judgment on this issue may be ascertained by the fact that in New York and New Jersey, persons who experience cardiac infarction while undergoing some unusual strain while at work are now allowed workmen's compensation benefits.

In the case of rheumatic fever and rheumatic heart disease the evidence clearly confirms the importance of socio-economic factors. Long before rheumatic fever was associated with streptococcal infections, it was observed that the prevalence of the disease was greatest among poor people living within poverty-stricken sections of communities. Findings made in Kiel and Leipzig as early as 1885 have been frequently quoted, but for a long period, especially between 1910 and 1925, there was a marked lack of interest in the socio-economic aspects of the disease. Attention was then focused narrowly on the processes of infection to the exclusion of the broader sociological factors.

In the 1920's, however, studies began to consider again the relationship between rheumatic fever and living conditions, particularly poverty in cities. These researches first undertaken in Great Britain, sustained the general impression that rheumatic fever and rheumatic heart disease were relatively rare among the well-to-do but frequent in working-class populations. Their initial conclusion, however, that these diseases were more prevalent among the artisan class than among very poor workers, immediately provoked considerable controversy, and has since proved invalid. Whatever may have been the special circumstances which led to this judgment, supported in the United States by Wilson[21] on the basis of a limited study of a clinic population, recent statistical studies of Morris and Titmuss[22] in England do not confirm it.

In the United States the findings of Collins,[23] based on the

[21] Wilson, M. G., *Rheumatic Fever*, New York, 1940.
[22] Morris, J. N., Titmuss, R. M., "Epidemiology of Juvenile Rheumatism," *Lancet*, 2:159–63, 1942.
[23] Collins, S. D., The Incidence of Rheumatic Fever as Recorded in General Morbidity Surveys of Families, Supplement No. 198 to the *Public Health Reports*, Washington, 1947, p. 39–41.

National Health Survey and the supplementary Communicable Disease Survey of 1936, also invalidate the artisan theory of the disease. He found that the incidence and prevalence of rheumatic fever for ages 5 to 19 among the white canvassed population rose consistently as the economic status decreased, and with the exception of one income group, the same was true for heart disease. The rates were generally twice as high for persons on relief and, in the case of heart disease, were sometimes three and four times as high. The relative increase in the rates as income decreased, aside from the high relief rate, is slightly greater in new cases than in total prevalence.

Local studies in Cincinnati,[24] New Haven,[25] Denver,[26] and Philadelphia,[27] bear out the association of poverty and rheumatic fever. The much quoted studies by Wilson, Schweitzer and Lubschez,[28] dealing with the familial epidemiology of rheumatic fever do not contravene the evidence of the importance of environmental factors. Their data are limited to only 109 families in a clinic population excluding the well-to-do, and the range between the best and worst environments was too narrow for a difference to be demonstrable.

Many studies have been made associating rheumatic fever and rheumatic heart disease with urbanization, overcrowded housing and nutritional deficiency. More detailed studies have shown, however, that these are important not as specific factors but primarily because they are associated with poverty. The general effects of poverty upon rheumatic fever, for example, is shown by the fluctuations in the mortality rate of the British working classes as they moved from unemployment to employment after

[24] Wedum, A. G., and Wedum, B. G., "Rheumatic Fever in Cincinnati in Relation to Rentals, Crowding, Density of Population and Negroes." *American Journal Public Health*, 34:1065–1070, 1944.

[25] Paul, J. R., *Rheumatic Fever in New Haven*, Lancaster, Pa., 1941, p. 40.

[26] Wedum, B. G., Wedum, A. G., and Beagler, A. L., "Prevalence of Rheumatic Heart Disease in Denver School Children," *American Journal of Public Health* 35:1271–1281, 1945.

[27] Hedley, O. F., "Rheumatic Heart Disease in Philadelphia Hospitals," *Public Health Reports*, 55:1599–1619, 1940.

[28] Wilson, M. G., Schweitzer, M. D. and Lubschez, R., "The Familial Epidemiology of Rheumatic Fever, Genetic and Epidemiologic Studies," *Journal of Pediatrics*, 22:581–611, 1943.

1930. Full employment and higher wages favorably affected the course of mortality in spite of the deterioration in the housing situation.[29]

The fact that throughout the United States in almost all geographic divisions and individual states and in all age groups, whenever the death rates are based on large enough population numbers, the non-white children show a higher mortality for rheumatic heart diseases than do the white children, gives further evidence that rheumatic fever and heart diseases are influenced by adverse conditions of the social environment. Unfavorable social-environmental conditions arising from poverty, especially bad housing, lack of hospitalization, lack of public health education and hygiene abetted by the factor of discriminatory practices against Negroes, all contribute to spread the acute disease, to increase rheumatic complications and consequently to increase the death rates.

A comparison[30] of mortality rates from rheumatic fever and chronic rheumatic heart disease during 1939–1940 for persons under 25 years of age in cities of 100,000 or over, where diagnostic facilities are better, shows that in the North mortality from rheumatic fever among colored persons is about twice that among the white (4.6 per 100,000 compared to 2.4 per 100,000), while in the South, where mortality is lower, the death rate for colored persons is three times that among the white (3.8 per 100,000 compared to 1.3 per 100,000). In the case of chronic rheumatic heart disease, in the North the death rate for the colored was 16.2 per 100,000 compared to 10.8 per 100,000 for the whites, while in the South the rates were 7.6 per 100,000 and 2.8 per 100,000 respectively.

Socio-economic influences also account for the extremely high death rates for white children from rheumatic fever and rheumatic heart afflictions in the Mountain States where the relative high

---

[29] Morris, J. N. and Titmuss, R. M., "Health and Social Change: I. The Recent History of Rheumatic Heart Disease." *The Medical Officer*, 72:69–71, 77–79, 85–87, 1944. Glover, J. A., "War-Time Decline of Acute Rheumatism." *Lancet* 2:51–52, 1943.

[30] Collins, S. D., The Incidence of Rheumatic Fever as Recorded in General Morbidity Surveys of Families, Supplement No. 198 to the *Public Health Reports*. Washington, 1947, pp. 36, 37.

proportion of the population is persons of Mexican origin for whom socio-economic conditions are less favorable than for the remainder of the population classified as white.[31] The high rate among new immigrant groups, such as the Puerto Ricans may be ascribed in large part to their underprivileged social and economic status. Comparative data on other national groups is very fragmentary and inconclusive.[32]

In summary, authorities have come to conclude that one of the basic factors to be considered in the genesis of rheumatic fever and rheumatic heart disease is poverty itself and only secondarily its many specific manifestations, psychological as well as physical. This position is cogently stated by Morris and Titmuss[33]: "The upshot seems to be that . . . the whole life of the underprivileged child [is involved]. 'The destruction of the poor is their poverty.' In social medicine such multiple non-specific causation is not unexpected."

These data all point to one basic conclusion. Since cardiovascular diseases are, to a large extent, community products, they are a community responsibility. It will require the funded resources of all agencies in the community to conquer them.

[31] Wolff, George, "Childhood Mortality from Rheumatic Fever and Heart Diseases," *Children's Bureau Publication 322*, 1948, p. 2, 14, 17.
[32] They are reviewed by Paul, J. R., *The Epidemiology of Rheumatic Fever*, Second Edition, New York, 1943, pp. 67–70.
[33] Morris, J. N. and Titmuss, R. M., "Epidemiology of Juvenile Rheumatism," *Lancet*, 2:59–63, 1942.

Address delivered August 22, 1950 at the Health Education Institute on Heart Diseases sponsored by New York University College of Medicine, Bellevue Medical Center, the American Heart Association and the New York Heart Association and held at New York University School of Education. Reprinted from *Journal of Educational Sociology*, vol. 24, No. 8 (April, 1951), pp. 450–462.

The Need for National Health Legislation

Three monographs* which I have recently prepared for the Committee on Medicine and the Changing Order of the New York Academy of Medicine contain findings which I believe may be of interest to the members of your Committee in the course of your hearings on the Wagner-Murray-Dingell Bill.

These monographs, written while I was a member of the staff of the Academy Committee, are part of a series planned, in the Committee's words, to bring to light "not only the achievements but also the inadequacies in present-day medical practices—the uneven development of its different sectors, the prevailing incongruities and irrationalities, as well as the lag in the adjustment of medicine to the social needs of today... While the monographs form an integral part of the Committee's studies, their publication does not necessarily imply the Committee's endorsement of statements of fact or opinion which are entirely the responsibility of the authors."

The evidence presented in the initial monograph of the series, *American Medical Practice in the Perspectives of a Century* (1945), showed that social and scientific changes during the last century have made necessary fundamental changes in the organization of medical services. In a society which has shifted from a locally subsisting agricultural economy with handicraft production, to an urban, mechanized, industrial economy with concentrated ownership in which there are wide income variations, the traditional fee-for-service basis has proved inadequate. New health problems in both rural and urban communities have de-

* See Bibliography.

veloped with which this system cannot cope. It does not permit the full and effective utilization of medical knowledge, fails to provide high quality medical services for all the people, and does not adequately reward the physician for his professional services.

Urbanization and industrialization have contributed to the development of scientific medicine and toward its centralization in the modern hospital, and have facilitated access to medical care through the concentration of populations. Peoples previously without contact with medical science have been brought within the orbit of its influence and, as the medical profession has demonstrated its effectiveness, and its scientific competence has won public confidence, the demand for medical services has mounted. Simultaneously with the improvements in medical practice, brought about by the use of new diagnostic and curative procedures, instruments, and technologies, and the growing importance of the hospital, the costs of medical care have increased and have complicated the problems of its distribution. The maturation of medical science has at the same time led to the development of medical specialties, which have created important professional and financial problems in the relationship between the specialist and the general practitioner and between both groups of physicians and the patient.

Better medical science, together with improvements in the food supply and in sanitation, has reduced mortality rates and lengthened life expectancy and has thus changed the age composition of the population. Medical progress has also lowered illness rates and improved the health of the population. By the conquest of communicable diseases medicine has decreased considerably the disruptions in social life brought about by disastrous epidemics. It is this very substantial achievement of medicine that has engendered many of its present problems.

While an ever larger portion of the population is insisting on its right to share in the advances of medicine that make longer and healthier lives possible, medicine of quality because of its costs has become increasingly beyond the reach of a large majority of the people. Modern medicine has proven its scientific efficacy to such a degree that when any segment of the population is deprived of its benefits, it recognizes that it is seriously at a disadvantage. The problems of medical practice that are agitating the public today are therefore primarily concerned with the provision of a high quality of curative and preventive medical service to all the people, whether they belong to low or high income groups, whether they be rural or urban residents, Negro or white.

At present this ideal is far from being realized. Low-income, rural and Negro groups now receive fewer medical and hospital services than do the high-income, the urban and the white populations in spite of the fact that they have higher sickness and mortality rates. The factor of prohibitive costs of medical services under the present system is the primary cause of these discrepancies.

Medical care cannot be considered as having reached a minimum level of adequacy in quantity and quality until the morbidity and mortality rates of the population as a whole correspond to the lowest rates now prevailing in wealthy, urban white groups. Yet all comprehensive surveys of the extent of medical care indicate that the proportions of illnesses attended by physicians is smallest among members of families at the bottom of the economic scale and that it increases as family income increases. Moreover, the trend in the location of physicians is away from the poorer rural areas which are unable to finance hospitals, leaving the people in these areas without adequate facilities and services. Further, the absence of adequate medical care is clearly one of the important causes of the fact that in 1944 while the tuberculosis death rate for whites was 33.7 per 100,000 population, the rate for Negroes was 106.2 per 100,000, which is higher than the white rate of 1920.

At the same time that the consumer is not adequately served, it is shown by studies of the income of physicians, that the present system of distributing medical services does not yield to the majority of the medical profession, financial returns commensurate with their investment in education and training. This fact has been obscured by the conditions prevailing during the war when there was a shortage of physicians, but with the return of medical men from the armed services the problem of adequate income for physicians has again arisen. The vast majority of physicians as well as the public require reorganization of the methods of financing and distributing medical care.

What should be the nature of this reorganization? Do voluntary prepayment medical plans promise an adequate solution? On the basis of my research in the preparation of the chapter on prepayment plans for medical services in my second monograph in the series, entitled *Medicine in Industry* (1946), I have become convinced that the multiplication of voluntary prepayment plans is wasteful and cannot meet the medical needs of the American people. In spite of the fact that voluntary plans have been functioning for many years in this country, they now offer a measure of protection against the costs of sickness to only a small fraction of the population of the country and provide direct medical services to a negligible percentage of the total. The publicity they have received is entirely out of proportion to their actual accomplishment. They have been largely expedients utilized by industry when necessary in areas where private medical services have been inadequate to meet medical needs requisite to maintain the uninterrupted production of goods, or have been plans by medical societies which, except in one state, have very few subscribers. They are expensive for what they offer the patients and far too costly to be included in the budgets of the majority of the population. Instead of there being an expansion in the scope of the medical services offered in these plans during recent years, there has been a contraction, that is, most plans now provide fewer services than did earlier voluntary plans. Such plans involve very difficult problems of administration, and medical services, with few exceptions, are limited to local areas at a time when there is increased mobility of the population from area to area.

It appears to me, therefore, that those who advocate voluntary plans as a solution to the very real problems of bringing high-quality medical care to all the people of America, ignore the significant evidence of their inadequacies which any survey of the functioning of present plans clearly reveals.

Those who argue against government participation in medicine, cannot be oblivious to the fact that government has been in medicine for many decades. I have surveyed the extent of such medical services financed by local, state and federal governments in my book *Medical Services by Government* and have found that vast sums are now spent in this field. The time has come for a comprehensive national health program expanding local and state services and bringing them within the scope of a national program.

There has been considerable increase during recent years in state expenditures for medical care, but proponents of state rather than federal action have encountered substantial difficulty in realizing their objectives because state authorities have been hesitant to introduce services that would raise state tax rates lest industry migrate to other states to avoid payment of such taxes. Similar difficulties have traditionally impeded efforts to increase financial support for government medical services on a local level.

While the financial contributions of the Federal Government to the support of medical care through grants-in-aid have been growing both absolutely and relatively, there has been apparent at the same time an attempt to decentralize the administration of the services financed by these funds, in order to permit wide local variations under basic national and state standards and supervision. The ultimate application of all medical services financed by government funds is local, and responsible participation by local government authorities and by local professional groups has been found to be imperative for the success of any program.

Experience has shown that the professional aspects of medical care programs are best developed under the direction of medical personnel. An increasing number of physicians have tended during the last few years to orient themselves to the idea of government responsibility for the payment of medical care which they previously furnished free or at reduced rates, and are showing greater willingness to participate in government medical programs and to accept primary responsibility for the supervision of these programs. On the other hand, when government spends tax money for services, it is responsible to the public for the proper allocation of these funds. For this reason government supervision of certain administrative procedures, including fee schedules and standards of service given, appears to be inevitable in the interest of the patients, the medical profession, and the general public.

In recent years patients' fees in local government general hospitals have met an increasing proportion of the operating costs of such hospitals. At the same time, government contributions to the maintenance of volunteer hospitals have grown, particularly during the war when it was impossible to augment existing government facilities sufficiently to meet requirements. As patients have contributed more often and in larger amounts to their hospital and medical expenses, they have become increasingly interested in prepayment insurance plans which take government medical services out from under the shadow of poor-law administration, under which they have traditionally functioned in local communities. In the controversy on the relative merits of financing government medical care by general tax funds or by contributory prepayment insurance plans, or by a combination of both, attention must be paid to the fact that there is increasing resentment against the application of means tests to establish eligibility for government medical services as well as against the stigma of charity associated with services financed from general tax funds. An ever larger number of people are therefore supporting prepayment medical plans under the auspices of the Federal Government such as proposed in Senate Bill 1606.

In summary, my researches for these monographs, as well as for my earlier work, *Society and Medical Progress* (1941), have led me to conclude that the present organization of medical services falls far short of meeting the health needs of the American people; that the system of voluntary prepayment plans proposed by the opponents of the national health program are, and will continue to be, totally unable to cope with the demands of the situation and that a national prepayment health insurance plan under government auspices, supplemented by federal grants-in-aid, is imperative.

The problem with which your Committee is concerned has been recognized as an acute one since the 1920's. In the interim, repeated surveys have been made of medical personnel, of medical facilities and of health needs; administrative experience in health problems has been acquired, particularly by the strengthening of the United States Public Health Service through the Social Security Act; and broadening public support for a national health program has developed. The time for legislative action has come. America now lags behind all other industrial countries in protecting its human resources which are the major source of the nation's strength. This health legislation is literally, not figuratively, a matter of life or death to millions.

Statement before the U. S. Senate Committee on Labor and Public Welfare on the Wagner-Murray-Dingell Bill, April 23, 1946.

Toward a Sociology of Medicine

Criticisms of sociology have been of two general varieties. There have been those who have been scornful of its abstract theory spinning, its formulation of categories without content and of generalizations without purpose other than seemingly to afford their makers with intellectual exercise in semantic subtlety. Others have been critical of the banality of its illustrative matter, the inconsequentiality of the problems it tackles concretely. It has been felt that sociology has dealt with problems too large to handle with its present skills or those too trivial to bother with, out of a larger context. These antithetical criticisms have had one basic premise in common. They have assumed that if sociology is to justify its designation as a science, it must contribute insights, principles, theories, and methods which will permit more effective prediction of human behavior and of cultural change and facilitate manipulation and control of social situations.

The field of sociology of medicine offers a stimulating area of research for sociologists who accept this definition of the function of their discipline. Its problems are vital ones and its data are sufficiently capable of controlled observation to enable the sociologists to test the validity of current concepts and to permit the formulation of new principles. Its range of problems are amply diverse to engage the attention of sociologists interested in historical, anthropological, institutional approaches; in studies of acculturation and cultural change; in research on the behavior of small or large groups involving leadership, bureaucracy, cooperation, competition, and other social processes; in community studies; in social classes and social structures; in demography and ecology; in mass communication; in attitude studies; in culture and personality; in social control and sanctions, in fact, in the entire gamut of conventional topics under which sociologists are prone to classify their major interests. The sociology of medicine permits the fruitful marriage of theory and practice; it is both speculative and practical, analytical and constructive.

In projecting the recognition in college curricula of the sociology of medicine it is not proposed that it be confined within the conceptual frame of the tradition of what has come to be called social medicine. It is worth noting in passing as sociologically significant that the idea of medicine as a social science arose during the struggles of the middle class for political and social rights in Germany during the 1840's, which had repercussions in a medical reform movement. It was at that time that the German physician, Salomon Neumann, formulated its basic premise that "medical science is intrinsically and essentially a *social* science, and as long as this is not recognized in practice we shall not be able to enjoy its benefits, and shall have to be satisfied with an empty shell and a sham."[1] After a short period in Germany during which this sentiment captured the interest of a group of notable physicians and suffused their work with heightened social sensitivities and social responsibility, it almost passed out of currency when the middle class attained its objectives. It was revived in England and the United States as a by-product of the pressures of the working class for social security legislation and for wider recognition of their democratic right to share more fully in the vast economic and cultural advances of the period. In both cases social medicine was associated with progressive movements that brought larger groups of people into the orbit of medical services, as they widened the conception of social participation and responsibility and put greater demands upon those who possessed political, social and financial power.

Social medicine is no longer a bold idea. There is now an Institute of Social Medicine at Oxford and a chair of social med-

---

[1] Cited by George Rosen, "Approaches to a Concept of Social Medicine. A Historical Survey," in Milbank Memorial Fund, *Backgrounds of Social Medicine* (New York, 1949), p. 9.

icine at Edinburgh, and a *British Journal of Social Medicine*. In 1947 a short Institute on Social Medicine was held by the New York Academy of Medicine. There are various lecturers in social medicine at American medical schools. In 1950 Leonard A. Scheele, Surgeon General of the U. S. Public Health Service could declare that "all public health workers, worthy of the name, recognize a social component in the health problems that confront them."[2]

Yet the concept of social medicine remains vague and ill-defined. In its most developed form it remains largely a groping effort on the part of the medical profession and other health workers to deal with the fact that a patient is a personality, has a family and is a member of society, when considering his health and diseases. It does not seem too audacious to assume that since this is already taken for granted by sociologists who have not been obliged to work their way tortuously from an absorption with specific diseases of special organs to an understanding of the patient as a whole and to the social context of health and disease, we may demand more mature formulations of principles and more concrete guidance from a sociology of medicine. The historic interest of sociologists in comparable fields involving the relation of humans to their environment provides special funded knowledge that should facilitate progress in this area.

The time is opportune for the emergence of a sociology of medicine. Recent social developments and prodigious advances in medical science and public health have led to the transformation of medical practice, with consequences that make the help of the sociologist imperative. Issues requiring the help of the sociologist arise because medicine functions in a changing social context resulting from concentration of economic power; technological developments that involve urbanization with its housing, educational and recreational problems and changing levels of living; mechanization with its effects on working conditions and industrial and occupational hazards; the passing of the closely knit neighborhood and of the integrated community that

---

[2] Leonard A. Scheele, "Cooperation Between Health and Welfare Agencies. A Health Officer's View," *Public Health Reports*, Vol. 66, February 9, 1951, p. 163.

influences standards of social responsibility, and the authority and competence of local handling of social services. Among the important developments in medicine and public health are: (1) broadening of the concepts and skills of medical science; (2) growth of medical specialization; (3) rise of the modern hospital and health center; (4) aging of the population; (5) movements for more effective distribution of medical services; (6) possibility of the realization of a functioning program of preventive medicine. The relevance of each of these developments to a sociology of medicine will be considered briefly.

1. Medical science in going beyond exclusive concern with communicable diseases involving external agents of infection to devote increased interest in deficiency and degenerative diseases has focused attention more decisively upon the patient as a person, as a member of a family, of a status group, and of a social class. This requires fuller understanding on the part of the physician of the impact of culture upon the patient in such matters as the significance of economic and psychological strains, of poverty and its sequelae, of class and other social coercions, of irrational sanctions and dreads, of cultural prides and prejudice, of the influence of war tensions upon disease incidence, of the disparity between social myths and cultural realities, and of the consequences of the struggle for survival and status in a competitive, class-structured society, the acquisitive values of which pervade and influence directly or indirectly all phases of the American cultural pattern and the life cycle of the patient.

2. Medical specialization consequent upon advances in medical knowledge, has posed important sociological problems involving professional status and role, interprofessional relationships, the relation between the specialist and the general practitioner, and the development of group practice, the effectiveness of the patient-doctor relationships, medical ethics, and the place of the cultist in the contemporary medical scene.

3. The rise of the modern hospital and health center as the primary agency of medical practice, research and teaching has raised a host of sociological problems that have theoretical as well as practical interest. These include where a hospital should be located and what its size should be to be most effective, and

what its tie-up to the community should be. There are also the problems of authority relations between the staff and the lay boards of directors, between the professional and administrative staff, between physicians and nurses and technicians and medical social workers, and between physicians in the practice of group medicine within the hospital. The relation of the hospital to voluntary health associations and to prepayment plans invites the aid of the sociologist as do the problems of hospital *esprit de corps* and the formulation of codes of hospital ethics.

4. The aging of the population has wide consequences. Here it will be noted only that it increases the rate of chronic diseases and thus changes the physician-patient relationship, which varies greatly depending upon the age and nature of the illness of the patient.

5. There are many sociological problems in the quest for more effective distribution of medical services to bridge the gap between medical knowledge and medical practice for all persons in society whether they belong to low or high income groups or are on relief, whether they reside in rural or urban areas, whether they are white or Negro. The ensuing controversies over proposals for the solution of this problem involve inquiries into the relation of the medical profession to the State; the relation of medical services to public welfare; the relation of curtailment of social services to war preparations; the relation of the local to state and federal governments; the dynamics of social movements; the function of pressure groups; the techniques of propaganda; the measurement of public sentiments; the tenacity and the vested interests of established groups and practices; the power relationships within such professional organizations as the American Medical Association and devices of control which such organizations utilize.

6. Programs of preventive medicine are in transition from potential to actual realization. The focus of medicine is changing from the control of disease to the maintenance of health. Health education which would facilitate this achievement has therefore become more important as a factor in health services. Sociologists can be helpful in this field which has long been plagued with irrational myths, rituals and cults. Sociological

histories of these cults that analyze the insecurities to which they appeal and the interests that utilize them make excellent studies. Moreover, problems of changing food habits, of methods of preventing contagion, of determining the occasions to consult a physician, and of alerting against industrial and home hazards, involve skill in the manipulation of tenacious attitudes and behavior patterns. Controls over communicable diseases, of the water supplies, waste disposal, and smoke and smog are sociological community problems. Social engineering and planning are implicit in any basic program for the prevention of industrial accidents and occupational disease and for assuring healthful working conditions in mines, mills, and factories. Moreover effective promotion of legislation in this field requires a knowledge of social structure and social classes and of all phases of political sociology.

Studies have been made by sociologists for at least the last 25 years which impinge and throw light on all the fields suggested in this attenuated and by no means definitive listing. Some extend beyond these categories into the area of the sociology of knowledge such as historical studies of the impact of diverse social economies and culture patterns upon medical science and the role and status of the physician, and of medical change upon other sciences and upon cultural change; and research in the cultural and scientific backgrounds of medical innovations and factors which impede or accelerate receptivity in professional circles and among the general public.

The time has come to systematize these studies into a body of knowledge and a definite academic discipline. Lecture courses and seminars should be introduced into university curricula that will stimulate wider interest and further research studies. A demand is beginning to develop for trained personnel in this field. It is the task of sociology departments to stimulate and satisfy such a demand.

Address delivered at Annual Meeting of Eastern Sociological Society held at Yale University, March 31, 1951.

Bibliography

Supplementing the Selected Writings of Bernhard J. Stern

BOOKS

General Anthropology, (with Melville Jacobs) Second Edition of *Introduction to Anthropology*, 1947), New York, Barnes and Noble, 1952.
When Peoples Meet: A Study of Race and Culture Contacts, with Alain Locke) New York, 1942, Rev. ed., New York, Hynds, Hayden & Eldridge, 1946.
The Family Past and Present, New York, Appleton Century, 1938.
The Lummi Indians of Northwest Washington, New York, Columbia University Press, 1934.
Lewis Henry Morgan: Social Evolutionist, Chicago, University of Chicago Press, 1931.
Medical Services by Government, New York, Commonwealth Fund, 1946.
Medicine in Industry, New York, Commonwealth Fund, 1946.
American Medical Practice in the Perspectives of a Century, New York, Commonwealth Fund, 1945.
The Health of a Nation (co-author with Michael M. Davis) Washington, National Education Association, 1943.
Society and Medical Progress, Princeton, New Jersey, Princeton University Press, 1941. Eng. ed. London Scientific Book Club, 1944.
Social Factors in Medical Progress, New York, Columbia University Press, 1927.
Should We Be Vaccinated?, A Survey of the Controversy in its

Historical and Scientific Aspects, New York, Harper and Brothers, 1927.

EDITOR OF

Young Ward's Diary, New York, Putnam, 1935.
Encyclopedia of the Social Sciences, 15 vols., New York, Macmillan. Assistant Editor beginning Vol. III (1930-1934)
The Letters of Ludwig Gumplowicz to Lester F. Ward, Supplement 1, *Sociologus* Leipzig, C. L. Hirschfeld Verlag, 1933.
"The Ward-Ross Correspondence," *American Sociological Review,* June 1938, Vol. III, No. 3, p. 362-401; October 1946, Vol. XI, no. 5, p. 593-605; December 1946, Vol. XI, no. 6, p. 734-748; December 1947, Vol. XII, No. 6, p. 703-720; February 1948, Vol. XIII, No. 1, p. 82-94; February 1949, Vol. XIV, No. 1, p. 88-119.
"Letters of Alfred Russell Wallace to Lester F. Ward," *The Scientific Monthly,* April 1935, Vol. XI, p. 375-379.
"The Letters of Albion W. Small to Lester F. Ward," *Social Forces,* December 1933, Vol. 12, No. 2, p. 163-173; March 1935, Vol. 13, No. 3, p. 323-340; September 1936, Vol. XV, No. 2, p. 174-186; March 1937, Vol. XV, No. 3, p. 305-327. Published in one volume Baltimore, Waverly Press, 1937.
"Giddings, Ward, and Small: An Interchange of Letters," *Social Forces,* March 1932, Vol. X, No. 3, p. 305-317.
"Selections from the Letters of Lorimer Fison and A. W. Howitt to Lewis Henry Morgan," *American Anthropologist,* April 1930, Vol. 32, No. 2, p. 257-279; July-September 1930, Vol. XXXII, No. 3, p. 419-453.
Understanding the Russians, (with Samuel Smith) New York, Barnes and Noble, 1947.

ARTICLES

"Resistance to the Adoption of Technological Innovations," *Technological Trends and National Policy,* Washington, Government Printing Office, 1937, p. 39-66.
"Darwin on Spencer," *The Scientific Monthly,* February 1928, Vol. XXVI, p. 180-181.

"An Indian Shaker and Healing Service," *Social Forces*, March 1929, Vol. VII, No. 3, p. 432-434.
"Culture in a Democratic Society," *The American Teacher*, October 1939, Vol. XXIV p. 16-18.
"Culture in a Democracy," Proceedings, Annual Education Conference Sponsored by the Teachers' Union, 1939.
"Patterns of Cooperation and Competition," *Child Study*, May 1938, Vol. XV No. 8, p. 239-243.
"Erich Fromm's Escape From Freedom," *Journal of Genetic Psychology*, September 1943, Vol. LXIII, p. 189-196.
"White on Boas," *American Journal of Sociology*, May 1948, Vol. LIII, p. 496.
"Soviet Policy on National Minorities," *American Sociological Review*, June 1944, Vol. IX, No. 3, p. 229-235.
"Does Genetic Endowment Vary by Socio-Economic Group?" *Science*, June 23, 1950, Vol. III p. 697-698.
"Income and Health," *Science and Society*, December 1941, Vol. V, p. 195-206.
"Possible Health Teaching Objectives and Evaluation of their Attainment," *Science Education*, February 1946, Vol. XXX, No. 1, p. 24-35.
"Activities Useful in the Study of the Maintenance of Health," *Science Education*, April-May 1945, Vol. XXIX, No. 3, p. 1-10.
"Health Education: Its Importance and Subject Matter," *Science Education*, March 1945, Vol. XXIX, No. 2, p. 61-72.
"Women, Position of in Historical Societies," *Encyclopedia of the Social Sciences*, Vol. 15, p. 442-446.
"Writing," *Encyclopedia of the Social Sciences*, Vol. XV, p. 500-502.
"Intermarriage," *Encyclopedia of the Social Sciences*, Vol. VII, p. 151-155.

UNPUBLISHED MONOGRAPHS

Historical Materials on Innovations in Higher Education, compiled and interpreted for the Planning Project for Advanced Training in Social Research, Columbia University, 1952-1953.
The Proposed Industrial Hospital and Rehabilitation Center of the State Insurance Fund of Puerto Rico. A Report to the

Governor of Puerto Rico. Prepared for the State Insurance Fund of Puerto Rico, September 1948.

The Socio-Economic Environment and Cardiovascular-Renal Diseases. Prepared for the New York Heart Association, July 1949.

The Negro in Adult Education. Prepared for the Carnegie-Myrdal Study of the Negro in America, 1940.

Index

Adams, Abigail, 270
Adams, John, 270
Agricultural peoples, 26, 28, 221-23, 236, 286, 288, 290, 291
Algonquin Indians, 171
American Association for the Advancement of Science, 42, 102, 156
American family; *see* the Family
American Indians, 213, 214, 230; *see also* Crow, Hopi, Iroquois, Navajo, Plains, Pueblo, Algonquin, Sioux
American Universities, 36, 39, 134, 138-40, 145, 153-55, 324
Ancient Society, 161, 164, 166, 174, 177, 178, 179, 183, 184, 186, 189, 233
Anthropologists, 15, 21, 188, 208, 212, 217, 284, 292, 317
Anthropology, 221, 226, 228, 283, 286
Anthropology, physical, 208, 307
Arnold, Thurman, 104, 116, 118
Artificial insemination, 318
Asepsis, 362-72
Atomic energy, 42, 123-25, 141, 151, 156

Bachofen, J. J., 163
Bancroft, H. H., 175, 176
Bandelier, Adolph, 169, 175, 189
Bateson, William, 4, 5
Bebel, August, 163
Bernard, L. L., 6
Biological factor, 3, 4, 12, 324
Biological sciences, 307-14
Boas, Franz, 8, 10, 12, 208-41, 323
Body snatching, 350-53
Bone, Homer, 112
Bonner, D. M., 335, 339
Brandeis, Louis D., 63, 64, 85
Briffault, R., 4
Bronk, D. W., 42

Capitalism, 56-59, 61, 62, 68, 71, 74, 133, 206, 238, 242-59, 267, 272, 282, 295, 297, 298
Cardiovascular diseases, socio-economic aspects, 401-11
Caspari, E., 341, 342
Chadwick, Edward, 389-91, 393
Childe, V. Gordon, 29, 291, 292
Church, role of, 265, 347, 348, 350, 354, 355, 377
Circulation of the blood, 347, 353, 356, 357

Clans, 22, 286, 287, 291, 293
Class structure, 19, 62, 204
Classes; *see* Social classes
Communist Manifesto, 277-79, 303
Comte, Auguste, 191-99, 201
Cornell University, 39, 135
Crow Indians, 182, 187
Cultural, the, 3-14, 15-22
Cultural change, 263-76
Culture, 3-8, 11, 12, 16-22, 32, 188-89, 220-21, 326-27
Culture traits, 5, 9, 10, 21, 231, 232
Cultures of peoples, 209-20

Darwin, Charles, 173, 180, 186, 291
Davis, W. Allison, 321, 322
Determinism,
  geographic, 219-20
  biological, 308
Dissection, 347-52
Dobzhansky, T., 325-27
Dühring, Eugen, 24
Durkheim, Emile, 3, 15

École Polytechnique, 37
Economic factor, influence of, 23-32, 220-26, 403-11
Edison, Thomas A., 5, 77, 87, 99, 100
Engels, Friedrich, 19, 21-24, 161, 185-86, 198, 268, 277-303
Environment, 208-19, 308-14, 316-27
Epidemics, 372-78, 382, 386-94
Eugenics controversy, 4, 203, 218, 316-19

Evolutionism of
  A. Comte, 192
  L. H. Morgan, 226-29

Factory system, 270, 271, 388, 389
Fairchild, Henry P., 34
Family, the 179, 180, 222, 263-303
Farrington, Benjamin, 30, 31
Fascism, 218, 239, 241, 242-59, 264, 275, 317
Feudal family; *see* Family
Feuerbach, Ludwig, 19, 21
Fison, Lorimer, 163, 165, 284, 285
Food-gathering peoples, 26, 28, 221-23, 236, 286-88, 290
Freedom of
  assemblage, 243
  press, 243
  speech, 243
  scientific research, 153-59
Functionalists, 21, 22

Galen, 348, 349, 353, 355, 358, 359, 362
Garrison, F. H., 345, 346, 368
Genetics, 307, 316-27, 328-42
Germ theory, 366-72, 383
Giddings, Franklin H., 34
Gilman, Daniel C., 39, 134, 135
Goldenweiser, A., 5, 11, 21, 229, 230
Guilds, 54, 55, 56

Hamilton, Walton, 103
Hansen, M. L., 34
Harvard Business School, 40, 149
Harvey, William, 31, 347, 353, 355-60, 396, 397

INDEX 431

Heredity, 7, 15, 208-19, 307, 309-14, 316-27, 329-42
Herskovits, Melville J., 4, 218
Historical Materialism, 18-32, 220, 224, 226, 236
Hogben, Lancelot, 337
Holmes, Oliver Wendell, 361-65
Holmes, S. J., 331, 334
Homo sapiens, 3, 12, 18
Hopi Indians, 10
Howitt, Alexander, 163, 284, 285
Human growth, 323, 325
Human types, 209, 213-18
Huntington, Ellsworth, 4

Ickes, Harold L., 116-18
Industrial Revolution, 56, 58, 73, 74, 268, 279
Innovations in medicine, opposition to, 345 ff., 353, 355-58, 360-85
Integrative levels, 16-21
Intelligence tests, 308, 310, 320-22
Inventions, 21, 47, 61, 63, 71, 75-99, 105, 107, 326
Inventors, 65-67, 86, 120
Iroquois Indians, 164, 168-71, 174, 175

Jenks, Leland H., 33-35
Jacobs, Melville, 24
Jenner, Edward, 373, 376
Jennings, H. S., 336
Johns Hopkins University, 39, 134, 135

Kautsky, Karl, 161
Keller, A. E., 19
Kinship systems, 22, 171-83, 187, 189, 287-94

Kinship terms, 174, 179, 180, 187, 286, 287
Koehler, W., 8
Kroeber, A. L., 3, 7, 8, 12, 15, 174, 183, 292

Language, 7, 8, 209, 230, 234
Lawrence Scientific School, 38
League of the Iroquois, 170, 171, 183
Lenin, V. I., 19, 302
Liebig, Justus von, 37
Lincoln, Abraham, 103, 137
Lister, Joseph, 365, 372
Lowie, R. H., 3, 12, 174, 180-83, 187, 227, 237, 292
Lubbock, Sir John, 172, 173
Luddites, 60
Lundberg, G. A., 20
Lysenko, T., 318-42

Machine wrecking, 59, 60
Maine, Henry, 173, 183
Malinowski, B., 9, 13, 22
Marett, R. R., 17, 18
Marriage, 265, 280-82, 284, 285-87, 296
Marx, Karl, 3, 15, 19, 21, 23, 56, 59, 60, 163, 185, 186, 192, 198, 201, 268, 277-79, 294-98, 301-303
Marxism, 18, 21-24, 194, 199, 205, 221, 224, 225, 237, 238, 277-303, 317
Marxists; see Marxism
McCready, Benjamin W., 392
Medical education, 347, 349
Medical profession, 395-400
Medical services, distribution of, 412-18, 423 ff.

Medicine, Social aspects of, 308, 344-424
Medieval society, 53-55
Mendelian principles, 316-18, 332, 334, 337, 338, 341, 342
Merton, Robert K., 31, 76, 136, 137
Mill, John Stuart, 192, 193
Mode of production, 23-28, 236, 294
Morgan, Lewis Henry, 4, 163-90, 232, 233, 279, 280, 283-85, 287, 291, 293
Morgan, Thomas Hunt, 307, 328, 332, 342
Morrill Act of 1862, 40, 135
Mortality rates, 398-99, 403-10
Mueller, Max, 4
Muller, H. J., 317, 318, 338, 339
Murdock, George, 20, 292
Murray-Wagner-Dingell, Senate bill, 412-18
Myrdal, Gunnar, 22, 35

National Academy of Sciences, 137
National health legislation, need for, 412-18
National Health Survey, 272, 385, 403, 404, 409
National Research Council, 137, 138, 156
National Science Foundation, 148-49
Naturphilosophie, 37
Navajo Indians, 10, 182
Nazis, 250-52, 298-99
Negroes, 270, 310, 316, 322, 325; health of, 398, 406, 407, 410, 413
Norton, John P., 38

Ogburn, W. F., 3, 11
Origin of the Family, 277, 279, 283, 297

Pasteur, 365, 366, 373, 382, 383
Patents, 63, 64, 65, 75-99, 103-14
Pavlov, 47
Pearson, Karl, 316, 317
Percussion, opposition to, 360, 361
Physician-patient relationship, 345, 346, 377, 383
Physician and society, 395-400
Plains Indians, 10, 183
Pledge, H. T., 31
Positivism, 194-97, 201
Primitive societies, 283-93
Psychiatry, 308, 311
Psychological processes, 15, 16, 17, 47, 227
Public health, 377, 379-81, 383, 386-94
Pueblo Indians, 10, 175
Puerperal fever, 363, 365

Race, 208-19, 313
Resistance to change, 47, 48, 52, 59, 75-99, 345-85
Rivers, W. H. R., 12, 13, 161, 185
Roemer, M. I., 405
Roosevelt, Franklin D., 40, 87, 138
Ross, E. A., 34, 205
Rush, Benjamin, 378

Scientific research, expenditures for, 143-50
Scientific research, freedom of, 133-59
Scientists, 36, 38, 41-43, 155-59, 240

INDEX 433

Semmelweis, I., 362-65
Shattuck, Lemuel, 378, 393
Sheffield Scientific School, 38, 135
Silliman, Benjamin, 38
Sinclair, Upton, 6
Singer, Charles J., 31
Sioux Indians, 178, 182
Small, Albion, 34
Smith, G. Elliott, 12
Smith, T. Southwood, 389, 390, 393
Social Darwinism, 308, 312, 313, 317
Social evolution, 226-29
Social, the, 3-14
Social classes, 203, 204, 206, 237, 238, 271, 313, 322, 388, 420
Social organization, 30, 177-84, 187, 264, 287-94
Social sciences, 20, 307-14
Social scientists, 15, 16, 283, 314
Sociological studies, 30, 324, 325
Sociologists, position of, 6, 15, 16-21, 33-35, 188, 272, 275, 276, 299, 312, 317
Sociology, 13, 20, 33, 35, 191, 192, 199-202, 205-07, 312; of heart disease, 401-11; of medicine, 419-24
Soviet Union, 44, 50, 62, 67, 71-74, 131, 186, 240, 274, 320
Spencer, Herbert, 173, 234
Spier, Leslie, 10, 173, 324
Stamp, Sir Josiah, 50, 72, 9&
Stern, Curt, 319-22, 334, 335
Stethoscope, opposition to, 361
Sub-human groups, 6-9
Sumner, William G., 3, 19
Superorganic, 7, 15, 19
Sydenham, Thomas, 359, 382

Technological changes, effect of, 271, 279, 297-300, 302
Technology, role of, 47, 50, 58, 61, 71, 75-99, 122-32, 297; innovations in, 48, 49, 51-58, 61-67
Temporary National Economic Committee, 103, 114, 130, 255, 256
Thomas, W. I., 3
Totemism, 229-30
Tylor, Edward B., 15, 173, 317

Vaccination, 373-76, 383
Vesalius, 31, 348, 349, 353
Virchow, R., 365, 383

Wallace, Alfred Russell, 206
War Production, 102-21, 125
Ward, C. Osborne, 201
Ward, Lester F., 3, 34, 192, 200-207, 317, 330
Weismann's germ plasm theory, 329-32, 342
White, Andrew D., 39
Woman
  position of, 364-75, 280, 287-92
  equality of, 273, 282, 283, 301
  as wage-earner, 268, 272, 273, 295, 298-302
Work, Lincoln T., 40, 149
World War I, 134, 258
World War II, 40, 102-21, 124, 136, 137, 138, 141, 142, 151, 300-01, 323
Writing, 30, 52

Yale University, 38, 134
Yerkes, R. M., 8